WITHDRAWN

LIVE FROM THE
CAMPAIGN TRAIL

# LIVE FROM THE CAMPAIGN TRAIL

*The Greatest Presidential Campaign Speeches*
*of the Twentieth Century and*
*How They Shaped Modern America*

## Michael A. Cohen

Walker & Company
New York

Published by Walker Publishing Company, Inc., New York
Distributed to the trade by Macmillan

All papers used by Walker & Company are natural, recyclable products made
from wood grown in well-managed forests. The manufacturing processes
conform to the environmental regulations of the country of origin.

Library of Congress Cataloging-in-Publication Data

Cohen, Michael A., 1971–
   Live from the campaign trail : the greatest presidential campaign speeches
of the twentieth century and how they shaped modern America / Michael
A. Cohen.—1st U.S. ed.
      p.  cm.
   ISBN-13: 978-0-8027-1697-2 (alk. paper)
   ISBN-10: 0-8027-1697-0
   1. Campaign speeches—United States—History—20th century.
2. Campaign speeches—United States—History—20th century—Sources.
3. Political campaigns—United States—History—20th century. 4. Political
campaigns—United States—History—20th century—Sources. 5. Presidents—United States—Election—History—20th century. 6. Presidents—
United States—Election—History—20th century—Sources. 7. Speeches,
addresses, etc., American. 8. Political culture—United States—History—
20th century. 9. United States—Politics and government—20th century.
I. Title.
   E743.C57 2008
   324.97309'04—dc22                                    2008001273

Visit Walker & Company's Web site at www.walkerbooks.com

First U.S. edition 2008

1   3   5   7   9   10   8   6   4   2

Typeset by Westchester Book Group
Printed in the United States of America by Quebecor World Fairfield

To Mom and Dad

# CONTENTS

# A NOTE ON SPEECH TEXTS

Virtually all the speech texts in this book have been edited in some measure. The reason is one of simple physics. If these speeches were printed fully, the book you are holding not only would be much bigger but also would be much heavier and far more unwieldy. In order to keep this volume at a manageable length, editing the speeches was a regrettable but necessary decision.

In most cases, the edits to these speeches are minor, focusing on introductions, acknowledgments, site references, and so on. In some cases, more substantive edits have been made. For example, Theodore Roosevelt's "New Nationalism" speech is more than eight thousand words, and Herbert Hoover's "Rugged Individualism" is of similar length. Both of these speeches have been rather dramatically reduced. Others received far less significant editing. Nonetheless, every effort has been taken to maintain the narrative flow and thematic content of each speech. The materials deleted were not essential to understanding the overall message of the speech. Finally, any edits that have been made, whether a few paragraphs or a few words, are referenced in the text by ellipses.

These edits notwithstanding, the existence of digital technology does provide us with alternatives. At the Web site www .livefromthetrail.com you can find links to the full text of every speech in this book.

# INTRODUCTION

*Of all the talents bestowed upon men, none is so precious as the gift of oratory. He who enjoys it wields a power more durable than that of a great king. He is an independent force in the world. Abandoned by his party, betrayed by his friends, stripped of his offices, whoever can command this power is still formidable.*

*Many have watched its effects. A meeting of grave citizens, protected by all the cynicism of these prosaic days, is unable to resist its influence. From unresponsive silence they advance to grudging approval and thence to complete agreement with the speaker. The cheers become louder and more frequent; the enthusiasm momentarily increases; until they are convulsed by emotions they are unable to control and shaken by passions of which they have resigned the direction.*

—WINSTON CHURCHILL,
"THE SCAFFOLDING OF RHETORIC," 1897

THE POWER OF oration Winston Churchill so eloquently describes is as old as politics itself. From the wondrous speeches of Demosthenes and Pericles in ancient Athens to the fierce debates of the Roman Senate, great orators have used stirring rhetoric to shape human events. More powerful than the written word, great speeches are capable of stirring feelings, capturing emotions, and driving listeners to action. But if history shows us anything, it is that great rhetoric alone does not move men or women toward what Lincoln called "the better angels of our nature." Words alone cannot accomplish such a feat—but ideas can and ideas do, and that is what this book is about: the ideas that have shaped our political discourse in the twentieth century and transformed modern America.

At its core a great speech brings together both memorable words and powerful ideas. Think of the Reverend Martin Luther King Jr. at the March on Washington in 1963, projecting the inspirational dream of a color-blind America in the captivating and moving image of his four little children one day living in a nation where "they will not be judged by the color of their skin but by the content of their character." When a speechwriter combines words and ideas into something both evocative and exciting, what General Douglas MacArthur once called "a thirsty ear" will readily and appreciatively soak it up.

However, in an age of extraordinary and pervasive technological advancement, oratory might seem like a quaint political skill when compared to a poignant or catty thirty-second television advertisement, a spicy blog post, or even that standby of modern speechmaking, the PowerPoint presentation. But as the words and ideas in this collection demonstrate, speeches and speechwriting remain an essential element of our national conversation. They are not only the most basic means by which our political leaders transmit ideas and seek to shape public opinion but they are the most fundamental way that our political leaders energize and lead a sometimes indifferent electorate.

For that reason, political speechwriting is a unique and revelatory prism for viewing history. Speeches are never delivered in a vacuum. There is always an objective and a goal, and the best speeches are seamlessly linked to the passions of the time and place in which they are delivered—think of Marc Antony asking in the wake of Caesar's assassination, "Friends, Romans, countrymen, lend me your ears"; think of Winston Churchill, in England's darkest moment, pledging his "blood, toil, tears and sweat" to the cause of victory; think in modern times of John F. Kennedy demanding that a new generation of Americans, at the dawn of a new era in this nation's history, "ask not what your country can do for you, but what you can do for your country." The speeches in this collection not only demonstrate the power of speechwriting and speechmaking to inspire and motivate the American people but they also are a repository of the ideas that have shaped our national discourse. A great speech is more than memorable oratory; it is a living and breathing document of history.

## SPEECHWRITING AND DEMOCRACY

So why campaign speeches? Should we take to heart the admonition of the American statesman Henry Stimson, who once derisively noted that "a man's campaign speeches are no proper subject for the study of a friendly biographer"?[1] Certainly, many campaign speeches are ephemeral, floating out of the speechgiver's mouth, over the heads of the assembled, and into the ether, soon to be forgotten—but so too, usually, are the candidates who deliver such remarks. The speeches in this book do not fall into such a category. Instead, they remind us that speechmaking is fundamental to the strength and vitality of democracy.

After all, memorable speechwriting has its greatest relevance and is held in highest esteem in a democratic society. Campaign speechmaking is an inherent element of any political system that demands its political leaders serve at the pleasure of the electorate and, most of all, with its permission. After all, what is democracy without the power of persuasion—the pointed words, the captivating ideas, and the inspiring visions of the future? Great speeches have the power to light a fire under the party faithful or motivate undecided voters to cast a ballot on Election Day. They grab listeners by both the heart and the head, putting people's inchoate and jumbled feelings about the future of their nation into a seamless and powerful narrative, leading them, as Churchill reminds us, from "grudging approval" to "complete agreement" and finally emotions and passions they are "unable to control."

While presidents, senators, governors, and even congressmen must (or at least should) show decorum and statesmanship while in their elected offices, on the campaign trail the rules speak to a wholly different reality: a primal, competitive meeting place where great ideas stirring national rhetoric and aspirations for the future are fervently debated, dissected, and discussed. Nowhere is that more true than on the presidential campaign trail.

Writing in 1832, Alexis de Tocqueville spoke of the national excitement that is generated in the United States by a presidential campaign:

> For a long while before the appointed time has come, the election becomes the important and, so to speak, the all-engrossing topic of discussion. Factional ardor is redoubled, and all the artificial passions which the imagination can create in a happy and peaceful land are agitated and brought to light . . . As the election draws near, the activity of intrigue and the agitation of the populace increase; the citizens are divided into hostile camps, each of which assumes the names of its favorite candidate; the whole nation glows with feverish excitement; the election is the daily theme of the press, the subject of every private conversation, the end of every thought and every action, the sole interest of the present. It is true that

as soon as the choice is determined, this ardor is dispelled, calm returns, and the river, which had nearly broken its banks, sinks to its usual level; but who can refrain from astonishment that such a storm should have arisen.[2]

Tocqueville was writing about the 1832 election, which featured the Democrat president Andrew Jackson against his Whig opponent, Henry Clay. It wasn't exactly a barn burner of a race, as Jackson won reelection handily. But the emotions of any presidential race are genuine, and they reflect a level of passion and intensity unique to democracy. As Tocqueville suggests, presidential candidacies become vessels for the hopes, dreams, and fears of their supporters. When the American people choose a president they are doing far more than simply picking a single man or woman to run this nation—they are voting for an idea and a vision of what they believe America is and, above all, what it can be. Indeed, America's democratic legacy and our adherence to it, even in the midst of a convulsive civil war, speaks to the fundamental importance of elections and campaigns in our national tradition. (The Confederate States of America held elections throughout the Civil War, for both president and the Confederate Congress.)

The cynical may retort that campaigns are nasty, brutish affairs, full of slickness, rhetorical excess, and mean-spiritedness. Campaigns, they argue, appeal to the lowest common denominator and have as much to do with public relations as with great ideas. Unfortunately, these notions have, for many Americans, come to define our election process. There is truth in these words, but they tell an incomplete story. Throughout our history, the best and most successful presidential candidates have largely recognized not only the intelligence of the electorate but also their desires and needs as Americans, and have spoken to these attributes rather than seeking to infantilize voters. Elections have been and remain about so much more than the cynical would have us believe, and these speeches are the living proof.

Presidential campaigns represent a quadrennial opportunity for Americans to debate not only the great ideas roiling their nation but also the fundamental conception of how they view their more than 230-year experiment in democracy. If American nationalism is, as some would argue, a civic religion, then the presidential campaign trail is truly this nation's hallowed ground.

## THE IDEA OF AMERICA

Writing about the 1980 election, the legendary political scribe Theodore White said, "What had come to issue . . . was the nature of the federal government's power. The campaign was about the consequences and reach of government, about the murky limits that separate the public interest from the individual right. It was about America's pride, and America's role in the turbulent outer world."[3] Without realizing it, White was hardly describing just one election; he was describing a century of American political history.

For much of the twentieth century, Americans have passionately debated two fundamental questions on the campaign trail— what is the role of government in the lives of the American people, and what is America's proper role and responsibility in the world. How presidential candidates have sought to address these two questions serves as the foundation of this book.

In 1896 William Jennings Bryan sparked a century-long national debate about the essential responsibilities of government by calling on the Democratic Party to stand with the workingman. In the 1910s, Woodrow Wilson and Teddy Roosevelt tussled over the nature of progressivism and activist government. In the 1920s and 1930s, Warren Harding and Herbert Hoover ex-

tolled the virtues of "rugged individualism" and laissez-faire economics, while Franklin Delano Roosevelt birthed the modern welfare state as he called for the federal government to play a larger role in creating economic opportunities for the American people.

In the 1940s and 1950s, Roosevelt and Dwight D. Eisenhower set America's postwar internationalist course by doing battle with, and ultimately defeating, the nation's long-standing isolationist impulse. In the 1950s and 1960s, Adlai Stevenson and John F. Kennedy demanded national sacrifice and vigilance in the fight against Communism, while Barry Goldwater called for a more openly confrontational stance with the Soviet Union. In the 1970s and 1980s, Ronald Reagan took up the conservative mantle, beseeching the American people to join a "national crusade to make America great again" at the same time the Democrats, led by George McGovern, were making an equally passionate call for them to "come home." In the 1990s, after years of conservative attacks on an expanding federal government, Bill Clinton turned away from the liberal platitudes of the Democratic Party's past and announced an end to the "era of big government."

As these great debates suggest, presidential contenders have rarely mired themselves in the minutiae of specific policy choices. Instead, candidates have largely spoken to broad principles and ideas defining not only their political philosophy but also that of their political party. Indeed, it is how Americans understand these broad principles—and how the pendulum of national elections swings to the right or left or rests in the middle—that defines our election process. There is a rhythm to American politics in the twentieth century, and the national pendulum has generally swung in one direction or another—but never that terribly far. America has never fallen prey to the politics of dogmatism, doctrinarism, or, worse, radicalism. Amidst the great debates of our nation's history there has been a startling pragmatism in American politics,

even if that pragmatism has been tethered to an occasionally fulsome and even exceptionalist political ideology.

## CHANGING HISTORY

Many of the speeches in this collection were delivered during watershed times in America's history—true before-and-after moments when the American people were given distinctive visions of what kind of nation the United States should be, and went to the ballot box to choose accordingly. But beyond providing insight into the history of the past century, these speeches also tell us about where we are today in American politics and the path we took to get there.

So much of how we understand politics today comes from the ideas and images of the two political parties enshrined in the twentieth century's best political speechwriting. William Jennings Bryan's attack on "idle holders of idle capital" in 1896, Woodrow Wilson's defense of the "man on the make" against the "juggernaut" of corporate influence in 1912, and Harry Truman's rhetorical assault against the Republican reactionary with "a calculating machine where his heart ought to be" in 1948 mimic the populist attacks on the moneyed and special interests that we hear from Democratic politicians today. At the same time, FDR's call for "bold, persistent experimentation" in government and his pledge of a "New Deal for the American people" remain the lodestars of American liberalism and still define the political philosophy of the Democratic Party.

Revulsion at the excesses of Vietnam by antiwar liberals and subsequent attacks on the postwar international consensus in the 1960s and '70s continue to roil internal debates in the Democratic Party—and of course also provide a club for Republicans to attack Democrats on national security issues. It is hardly coincidental that in 2004 a senior administration official in the Bush White House would say of internecine party battles over the war in Iraq that "it's never stopped being 1968" for Democrats.

On the Republican side, the basic economic conservatism of Herbert Hoover in 1928 is being revisited today as Republican candidates for president attack the "socialist" plans of their opponents. Barry Goldwater's 1964 paean to extremism in defense of liberty eerily matches the tough, take-no-prisoners rhetoric of President George W. Bush's 2004 campaign speeches describing the war on terrorism. George Wallace's attacks on a "left-wing monster" and Richard Nixon's defense of the "forgotten majority" became the template for two generations of conservative broadsides against activist government and American liberalism. In the 1980s, Ronald Reagan perfected this basic message of conservative populism and we are still hearing variations of this political theme on the modern campaign trail. Finally, Dan Quayle's attack on the TV character Murphy Brown and Pat Buchanan's declaration of a "cultural war" in America presaged the "values" debate, becoming as seemingly important to American politics today as health care and foreign policy. Quite simply, the words of the past continue to shape the way we think about politics in 2008 and beyond.

## RACE, RELIGION, AND RIGHTS

Of course, for all the constants in America's campaign narrative, new and important issues—some of which speak to the most essential notions of America's founding creed—have consistently arisen on the campaign trail. Beginning in 1948 with Hubert Humphrey's seminal call for the Democratic Party to "step into the bright sunshine of human rights," the government's responsibility in ensuring the full application of civil rights for African Americans began to emerge as a question of extraordinary significance. For Democrats, the issue of race ripped the party in half, splitting northern liberals from the party's once uncontested southern base. Shameless politicians, such as Alabama governor George Wallace, played on the worst impulses of the American people to score political victories. National Republican leaders used the excesses of the Great Society programs of the 1960s and the perceived liberal focus on the rights of poor minorities versus those of the middle class to spark a conservative revolt against activist government. The result, however, was a coded, often nasty national conversation on race that rubbed raw the wound of America's two-century-long racial divide. Even today, the issue of race remains fundamental to understanding the evolution of American politics in the twentieth century and beyond.

One of the greatest transformations in campaign rhetoric has been the discussion of religious faith. In 1960 John F. Kennedy was forced to remind the American people that being Catholic did not disqualify him from also being president of the United States. At the time, Kennedy argued that religion and politics must be kept absolutely separate. Were he alive today, Kennedy would be amazed at how things have changed.

In the 1980s and '90s, as social issues began to take on new resonance, the American people began a serious (and often divisive debate) about the role of morality and values in our national politics. In 1992 Pat Buchanan and Vice President Dan Quayle extolled the virtues of "traditional" family values. In 1998 the president's sexual behavior became the subject of great national debate, and in 2004 a plurality of voters ranked moral values as the key impetus for their ballot choice. By 2007, NBC's Tim Russert would ask presidential candidates in a Democratic debate about their favorite Bible verse—and few observers would bat an eye over this extraordinary intrusion of personal faith into the campaign process.

## CAMPAIGN ORATORY AS A MODERN PHENOMENON

In a very real sense, the issues that have divided America in the twentieth century stand in stark contrast to those that divided

America in much of the nineteenth century. America then was hardly a global power, and questions of the proper role of government and the appropriateness of an activist and engaged federal government were largely absent from campaign debates. Indeed, something else was missing as well—candidates.

Throughout much of the nineteenth century, presidents, not to mention presidential candidates, rarely gave speeches, instead leaving campaign action to lesser party leaders. Most candidates preferred to remain on their "front porch" and have the voters come to them. For sitting presidents it was considered particularly unseemly, even beneath the seriousness of the office, to personally ask the voters for their support. In 1888, for example, Grover Cleveland not only refused to campaign but also forbade his cabinet from hitting the trail. Small wonder he lost his bid for reelection.

There is of course an exception to this rule. The most important campaign speech in American history was delivered by our greatest presidential speechwriter, Abraham Lincoln, at Cooper Union in New York City. There Lincoln made a passionate argument against the further expansion of slavery into the western territories and upheld the position of the Republican Party as the true party of freedom in America. The speech would take Lincoln out of the realm of political obscurity and smooth his path to the Republican nomination and eventually the White House. Nonetheless, the tradition against campaign speeches remained intact during the 1860 campaign. The Cooper Union speech was delivered in February, yet by the time Lincoln was nominated by the Republican Party for president he refused to give a single speech or further elaborate on his political views during the campaign.[4]

The brilliance of the Cooper Union speech notwithstanding, it is particularly fitting and proper to focus an examination of the great campaign speeches of American history on the twentieth century, because it was indeed during the century past when presidential campaign speechwriting took on a life of its own.

In 1896, Bryan became one of the first presidential candidates to actually venture onto the campaign trail and the first to barnstorm the nation, delivering more than six hundred speeches and speaking to more than five million Americans. Bryan's "Cross of Gold" speech and the subsequent campaign represented a new style of political campaigning and gave a new relevance to political oratory that would change the face of twentieth-century America. This seismic transformation made speechgiving by presidential candidates an essential element of modern political discourse. Candidates began actually asking the American people directly for their votes—and American politics and the vitality of our democracy have never been the same and, arguably, have never been better.

When Bryan spoke at the Democratic convention, where he was nominated, it was another of the political year's more unusual moments. Rarely before did candidates actually attend the party convention, and they never accepted their nomination in person. An elaborate ceremony would be planned for after the convention, at which time the nominee would be "notified" that he had been chosen. In 1932, Franklin Roosevelt would change all that, becoming not only the first presidential nominee to appear at a convention in person to accept the honor but also the first to fly in a plane to get there. From that point forward the spectacle of national conventions and the acceptance speech of the candidate would take on a rarefied air. Gone were the days when delegates argued and debated over who would be the nominee. Now, conventions have become akin to political coronations, and the televised acceptance speech has become the single most effective tool for candidates to get their campaign message and political philosophy out to voters. At the very least, it is the most viewed, read, and heard campaign speech of an entire modern presidential campaign.

## FINDING THE RIGHT WORDS

At their core, the best political speeches inspire their listeners. Many of the best rely on the accents and memories of the past. As you read on, you'll see many references to Lincoln: not only was he arguably our greatest president, but he was certainly the most quotable. Jefferson, Washington, and even revolutionary leaders such as Thomas Paine get their due as well. The politician who invokes these unimpeachable figures as well as the events of American folklore—Plymouth Rock, Gettysburg, Philadelphia 1776, Lexington and Concord, the Alamo, Normandy, and today September 11—will always find an appreciative audience. Casting one's plans for the future in the bright and vivid light of historical precedent is generally a winning strategy.

However, the best political speeches invoke not simply the past but also the hopefulness of the future. The occasional mean-spirited attack will succeed—think of Harry Truman in 1948. But contrary to the conventional wisdom, rarely does the negative attack alone bring victory in November. This is not to say that politicians don't build straw men out of their opponent's liabilities and negative political stereotypes. Nearly all the more successful ones do, and for good reason—there are few ways to make yourself look better than to point out the iniquities and failings of your opponent.

But ultimately, like voters everywhere, Americans want something to cast their ballot *for*, as opposed to simply finding something to vote *against*. As the old saying goes, you can't beat something with nothing.

Voters expect their presidential candidates to inspire them, to give them hope for their future, and above all to lead. For decades, it was the Democrats who had the lock on inspirational visions, while the Republicans played the role of the national scold. It might explain why so many of the best speeches in this collection were delivered by Democrats. Or maybe it's because, as Ralph Waldo Emerson suggests, "conservatism stands on man's confessed limitations; reform on his indisputable infinitude."[5] With Ronald Reagan, however, Republicans finally began to cloak their conservative message in populist and optimistic tones, while Democrats began to sound whiny and pessimistic.

To be sure, the speeches accumulated here do not include all the great campaign speeches of the twentieth century. If space allowed, this collection would have included such gems as Ronald Reagan's "Time for Choosing" conservative manifesto from the 1964 campaign, George H. W. Bush's 1988 acceptance speech at the Republican National Convention, Jeane Kirkpatrick's blistering attack on "Blame America Firsters" at the 1984 GOP convention, Claude Bowers's spellbinding keynote speech at the 1928 Democratic convention, Robert F. Kennedy's poignant eulogy to the slain Martin Luther King Jr., and Lyndon Johnson's stentorian declaration that he would not seek reelection in 1968. Of course, countless additional speeches by Franklin Roosevelt, Adlai Stevenson, and Theodore Roosevelt would, in an ideal world, be in this book as well.

The absence of these addresses in no way shortchanges the speeches that are included. Each has in some manner influenced and shaped American politics and American history in this, the "American century." All the great (and even some of the not-so-great) orators of the twentieth century are here: from the eloquent (Mario Cuomo and John F. Kennedy) to the tub-thumping (William Jennings Bryan and Theodore Roosevelt), from the great communicators (Franklin Delano Roosevelt and Ronald Reagan) to the plainspoken (Harry Truman and Barry Goldwater), from the learned (Adlai Stevenson and Woodrow Wilson) to the long-winded (Jesse Jackson and Bill Clinton), from the liberal (Hubert Humphrey) to the conservative (Herbert Hoover), from the peacenik (George McGovern) to the military man (Dwight Eisenhower), and from the infamous (George Wallace and Pat Buchanan) to the mediocre (Warren Harding and Dan Quayle) and the maudlin (Richard Nixon).

Whatever their varied backgrounds, political affiliations, or speaking styles, they have one thing in common: their words and ideas have helped to shape the America that we know today. In some small manner, each of the speeches in this collection reflects a century of American political debate about the proper role of government and the responsibilities of the United States in a globalized and interconnected world. These are exactly the types of debates that we can expect to continue in the years to come.

More than 170 years ago Tocqueville said that democracy does not necessarily lead to the "most skilled government," and that is true even today. But Tocqueville also reminded us that democracy produces "what the ablest governments are frequently unable to create: namely, an all-pervading and restless activity, a super-abundant force, and an energy which is inseparable from it and which may, however unfavorable circumstances may be, produce wonders. These are the true advantages of democracy." They are also the fundamental elements of America's campaign trail and the battles that have been waged there in the twentieth century. May those battles continue every four years, when the American people and the men and women who seek to lead them meet once again . . . on the trail.

## Chapter 1

## THE GREAT COMMONER

William Jennings Bryan Delivers the Most Influential
Speech in American Political History: 1896

A T FIRST GLANCE, it may seem odd to begin a book that
looks at the great speeches of the twentieth century with a
speech that was delivered in the nineteenth century. But just as
the 1930s began when Franklin Roosevelt was elected president,
the 1960s ended when Richard Nixon resigned the presidency,
and the twenty-first century started on September 11, 2001, the
political history of the twentieth century began on a sultry July
day in Chicago in the year 1896.

The harbinger of this political revolution was a former two-term
congressman from Nebraska named William Jennings Bryan.
Renowned far and wide as an unrivaled orator, Bryan was a dark
horse candidate to become the Democratic Party's presidential
nominee. He was generally considered too populist and inexperienced to merit any serious consideration. But, as Bryan would soon
prove, great oratory has a tendency to create its own political reality.

Bryan would leave Chicago as the standard-bearer of the Democratic Party, the youngest presidential nominee in the country's
history, and a new force in American politics. The source of his
meteoric rise: the immortal "Cross of Gold" speech, which would

transform the Democratic Party and in turn the country. There is no better place to begin an examination of the greatest campaign speeches of the twentieth century than with the "Cross of Gold." It is the single most influential and electrifying campaign speech in American political history.

## THE POPULIST RISES

Raised in a farming community in Illinois, William Jennings Bryan was the child of parents who were both Andrew Jackson Democrats and deeply devout Christians. All three influences came to shape his public persona as an "agrarian rebel" as he couched his spellbinding rhetoric in both populist and biblical tones.[1] Bryan once wrote of his father, Silas Bryan, "He saw no necessary conflict—and I have never been able to see any—between the principles of our government and the principles of Christian faith."[2] For Bryan, the Bible was as much the framework for his political beliefs as the Constitution or the Declaration of Independence.[3] Like many populist leaders of the era, Bryan fundamentally saw politics as a moral exercise, and he viewed his political calling as that of a "voice of the people"—a descendant of Thomas Jefferson and Andrew Jackson, reflecting the needs and wishes of the common man against what he saw as the greed and selfishness of unabashed and rapacious nineteenth-century capitalism.

However, unlike other populist leaders, Bryan didn't just sense "popular feelings," he "embodied them," said historian Richard Hofstadter.[4] Although populism had gathered converts during the economic depression of the mid-1890s, the movement was as disjointed and "as rickety as the worst of the sharecropper homes."[5] While a number of populist-inclined representatives had won congressional seats and statehouses, and the nominee of the Populist Party, James Weaver, had won just under 10 percent of the vote in the 1892 presidential election, the party had yet to find a national voice and movement. Bryan would change all that by providing a national platform for the populist agenda. In his 1896 campaign for the presidency, Bryan would become the most renowned national politician of his era to speak directly on behalf of the welfare of the working masses.

The issue on which Bryan staked his call for political change was free silver. No one issue better reflected the glaring divides in turn-of-the-century America than bimetallism, or the question of whether America should adopt a silver or gold standard for its monetary policy. The silver-or-gold issue reflected a long-standing economic divide over the benefits of a strong dollar versus a weak one. Those who supported free silver extolled the benefits of an inflationary monetary policy, believing it would not only lead to an increase in wages but also help debtors pay off their obligations more easily and quickly. The "goldbugs" argued that a gold standard or "sound money" policy would remove uncertainty in financial markets, bring greater financial stability, and encourage greater bank lending. Moreover, since foreign markets used the gold standard, a move to silver would have a dangerous impact on trade. Of course, the debate was about more than monetary policy, as it took on class-like conceits, dividing the country between prairie and city, isolationist and internationalist, farmer and industrialist.

The silver standard had become the rallying cry of populists everywhere, while the gold standard reflected the establishment view of the nation's emerging industrial economy. For Bryan, that was reason enough to grasp on to the silver issue. The details were for Bryan a bit fuzzy. As he told a Nebraska crowd in 1892, "I don't know anything about free silver . . . The people of Nebraska are for free silver and I am for free silver. I will look up the argument later."[6] For a man who, like the hero of the Democratic

Party, Thomas Jefferson, believed the simple laborer and family farmer was the salt of the earth, what did the specifics matter?

As the Democrats assembled in Chicago it was still not clear which direction the party would take on the currency issue. After all, only four years earlier, Democrats had nominated the decidedly non-populist Grover Cleveland. This was a man who cared so little about popular opinion that he once noted, "While the people should patriotically and cheerfully support their government, its functions do not include support of the people." Not surprisingly, the Panic of 1893 turned him—and his conservative ideology—into an albatross around the neck of the Democratic Party, providing Bryan and his populist brethren with a clear political opportunity.

For more than sixteen months Bryan had traveled the country describing the virtues of a free silver platform.[7] He had made it his pet cause and he believed that it would pave the way toward the Democratic nomination. While publicly Bryan played it coy, privately he confidently told friends and political colleagues that he would leave Chicago the nominee of the party. Few, however, took this young upstart seriously. The night before he was to deliver the speech that would transform American democracy, Bryan went for a quiet dinner with his wife and a family friend. Outside the window of the restaurant, convention delegates marched under the banners of various candidates, none of which included the former congressman from Nebraska. But Bryan was undaunted. He turned to his wife and said, "These people don't know it, but they will be cheering for me just this way by this time tomorrow night. I will make the greatest speech of my life tomorrow."[8]

## THE "SILVER TONGUED" ORATOR SPEAKS

The next day as the delegates gathered to debate the bimetallism issue, Bryan was asked to address the convention in defense of silver.

Dressed in the garb of a westerner—a black alpaca suit, a low-cut vest, and a white lawn tie—Bryan bounded to the stage.[9] The crowd jumped to their feet and surged forward, their applause growing "like a forest fire in fury."[10] Bryan appealed for silence, but the pro-silver crowd would hear none of it. Delegates climbed on chairs as they waved their handkerchiefs and beat the floor.

Only after the crowd had wrung itself out screaming and shouting was Bryan able to begin. He did not disappoint. His commanding voice, which was said to be audible three city blocks away, boomed through the rafters of the cavernous convention hall. His first words quickly alerted his audience that the issue of silver was about more than mere currency. "I come to speak to you in defense of a cause holy as the cause of liberty—the cause of humanity," said Bryan.

The "Great Commoner" then proceeded to deliver a full-throated attack on not only the supporters of the gold standard but in fact the entire eastern establishment of the party. Bryan gave his rivals no quarter as he preached to the audience about the sanctity of the common man.

> The man who is employed for wages is as much a business man as his employer. The attorney in a country town is as much a business man as the corporation counsel in a great metropolis. The merchant at the cross roads store is as much a business man as the merchant of New York. The farmer who goes forth in the morning and toils all day, begins in the spring and toils all summer, and, by the application of brains and muscle to the natural resources of this country, creates wealth, is as much a business man as the man who goes upon the board of trade and bets upon the price of grain. The miners who go 1000 feet into the earth . . . are as much business men as the few financial magnates who, in a back room, corner the money market of the world.

Now that Bryan had established the equality of the working masses with the eastern industrialists, he made clear to which side the Democratic Party must assign its allegiance—with the farmer and laborer of small-town, Jeffersonian America.

We come to speak for that broader class of business men . . . We say not one word against those who live upon the Atlantic coast, but those hardy pioneers who braved all the dangers of the wilderness, who have made the desert to blossom as the rose—those pioneers away out there, rearing their children near to Nature's heart, where they can mingle their voices with the voices of the birds—out there where they have erected schoolhouses for the education of their young, and churches where they praise their Creator, and cemeteries where sleep the ashes of their dead, are as deserving of the consideration of this party as any people in this country.

These words speak to the transcendent nature of the "Cross of Gold." The speech fundamentally changed the tone and tenor of modern American political rhetoric. It recast the Democratic Party as the party of populism and the emerging progressive movement, making it the voice of working-class America. Bryan's words established a clear dividing line between East (industry) and West (agriculture), between reformers and conservatives, and above all between "the idle holders of idle capital" and "the struggling masses who produce the wealth and pay the taxes of the country." These contrasting viewpoints would set the stage for a century of political debates. Indeed, Americans have spent more than a century arguing over the issues that Bryan raised in July 1896.

Above all, at the dawn of the twentieth century, Bryan's words dramatized the divide between two perspectives on the proper role of government. "There are two ideas of government. There are those who believe that if you just legislate to make the well to do prosperous, their prosperity will leak through on those below. The Democratic idea, however, has been that if you legislate to make the masses prosperous their prosperity will find its way up through every class, and rest upon it," said Bryan. One can easily imagine hearing such words spoken today on the presidential campaign trail.

As the historian Michael Kazin argues, Bryan's words stand as among the first ever spoken by a national political leader that argued for the permanent expansion of the powers of the federal government on behalf of working-class Americans.[11] The dedicated Republican newspaper editor William Allen White, who viewed Bryan's nomination with enormous trepidation, would later begrudgingly say of Bryan, "It was the first time in my life and in the life of a generation in which any man large enough to lead a national party had boldly and unashamedly made his cause that of the poor and the oppressed."[12]

Yet Bryan was far from done. With the crowd whipped to a frenzy and unable to resist his urging, Bryan delivered his rhetorical coup de grâce, couched in language that stirred in his God-fearing audience images of Christ on the cross. It remains among the most famous utterances in American oratory:

> Having behind us the producing masses of this nation and the world; having behind us the commercial interests and the laboring interests, and all the toiling masses, we shall answer their demands for a gold standard by saying to them "You shall not press down upon the brow of labor this crown of thorns. You shall not crucify mankind upon a cross of gold."

As he spoke the words "crown of thorns," Bryan raised his hands to his temples as if to dramatize a crown upon his actual head.[13] He then stretched his arms wide and held them in a Christ-like pose. It was the height of political theater, and an eerie silence fell over the stunned crowd. Bryan's arms fell to his side and he humbly began to walk back to his seat.

Then all hell broke loose.

The effect on the crowd was cataclysmic. "Marc Antony never applied the match more effectively," said the Associated Press.[14] The crowd screamed itself hoarse, "until the volume of sounds broke like a gigantic wave."[15] One newsman compared the sound in the convention hall to "one great burst of artillery," while others said it was "almost frightening."[16] Delegates waved handkerchiefs, hats, umbrellas, and anything else they could get their hands on. Those in the galleries tore off their coats and flung them from the balconies into the gurgling crowd below. Grown men hugged and openly wept as tears streamed down their bearded cheeks.[17] Historian Richard Hofstadter tells the story of one pro-gold Democrat seated in the convention hall's galleries scoffing at Bryan's pro-silver words. Yet by the time the young orator concluded his remarks, this onetime skeptic was so overwhelmed he turned to a pro-silver Democrat seated nearby and screamed at him, "Yell for God's sake, yell," as he pulled him out of his chair.[18]

Writing for the *New York Journal,* the noted political commentator Henry George said of the astonishing scene, "With his first words, there began a scene which I think must be without parallel, not merely in the history of American conventions, but in the history of the world; a display of the power of well chosen speech to move and stir great masses of men that can hardly before have had its equal."[19] While George may have exaggerated, it is fair to say that never before and never since in American politics has a political speech had such an electrifying impact on an audience.

Not surprisingly, the silver plank to the party platform was passed and the thirty-six-year-old Bryan would become the Democratic nominee for president, transforming the Democrats into the party of liberalism and reform. It is an image that continues to define the party to this day.

## A NATION DIVIDED

However, not everyone was enthralled by Bryan's words. The *Kansas City Journal* ominously declared, "The politician who attempts to array one class against another; to influence the poor against the rich; to kindle the fires of revolution in the breasts of the people, is a demagogue and an enemy of his country. Such a man is William Jennings Bryan of Nebraska."[20]

Ultimately Bryan's incendiary rhetoric would doom his political prospects. The "Cross of Gold" contains some of the most important aspects of a great political speech. It has a well-defined and easily identifiable straw man (the eastern moneyed elite) and certainly has an inspirational element. But the rhetorical lift that the "Cross of Gold" speech provides is narrowly aimed and harshly divisive. Bryan depicted the battle over bimetallism as a "war" and those who opposed silver as the "enemy," and pledged that "we shall fight them [the defenders of the gold standard] to the uttermost."

Maybe there was no way for Bryan to significantly broaden his appeal outside of his base of agrarian, working-class voters, but to be sure, he didn't really try. He attacked his opponents not simply as wrong but as immoral and even irreligious. And Bryan did more than simply lambaste Republicans—he confronted an entire class of Americans, arguing that the farmer and small-town businessman was more deserving of support than those who lived on the Atlantic coast or in an urban area. At a time of rising industrialization and urbanization, Bryan's "Cross of Gold" was grounded in a vision of the nation's agrarian past that meant little to these Americans. (It is small wonder that Bryan would lose every state in the Northeast while sweeping the Rocky Mountain states, the Plains states, and the traditionally solid Democratic South.)

When GOP surrogates traveled the country denouncing Bryan as a dangerous radical and demagogue, their words resonated. While the "Cross of Gold" undoubtedly energized the Democratic delegates and likely won him the party's nomination, it also likely doomed any chance of Bryan becoming president. As many future American politicians would discover, the harsher and more divisive the campaign rhetoric, the greater the chance of failure at the ballot box. Populism may get the political juices flowing and whip some voters into a frenzy, but it rarely translates into success on Election Day.

Undaunted, Bryan left Chicago and hit the campaign trail—truly an unprecedented act. Previously, it was considered uncouth for a national candidate to speak directly to voters and ask for their support, but Bryan knew his strength came in his oration and personal magnetism. He barnstormed the nation, traveling more than eighteen thousand miles, delivering hundreds of speeches, and speaking to millions of people. No American had ever seen as vigorous a campaign for the White House. It represented a new style of political campaigning—and a new appreciation for the importance of political oratory—that would change the very nature of twentieth-century American politics. In contrast to Bryan's fervent campaigning, his opponent, William McKinley, conducted a front-porch campaign. The Republican candidate stayed at his home in Canton, Ohio, while a steady flow of visitors streamed into town to hear the candidate make his case for the White House. The contrast between the activist Bryan and the politically reposed McKinley could hardly be laid out more vividly.

Of course, Bryan would go on to lose the 1896 election. It would be the first of three unsuccessful runs for the White House. The populist and later the progressive movements, which Bryan gave lift to, would never truly dominate American politics, but their influence would be felt far and wide, from the eventual adoption of the federal income tax and popular election of U.S. senators to women's suffrage, regulation of the railroads, creation of the Department of Labor, and even the adoption of Prohibition.[21] Not only would Bryan's speech and subsequent campaign transform the Democratic Party, but his focus on government's role in lending a helping hand to the working masses would eventually give birth to the modern welfare state—and a century-long economic debate about the proper role of government in the lives of the American people. Quite simply, nothing in American politics was ever the same after the "Cross of Gold."

## *William Jennings Bryan Addresses the Democratic National Convention on the Issue of Bimetallism, Chicago, July 9, 1896*

Mr. Chairman and Gentlemen of the Convention—I would be presumptuous, indeed, to present myself against the distinguished gentlemen to whom you have listened if this were but a measuring of ability, but this is not a contest among persons. The humblest citizen in all the land when clad in the armor of a righteous cause is stronger than the whole hosts error can bring.

I come to speak to you in defense of a cause holy as the cause of liberty—the cause of humanity.

. . . Never before in the history of this country has there been witnessed such a contest as that through which we have passed. Never before in the history of American politics has a great issue been fought out as this issue has been by the voters themselves.

. . . In this contest brother has been arrayed against brother and father against son. The warmest ties of love and acquaintance and association have been disregarded. Old leaders have been cast aside when they refused to give expression to the sentiments of those whom they would lead, and new leaders have sprung up to give direction to this cause of truth. Thus has the contest been waged . . .

. . . When you come before us and tell us that we shall disturb your business interests we reply that you have disturbed our business interests by your course. We say to you that you have made too limited in its application the definition of "business man." The man who is employed for wages is as much a business man as his employer. The attorney in a country town is as much a business man as the corporation counsel in a great metropolis. The merchant at the cross roads store is as much a business man as the merchant of New York.

The farmer who goes forth in the morning and toils all day,

begins in the spring and toils all summer, and, by the application of brains and muscle to the natural resources of this country, creates wealth, is as much a business man as the man who goes upon the board of trade and bets upon the price of grain. The miners who go 1000 feet into the earth or climb 2000 feet upon the cliffs and bring forth from their hiding places the precious metals to be poured into the channels of trade are as much business men as the few financial magnates who, in a back room, corner the money market of the world.

We come to speak for that broader class of business men. Ah, my friends, we say not one word against those who live upon the Atlantic coast, but those hardy pioneers who braved all the dangers of the wilderness, who have made the desert to blossom as the rose—those pioneers away out there, rearing their children near to Nature's heart, where they can mingle their voices with the voices of the birds—out there where they have erected schoolhouses for the education of their young, and churches where they praise their Creator, and cemeteries where sleep the ashes of their dead, are as deserving of the consideration of this party as any people in this country.

It is for these that we speak. We do not come as aggressors. Our war is not a war of conquest. We are fighting in the defense of our homes, our families and posterity. We have petitioned and our petitions have been scorned. We have entreated and our entreaties have been disregarded. We have begged and they have mocked, and our calamity came.

We beg no longer, we entreat no more, we petition no more. We defy them!

The gentleman from Wisconsin has said he fears a Robespierre. My friend, in this land of the free you need fear no tyrant who will spring up from among the people. What we need is an Andrew Jackson, to stand, as Jackson stood, against the encroachments of aggrandized wealth.

They tell us that this platform was made to catch votes. We reply to them that changing conditions make new issues; that the principles upon which rest democracy are as everlasting as the hills, but that they must be applied to new conditions as they arise. Conditions have arisen, and we are attempting to meet those conditions.

... We say in our platform that we believe the right to coin money and issue money is a function of government. We believe it. We believe it is a part of sovereignty and can no more with safety be delegated to private individuals than we could afford to delegate to private individuals the power to make penal statutes or levy laws for taxation.

Mr. Jefferson, who was once regarded as good Democratic authority, seems to have a different opinion from the gentleman who has addressed us on the part of the minority. Those who are opposed to this proposition tell us that the issue of paper money is a function of the bank, and that the government ought to go out of the banking business. I stand with Jefferson rather than with them in holding, as he did, that the issue of money is a function of the government, and that the banks ought to go out of the government business.

They complain about that plank which declares against the life tenure in office. They have tried to strain it to mean that which it does not mean. What we oppose in that plank is the life tenure that is being built at Washington, which excludes from participation in the benefits the humbler members of our society.

... Now, my friends, let me come to the great paramount issue. If they ask us here why it is that we say more on the money question than we say upon the tariff question I reply that if protection has slain its thousands the gold standard has slain its tens of thousands. If they ask us why we did not embody all these things in our platform which we believe we reply to them that when we have restored the money of the constitution all other necessary re-

forms will be possible, and that until that is done there is no reform that can be accomplished.

Why is it that within three months such a change has come over
the sentiments of this country? Three months ago, when it was
confidently asserted that those who believe in the gold standard
would frame our platform and nominate another candidate, even
the advocates of the gold standard did not think that we could elect
a president, but they had good reason for the suspicion, because
there is scarcely a state here today asking the gold standard that is
not within the absolute control of the Republican party.

But note the change. Mr. McKinley was nominated at St.
Louis on a platform that declared for the maintenance of the gold
standard until it should be changed into bimetallism by an international agreement. Mr. McKinley was the most popular man
among the Republicans, and everybody three months ago in the
Republican party prophesied his election.

How is it today? Why, that man who used to boast that he
looked like Napoleon—that man shudders today when he thinks
that he was nominated on the anniversary of the battle of Water-
loo. Not only that, but as he listens he can hear with ever increasing distinctness the sound of the waves as they beat upon the
lonely shores of St. Helena.

Why this change? Ah, my friends, is not the change evident to
any one who will look at the matter? It is no private character,
however pure, no personal popularity, however great, that can protect from the avenging wrath of an indignant people the man who
will either declare that he is in favor of fastening the gold standard
upon this people, or who is willing to surrender the right of self-
government and place legislative control in the hands of foreign po-
tentates and powers.

We go forth confident that we shall win. Why? Because upon
the paramount issue in this campaign there is not a spot of ground
upon which the enemy will dare to challenge battle. Why, if they

tell us that the gold standard is a good thing, we point to their platform and tell them that their platform pledges the party to get rid of a gold standard and substitute bimetallism. If the gold standard is a good thing, why try to get rid of it?

I might call your attention to the fact that some of the very people who are in this convention today and who tell you that we ought to declare in favor of international bimetallism, and thereby declare that the gold standard is wrong and the principle of bimetallism is better—these very people four months ago were open and avowed advocates of the gold standard, and telling us that we could not legislate two metals together, even with all the world.

I want to suggest this truth, that if the gold standard is a good thing we ought to declare in favor of its retention, and not in favor of abandoning it, and if the gold standard is a bad thing, why should we wait until some other nations are willing to help us to let go?

Here is the line of battle: We care not upon which issue they force the fight. We are prepared to meet them on either issue, or on both. If they tell us that the gold standard is the standard of civilization, we reply to them that this, the most enlightened of all the nations of the earth, has never declared for a gold standard, and both the parties this year are declaring against it.

If the gold standard is the standard of civilization, why, my friends, should we not have it? So, if they come to meet us on that, we can present the history of our nation. More than that, we can tell them this, that they will search the pages of history in vain to find a single instance in which the common people of any land have ever declared themselves in favor of a gold standard. They can find where the holders of fixed investments have.

Mr. Carlisle* said in 1878 that this was a struggle between the idle holders of idle capital and the struggling masses who produce

---

*This refers to John G. Carlisle, the incumbent president Grover Cleveland's deeply unpopular secretary of the treasury.

the wealth and pay the taxes of the country, and, my friends, it is simply a question that we shall decide, upon which side shall the Democratic party fight? Upon the side of the idle holders of idle capital, or upon the side of the struggling masses? That is the question that the party must answer first, and then it must be answered by each individual hereafter.

The sympathies of the Democratic party, as described by the platform, are on the side of the struggling masses who have ever been the foundation of the Democratic party. There are two ideas of government. There are those who believe that if you just legislate to make the well to do prosperous, their prosperity will leak through on those below. The Democratic idea has been that if you legislate to make the masses prosperous their prosperity will find its way up through every class, and rest upon it.

You come to us and tell us that the great cities are in favor of the gold standard. I tell you that the great cities rest upon these broad and fertile prairies. Burn down your cities and leave our farms, and your cities will spring up again as if by magic; but destroy our farms and the grass will grow in the streets of every city in this country.

My friends, we shall declare that this nation is able to legislate for its own people on every question, without waiting for the aid or consent of any other nation on earth, and upon that issue we expect to carry every single state in this union.

. . . It is the issue of 1776 over again. Our ancestors were the 3,000,000 who had the courage to declare their political independence of every other nation upon earth. Shall we, their descendants, when we have grown to 70,000,000, declare that we are less independent than our forefathers? No, my friends, it will never be the judgment of this people.

Therefore, we care not upon what lines the battle is fought. If they say bimetallism is good, but we cannot have it until some nation helps us, we reply that instead of having a gold standard because England has we shall restore bimetallism and then let England have bimetallism because the United States has.

If they dare to come out and in the open defend the gold standard as a good thing we shall fight them to the uttermost. Having behind us the producing masses of this nation and the world; having behind us the commercial interests and the laboring interests, and all the toiling masses, we shall answer their demands for a gold standard by saying to them "You shall not press down upon the brow of labor this crown of thorns. You shall not crucify mankind upon a cross of gold."

*Chapter 2*

# THE NEW NATIONALISM VERSUS THE NEW FREEDOM

Theodore Roosevelt and Woodrow Wilson Debate the
Fundamental Question of American Capitalism:
1910–1912

F EW PRESIDENTIAL ELECTIONS have done more to shape
the course of American history than the 1912 race for the
White House. It was a campaign that matched three men who
had been or would be president: Theodore Roosevelt, Woodrow
Wilson, and the incumbent, William Howard Taft. It was a race
that would feature one of the strongest third-party performances
in American presidential history, with Roosevelt's Progressive
Party and Eugene Debs's Socialist Party receiving more than a
third of the popular vote. But above all, the 1912 campaign came
to represent a true dividing line in American politics—a before-
and-after moment that changed the political destiny of the nation.

In 1896, the choice on the campaign trail was between a pas-
sive view of government's role in the affairs of the American people (McKinley) and a far more activist one (Bryan). The 1912
election, on the other hand, was the first presidential election in
American history to offer two competing notions of *activist* government. At their core, Roosevelt's "New Nationalism" and

Wilson's "New Freedom" both made clear the need for government intervention in the economic affairs of the nation.[1] The question the two candidates would pose to the American people was what this engagement would look like.

On the surface, the contrast between Theodore Roosevelt's New Nationalism and Woodrow Wilson's New Freedom was not as great as it would seem. For example, both men rejected the positions of the more radical progressives, such as Debs. (William Allen White joked that the difference between the two candidates was "that fantastic imaginary gulf that always has existed between tweedle-dum and tweedle-dee.")[2] But on one crucial issue the two men strongly diverged—how to deal with America's increasingly powerful business trusts, the precursors to today's modern corporations. This disagreement would lay the foundation for a century-long economic and political debate, which continues to this day. The growing "bigness" of American business and its impact on the economic, political, and cultural life of the United States would become the defining issue of not only the 1912 campaign but also the Progressive Era.[3]

## ROOSEVELT AND THE NEW NATIONALISM

At the turn of the century, presidential elections generally didn't gather steam until the national conventions. But 1912 was no ordinary year. The race began in true measure more than two years before, when former president Teddy Roosevelt broke with current president William Howard Taft and the increasingly conservative Republican Party. Though he had been out of the White House for two years, few national figures exerted as great an influence over the national psyche as Roosevelt. Famed historian Arthur Schlesinger Jr. said of him, "With his squeaky voice, his gleaming teeth, his overpowering grin, and his incurable delight in self-dramatization, he brought everything he touched to life . . . He stirred the conscience of America."[4]

The former president had anointed the portly Taft as his successor but became bitterly disappointed in his protégé's abandonment of progressive values and embrace of conservatism. Fed up with Taft's rightward drift, Roosevelt headed to Osawatomie, Kansas, to deliver the first articulation of his emerging New Nationalism doctrine. This was a sacred spot for reformers, as Osawatomie was the town where abolitionist leader John Brown began his war against slavery in 1856. On this steamy late August afternoon, the small town's Main Street "was gay with Sears Roebuck gingham and fresh blue denim."[5] Said one local paper, "We put on our biled shirts, brought the galluses out of their hiding place, had our better halves darn our socks, put on our smile, and thank you, we are ready for plutocrat and peasant." More than thirty thousand people came out to hear the former president deliver one of his "thumping speeches"—and quite a speech it would be. Standing atop a kitchen table, Roosevelt spoke for more than ninety minutes.[6]

Inspired in large measure by Herbert Croly's recently published *The Promise of American Life*, Roosevelt's New Nationalism philosophy called on the American people to put the interests of the nation above their own "sectional or personal advantage."[7] Arguing that America faced a moment as consequential as the one it had faced on the eve of the Civil War, Roosevelt believed that America must devote itself to national unity and move beyond the parochial assumptions and attachments that drove so much of American politics.[8]

In echoing Alexander Hamilton's founding vision of a strong, centralized government, Roosevelt declared that the time had come for the federal government and a "vigorous Chief Executive" to exert its influence as the "steward of public welfare" and directly regulate the economy in order to ensure social justice. In words that surely made conservatives apoplectic, Roosevelt declared:

> The true friend of property, the true conservative, is he who insists that property shall be the servant and not the master of the commonwealth; who insists that the creature of man's making shall be the servant and not the master of the man who made it. The citizens of the United States must effectively control the mighty commercial forces which they have themselves called into being.

Under the New Nationalism, no longer would the pursuit of profit take precedence over "human welfare," and businesses would have to accept regulation in order to ensure that the needs of the populace were being met. "The object of government is the welfare of the people," Roosevelt asserted.

On a practical level, the New Nationalism called for a stronger executive branch to play a more meaningful and assertive role in national affairs. "The national government," said Roosevelt, "belongs to the whole American people, and where the whole American people are interested, that interest can be guarded effectively only by the national government."

This newly emboldened federal government would improve the lot of the American people through the implementation of a number of progressive policies, including the adoption of a graduated income and inheritance tax, the banishment of child labor, a reduction in tariffs, worker's compensation, and above all, increased power for the Interstate Commerce Commission in regulating those corporations conducting interstate business.[9] In short, government would become an activist force focused on uplifting the public welfare.

It was on the issue of the trusts, however, that Roosevelt refused to go as far as some progressives. Echoing Croly's belief that

large-scale businesses "contributed to American economic efficiency," Roosevelt didn't envision these economic powerhouses being broken up. He wanted them to be beholden to a strong federal executive.[10] This somewhat benign view of the trusts would become the central dividing line between Roosevelt and his eventual Democratic opponent, Woodrow Wilson.

But in 1910 that debate had yet to truly begin. Roosevelt's New Nationalism was above all a debate between progressivism and conservatism. Before Wilson had even hit the campaign trail, Roosevelt was seeking to move Republicans toward a progressive political agenda. Roosevelt was, in effect, launching his bid for the soul of the Republican Party.

While young progressives were enthralled by Roosevelt's words, conservatives were aghast. *Harper's Weekly* labeled the former president "a virtual traitor"; the *World* charged the New Nationalism was "an outburst of Marxian madness"; others compared him to tyrants such as Julius Caesar and Kaiser Wilhelm, among others.[11]

Their fears were well-founded. Roosevelt's New Nationalism agenda would not only lay the underpinnings for the modern welfare state but also strengthen and empower the executive branch, making possible the eventual implementation of progressive reforms. Indeed, many of the measures he advocated would be adopted by his 1912 opponent and would fundamentally alter and increase the role of the federal government in the lives of the American people. Roosevelt lost the battle in 1912, but in many respects his beliefs would win the war.

Roosevelt's insurgent campaign against Taft and the conservative wing of the party would fall short at the tumultuous 1912 Republican convention. While Roosevelt overwhelmed the deeply unpopular Taft in primary voting (including the incumbent president's home state of Ohio), Taft's control over the party apparatus ensured his renomination at the GOP convention in Chicago

Unwilling to accept what was largely a false defeat, Roo
launched a third-party campaign under the banner of the Prog.
sives, splitting the Republican coalition and virtually ensuring
Democratic victory on Election Day.

The decision by party bosses to stick with Taft and reject reform
would have far-reaching consequences for Republicans,
enshrining the century-long dominance of small-government conservatism in the party. Commented historian James Chace, "The
broken friendship between Taft and Roosevelt inflicted wounds
on the Republican Party that have never been healed. For the rest
of the century . . . the Republican Party was riven by the struggle
between reform and reaction."[12] In countless elections—1940,
1952, 1964, 1980, even 1992—these battles would rage among the
party faithful.

Yet, for all the intrigue on the GOP side, there was still a general election to be fought. While Taft remained in the race, it was
clear to all concerned (most of all the candidate himself) that he
could not win reelection. In fact, he spent much of the election
on the golf links rather than on the hustings. Instead, the race for
the White House in 1912 became an extraordinary debate on
progressivism, held on the campaign trail, between two very different conceptions of the appropriate role of government in the
lives of the American people.

## WILSON AND THE NEW FREEDOM

Woodrow Wilson is today known as one of the presidency's great
thinkers, and yet he was a politician whose back-and-forth political machinations sometimes reflected an individual more focused
on the forcefulness of his message than on its substance. As historian William Leuchtenburg said of the twenty-eighth president,
"Wilson felt that every significant political achievement resulted
from the leadership of an inspired statesman who has found the

precise words to move men. He was often less interested in finding the right solution to the problem than the right language."[13]
For Wilson, public rhetoric was at its core a tool for molding public opinion: "a president whom [the country] trusts can not only
lead it, but form it to his own views" by "giving direction to
opinion."[14] According to historian Eric Goldman, "Wilson's un-
doubted power over men did not come from any striking origi-
nality of thought or any great ability in reaching rapport with
other human beings. It came from God-lashed energies, a conta-
gious self-righteousness, a talent for finely chiseled oratory which
carried a constant implication that only the Devil would disagree."[15] At the very least, Wilson was a speechwriter's dream
come true.

Certainly, no presidential candidate in American history put together a more varied and fascinating collection of great campaign
speeches than Woodrow Wilson. Today, most candidates repeat
campaign remarks over and over again, articulating the same poll-
tested themes and messaging. But Wilson provided historians with
a treasure trove of orations. His collection of 1912 campaign
speeches—almost all given after Labor Day, the traditional kickoff
to the fall campaign, and most delivered extemporaneously—
demonstrates the breadth of Wilson's intellect, the suppleness of his
mind, and the true dynamics of his New Freedom platform. Pity
the editor who tries to choose just one of these speeches to hold up
as an example of Wilson's rhetorical prowess! But if 1912 was an
election primarily about the issue of the trusts, then Wilson's
address in Buffalo, New York, before as many as ten thousand
workers on Labor Day, September 2, 1912, is among the most important and influential—but it was not one that necessarily came
naturally.

Wilson ran for the presidency with a record that in the parlance of today's politics would most likely be characterized as that
of a flip-flopper. He left the Democratic Party in 1896 over the

nomination of William Jennings Bryan and once confessed that had he been alive during the American Revolution, he would have been a Tory. His makeup was seemingly that of a conservative (or so thought his early political backers), but upon winning the gubernatorial nomination in New Jersey, he embraced reform. By the time of the 1912 Democratic convention, he was bashing the "money trusts" and the big-business elites who had ironically greased the wheels of his political rise.[16]

A latecomer to progressivism, Wilson sought an issue that would allow him to differentiate his campaign from Roosevelt's. With the assistance of future Supreme Court justice Louis Brandeis, Wilson focused his political message on America's growing business trusts and government's role and responsibility in regulating them.[17]

For Wilson, the impact of the trusts was the crucial question of the campaign. He argued that because of their enormous size and growing economic power, they were limiting the opportunities and aspirations of the American people. "These great combined industries have been more inimical to organized labor than any other class of employers in the United States." Only by expanding competition and by marginalizing the power of the trusts would Americans enjoy a new burst of freedom. "I believe that the greatest force for peace," claimed Wilson, "the greatest force for righteousness, the greatest force for the elevation of mankind, is organized opinion, is the thinking of men, is the great force which is in the soul of men, and I want men to breathe a free and pure air."

To dramatize his point, Wilson used a resonant image—that of a new invention, the automobile. He argued that the monopolies were "so many cars of juggernaut" which were "being driven over men in such ways to crush them." Under a Roosevelt presidency, these juggernauts not only would be "licensed" but would even be "driven by commissioners of the United States," flattening everything in their path.

It was the perfect analogy for capturing the divide between the two candidates. While Roosevelt wanted a newly assertive federal government to step in directly and regulate the nation's economic behemoths (but still keep them in place), Wilson sought to weaken the trusts in order to ensure greater competition in the economy. As he put it succinctly, "Ours is a program of liberty, and theirs is a program of regulation." He would ridicule Roosevelt's approach, derisively claiming that under TR's plan the monopolies would be "in charge of the federal government." "Do you want to be taken care of by a combination of the government and the monopolies?" Wilson asked, reminding listeners that "the minute you are taken care of by the government you are wards, not independent men."

The differences between the two candidates on the trust question were as old as the nation itself and reflected the contrasting views of Hamilton and Thomas Jefferson, with his advocacy of state's rights, limited government, and a revolutionary belief in the purity of the toiling masses. Roosevelt derided Jefferson's "nervous fear of doing anything that may seem to be unpopular with the rank and file of the people," and he believed that America needed "Hamiltonian means," in order to achieve Jeffersonian goals for the nation.[18]

Wilson's conception of the New Freedom was firmly grounded in Jeffersonian thinking. In Wilson's New Freedom, it was the "man on the make" who represented the building block of not just the American economy but American society. At Buffalo, in language echoing Bryan, Wilson argued that "the wage earners of this country, in the broad sense, constitute the country." For Wilson, the New Freedom and greater economic competition would "take the shackles off American industry, the shackles of monopoly, and . . . reassert the power of American citizenship." As he plaintively asked the laborers gathered before him in Buffalo, "See to it that those who are sweating blood know that they must not sweat blood all their lives but that if they devote their energy they will devote it in hope and not in despair, as their own masters, and not as men's servants; as men who can look their fellow in the face and say: 'We also are of the free breed of American citizens.'"

In the end, the trust issue was indicative of a much larger debate about the future of America. After taking office as Wilson's vice president, Thomas Marshall would sum up well the fundamental issue at stake in 1912: "The people were told in the last campaign that trusts were a natural evolution and that the only way to deal with them was to regulate them. The people are tired of being told such things. What they want is the kind of opportunity that formerly existed in this country."[19]

Throughout its relatively short history, America had embodied a mind-set that reflected the ideal that success in life was the result of hard work, ambition, and perseverance. As Wilson would describe this reigning national impulse in a campaign rally in late October in New York City, America was committed to "ideals of absolutely free opportunity, where no man has any limitations except the limitations of his character and of his mind; where there is no distinction of class, no distinction of blood, no distinction of social status, but men win or lose on their merits."[20] It was this belief in traditional American values, which firmly anchored the New Freedom, that went a long way toward explaining its popularity vis-à-vis the far more radical doctrine of the New Nationalism.

In Wilson's view, the people's destiny, their liberty, and their entrepreneurship were being destroyed by the all-encompassing trusts. The solution was not to regulate these economic giants but instead to ensure that all participants in the economy could compete fairly. What the country needed was "free competition," not "illicit competition." If the trusts were to win the competitive battle, that was fine with Wilson. He had no problem with big companies, as long as they achieved such size through efficiency rather than unfair or illegal means. Such distinctions would allow Wilson to incongruously (but logically) argue "I am for big business" but "I am against the trusts."[21]

## DRAWING BATTLE LINES

Generations of reformers to come would hotly debate the contrasting approaches for balancing economic growth and social policy that were bandied about the campaign trail in 1912. Never again would an American election feature such a dynamic debate about the nature of activist government. Indeed from a political perspective, the campaign helped to establish century-long battle lines between the two parties and between liberalism and conservatism. Yet for all their disagreements Roosevelt and Wilson did share one thing in common: through their embrace of progressive ideals they "invented the activist modern presidency . . . Their legacy was the use of centralized power to create greater democracy," says Chace.[22]

Though he largely stayed off the campaign trail in 1912, delivering only two major speeches after August, President Taft also would have his say. At the official notification of his renomination he attacked the approaches of his opponents as "socialism" (a familiar GOP refrain) and sounded an age-old message of American individualism and entrepreneurship: "The fruits of energy, courage, enterprise, attention to duty, hard work, thrift, providence, restraints of appetite and passion will continue to have their reward under the present system."[23]

In September, he would take his attacks on Wilson and Roosevelt even further, mocking progressive politics. "A National Government cannot create good times," Taft derisively remarked. "It cannot make the rain to fall, the sun to shine, or the crops to grow, but it can, by pursuing a meddlesome policy, attempting to change economic conditions, and frightening the investment of capital, prevent a prosperity and a revival of business which otherwise might have taken place."[24]

On Election Day, Taft and the GOP were humiliated, winning only 23 percent of the vote and a meager eight electoral votes. Yet the conservatives won a Pyrrhic victory—control of the Republican Party. Taft's governing philosophy would be derided in 1912, but a century later it would continue to form the intellectual backbone of the party.

Even though Wilson's embrace of reform was not as passionate as that of his thrice-nominated Democratic predecessor, William Jennings Bryan, the contrast with Taft and the conservatives solidified the Democratic Party's position as the voice of progressivism and eventually liberalism in American politics. The extraordinary debate in 1912 between Wilson and Roosevelt would eventually be supplanted by a larger debate between liberalism and conservatism. The national conversation about the proper balance between liberal and conservative views on the role of government in helping tackle America's economic and social challenges was born in 1912. Nearly one hundred years later, it continues to rage on the campaign trail.

### *Theodore Roosevelt Defines His New Nationalism Platform, Osawatomie, Kansas, August 31, 1910*

We come here to-day to commemorate one of the epoch-making events of the long struggle for the rights of man—the long struggle for the uplift of humanity. Our country—this great republic—means nothing unless it means the triumph of a real democracy, the triumph of popular government, and, in the long run, of an economic system under which each man shall be guaranteed the opportunity to show the best that there is in him. That is why the history of America is now the central feature of the history of the world; for the world has set its face hopefully toward our democracy; and, O my fellow citizens, each one of you carries on your shoulders not only the burden of doing well for the sake of your own country, but the burden of doing well and of seeing that this nation does well for the sake of mankind.

. . . In every wise struggle for human betterment one of the main objects, and often the only object, has been to achieve in large measure equality of opportunity. In the struggle for this great end, nations rise from barbarism to civilization, and through it people press forward from one stage of enlightenment to the next. One of the chief factors in progress is the destruction of special privilege. The essence of any struggle for healthy liberty has always been, and must always be, to take from some one man or class of men the right to enjoy power, or wealth, or position, or immunity, which has not been earned by service to his or their fellows. That is what you fought for in the Civil War, and that is what we strive for now.

At many stages in the advance of humanity, this conflict between the men who possess more than they have earned and the men who have earned more than they possess is the central condition of progress. In our day it appears as the struggle of free men to gain and hold the right of self-government as against the special interests, who twist the methods of free government into machinery for defeating the popular will. At every stage, and under all circumstances, the essence of the struggle is to equalize opportunity, destroy privilege, and give to the life and citizenship of every individual the highest possible value both to himself and to the commonwealth.

. . . Practical equality of opportunity for all citizens, when we achieve it, will have two great results. First, every man will have a fair chance to make of himself all that in him lies; to reach the highest point to which his capacities, unassisted by special privilege of his own and unhampered by the special privilege of others, can carry him, and to get for himself and his family substantially what he has earned. Second, equality of opportunity means that the commonwealth will get from every citizen the highest service of which he is capable. No man who carries the burden of the special privileges of another can give to the commonwealth that service to which it is fairly entitled.

I stand for the square deal . . . I mean not merely that I stand for fair play under the present rules of the game, but that I stand for having those rules changed so as to work for a more substantial equality of opportunity and of reward for equally good service.

. . . Now, this means that our government, national and state, must be freed from the sinister influence or control of special interests . . . We must drive the special interests out of politics. That is one of our tasks to-day. Every special interest is entitled to justice . . . but not one is entitled to a vote in Congress, to a voice on the bench, or to representation in any public office. The Constitution guarantees protection to property, and we must make that promise good. But it does not give the right of suffrage to any corporation.

The true friend of property, the true conservative, is he who insists that property shall be the servant and not the master of the commonwealth; who insists that the creature of man's making shall be the servant and not the master of the man who made it. The citizens of the United States must effectively control the mighty commercial forces which they have called into being.

There can be no effective control of corporations while their political activity remains. To put an end to it will be neither a short nor an easy task, but it can be done. We must have complete and effective publicity of corporate affairs, so that the people may know beyond peradventure whether the corporations obey the law and whether their management entitles them to the confidence of the public. It is necessary that laws should be passed to prohibit the use of corporate funds directly or indirectly for political purposes; it is still more necessary that such laws should be thoroughly enforced. Corporate expenditures for political purposes, and especially such expenditures by public-service corporations, have supplied one of the principal sources of corruption in our political affairs.

It has become entirely clear that we must have government supervision of the capitalization, not only of public-service corporations, including, particularly, railways, but of all corporations doing an interstate business.

. . . Combinations in industry are the result of an imperative economic law which cannot be repealed by political legislation. The effort at prohibiting all combination has substantially failed. The way out lies, not in attempting to prevent such combinations, but in completely controlling them in the interest of the public welfare.

. . . The absence of effective state, and, especially, national, restraint upon unfair money getting has tended to create a small class of enormously wealthy and economically powerful men, whose chief object is to hold and increase their power. The prime need is to change the conditions which enable these men to accumulate power which it is not for the general welfare that they should hold or exercise . . . This, I know, implies a policy of a far more active governmental interference with social and economic conditions in this country than we have yet had, but I think we have got to face the fact that such an increase in governmental control is now necessary.

. . . We are face to face with new conceptions of the relations of property to human welfare, chiefly because certain advocates of the rights of property as against the rights of men have been pushing their claims too far. The man who wrongly holds that every human right is secondary to his profit must now give way to the advocate of human welfare, who rightly maintains that every man holds his property subject to the general right of the community to regulate its use to whatever degree the public welfare may require it.

But I think we may go still further. The right to regulate the use of wealth in the public interest is universally admitted. Let us admit also the right to regulate the terms and conditions of labor, which is the chief element of wealth, directly in the interest of the common good. The fundamental thing to do for every man is to give him a chance to reach a place in which he will make the greatest possible contribution to the public welfare. Understand what I say there. Give him a chance, not push him up if he will not be pushed. Help any man who stumbles; if he lies down, it is a poor job to try to carry him; but if he is a worthy man, try your best to see that he gets a chance to show the worth that is in him. No man can be a good citizen unless he has a wage more than sufficient to cover the bare cost of living, and hours of labor short enough so that after his day's work is done he will have time and energy to bear his share in the management of the community, to help in carrying the general load. We keep countless men from being good citizens by the conditions of life with which we surround them.

We need comprehensive workmen's compensation acts, both

state and national laws to regulate child labor and work for women, and, especially, we need in our common schools not merely education in book learning, but also practical training for daily life and work. We need to enforce better sanitary conditions for our workers and to extend the use of safety appliances for our workers in industry and commerce, both within and between the states. Also, friends, in the interest of the workingman himself we need to set our faces like flint against mob violence just as against corporate greed; against violence and injustice and lawlessness by wage workers just as much as against lawless cunning and greed and selfish arrogance of employers.

If I could ask but one thing of my fellow countrymen, my request would be that, whenever they go in for reform, they remember the two sides, and that they always exact justice from one side as much as from the other. I have small use for the public servant who can always see and denounce the corruption of the capitalist, but who cannot persuade himself, especially before election, to say a word about lawless mob violence. And I have equally small use for the man, be he a judge on the bench, or editor of a great paper, or wealthy and influential private citizen, who can see clearly enough and denounce the lawlessness of mob violence, but whose eyes are closed so that he is blind when the question is one of corruption in business on a gigantic scale. Also remember what I said about excess in reformer and reactionary alike. If the reactionary man, who thinks of nothing but the rights of property, could have his way, he would bring about a revolution; and one of my chief fears in connection with progress comes because I do not want to see our people, for lack of proper leadership, compelled to follow men whose intentions are excellent, but whose eyes are a little too wild to make it really safe to trust them.

. . . I do not ask for overcentralization; but I do ask that we work in a spirit of broad and far-reaching nationalism when we work for what concerns our people as a whole. We are all Americans. Our common interests are as broad as the continent. I speak to you here in Kansas exactly as I would speak in New York or Georgia, for the most vital problems are those which affect us all alike. The national government belongs to the whole American people, and where the whole American people are interested, that interest can be guarded effectively only by the national government. The betterment which we seek must be accomplished, I believe, mainly through the national government.

The American people are right in demanding that New Nationalism, without which we cannot hope to deal with new problems. The New Nationalism puts the national need before sectional or personal advantage. It is impatient of the utter confusion that results from local legislatures attempting to treat national issues as local issues. It is still more impatient of the impotence which springs from overdivision of governmental powers, the impotence which makes it possible for local selfishness or for legal cunning, hired by wealthy special interests, to bring national activities to a deadlock. This New Nationalism regards the executive power as the steward of the public welfare. It demands of the judiciary that it shall be interested primarily in human welfare rather than in property, just as it demands that the representative body shall represent all the people rather than any one class or section of the people. I believe in shaping the ends of government to protect property as well as human welfare.

. . . The object of government is the welfare of the people. The material progress and prosperity of a nation are desirable chiefly so far as they lead to the moral and material welfare of all good citizens. Just in proportion as the average man and woman are honest, capable of sound judgment and high ideals, active in public affairs—but, first of all, sound in their home life, and the father and mother of healthy children whom they bring up well—just so far, and no farther, we may count our civilization a success. We must have—I believe we have already—a genuine and permanent moral awakening, without which no wisdom of legislation or administration really means anything; and, on the other hand, we must try to secure the social and economic legislation without which any improvement due to purely moral agitation is necessarily evanescent.

. . . No matter how honest and decent we are in our private lives, if we do not have the right kind of law and the right kind of administration of the law, we cannot go forward as a nation. That is imperative; but it must be an addition to, and not a substitution for, the qualities that make us good citizens. In the last analysis, the most important elements in any man's career must be the sum of those qualities which, in the aggregate, we speak of as character. If he has not got it, then no law that the wit of man can devise, no administration of the law by the boldest and strongest executive, will avail to help him. We must have the right kind of character—character that makes a man, first of all, a good man in the home, a good father, a good husband—that makes a man a good neighbor. You must have that, and, then, in addition, you must have the kind of law and the kind of administration of the law which will give to those qualities in the private citizen the best possible chance for development. The prime problem of our nation is to get the right type of good citizenship, and, to get it, we must have progress, and our public men must be genuinely progressive.

## *Woodrow Wilson Kicks Off His Campaign for the White House, Buffalo, September 2, 1912*

I feel that it is an honor and a privilege to address an audience like this and yet I feel, more than the honor of the occasion, the responsibility of it. Because I have learned from occupying a responsible executive position that the thing that grips a man most is what he promised the people that he would attempt before he was elected.

When I was engaged in the campaign before my election as governor of New Jersey, I made a good many promises. And I think that a great many people who heard me supposed that it was the usual thing that these promises were made in order to get votes, and that the man who made them did not feel the full responsibility of keeping them after he was elected. I don't know what the reason is, perhaps because I went into politics rather late in life, but I felt that every promise I made in that campaign I was bound to try to fulfill. No man can promise more than that he will do his best.

. . . Why is it that the people of this country are in danger of being discontented with the parties that have pretended to serve them? It is because in too many instances their promises were not matched by their performances and men began to say to themselves, "What is the use of going to the polls and voting? Nothing happens after the election." Is there any man within the hearing of my voice who can challenge the statement that any party that has forfeited the public confidence has forfeited it by its own non-performance?

. . . I want to speak upon this occasion, of course, on the interests of the workingman, of the wage earner, not because I regard the wage earners of this country as a special class, for they are not. After you have made a catalogue of the wage earners of this country, how many of us are left? The wage earners of this country, in the broad sense, constitute the country. And the most fatal thing that we can do in politics is to imagine that we belong to a special class, and that we have an interest which isn't the interest of the whole community. Half of the difficulties, half of the injustices of our politics have been due to the fact that men regarded themselves as having separate interests which they must serve even though other men were done a great disservice by their promoting them.

We are not afraid of those who pursue legitimate pursuits provided they link those pursuits in at every turn with the interest of the community as a whole; and no man can conduct a legitimate business, if he conducts it in the interest of a single class. I want, therefore, to look at the nation as a whole today . . . not divide it up into sections and classes, but I want particularly to discuss with you today the things which interest the wage earner.

. . . I want as a means of illustration, not as a means of contest, to use the platform of the third party as the means of expounding what I have to say today. I want you to read that platform very carefully, and I want to call your attention to the fact that it really consists of two parts. In one part of it, it declares the sympathy of the party with a certain great program of social reform, and promises that all the influence of that party, of the members of that party, will be used for the promotion of that program of social reform. In the other part, it itself lays down a method of procedure, and what I want you to soberly consider is whether the method of procedure is a suitable way of laying the foundations for the realization of that social program . . . the betterment of the condition of men in this occupation and the other, the protection of women, the shielding of children, the bringing about of social justice here, there, and elsewhere.

. . . There is a central method, a central purpose, in that platform from which I very seriously dissent. I am a Democrat as distinguished from a Republican because I believe (and I think that it is generally believed) that the leaders of the Republican party—for I always distinguish them from the great body of the Republican voters who have been misled by them . . . have allowed themselves to become so tied up in alliances with special interests that they are not free to serve us all. And that the immediate business, if you are to have any kind of reform at all, is to set your government free, is to break it away from the partnerships and alliances and understandings and purchases which have made it impossible for it to look at the country as a whole and made it necessary to serve special interests one at a time. Until that has been done, no program of social reform is possible because a program of social reform depends upon universal sympathy, universal justice, universal cooperation. It depends upon our understanding one another and serving one another.

What is the program of the third party with regard to the disentanglement of the government? Mr. Roosevelt has said, and up to a certain point I sympathize with him, that he does not object, for example, to the system of protection except in this circumstance—that it has not inured to the benefit of the workingman of this country. It is very interesting to have him admit that because the leaders of the Republican party have been time out of mind putting this bluff up on you men that the protective policy was for your sake, and I would like to know what you ever got out of it that you didn't get out of the better effort of organized labor? I have yet to learn of any instance where you got anything without going and taking it. And the process of our society instead of being a process of peace has sometimes too much resembled a process of war because men felt obliged to go and insist in organized masses upon getting the justice which they couldn't get any other way.

It is interesting, therefore, to have Mr. Roosevelt admit that not enough of the "prize money," as he frankly calls it, has gone into the pay envelope . . . But Mr. Roosevelt says that his [object] will be to see that a larger proportion gets into the pay envelope. And how does he propose to do it? . . . I don't find any suggestion anywhere in that platform of the way in which he is going to do it, except in one plank. One plank says that the party will favor a minimum wage for women; and then it goes on to say by a minimum wage it means a living wage, enough to live on.

I am going to assume, for the sake of argument, that it proposed more than that, that it proposed to get a minimum wage for everybody, men as well as women; and I want to call your attention to the fact that just as soon as a minimum wage is established by law, the temptation of every employer in the United States will be to bring his wages down as close to that minimum as he dares, because you can't strike against the government of the United States. You can't strike against what is in the law. You can strike against what is in your agreement with your employer, but if underneath that agreement there is the steel and the adamant of federal law, you can't tamper with that foundation. And who is going to pay these wages? You know that the great difficulty about wages . . . is that the control of industry is getting into fewer and fewer hands. And that, therefore, a smaller and smaller number of men are able to determine what wages shall be. In other words, one of the entanglements of our government is that we are dealing not with a community in which men may take their own choice of what they shall do, but in a community whose industry is very largely governed by great combinations of capital in the hands of a comparatively small number of men; that, in other words, we are in the hands, in many industries, of monopoly itself. And the only way in which the workingman can gain more wages is by getting them from the monopoly.

Very well then, what does this platform propose to do? Break up the monopolies? Not at all. It proposes to legalize them. It says in effect: You can't break them up; the only thing you can do is to put them in charge of the federal government. It proposes that they shall be adopted and regulated. And that looks to me like a consummation of the partnership between monopoly and government. Because, when once the government regulates monopoly, then monopoly will have to see to it that it regulates the government. This is a [beautiful] circle of change.

We now complain that the men who control these monopolies control the government, and it is in turn proposed that the government should control them. I am perfectly willing to be controlled if it is I, myself, who controls me. If this partnership can be continued, then this control can be manipulated and adjusted to its own pleasure. Therefore, I want to call your attention to this fact that these great combined industries have been more inimical to organized labor than any other class of employers in the United States. Is not that so?

These monopolies that the government, it is proposed, should adopt are the men who have made your independent action most difficult. They have made it most difficult that you should take care of yourselves; and let me tell you that the old adage that God takes care of those who take care of themselves is not gone out of date. No federal legislation can change that thing. The minute you are taken care of by the government you are wards, not independent men. And the minute they are legalized by the government, they are protégés and not monopolies. They are the guardians and you are the wards. Do you want to be taken care of by a combination of the government and the monopolies?

. . . Now, I say, gentlemen, that a party that proposes that program cannot, if it carries out that program, be forwarding these other industrial purposes of social regeneration, because they have crystallized, they have hardened, they have narrowed the government which is to be the source of this thing. After all this is done who is to guarantee to us that the government is to be pitiful, that the government is to be righteous, that the government is to be just? Nothing will then control the power of the government except open revolt, and God forbid that we should bring about a state of politics in which open revolt should be substituted for the ballot box.

I believe that the greatest force for peace, the greatest force for righteousness, the greatest force for the elevation of mankind, is organized opinion, is the thinking of men, is the great force which is in the soul of men, and I want men to breathe a free and pure air. And I know that these monopolies are so many cars of juggernaut which are in our very sight being driven over men in such ways as to crush their life out of them. And I don't look forward with pleasure to the time when the juggernauts are licensed. I don't look forward with pleasure to the time when the juggernauts are driven by commissioners of the United States. I am willing to license automobiles, but not juggernauts, because if any man ever dares take a joy ride in one of them, I would like to know what is to become of the rest of us; because the road isn't wide enough for us to get out of the way. We would have to take to the woods and then set the woods afire. I am speaking partly in pleasantry but underneath, gentlemen, there is a very solemn sense in my mind that we are standing at a critical turning point in our [choice].

Now you say on the other hand, what do the Democrats propose to do? I want to call your attention to the fact that those who wish to support these monopolies by adopting them under the regulation of the government of the United States are the very men who cry out that competition is destructive. They ought to know because it is competition as they conducted it that destroyed our economic freedom. They are certainly experts in destructive competition. And the purpose of the Democratic leaders is this: not to legislate competition into existence again—because statutes can't make men do things—but to regulate competition.

What has created these monopolies? Unregulated competition. It has permitted these men to do anything that they chose to do to squeeze their rivals out and to crush their rivals to the earth. We know the processes by which they have done these things. We can prevent those processes by remedial legislation, and that remedial legislation will so restrict the wrong use of competition that the right use of competition will destroy monopoly. In other words, ours is a program of liberty and theirs is a program of regulation. Ours is a program by which we find we know the wrongs that have been committed and we can stop those wrongs. And we are not going to adopt into the governmental family the men who forward the wrongs and license them to do the whole business of the country.

. . . The only way the United States is ever going to be taken care of is by having the voice of all the men in it constantly clamorous for the recognition of what is justice as they see life. A little group of men sitting every day in Washington City is not going to have a vision of your lives as a whole. You alone know what your lives are. I say, therefore, take the shackles off of American industry, the shackles of monopoly, and see it grow into manhood, see it grow out of the enshackled childishness into robust manliness, men being able to take care of themselves, and reassert the great power of American citizenship.

These are the ancient principles of government the world over. For when in the history of labor, here in this country or in any other, did the government present its citizens with freedom and with justice? When has there been any fight for liberty that wasn't a fight against this very thing, the accumulation of regulative power in the hands of a few persons? I, in my time, have read a good deal of history and, if I were to sum up the whole history of liberty, I should say that it consisted at every turn in human life in resisting just such projects as are now proposed to us. If you don't believe it, try it. If you want a great struggle for liberty that will cost you blood, adopt this program, put yourselves at the disposition of a Providence resident in Washington and then see what will come of it.

Ah, gentlemen, we are debating very serious things. And we are debating this: Are we going to put ourselves in a position to enter upon a great program of understanding one another and helping one another? I can't understand you unless you talk to me. I can't understand you by looking at you. I can't understand you by reading books. With apologies to the gentlemen in front of me, I couldn't even understand you by reading the newspapers. I can understand you only by what you know of your own lives and make evident in your own actions. I understand you only in proportion as you "hump" yourselves and take care of yourselves, and make your force evident in the course of politics. And, therefore, I believe in government as a great process of getting together, a great process of debate.

. . . You know I have been considered as disqualified for politics because I was a school teacher. But there is one thing a school teacher learns that he never forgets, namely, that it is his business to learn all he can and then to communicate it to others. Now, I consider this to be my function. I have tried to find out how to learn things and learn them fast. And I have made up my mind that for the rest of my life I am going to put all I know at the disposal of my fellow citizens . . .

I have undertaken the duty of constituting myself one of the attorneys for the people in any court to which I can get entrance. I don't mean as a lawyer, for while I was a lawyer, I have repented. But I mean in the courts of public opinion wherever I am allowed, as I am indulgently allowed today, to stand on a platform and talk to attentive audiences—for you are most graciously attentive—I want to constitute myself the spokesman so far as I have the proper table of contents for the people whom I wish to serve; for the whole strength of politics is not in the leader but in the followers. By leading I do not mean telling other people what they have got to do. I [mean] finding out what the interests of the community are agreed to be, and then trying my level best to find the methods of solution by common counsel. That is the only feasible program of social uplift that I can imagine, and, therefore, I am bound in conscience to fight everything that crystallizes things so at the center that you can't break in.

It is amazing to me that public-spirited, devoted men in this country have not seen that the program of the third party proclaims purposes and in the same breath provides an organization of government which makes the carrying out of those purposes impossible. I would rather postpone my sympathy for social reform until I had got in a position to make things happen. And I am not in a position to make things happen until I am part of a free organization which can say to every interest in the United States: "You come into this conference room on an equality with every other interest in the United States, and you are going to speak here with open doors. There is to be no whispering behind the hand. There is to be no private communication. What you can't afford to let the country hear had better be left unsaid."

What I fear, therefore, is a government of experts. God forbid that in a democratic country we should resign the task and give the government over to experts. What are we for if we are to be [scientifically] taken care of by a small number of gentlemen who are the only men who understand the job? Because if we don't understand the job, then we are not a free people. We ought to resign our free institutions and go to school to somebody and find out what it is we are about. I want to say I have never heard more penetrating debate of public questions than I have sometimes been privileged to hear in clubs of workingmen; because the man who is down against the daily problem of life doesn't talk about it in rhetoric; he talks about it in facts. And the only thing I am interested in is facts. I don't know anything else that is as solid to stand on.

I beg, therefore, that in the election that is approaching you will serve your own interests by discriminatingly serving the whole country and holding [it as your ultimate aim] to see to it that liberty, the initiative of the individual, the initiative of the group, the freedom of enterprise, the multiplicity of American undertakings, is the foundation of your judgment. Do not let America get tied up into little coteries; see to it that every door is open to the youngster as well as to the older man that has made his way. See to it that those who are swimming against the stream have some little glimpses of the [shore]. See to it that those who are sweating blood know that they must not sweat blood all their lives but that if they devote their energy they will devote it in hope and not in despair, as their own masters, and not as men's servants; as men who can look their fellows in the face and say: "We also are of the free breed of American citizens." For, gentlemen, we are at this juncture recovering the ideals of American politics, nothing else. By forgetfulness, by negligence, by criminal discrimination against one another, we have allowed our government to come to such a pass that it does not serve us all without discrimination; and we are about to recover it.

I am not here to commend one party above another. I am here to commend one purpose rather than another, and to challenge every man to vote, not as he has been in the habit of voting, merely because that has been his habit, but as he deems the interests of the community to demand not only, as he believes will be most effective in the long run. In other words, choose measures, choose paths, choose men and, if you please, forget that there are parties.

. . . It is very embarrassing to me, I will tell you frankly, to appear as one who solicits your votes. I would a great deal rather get elected first and then come back to you and say, "Now, what are we going to do?" . . . And I had rather argue politics in the plural than in the singular. It is a lonely business arguing it in the singular. All that you can promise in the singular is that there will be a good deal doing, that you won't allow yourself to be fooled even by your own party, and that the pledges you take upon yourself you take yourself individually and will do your best to carry out whether anybody else goes with you or not. But I am not afraid of that. If the American people elect a man President and say, "You go on and do those things," nobody is going to head him off because there is a force behind him which nobody dares resist—that great impulse of just opinion without which there is no pure government at all.

I do not know any other appeal, therefore, than this appeal to you as Americans, as men who constitute the bone and sinew of American citizenship and [who], when you address yourselves to the discussion of public affairs, know what the realities are and are not deceived by the appearances. Let us get together and [save] the government of the United States.

## Chapter 3

# A "RETURN TO NORMALCY"

## Warren Harding Soothes
## a Restive Nation: 1920

I F ONE WERE to place a dozen presidential historians in a room,
they would likely agree on a couple of basic facts: George
Washington, Abraham Lincoln, and Franklin Roosevelt were the
nation's greatest presidents—and Warren Harding was the worst.
It was a view shared, in part, by the man himself, who once said,
"I am not fit for this office and should never have been here."

Yet in a crowded GOP field seeking the presidency in 1920,
Harding distinguished himself with one of the more effective
and timely campaign speeches in American history. His call for a
"return to normalcy" became the winning theme of the 1920
campaign and led to one of the greatest victories in American
presidential history. Harding would capture more than 60 percent of the popular vote—the biggest margin in a national election since the dawn of the two-party system.

The key to Harding's success was a fundamental convergence
between his own conservative views and those of the American
electorate. In 1912, millions had cast their vote for the reform candidacies of Theodore Roosevelt and Woodrow Wilson. But, after
eight years of progressive politics, military involvement in World

War I, and the subsequent battles over peace negotiations and the issue of America's engagement in the League of Nations, Americans wanted to return to quieter times. As one observer noted of the American people, "They were done with wheatless days, meatless meals, gasless Sundays, and all the restraints and controls of war-time."[1] The same progressive themes that sparked such enthusiasm and hope in 1912 brought hostility and anger in 1920.

Above all, Americans wanted a change from the universally disliked President Woodrow Wilson and the Democratic Party. Wilson had seemingly upset everyone in America, from the nationalists who opposed the League of Nations and the "drys" who supported Prohibition to a whole host of immigrant groups including German and Irish Americans.[2] Yet, while change in American politics usually reflects a desire for bold action, in 1920 it had the exact opposite effect. What voters wanted in 1920 was "quietude, a period of healing, a chance to pursue private affairs without governmental interference, and a chance to forget public affairs."[3] If Americans were seeking a respite, they couldn't have chosen much better than Warren G. Harding. A former newspaper editor and a one-term senator from Ohio, Harding was anything but a political or policy-making dynamo.

As for his speeches, *stirring* was not exactly the word that came to mind. While Harding was known for having a "melodic" and ringing voice, the words often left something to be desired.[4] Former secretary of the treasury William McAdoo, a runner-up for the Democratic nomination in 1920 to Ohio governor James M. Cox, called Harding's speeches "an army of pompous phrases moving over the landscape in search of an idea. Sometimes these meandering words actually capture a staggering thought and bear it triumphantly, a prisoner in their midst, until it died of servitude and over work."[5] Newspaper columnist H. L. Mencken equated Harding's oration with "a string of wet sponges," "stale bean soup," and "dogs barking idiotically through endless nights."[6] He described his speeches as akin to a "hippopotamus struggling to free itself from a slough of molasses."[7]

Yet, for all the harsh critiques, Harding ran a nuanced and calculated nomination campaign. Having announced his candidacy in December 1919, he carefully cultivated Republican delegates and effectively positioned himself as the logical second or third choice in case of deadlock at the Republican convention.

Although he performed abysmally in several of the early GOP primary beauty contests, he was bolstered by his strong-willed wife, Florence, and stayed in the race. As the favorite son of Ohio, a state that had produced seven presidents, the senator from the Buckeye State enjoyed a natural political advantage.

## A TEPID CALL TO ARMS

In a speech to the Home Market Club in Boston, Harding laid out his political manifesto for the coming Republican nominating convention. It was couched in the weary rhetoric, soaring platitudes, suspect analogies, meandering phrases, and clunky alliterations he seemed to cherish.[8] He presciently noted at the outset that years of war had had a tumultuous impact on the nation: "Poise has been disturbed and nerves have been racked, and fever has rendered men irrational."

So what is the tonic for what ails America? In alliterative glory, Harding spelled out his solution: "not heroics, but healing; not nostrums, but normalcy; not revolution, but restoration; not agitation, but adjustment; not surgery, but serenity; not the dramatic, but the dispassionate; not experiment, but equipoise; not submergence in internationality, but sustainment in triumphant nationality."

The key word in this statement of understated aspirations is *normalcy*—a word that Harding is often credited with coining. His original speech featured the word *normality*, but instead he said *normalty* and amused reporters changed it to *normalcy*. Harding's malapropisms notwithstanding, in the midst of the flowery prose was a simple yet powerful political message—no to progressivism, no to international engagement, yes for a return to America's simpler days.

By invoking the glories of the past, Harding attacked the excesses of progressivism and the flurry of legislation and efforts at social change that defined the Wilson era. While on one hand progressivism represented an abiding national desire for economic and political reform, there was another, less popular side—the focus by some in the progressive movement on remaking the nation and imposing unprecedented social change. These initiatives ran the gamut from the temperance movement to attacks on prostitution and divorce as well as the promotion of women's rights. It was this element of progressivism that caused many Americans to recoil, and the backlash of 1920 was sparked in some measure by these efforts at far-reaching social transformation.[9]

Harding spoke directly to this issue in calling not only for a return to the basic American value of hard work but also for government to minimize its role in "guiding" the lives of the American people:

> The world needs to be reminded that all human ills are not curable by legislation, and that quantity of statutory enactments and excess of government offer no substitute for quality of citizenship. The problems of maintained civilization are not to be solved by a transfer of responsibility from citizenship to government, and no eminent page in history was ever drafted by the standards of mediocrity. More, no government is worthy of the name which is directed by influence on the one hand, or moved by intimidation on the other.

Harding went on to argue that "out of the supreme tragedy" of war "must come a new order." Harding asserted that "war has not abolished work . . . Nor has it provided a governmental panacea for human ills, or the magic touch that makes failure a success. Indeed, it has revealed no new reward for idleness, no substitute for the sweat of a man's face in the contest for subsistence and acquirement."

There is an extraordinary tone of self-denial in Harding's words along with a veneration of the small-town virtues of religious faith, honest labor, and patriotic fervor that still dominated much of American society.[10] "We might try repairs on the old clothes and simplicity for the new," Harding argued in a paean to the values of the past. "I know the tendency to wish the thing denied, I know the human hunger for a new thrill, but denial enhances the ultimate satisfaction, and stabilizes our indulgence. A blasé people is the unhappiest in all the world." These are the words of a true American individualist—embracing the notion that only through hard work and self-sacrifice can the country ensure economic prosperity. But Harding was also suggesting that America would be far better if it cast aside its progressive inclinations and returned to a more traditional political ideology.

To be sure, Warren Harding wasn't a strong believer in self-denial in his own life. He carried on numerous affairs, drank heavily, likely fathered an illegitimate child, actively played the stock market (even from the White House), and was known for hosting one of the best poker games in Washington. Still, Americans wanted to put the tumult of the 1910s and Woodrow Wilson behind them. They wanted normalcy and repose. Harding gave them just that chance. As he noted in his address, "My best judgment of America's needs is to steady down, to get squarely on our feet, to make sure of the right path."

That journey would start with America's standing in the world. No one issue roiled the electorate more than foreign affairs, in particular Wilson's ongoing efforts to get the Senate to guarantee America's entry into the League of Nations. Many Republicans, who were long suspicious of the "foreign entanglements" that George Washington had warned about in his farewell address, strongly opposed the League. Harding's opposition was more muted. He had called for an "association of nations" to pacify pro-League Republicans, but had earlier expressed his intention to vote against the League in the Senate, without specific changes to the treaty (changes to which Wilson would not agree). Indeed, his views on foreign policy were best summed up by his campaign mantra of "Americanism"—which was, for the most part, little more than a fancy new name for an old policy: isolationism.

If we can prove a representative popular government under which a citizenship seeks what it may do for the government and country rather than what the country may do for individuals, we shall do more to make democracy safe for the world than all armed conflict ever recorded . . . Let us stop to consider that tranquility at home is more precious than peace abroad, and that both our good fortune and our eminence are dependent on the normal forward stride of all the American people.

Poignant words, but they were an unambiguous call for America to remain within its borders and allow the rest of the world to solve its own problems—while the United States served as a shining example of democracy in action. Nimbly, Harding flipped around Wilson's argument upon America's entry into World War I that the nation must go to war to make the world "safe for democracy," arguing that the best way to achieve this goal was to ensure the strength of representative government at home.

Ironically, the first half of the above passage is reminiscent of President John F. Kennedy's seminal call from his inaugural address, "Ask not what your country can do for you, ask what you can do for your country." Suffice to say, however, Harding and Kennedy meant two very different things. While Kennedy wanted to usher in a new era of self-sacrifice and patriotism, Harding was calling for a return to limited government, where the state's responsibilities to its citizens would be further constrained. (In fact, for years afterward, Democratic candidates from Truman to Kennedy would mock Harding's "normalcy" refrain as a symbol of Republicans' passivity and knee-jerk opposition to any sort of government activism.)

Harding emerged from a deadlocked GOP convention to claim the party's nomination. His win would bring even more harsh invective against the Republican nominee. The *New York World* called him "weak and colorless and mediocre" and claimed he had "never had an original idea."[11] The *New York Post* called his nomination "an affront to the intelligence and conscience of the American people."[12] The *Nation* minced few words, calling him "a dummy," "an animated automaton," and "a marionette that moves when the strings are pulled."[13]

But not every paper was so harsh. In the *New York Times*, Rupert Hughes would offer this hilarious, if backhanded, praise of Harding: "His words are as plain and familiar and simple as bread, as refreshing as water. There is not much style about good bread, but it is much easier to make fancy cakes than good bread. And it is easier to concoct heady drinks, colored pops and poisonous hooch than to provide wells of pure, cool water . . . Harding is the possessor of a splendid style, and that style is the expression of just the personality most needed and most welcome in the chaotic turbulence that follows the world quake and the tidal wave."[14]

Millions of Americans responded to Harding's simple message. Like his Ohio predecessor, President William McKinley, Harding launched a so-called front-porch campaign from his hometown in Marion, Ohio. Between July 22 and the end of September, he received more than six hundred thousand visitors who came to hear his soothing, inoffensive words.[15] Eventually, Harding would venture out to the campaign trail and deliver more than one hundred speeches.[16] His opponent, Cox, barnstormed the country, but to little avail. As one observer wryly noted, "Seldom did a major candidate for the presidency campaign so vigorously, speak so frequently, and persuade such a small percentage (34.5%) of citizens to vote for him as did Cox."[17] The election results heartily ratified the American people's deep desire for change. Harding won in a historic landslide, taking every state outside the solidly Democratic South.

For all his electoral success, Harding's presidency was a shining mediocrity, and, as his wife had feared, the stress of the nation's highest office eventually would be his demise. He suffered a heart attack during a western tour and passed away in San Francisco on August 2, 1923. As the train bearing the president's body traversed the nation back to Washington, an estimated nine million Americans stood along railroad tracks to offer their silent homage to the nation's fallen and much beloved president.

While Harding's presidency is neither little remembered nor much noted today, his election ushered in a temporary reprieve from the reformist calls of Bryan, Roosevelt, and Wilson. At the time, the famed progressive leader Hiram Johnson bemoaned Harding's victory but never lost faith in the goals of progressivism. "In the end," he declared, "there will be a revolution, but it will not come in my time."[18] Johnson would be proven wrong. A mere decade later the nation would experience a series of cataclysmic events that would wash away Harding's idyllic vision of past American glory and lead to Franklin Roosevelt's New Deal, ensuring that the nation's future would look quite different from its past.

## Senator Warren Harding Lays Out His Platform for the 1920 Election, Boston, May 14, 1920

There isn't anything the matter with the world's civilization except that humanity is viewing it through a vision impaired in a cataclysmal war. Poise has been disturbed and nerves have been racked, and fever has rendered men irrational; sometimes there have been draughts upon the dangerous cup of barbarity and men have wandered far from safe paths, but the human procession still marches in the right direction.

Here, in the United States, we feel the reflex, rather than the hurting wound, but we still think straight, and we mean to act straight, and mean to hold firmly to all that was ours when war involved us, and seek the higher attainments which are the only compensations that so supreme a tragedy may give mankind.

America's present need is not heroics, but healing; not nostrums, but normalcy; not revolution, but restoration; not agitation, but adjustment; not surgery, but serenity; not the dramatic, but the dispassionate; not experiment, but equipoise; not submergence in internationality, but sustainment in triumphant nationality. It is one thing to battle successfully against world domination by military autocracy, because the infinite God never intended such a program, but it is quite another thing to revise human nature and suspend the fundamental laws of life and all of life's acquirements.

. . . This republic has its ample tasks. If we put an end to false economics which lure humanity to utter chaos, ours will be the commanding example of world leadership today. If we can prove a representative popular government under which a citizenship seeks what it may do for the government rather than what the government may do for individuals, we shall do more to make democracy safe for the world than all armed conflict ever recorded. The world needs to be reminded that all human ills are not curable by legislation, and that quantity of statutory enactment and excess of government offer no substitute for quality of citizenship.

The problems of maintained civilization are not to be solved by a transfer of responsibility from citizenship to government, and no eminent page in history was ever drafted by the standards of mediocrity. More, no government is worthy of the name which is directed by influence on the one hand, or moved by intimidation on the other.

Nothing is more vital to this republic to-day than clear and intelligent understanding. Men must understand one another, and government and men must understand each other. For emergence from the wreckage of war, for the clarification of fevered minds, we must all give and take, we must both sympathize and inspire, but must learn griefs and aspirations, we must seek the common grounds of mutuality.

There can be no disguising everlasting truths. Speak it plainly, no people ever recovered from the distressing waste of war except through work and denial. There is no other way. We shall make no recovery in seeking how little men can do, our restoration lies in doing the most which is reasonably possible for individuals to do . . . War wasted hundreds of billions, and depleted world store-houses, and cultivated new demands, and it hardened selfishness and gave awakening touch to elemental greed. Humanity needs renewed consecrations to what we call fellow citizenship.

Out of the supreme tragedy must come a new order and a higher order, and I gladly acclaim it. But war has not abolished work, has not established the processes of seizure or the rule of physical might. Nor has it provided a governmental panacea for human ills, or the magic touch that makes failure a success. Indeed, it has revealed no new reward for idleness, no substitute for the sweat of a man's face in the contest for subsistence and acquirement.

. . . My best judgment of America's needs is to steady down, to get squarely on our feet, to make sure of the right path. Let's get out of the fevered delirium of war, with the hallucination that all the money in the world is to be made in the madness of war and the wildness of its aftermath. Let us stop to consider that tranquility at home is more precious than peace abroad, and that both our good fortune and our eminence are dependent on the normal forward stride of all the American people.

. . . It is utter folly to talk about reducing the cost of living without restored and increased efficiency or production on the one hand and more prudent consumption on the other. No law will work the miracle. Only the American people themselves can solve the situation. There must be the conscience of capital in omitting profiteering, there must be the conscience of labor in efficiently producing, there must be a public conscience in restricting outlay and promoting thrift.

Sober capital must make appeal to intoxicated wealth, and thoughtful labor must appeal to the radical who has no thought of the morrow, to effect the needed understanding . . . We ought to dwell in the heights of good fortune for a generation to come, and I pray that we will, but we need a benediction of wholesome common sense to give us that assurance.

I pray for sober thinking in behalf of the future of America. No worth-while republic ever went the tragic way to destruction, which did not begin the downward course through luxury of life and extravagance of living. More, the simple living and thrifty people will be the first to recover from a war's waste and all its burdens, and our people ought to be the first recovered. Herein is greater opportunity than lies in alliance, compact or supergovernment. It is America's chance to lead in example and prove to the world the reign of reason in representative popular government where people think who assume to rule.

No overall fad will quicken our thoughtfulness. We might try repairs on the old clothes and simplicity for the new. I know the tendency to wish the thing denied, I know the human hunger for a new thrill, but denial enhances the ultimate satisfaction, and stabilizes our indulgence. A blasé people is the unhappiest in all the world.

It seems to me singularly appropriate to address this membership an additional word about production. I believe most cordially in the home market first for the American product. There is no other way to assure our prosperity. I rejoice in our normal capacity to consume our rational, healthful consumption.

We have protected our home market with war's barrage. But the barrage has lifted with the passing of the war. The American people will not heed to-day, because world competition is not yet restored, but the morrow will soon come when the world will seek our markets and our trade balances, and we must think of America first or surrender our eminence.

The thought is not selfish. We want to share with the world in seeking becoming restoration. But peoples will trade and seek wealth in their exchanges, and every conflict in the adjustment of peace was founded on the hope of promoting trade conditions. I heard expressed, before the Foreign Relations Committee of the Senate, the aspirations of nationality and the hope of commerce to develop and expand aspiring peoples. Knowing that those two thoughts are inspiring all humanity, as they have since civilization began, I can only marvel at the American who consents to surrender either. There may be conscience, humanity and justice in both, and without them the glory of the republic is done.

I want to go on, secure and unafraid, holding fast to the American inheritance and confident of the supreme American fulfillment.

## Chapter 4

# "RUGGED INDIVIDUALISM"
# VERSUS "BOLD, PERSISTENT
# EXPERIMENTATION"

### Herbert Hoover and Franklin Roosevelt Debate
### the Role of Government in the Lives of the
### American People: 1928–1932

FOR ALL ITS legislative and programmatic success, progressivism never fully transformed American society. As the election of Warren Harding in 1920 and Calvin Coolidge in 1924 demonstrated, the nation's reformist inclination was always at odds with the abiding faith of the American people in limited government and, above all, individualism. Individualism (a term coined by Alexis de Tocqueville), or the ability of each citizen to shape his or her destiny free of government intervention or assistance, remained one of the most powerful and resonant concepts in American society.[1] It was seen not only as the very basis of the country's economic success but also as the crucial building block of a free society. Andrew Carnegie called individualism the very "foundation" of the human race, and it would come to define the unprecedented prosperity and social change of the Roaring Twenties.[2]

By 1920, the country's exhaustion from progressivism led

many Americans to once again embrace the ideal of individual freedom as well as personal fulfillment and pleasure. These societal changes were, not surprisingly, mimicked in economic and political terms. Industrial development and the transition to a peacetime economy were driven by a laissez-faire economic model, which largely placed the needs of big business above those of labor. Yet most Americans were unconcerned. A new ism—namely, consumerism—was becoming their watchword. As mass production made automobiles, radios, and a host of new consumer items accessible to ordinary Americans, the reform battles of the previous decade fell by the wayside.

In an oft-cited quote, then-president Calvin Coolidge asserted that "the business of America is business." But it was another Coolidge quote that even more accurately reflected the mood of the time: "To the individual has been left the power and responsibility, the foundation for the rule of the people." Government's responsibility was "the recognition of the rights of the development of the individual."[3] Coolidge saw little role for the federal government, believing that its fundamental responsibility lay in serving the needs of the private sector. "The law that builds up the people is the law that builds up industry . . . the Government can do more to remedy the economic ills of the people by a system of rigid economy in public expenditure than can be accomplished through any other action," said Coolidge.[4] This was no friend of the progressive movement.

Despite Coolidge's doctrinaire views, it was the man that followed him in the White House, Herbert Hoover, who would be more clearly identified with the individualism and unfettered capitalism of the Roaring Twenties—but for all the wrong reasons.

## An American Individualist

Hoover was the embodiment of American individualism (he even wrote a book by that name)—a self-made man who had emerged from a meager upbringing to become an individual of both vast wealth and great national reputation. Though he maintained strong progressive impulses, having supported Roosevelt in 1912, at his core Hoover was an individualist who, while sympathetic to the notion that America must "safeguard to every individual an equality of opportunity," still embraced a social Darwinist notion of personal achievement and success.[5] He wasn't alone. On the eve of the 1928 presidential election, Hoover's beliefs were in line with those of most Americans. For a man whose name is today the butt of political jokes and who is seen as a virtual Nero fiddling while America burned, Hoover was, at the time, very much in tune with his countrymen.

As the historian Richard Hofstadter says of America's thirty-first president, "The things Hoover believed in—efficiency, enterprise, opportunity, individualism, substantial laissez-faire, personal success, material welfare—were all in the dominant American tradition. The ideas he represented—ideas that to so many people made him seem hateful or ridiculous after 1929—were precisely the same ideas that in the remoter past of the nineteenth century and the more immediate past of the New Era had had an almost irresistible lure for the majority of Americans."[6]

It's little wonder that Hoover's most famous and influential speech was one that unabashedly embodied these beliefs—what he called the "rugged individualism" of American capitalism. Speaking before a packed Madison Square Garden on the eve of the 1928 election, Hoover used the speech as an opportunity to not only take credit for the decade's great economic prosperity (under GOP leadership) but also warn of the grave dangers in making government a player instead of an "umpire" in the economic game. "It would impair the very basis of liberty and freedom," claimed Hoover.

Hoover contrasted the success of American capitalism in the 1920s with the "socialist" and statist economic models of Europe, sounding a resounding message of American exceptionalism.

> During one hundred and fifty years we have builded up a form of self-government and a social system which is peculiarly our own. It differs essentially from all others in the world. It is the American system . . . It is founded upon the conception that only through ordered liberty, freedom, and equal opportunity to the individual will his initiative and enterprise spur on the march of progress. And in our insistence upon equality of opportunity has our system advanced beyond all the world.

During World War I, the United States came to rely more heavily on government involvement in the workings of the economy, but Hoover insisted that only through GOP leadership had the nation been able to return to its normal and most successful economic model. "When the Republican Party came into full power it went at once resolutely back to our fundamental conception of the state and the rights and responsibilities of the individual . . . it restored confidence and hope in the American people, it freed and stimulated enterprise."

Hoover went on to explicitly warn of the dangers of bringing government too closely into the working of business:

> It is a false liberalism that interprets itself into the government operation of commercial business. Every step of bureaucratizing of the business of our country poisons the very roots of liberalism—that is, political equality, free speech, free assembly, free press, and equality of opportunity. It is not the road to

more liberty, but to less liberty. Liberalism should not be striving to spread bureaucracy but striving to set bounds to it.

While these views are regularly shared by many modern conservatives, few have expressed the ideology of small-government conservatism as eloquently and as intelligently as Hoover. The notion of limited government is hardly dead—far from it. But the difference here is one of tone. While today some conservatives speak of shrinking government to such a small size that it can be drowned in a bathtub, Hoover based his economic conservatism on the notion of individualism and argued that expanding the reach of government would limit the freedom of the American people.

Today, such views are often expressed in populist terms, extolling the virtues of the free market and demeaning the big-government bureaucracy that was an outgrowth of the New Deal and Great Society. These modern debates are predicated more on a negative—the excesses and disconnect of government bureaucracy. But in 1928, Hoover argued passionately (or as passionately as he was capable of expressing it) on behalf of the capitalist system not only for its economic potential but also for the limitless opportunities that he believed it provided.

Riding this message of economic freedom and a vibrant and growing economy (as well as a healthy dose of race-baiting and anti-Catholic politicking), Hoover easily trounced his over-matched opponent, New York governor Al Smith. But Hoover's economic conservatism would prove disastrous for his presidency and the Republican Party not just four years later but for two generations to come.

When the Great Depression wiped out Wall Street and put millions out of work, Hoover stubbornly rejected calls for a wider government effort to help alleviate its worst effects. To be sure, the image of Hoover as completely oblivious to the economic calamity that befell the nation is unfair. He was the first president to eschew the laissez-faire model during an economic downturn and bring the federal government to bear in helping those most hurt.[7]

But these were limited efforts, and like any true ideologue, Hoover was unable to fully shed his political and economic philosophy, offering only private or voluntary solutions to the nation's growing and seemingly intractable economic problems. For example, he opposed public relief measures on the grounds that such steps "would have injured the spiritual responses of the American people."[8] Almost overnight Hoover became an anachronism, his doctrinaire economic views largely discredited in the eyes of millions of Americans. The patron saint of "rugged individualism" had neither the wherewithal nor the inclination to turn the forces of government loose in helping the nation out of its economic malaise.

By the time of his race for reelection in 1932, America was at its lowest point since the Civil War. Hoover's recalcitrance provided an opportunity for the Democratic nominee to propose genuine change—and that's exactly what Franklin Roosevelt did. But what comes across in his 1932 campaign for the White House is less an economic doctrine of big government than a call for activist and bold leadership.

In a seminal address on May 22, 1932, at Oglethorpe University in Georgia, Roosevelt laid out the approach that would come to define his campaign for the White House: "The country needs and, unless I mistake its temper, the country demands bold, persistent experimentation. It is common sense to take a method and try it: If it fails, admit it frankly and try another. But above all, try something." A greater contrast with the seemingly paralyzed Hoover and a more defining explanation of FDR's temperament is nearly impossible to imagine. Above all, these hopeful words came to define Roosevelt's administration and his extraordinary appeal to the American people. As one of FDR's key advisers, Rexford Tugwell, would later say of the remarks, it was "the sincerest, most unpolitical statement of Roosevelt's attitudes and convictions."[9]

## FLIGHT TO CHICAGO

Even in an era before the advent of television, Roosevelt understood the power of political theater. Not long after the Democratic nomination was officially his, the convention's chairman, Thomas Walsh, announced that if the delegates would stay in session, Roosevelt would come to the party convention in Chicago. The effect on the crowd was electric. According to his speechwriter Samuel Rosenman, Roosevelt "wanted to let people know that his approach was going to be bold and daring; that if elected he would be ready to act—and act fast."[10]

Not only was Roosevelt offering to be the first presidential nominee to accept his nomination in person, he was going to board a plane to do it. Very few Americans had traveled by air in 1932, not even a sitting president or a candidate for the job. Air travel at the time was not exactly a walk in the park, but Roosevelt, who had flown as assistant secretary of the navy, had little concern.[11] He dozed off during parts of the nine-hour journey from Albany, New York, which included two stops for refueling along the way.[12]

When he finally arrived at the airport in Chicago, Roosevelt was met with a tumultuous response. More than ten thousand well-wishers greeted the nominee. As the plane touched down and Roosevelt emerged on a flag-draped ramp, the crowd went wild, breaking down a restraining fence and so jostling the candidate they knocked off his glasses. (Another eager spectator stole his hat as a souvenir.) It was akin to the Beatles arriving in New York in 1964: the extraordinary response was like none ever before given to a presidential candidate.[13] To be sure, the drama was far from complete: there was still the issue of his speech.

Roosevelt's speechwriter Raymond Moley had drafted an initial set of remarks, approximately nine thousand words long, with significant input from Roosevelt. As was generally the case, Moley did not craft a peroration, as Roosevelt preferred to write those in longhand, on his own. Then Moley took a leap of faith that would normally paralyze every speechwriter with fear—he left the speech in the hands of others and ventured to Chicago for the convention. Back in Albany, Roosevelt and Rosenman cut the remarks down to size but, to Moley's enormous relief, left the speech's substance largely in place.[14]

FDR's top political adviser, Louis Howe, who was probably more responsible than any other person for Roosevelt's political ascent, hated the speech. It didn't help things that Howe couldn't stand Rosenman and resented his growing prominence as a key Roosevelt aide. After reading the speech, Howe screamed, "Good God, do I have to do everything myself? I see Sam Rosenman in every paragraph of this mess."[15] He dictated a new draft, which he then shoved into the hands of Roosevelt at the airport. In a nifty bit of multitasking, Roosevelt read through Howe's revised remarks as he was being driven through Chicago, at the same time waving and smiling to the crowds that lined the streets.[16]

As he waited in the wings to deliver a speech that would transform the nation and define an era, Roosevelt attached the first page of Howe's remarks to the Rosenman draft and walked onstage. As Jonathan Alter noted, "Like so much else in Franklin Roosevelt's future, this was slapdash, cavalier—and exactly the kind of improvisation that would serve him so well when he entered the White House the following year."[17]

The unprecedented nature of Roosevelt's dramatic flight to Chicago was captured in his acceptance address, which forthrightly

promised a "New Deal" for the American people under Democratic leadership. In both this speech and his later address to the
Commonwealth Club in San Francisco in September 1932, FDR
laid out the very broad outlines of his policy agenda, crested
above all by his earlier call for "bold, persistent experimentation."
At the Democratic convention, FDR articulated the belief that
the federal government "has always had and still has a continuing
responsibility for the broader public welfare." Progressive leaders
had been making a similar pitch for more than thirty years, to little avail at the ballot box. But where Bryan and TR failed, Roosevelt, by promising less radical change, found great success.

To this day, there remains an unresolved debate as to exactly
how specific FDR was during the 1932 campaign about the policies to come in his presidency. It's not by accident. As Eric Goldman described FDR's often scattershot statements, "Some of the
campaign sounded as if he intended to use the old cards of government economy, sound currency, and antitrust action, while
other speeches suggested a crisp new pack."[18]

His acceptance speech provides a perfect example. On one
hand, he laid out several specific policy prescriptions, such as
mortgage assistance and securities regulation, but these concepts
were underdeveloped. He extolled the virtues of public works
projects, but hardly gave full measure to the many such programs
that would come to define the New Deal. Yes, Roosevelt laid out
a few policy initiatives, but they only hinted at the breadth and
depth of the actions he would take as president.

In fact, FDR focused several of his policy prescriptions on the
plight of American farmers, noting that half of all Americans "are
dependent on agriculture" and offering them more direct government support. He decried the "impregnable barbed wire entanglement" of GOP tariffs, which he claimed, in a bit of hyperbole,
"have isolated us from all the other human beings in all the rest of
the round world." He called for a thrifty government, articulating

his desire to "abolish useless offices" and curb government spending. (This passage would ironically be co-opted by Ronald Reagan forty-eight years later to bolster his own conservative economic views.) The Democratic platform that he endorsed still called for balancing the budget, and the same man who would later become the father of activist government and the modern welfare state would at Pittsburgh's Forbes Field in October 1932 bash President Hoover for "reckless and extravagant spending" and pledge a smaller, leaner federal government.[19] For all the supposed radicalism of FDR's New Deal agenda, on the campaign trail it was presented in a far more conservative light than many have acknowledged. Even Roosevelt understood that the American people's desire for activist government had its limits.

Roosevelt's focus was less on policy and more on making it clear that a Democratic administration would represent a new focus for American government. "The people of this country want a genuine choice this year, not a choice between two names for the same reactionary doctrine. Ours must be a party of liberal thought, of planned action, of enlightened international outlook, and of the greatest good to the greatest number of our citizens."

What alternative did Republicans provide? Here FDR played the populist card to the hilt. According to Roosevelt, the GOP offered a view on economic and social life where "a favored few are helped and hopes that some of their prosperity will leak through, sift through, to labor, to the farmer, to the small business man. That theory belongs to the party of Toryism." This was language straight out of the "Cross of Gold."

The New Deal represented a seminal break from the "rugged individualism" of the past. Roosevelt was arguing that all Americans had a stake in the well-being of their fellow countrymen: "Never in history have the interests of all the people been so united in a single economic problem." And FDR went to great lengths to portray his call for "a nation of interdependence" versus "a nation of independence" (i.e., individualism) as a veritable changing of the political guard. The contrast between the two parties could not have been greater, a fact that Roosevelt constantly reminded his audience of:

> Never before in modern history have the essential differences between the two major American parties stood out in such striking contrast as they do today. Republican leaders not only have failed in material things, they have failed in national vision, because in disaster they have held out no hope, they have pointed out no path for the people to climb back to places of security and safety in our American life.

And then in the speech's most memorable passage, Roosevelt coined a phrase that was in fact a mere throwaway line from FDR's speechwriters and yet would come to define this new era in American history, "I pledge you, I pledge myself, to a new deal for the American people." Placing the moment in an epic and historic light, he told the thousands in Chicago and the millions listening at home on their radios, "This is more than a political campaign; it is a call to arms. Give me your help, not to win votes alone, but to win in this crusade to restore America to its own people."

## COMMONWEALTH CLUB

The spectacle of Roosevelt appearing in person to accept the Democratic nomination gave a dramatic boost to his candidacy. To many it seemed this was Roosevelt's campaign to lose. But that did not stop him from hitting the campaign trail hard and barnstorming the nation. He ignored the advice of his running mate, John Garner, who told FDR, "All you have to do is stay alive 'til November."[20]

While most of the candidate's speeches were political in nature, Roosevelt would take a philosophical turn in September 1932 at the Commonwealth Club in San Francisco. There he laid out a political and economic philosophy that sought nothing less than to put a stake through the heart of Hoover-style conservatism. The speech defies easy explanation, because it was in so many respects the "least characteristically Rooseveltian address of the 1932 campaign."[21] This was not the great crusade or call to arms of FDR's acceptance or even inaugural speech. Yet the Commonwealth Club speech is considered by many historians to be one of the great campaign speeches of twentieth-century political oratory because it supposedly laid out FDR's New Deal agenda and approach. It's not and it didn't. It lacked the brimming optimism and soaring ideals of FDR's best rhetoric. In fact, there is little evidence that he gave the remarks more than a cursory glance before delivering them.[22]

Nonetheless, there are important ideas in the Commonwealth Club speech that provide an instructive road map for the New Deal policies to come. The speech was not a true campaign address; it reads more like a lecture. Drafted by FDR's adviser Adolf Berle, who had recently written a scathing attack on corporate America titled *Modern Corporation and Private Property*, it is the closest that Roosevelt would come to debating the issue of individualism on the campaign trail.

At the outset, he argued, "The issue of government has always been whether individual men and women will have to serve some system of government or economics, or whether a system of government and economics exists to serve individual men and women."

Roosevelt related this issue to the original debate between two of America's founding fathers: Hamilton, with his definition of the "autocratic strength of the government," and Jefferson, with his more egalitarian model. In the end, Jefferson's vision was the victor and "individualism was made the great watchword of American life." While Roosevelt would largely reject the Jeffersonian notion of the small-town merchant and yeoman farmer as the focal point of the American economy, there was another element to Jefferson's "victory" that Roosevelt would embrace—the idea of government action to *protect* individualism.

Roosevelt noted that the cult of individualism and the spirit of unfettered capitalism ushered in a golden era in American life, but with a cost. "It was thought that no price was too high to pay for the advantages which we could draw from a finished industrial system . . . The financiers who pushed the railroads to the Pacific were always ruthless, often wasteful, and frequently corrupt; but they did build railroads."

Government's role during this period was "not to interfere but to assist in the development of industry." According to FDR, such indifference might have been acceptable when America was still claiming and developing new land in its unquenchable Manifest Destiny. But no more; "equality of opportunity as we have known it no longer exists. Our industrial plant is built . . . our last frontier has long since been reached, and there is practically no more free land." As a result, "we are now providing a drab living for our own people." In short, the government models of the past must adapt to the new realities of the American economy. Echoing Wilson's "New Freedom," Roosevelt warned that the "independent businessman is running a losing race" and that American business risked being dominated by a mere "dozen corporations." Roosevelt makes clear that the "operation of the speculator, the manipulator, even the financier" must, if necessary, be restricted in order to ensure that individualism is "protected."

According to FDR, the "day of the great promoter or financial Titan, to whom we granted anything if only he would build, or develop, is over." Indeed, Roosevelt called for a new economic order:

> Our task now is not discovery or exploitation of natural re-
> sources, or necessarily producing more goods. It is the soberer,
> less dramatic business of administering resources and plants al-
> ready in hand, of seeking to reestablish foreign markets for
> our surplus production, of meeting the problem of undercon-
> sumption, of adjusting production to consumption, of distrib-
> uting wealth and products more equitably, of adapting existing
> economic organizations to the service of the people. The day
> of enlightened administration has come.

Rarely has an economic revolution been framed so tepidly and, to some extent, misguidedly. The theory underpinning this analy-sis was known as the "mature economic thesis," and it was an al-together pessimistic appraisal of the American economy and American ingenuity. As historian Davis W. Houck argues, its ba-sic underlying principle was that "capitalism's best days are in the past" and what America needed was not a new shot of entrepre-neurship but a wave of technocrats to "administer resources."[23] Here we see one of the true flaws of the New Deal: an overre-liance on "enlightened administration" and keep-busy public works projects instead of a true entrepreneurially geared eco-nomic initiative.[24] The New Deal would bring the nation out of the Great Depression and restore hope, but it would not necessar-ily provide the underpinnings of a great economic renewal. That would come later, in the guise of world war.

Roosevelt also offered the voters a more hopeful message, not-ing that "a right to life" also includes "a right to make a comfort-able living." Indeed, he even presented his own vision of individualism, asserting that government had a responsibility to help ensure that a system in which "every individual may find safety if he wishes it; in which every individual may attain such power as his ability permits, consistent with his assuming the accompanying responsibility." But these were not necessarily new themes. They had been developed in both the Oglethorpe speech and his acceptance address in Chicago.

At times, Roosevelt reflected a decidedly conservative tone. While he described a governmental role for "an economic declaration of rights" and "an economic constitutional order," he believed it should assist in the process, not be actively engaged.[25] Roosevelt argued, "The government should assume the function of government regulation only as a last resort, to be tried only when private initiative, inspired by high responsibility, with such assistance and balance as government can give, has finally failed." Four years later, at his renomination in Philadelphia, these ideas would practically seem quaint, as FDR adopted a far more radical agenda. For those who view the New Deal as the birth of activist big government, these are not words that bring that future to mind.

In this speech Roosevelt was dipping his toe in the water of a powerful new concept of liberalism and an expanded role for government but he was not yet willing to dive into the pool. It was still 1932, Americans remained suspicious of government, and after all, he still had to get elected. Many have rightly come to see FDR's election as the birth of modern liberalism, but that wasn't the key message of his campaign, which was far more focused on bringing boldness and experimentation to the halls of government. As Hofstadter noted, "At the heart of the New Deal there was not a philosophy but a temperament."[26] In the end, Roosevelt "trusted no system except the system of endless experimentation."[27]

Nonetheless, with both these speeches, Roosevelt cast the election as a clear and unmistakable choice between the "rugged individualism" of Hoover and his own experimentalist, progressive agenda. In a landslide the American people chose FDR's vision. The result was an election victory that would represent a transformative change in how Americans viewed their government. FDR's campaign oratory slowly but surely moved the country away from laissez-faire to a new liberal economic model and activist conception of government that would lead to the welfare state we know today. That debate, captured in these speeches, remains crucial to understanding American politics in the twentieth century and the two parties' contrasting points of view on the role and responsibilities of the federal government.

## Herbert Hoover Describes the "Rugged Individualism" of American Capitalism, New York, October 23, 1928

This campaign now draws near a close. The platforms of the two parties defining principles and offering solutions of various national problems have been presented and are being earnestly considered by our people.

After four months' debate it is not the Republican Party which finds reason for abandonment of any of the principles it has laid down or of the views it has expressed for solution of the problems before the country. The principles to which it adheres are rooted deeply in the foundations of our national life. The solutions which it proposes are based on experience with government and on a consciousness that it may have the responsibility for placing those solutions in action.

. . . The Republican Party has ever been a party of progress. I do not need to review its seventy years of constructive history. It has always reflected the spirit of the American people. Never has it done more for the advancement of fundamental progress than during the past seven and one-half years since we took over the government amidst the ruin left by war.

It detracts nothing from the character and energy of the American people, it minimizes in no degree the quality of their accomplishments to say that the policies of the Republican Party have played a large part in recuperation from the war and the building of the magnificent progress which shows upon every hand today. I say with emphasis that without the wise policies which the Republican Party has brought into action during this period, no such progress would have been possible.

. . . Only through keen vision and helpful co-operation by the government has stability in business and stability in employment been maintained during this past seven and one-half years. There always are some localities, some industries, and some individuals who do not share the prevailing prosperity. The task of government is to lessen these inequalities.

Never has there been a period when the Federal Government has given such aid and impulse to the progress of our people, not alone to economic progress but to the development of those agencies which make for moral and spiritual progress.

But in addition to this great record of contributions of the Republican Party to progress, there has been a further fundamental contribution—a contribution underlying and sustaining all the others—and that is the resistance of the Republican Party to every attempt to inject the government into business in competition with its citizens.

After the war, when the Republican Party assumed administration of the country, we were faced with the problem of determination of the very nature of our national life. During one hundred and fifty years we have builded up a form of self-government and a social system which is peculiarly our own. It differs essentially from all others in the world. It is the American system. It is just as definite and positive a political and social system as has ever been developed on earth. It is founded upon a particular conception of self-government in which decentralized local responsibility is the very base. Further than this, it is founded upon the conception that only through ordered liberty, freedom, and equal opportunity to the individual will his initiative and enterprise spur on the march of progress. And in our insistence upon equality of opportunity has our system advanced beyond all the world.

During the war we necessarily turned to the government to solve every difficult economic problem. The government having absorbed every energy of our people for war, there was no other solution. For the preservation of the state the Federal Government became a centralized despotism which undertook unprecedented responsibilities, assumed autocratic powers, and took over the business of citizens. To a large degree we regimented our whole people temporarily into a socialistic state. However justified in time of war, if continued in peace-time it would destroy not only our American system but with it our progress and freedom as well.

When the war closed, the most vital of all issues both in our own country and throughout the world was whether governments should continue their war-time ownership and operation of many instrumentalities of production and distribution. We were challenged with a peace-time choice between the American system of rugged individualism and a European philosophy of diametrically opposed doctrines—doctrines of paternalism and state socialism. The acceptance of these ideas would have meant the destruction of self-government through centralization of government. It would have meant the undermining of the individual initiative and enterprise through which our people have grown to unparalleled greatness.

The Republican Party from the beginning resolutely turned its face away from these ideas and these war practices . . . When the Republican Party came into full power it went at once resolutely back to our fundamental conception of the state and the rights and responsibilities of the individual. Thereby it restored confidence and hope in the American people, it freed and stimulated enterprise, it restored the government to its position as an umpire instead of a player in the economic game. For these reasons the American people have gone forward in progress while the rest of the world has halted, and some countries have even gone backward. If anyone will study the causes of retarded recuperation in Europe, he will find much of it due to the stifling of private initiative on one hand, and overloading of the government with business on the other.

There has been revived in this campaign, however, a series of proposals which, if adopted, would be a long step toward the abandonment of our American system and a surrender to the destructive operation of governmental conduct of commercial business. Because the country is faced with difficulty and doubt over certain national problems—that is, prohibition, farm relief, and electrical power—our opponents propose that we must thrust government a long way into the businesses which give rise to these problems. In effect, they abandon the tenets of their own party and turn to state socialism as a solution for the difficulties presented by all three.

. . . There is, therefore, submitted to the American people a question of fundamental principle. That is: shall we depart from the principles of our American political and economic system, upon which we have advanced beyond all the rest of the world, in order to adopt methods based on principles destructive of its very foundations? And I wish to emphasize the seriousness of these proposals. I wish to make my position clear; for this goes to the very roots of American life and progress.

I should like to state to you the effect that this projection of government in business would have upon our system of self-government and our economic system. That effect would reach to the daily life of every man and woman. It would impair the very basis of liberty and freedom not only for those left outside the fold of expanded bureaucracy but for those embraced within it.

Let us first see the effect upon self-government. When the Federal Government undertakes to go into commercial business it must at once set up the organization and administration of that business, and it immediately finds itself in a labyrinth, every alley of which leads to the destruction of self-government.

. . . Our government to succeed in business would need become in effect a despotism. There at once begins the destruction of self-government.

. . . There is no better example of the practical incompetence of government to conduct business than the history of our railways. During the war the government found it necessary to operate the railways. That operation continued until after the war. In the year before being freed from government operation they were not able to meet the demands for transportation. Eight years later we find them under private enterprise transporting fifteen per cent more goods and meeting every demand for service. Rates have been reduced by fifteen per cent and net earnings increased from less than one per cent on their valuation to about five per cent. Wages of employees have improved by thirteen per cent. The wages of railway employees are today one hundred and twenty-one per cent above pre-war, while the wages of government employees are today only sixty-five per cent above pre-war. That should be a sufficient commentary upon the efficiency of government operation.

. . . The government in commercial business does not tolerate amongst its customers the freedom of competitive reprisals to which private business is subject. Bureaucracy does not tolerate the spirit of independence; it spreads the spirit of submission into our daily life and penetrates the temper of our people not with the habit of powerful resistance to wrong but with the habit of timid acceptance of irresistible might.

Bureaucracy is ever desirous of spreading its influence and its power. You cannot extend the mastery of the government over the daily working life of a people without at the same time making it the master of the people's souls and thoughts. Every expansion of government in business means that government in order to protect itself from the political consequences of its errors and wrongs is driven irresistibly without peace to greater and greater control of the nation's press and platform. Free speech does not live many hours after free industry and free commerce die.

It is a false liberalism that interprets itself into the government operation of commercial business. Every step of bureaucratizing of the business of our country poisons the very roots of liberalism—that is, political equality, free speech, free assembly, free press, and equality of opportunity. It is the road not to more liberty, but to less liberty. Liberalism should be found not striving to spread bureaucracy but striving to set bounds to it. True liberalism seeks all legitimate freedom first in the confident belief that without such freedom the pursuit of all other blessings and benefits is vain. That belief is the foundation of all American progress, political as well as economic.

Liberalism is a force truly of the spirit, a force proceeding from the deep realization that economic freedom cannot be sacrificed if political freedom is to be preserved. Even if governmental conduct of business could give us more efficiency instead of less efficiency, the fundamental objection to it would remain unaltered and unabated. It would destroy political equality. It would increase rather than decrease abuse and corruption. It would stifle initiative and invention. It would undermine the development of leadership. It would cramp and cripple the mental and spiritual energies of our people. It would extinguish equality and opportunity. It would dry up the spirit of liberty and progress. For these reasons primarily it must be resisted. For a hundred and fifty years liberalism has found its true spirit in the American system, not in the European systems.

I do not wish to be misunderstood in this statement. I am defining a general policy. It does not mean that our government is to part with one iota of its national resources without complete protection to the public interest. I have already stated that where the government is engaged in public works for purposes of flood control, of navigation, of irrigation, of scientific research or national defense, or in pioneering a new art, it will at times necessarily produce power or commodities as a by-product. But they must be a by-product of the major purpose, not the major purpose itself.

Nor do I wish to be misinterpreted as believing that the United

States is free-for-all and devil-take-the-hindmost. The very essence of equality of opportunity and of American individualism is that there shall be no domination by any group or combination in this republic, whether it be business or political. On the contrary, it demands economic justice as well as political and social justice. It is no system of laissez faire.

. . . I have witnessed not only at home but abroad the many failures of government in business. I have seen its tyrannies, its injustices, its destructions of self-government, its undermining of the very instincts which carry our people forward to progress. I have witnessed the lack of advance, the lowered standards of living, the depressed spirits of people working under such a system . . .

Our people have the right to know whether we can continue to solve our great problems without abandonment of our American system. I know we can. We have demonstrated that our system is responsive enough to meet any new and intricate development in our economic and business life. We have demonstrated that we can meet any economic problem and still maintain our democracy as master in its own house, and that we can at the same time preserve equality of opportunity and individual freedom.

In the last fifty years we have discovered that mass production will produce articles for us at half the cost they required previously. We have seen the resultant growth of large units of production and distribution. This is big business. Many businesses must be bigger, for our tools are bigger, our country is bigger. We now build a single dynamo of a hundred thousand horsepower. Even fifteen years ago that would have been a big business all by itself. Yet today advance in production requires that we set ten of these units together in a row.

The American people from bitter experience have a rightful fear that great business units might be used to dominate our industrial life and by illegal and unethical practices destroy equality of opportunity.

Years ago the Republican administration established the principle that such evils could be corrected by regulation. It developed methods by which abuses could be prevented while the full value of industrial progress could be retained for the public. It insisted upon the principle that when great public utilities were clothed with the security of partial monopoly, whether it be railways, power plants, telephones or what not, then there must be the fullest and most complete control of rates, services, and finances by government or local agencies. It declared that these businesses must be conducted with glass pockets.

. . . The wisdom of our forefathers in their conception that progress can only be attained as the sum of the accomplishment of free individuals has been reinforced by all of the great leaders of the country . . . Jackson, Lincoln, Cleveland, McKinley, Roosevelt, Wilson and Coolidge have stood unalterably for these principles.

And what have been the results of our American system? Our country has become the land of opportunity to those born without inheritance, not merely because of the wealth of its resources and industry but because of this freedom of initiative and enterprise. Russia has natural resources equal to ours. Her people are equally industrious, but she has not had the blessings of one hundred and fifty years of our form of government and of our social system.

By adherence to the principles of decentralized self-government, ordered liberty, equal opportunity, and freedom to the individual, our American experiment in human welfare has yielded a degree of well-being unparalleled in all the world. It has come nearer to the abolition of poverty, to the abolition of fear of want, than humanity has ever reached before. Progress of the past seven years is the proof of it.

. . . I cannot believe that the American people wish to abandon or in any way to weaken the principles of economic freedom and self-government which have been maintained by the Republican Party and which have produced results so amazing and so stimulating to the spiritual as well as to the material advance of the nation . . .

We still have great problems if we would achieve the full economic advancement of our country. In these past few years some groups in our country have lagged behind others in the march of progress. I refer more particularly to those engaged in the textile, coal, and the agricultural industries. We can assist in solving these problems by co-operation of our government. To the agricultural industry we shall need to advance initial capital to assist them to stabilize their industry. But this proposal implies that they shall conduct it themselves, and not the government. It is in the interest of our cities that we shall bring agriculture and all industries into full stability and prosperity. I know you will gladly cooperate in the faith that in the common prosperity of our country lies its future.

. . . The foundations of progress and prosperity are dependent as never before upon the wise policies of government, for government now touches at a thousand points the intricate web of economic and social life. Under administration by the Republican Party in the last seven and one-half years our country as a whole has made unparalleled progress and this has been in generous part reflected to this great city. Prosperity is no idle expression. It is a job for every worker; it is the safety and the safeguard of every business and every home. A continuation of the policies of the Republican Party is fundamentally necessary to the further advancement of this progress and to the further building up of this prosperity.

I have dwelt at some length on the principles of relationship between the government and business. I make no apologies for dealing with this subject. The first necessity of any nation is the smooth functioning of the vast business machinery for employment, feeding, clothing, housing, and providing luxuries and comfort to a people. Unless these basic elements are properly organized and function, there can be no progress in business, in education, literature, music, or art. There can be no advance in the fundamental ideals of a people. A people cannot make progress in poverty.

. . . The greatness of America has grown out of a political and social system and a method of control of economic forces distinctly its own—our American system—which has carried this great experiment in human welfare further than ever before in all history. We are nearer today to the ideal of the abolition of poverty and fear from the lives of men and women than ever before in any land. And I again repeat that the departure from our American system by injecting principles destructive to it which our opponents propose will jeopardize the very liberty and freedom of our people, will destroy equality of opportunity, not alone to ourselves but to our children.

To me the foundation of American life rests upon the home and the family. I read into these great economic forces, these intricate and delicate relations of the government with business and with our political and social life, but one supreme end—that we reinforce the ties that bind together the millions of our families, that we strengthen the security, the happiness, and the independence of every home.

My conception of America is a land where men and women may walk in ordered freedom in the independent conduct of their occupations; where they may enjoy the advantages of wealth, not concentrated in the hands of the few but spread through the lives of all; where they build and safeguard their homes, and give to their children the fullest advantages and opportunities of American life; where every man shall be respected in the faith that his conscience and his heart direct him to follow; where a contented and happy people, secure in their liberties, free from poverty and fear, shall have the leisure and impulse to seek a fuller life.

Some may ask where all this may lead beyond mere material progress. It leads to a release of the energies of men and women from the dull drudgery of life to a wider vision and a higher hope. It leads to the opportunity for greater and greater service, not alone from man to man in our own land, but from our country to the whole world. It leads to an America, healthy in body, healthy in spirit, unfettered, youthful, eager—with a vision searching beyond the farthest horizons, with an open mind, sympathetic and generous. It is to these higher ideals and for these purposes that I pledge myself and the Republican Party.

## *Franklin D. Roosevelt Offers a "New Deal" to the American People, Chicago, July 2, 1932*

I appreciate your willingness after these six arduous days to remain here, for I know well the sleepless hours which you and I have had. I regret that I am late, but I have no control over the winds of Heaven and could only be thankful for my Navy training.

The appearance before a National Convention of its nominee for President, to be formally notified of his selection, is unprecedented and unusual, but these are unprecedented and unusual times. I have started out on the tasks that lie ahead by breaking the absurd traditions that the candidate should remain in professed ignorance of what has happened for weeks until he is formally notified of that event many weeks later.

My friends, may this be the symbol of my intention to be honest and to avoid all hypocrisy or sham, to avoid all silly shutting of the eyes to the truth in this campaign. You have nominated me and I know it, and I am here to thank you for the honor.

Let it also be symbolic that in so doing I broke traditions. Let it be from now on the task of our Party to break foolish traditions. We will break foolish traditions and leave it to the Republican leadership, far more skilled in that art, to break promises.

Let us now and here highly resolve to resume the country's interrupted march along the path of real progress, of real justice, of real equality for all of our citizens, great and small. Our indomitable leader in that interrupted march is no longer with us, but there still survives today his spirit. Many of his captains, thank God, are still with us, to give us wise counsel. Let us feel that in everything we do there still lives with us, if not the body, the great indomitable, unquenchable, progressive soul of our Commander-in-Chief, Woodrow Wilson.

. . . As we enter this new battle, let us keep always present with us some of the ideals of the Party: The fact that the Democratic

Party by tradition and by the continuing logic of history, past and present, is the bearer of liberalism and of progress and at the same time of safety to our institutions. And if this appeal fails, remember well, my friends, that a resentment against the failure of Republican leadership—and note well that in this campaign I shall not use the words "Republican Party," but I shall use, day in and day out, the words, "Republican leadership"—the failure of Republican leaders to solve our troubles may degenerate into unreasoning radicalism.

The great social phenomenon of this depression, unlike others before it, is that it has produced but a few of the disorderly manifestations that too often attend upon such times.

Wild radicalism has made few converts, and the greatest tribute that I can pay to my countrymen is that in these days of crushing want there persists an orderly and hopeful spirit on the part of the millions of our people who have suffered so much. To fail to offer them a new chance is not only to betray their hopes but to misunderstand their patience.

To meet by reaction that danger of radicalism is to invite disaster. Reaction is no barrier to the radical. It is a challenge, a provocation. The way to meet that danger is to offer a workable program of reconstruction, and the party to offer it is the party with clean hands.

This, and this only, is a proper protection against blind reaction on the one hand and an improvised, hit-or-miss, irresponsible opportunism on the other.

There are two ways of viewing the Government's duty in matters affecting economic and social life. The first sees to it that a favored few are helped and hopes that some of their prosperity will leak through, sift through, to labor, to the farmer, to the small business man. That theory belongs to the party of Toryism, and I had hoped that most of the Tories left this country in 1776.

But it is not and never will be the theory of the Democratic Party. This is no time for fear, for reaction or for timidity. Here and now I invite those nominal Republicans who find that their conscience cannot be squared with the groping and the failure of their party leaders to join hands with us; here and now, in equal measure, I warn those nominal Democrats who squint at the future with their faces turned toward the past, and who feel no responsibility to the demands of the new time, that they are out of step with their Party.

Yes, the people of this country want a genuine choice this year, not a choice between two names for the same reactionary doctrine. Ours must be a party of liberal thought, of planned action, of enlightened international outlook, and of the greatest good to the greatest number of our citizens.

Now it is inevitable—and the choice is that of the times—it is inevitable that the main issue of this campaign should revolve about the clear fact of our economic condition, a depression so deep that it is without precedent in modern history. It will not do merely to state, as do Republican leaders to explain their broken promises of continued inaction, that the depression is worldwide. That was not their explanation of the apparent prosperity of 1928. The people will not forget the claim made by them then that prosperity was only a domestic product manufactured by a Republican President and a Republican Congress. If they claim paternity for the one they cannot deny paternity for the other.

I cannot take up all the problems today. I want to touch on a few that are vital. Let us look a little at the recent history and the simple economics, the kind of economics that you and I and the average man and woman talk.

In the years before 1929 we know that this country had completed a vast cycle of building and inflation; for ten years we expanded on the theory of repairing the wastes of the War, but actually expanding far beyond that, and also beyond our natural and normal growth. Now it is worth remembering, and the cold figures of finance prove it, that during that time there was little or no drop in the prices that the consumer had to pay, although those same figures proved that the cost of production fell very greatly; corporate profit resulting from this period was enormous; at the same time little of that profit was devoted to the reduction of prices. The consumer was forgotten. Very little of it went into increased wages; the worker was forgotten, and by no means an adequate proportion was even paid out in dividends—the stockholder was forgotten.

And, incidentally, very little of it was taken by taxation to the beneficent Government of those years.

What was the result? Enormous corporate surpluses piled up— the most stupendous in history. Where, under the spell of delirious speculation, did those surpluses go? Let us talk economics that the figures prove and that we can understand. Why, they went chiefly in two directions: first, into new and unnecessary plants which now stand stark and idle; and second, into the call-money market of Wall Street, either directly by the corporations, or indirectly through the banks. Those are the facts. Why blink at them?

Then came the crash. You know the story. Surpluses invested in unnecessary plants became idle. Men lost their jobs; purchasing power dried up; banks became frightened and started calling loans. Those who had money were afraid to part with it. Credit contracted. Industry stopped. Commerce declined, and unemployment mounted.

And there we are today.

Translate that into human terms. See how the events of the past three years have come home to specific groups of people: first, the group dependent on industry; second, the group dependent on agriculture; third, and made up in large part of members of the first two groups, the people who are called "small investors and depositors." In fact, the strongest possible tie between the first two groups, agriculture and industry, is the fact that the savings and to a degree the security of both are tied together in that third group—the credit structure of the Nation.

Never in history have the interests of all the people been so united in a single economic problem. Picture to yourself, for instance, the great groups of property owned by millions of our citizens, represented by credits issued in the form of bonds and mortgages—Government bonds of all kinds, Federal, State, county, municipal; bonds of industrial companies, of utility companies; mortgages on real estate in farms and cities, and finally the vast investments of the Nation in the railroads. What is the measure of the security of each of those groups? We know well that in our complicated, interrelated credit structure if any one of these credit groups collapses they may all collapse. Danger to one is danger to all.

How, I ask, has the present Administration in Washington treated the interrelationship of these credit groups? The answer is clear: It has not recognized that interrelationship existed at all. Why, the Nation asks, has Washington failed to understand that all of these groups, each and every one, the top of the pyramid and the bottom of the pyramid, must be considered together, that each and every one of them is dependent on every other; each and every one of them affecting the whole financial fabric?

Statesmanship and vision, my friends, require relief to all at the same time.

Just one word or two on taxes, the taxes that all of us pay toward the cost of Government of all kinds.

I know something of taxes. For three long years I have been going up and down this country preaching that Government—Federal and State and local—costs too much. I shall not stop that preaching. As an immediate program of action we must abolish useless offices. We must eliminate unnecessary functions of Government—functions, in fact, that are not definitely essential to the continuance of Government. We must merge, we must consolidate subdivisions of Government, and, like the private citizen, give up luxuries which we can no longer afford.

. . . I propose to you, my friends, and through you, that Government of all kinds, big and little, be made solvent and that the example be set by the President of the United States and his Cabinet.

And talking about setting a definite example, I congratulate this convention for having had the courage fearlessly to write into its declaration of principles what an overwhelming majority here assembled really thinks about the 18th Amendment. This convention wants repeal. Your candidate wants repeal. And I am confident that the United States of America wants repeal.

. . . And now one word about unemployment, and incidentally about agriculture. I have favored the use of certain types of public works as a further emergency means of stimulating employment and the issuance of bonds to pay for such public works, but I have pointed out that no economic end is served if we merely build without building for a necessary purpose. Such works, of course, should insofar as possible be self-sustaining if they are to be financed by the issuing of bonds. So as to spread the points of all kinds as widely as possible, we must take definite steps to shorten the working day and the working week.

Let us use common sense and business sense. Just as one example, we know that a very hopeful and immediate means of relief, both for the unemployed and for agriculture, will come from a wide plan of the converting of many millions of acres of marginal and unused land into timberland through reforestation. There are tens of millions of acres east of the Mississippi River alone in abandoned farms, in cut-over land, now growing up in worthless brush. Why, every European Nation has a definite land policy, and has had one for generations. We have none. Having none, we face a future of soil erosion and timber famine. It is clear that economic foresight and immediate employment march hand in hand in the call for the reforestation of these vast areas.

In so doing, employment can be given to a million men. That is the kind of public work that is self-sustaining, and therefore capable of being financed by the issuance of bonds which are made secure by the fact that the growth of tremendous crops will provide adequate security for the investment.

Yes, I have a very definite program for providing employment by that means. I have done it, and I am doing it today in the State of New York. I know that the Democratic Party can do it successfully in the Nation. That will put men to work, and that is an example of the action that we are going to have.

Now as a further aid to agriculture, we know perfectly well— but have we come out and said so clearly and distinctly?—we should repeal immediately those provisions of law that compel the Federal Government to go into the market to purchase, to sell, to speculate in farm products in a futile attempt to reduce farm surpluses. And they are the people who are talking of keeping Government out of business. The practical way to help the farmer is by an arrangement that will, in addition to lightening some of the impoverishing burdens from his back, do something toward the reduction of the surpluses of staple commodities that hang on the market. It should be our aim to add to the world prices of staple products the amount of a reasonable tariff protection, to give agriculture the same protection that industry has today.

. . . One more word about the farmer, and I know that every delegate in this hall who lives in the city knows why I lay emphasis on the farmer. It is because one-half of our population, over 50,000,000 people, are dependent on agriculture; and, my friends, if those 50,000,000 people have no money, no cash, to buy what is produced in the city, the city suffers to an equal or greater extent.

That is why we are going to make the voters understand this

year that this Nation is not merely a Nation of independence, but it is, if we are to survive, bound to be a Nation of interdependence— town and city, and North and South, East and West. That is our goal, and that goal will be understood by the people of this country no matter where they live.

. . . Out of all the tons of printed paper, out of all the hours of oratory, the recriminations, the defenses, the happy-thought plans in Washington and in every State, there emerges one great, simple, crystal-pure fact that during the past ten years a Nation of 120,000,000 people has been led by the Republican leaders to erect an impregnable barbed wire entanglement around its borders through the instrumentality of tariffs which have isolated us from all the other human beings in all the rest of the round world. I accept that admirable tariff statement in the platform of this convention. It would protect American business and American labor. By our acts of the past we have invited and received the retaliation of other Nations. I propose an invitation to them to forget the past, to sit at the table with us, as friends, and to plan with us for the restoration of the trade of the world.

Go into the home of the business man. He knows what the tariff has done for him. Go into the home of the factory worker. He knows why goods do not move. Go into the home of the farmer. He knows how the tariff has helped to ruin him.

At last our eyes are open. At last the American people are ready to acknowledge that Republican leadership was wrong and that the Democracy is right.

My program, of which I can only touch on these points, is based upon this simple moral principle: the welfare and the soundness of a Nation depend first upon what the great mass of the people wish and need; and second, whether or not they are getting it.

What do the people of America want more than anything else? To my mind, they want two things: work, with all the moral and spiritual values that go with it; and with work, a reasonable measure of security—security for themselves and for their wives and children. Work and security—these are more than words. They are more than facts. They are the spiritual values, the true goal toward which our efforts of reconstruction should lead. These are the values that this program is intended to gain; these are the values we have failed to achieve by the leadership we now have.

Our Republican leaders tell us economic laws—sacred, inviolable, unchangeable—cause panics which no one could prevent. But while they prate of economic laws, men and women are starving. We must lay hold of the fact that economic laws are not made by nature. They are made by human beings.

Yes, when—not if—when we get the chance, the Federal Government will assume bold leadership in distress relief. For years Washington has alternated between putting its head in the sand and saying there is no large number of destitute people in our midst who need food and clothing, and then saying the States should take care of them, if there are. Instead of planning two and a half years ago to do what they are now trying to do, they kept putting it off from day to day, week to week, and month to month, until the conscience of America demanded action.

I say that while primary responsibility for relief rests with localities now, as ever, yet the Federal Government has always had and still has a continuing responsibility for the broader public welfare. It will soon fulfill that responsibility.

. . . Out of every crisis, every tribulation, every disaster, mankind rises with some share of greater knowledge, of higher decency, of purer purpose. Today we shall have come through a period of loose thinking, descending morals, an era of selfishness, among individual men and women and among Nations. Blame not Governments alone for this. Blame ourselves in equal share. Let us be frank in acknowledgment of the truth that many amongst us have made obeisance to Mammon, that the profits of speculation, the easy road without toil, have lured us from the old barricades. To return to higher standards we must abandon the false prophets and seek new leaders of our own choosing.

Never before in modern history have the essential differences between the two major American parties stood out in such striking contrast as they do today. Republican leaders not only have failed in material things, they have failed in national vision, because in disaster they have held out no hope, they have pointed out no path for the people below to climb back to places of security and of safety in our American life.

Throughout the Nation, men and women, forgotten in the political philosophy of the Government of the last years look to us here for guidance and for more equitable opportunity to share in the distribution of national wealth.

On the farms, in the large metropolitan areas, in the smaller cities and in the villages, millions of our citizens cherish the hope that their old standards of living and of thought have not gone forever. Those millions cannot and shall not hope in vain.

I pledge you, I pledge myself, to a new deal for the American people. Let us all here assembled constitute ourselves prophets of a new order of competence and of courage. This is more than a political campaign; it is a call to arms. Give me your help, not to win votes alone, but to win in this crusade to restore America to its own people.

## Franklin D. Roosevelt Addresses the Commonwealth Club, San Francisco, September 23, 1932

I want to speak not of politics but of government. I want to speak not of parties, but of universal principles. They are not political, except in that larger sense in which a great American once expressed a definition of politics, that nothing in all of human life is foreign to the science of politics.

. . . Sometimes, my friends, particularly in years such as these, the hand of discouragement falls upon us. It seems that things are in a rut, fixed, settled, that the world has grown old and tired and very much out of joint. This is the mood of depression, of dire and weary depression.

But then we look around us in America, and everything tells us that we are wrong. America is new. It is in the process of change and development. It has the great potentialities of youth and particularly is this true of the great West, and of this coast, and of California.

I would not have you feel that I regard this as in any sense a new community. I have traveled in many parts of the world, but never have I felt the arresting thought of the change and development more than here, where the old, mystic East would seem to be near to us, where the currents of life and thought and commerce of the whole world meet us. This factor alone is sufficient to cause man to stop and think of the deeper meaning of things, when he stands in this community.

. . . I want to invite you, therefore, to consider with me in the large, some of the relationships of government and economic life that go deeply into our daily lives, our happiness, our future and our security.

The issue of government has always been whether individual men and women will have to serve some system of government or economics, or whether a system of government and economics exists to serve individual men and women. This question has persistently dominated the discussion of government for many generations.

. . . When we look about us, we are likely to forget how hard people have worked to win the privilege of government. The growth of the national governments of Europe was a struggle for the development of a centralized force in the nation, strong enough to impose peace upon ruling barons. In many instances the victory of the central government . . . was a haven of refuge to the individual. The people preferred the master far away to the exploitation and cruelty of the smaller master near at hand.

But the creators of national government were perforce ruthless men. They were often cruel in their methods, but they did strive steadily toward something that society needed and very much wanted, a strong central state able to keep the peace, to stamp out civil war, to put the unruly nobleman in his place, and to permit the bulk of individuals to live safely. The man of ruthless force had his place in developing a pioneer country, just as he did in fixing the power of the central government in the development of the nations.

Society paid him well for his services and its development. When the development among the nations of Europe, however, had been completed, ambition and ruthlessness, having served their term, tended to overstep their mark.

There came a growing feeling that government was conducted for the benefit of a few who thrived unduly at the expense of all. The people sought a balancing—a limiting force. There came gradually, through town councils, trade guilds, national parliaments, by constitution and by popular participation and control, limitations on arbitrary power.

Another factor that tended to limit the power of those who ruled, was the rise of the ethical conception that a ruler bore a responsibility for the welfare of his subjects.

The American colonies were born in this struggle. The American Revolution was a turning point in it. After the Revolution the struggle continued and shaped itself in the public life of the country. There were those who because they had seen the confusion which attended the years of war for American independence surrendered to the belief that popular government was essentially dangerous and essentially unworkable. They were honest people, my friends, and we cannot deny that their experience had warranted some measure of fear. The most brilliant, honest and able exponent of this point of view was Hamilton. He was too impatient of slow-moving methods. Fundamentally he believed that the safety of the republic lay in the autocratic strength of its government, that the destiny of individuals was to serve that government, and that fundamentally a great and strong group of central institutions, guided by a small group of able and public spirited citizens, could best direct all government.

But Mr. Jefferson, in the summer of 1776, after drafting the Declaration of Independence turned his mind to the same problem and took a different view . . . Government to him was a means to an end, not an end in itself; it might be either a refuge and a help or a threat and a danger, depending on the circumstances.

. . . People, he considered, had two sets of rights, those of "personal competency" and those involved in acquiring and possessing property. By "personal competency" he meant the right of free thinking, freedom of forming and expressing opinions, and freedom of personal living, each man according to his own lights. To insure the first set of rights, a government must so order its functions as not to interfere with the individual. But even Jefferson realized that the exercise of property rights might so interfere with the rights of the individual that the government, without whose assistance the property rights could not exist, must intervene, not to destroy individualism, but to protect it.

You are familiar with the great political duel which followed; and how Hamilton, and his friends, building toward a dominant centralized power were at length defeated in the great election of 1800, by Mr. Jefferson's party. Out of that duel came the two parties, Republican and Democratic, as we know them today.

So began, in American political life, the new day, the day of the individual against the system, the day in which individualism was made the great watchword of American life. The happiest of economic conditions made that day long and splendid. On the Western frontier, land was substantially free. No one, who did not shirk the task of earning a living, was entirely without opportunity to do so. Depressions could, and did, come and go; but they could not alter the fundamental fact that most of the people lived partly by selling their labor and partly by extracting their livelihood from the soil, so that starvation and dislocation were practically impossible. At the very worst there was always the possibility of climbing into a covered wagon and moving west where the untilled prairies afforded a haven for men to whom the East did not provide a place. So great were our natural resources that we could offer this relief not only to our own people, but to the distressed of all the world; we could invite immigration from Europe, and welcome it with open arms. Traditionally, when a depression came a new section of land was opened in the West; and even our temporary misfortune served our manifest destiny.

It was in the middle of the nineteenth century that a new force was released and a new dream created. The force was what is called the industrial revolution, the advance of steam and machinery and the rise of the forerunners of the modern industrial plant. The dream was the dream of an economic machine, able to raise the standard of living for everyone; to bring luxury within the reach of the humblest; to annihilate distance by steam power and later by electricity, and to release everyone from the drudgery of the heaviest manual toil. It was to be expected that this would necessarily affect government. Heretofore, government had merely been called upon to produce conditions within which people could live happily, labor peacefully, and rest secure. Now it was called upon to aid in the consummation of this new dream. There was, however, a shadow over the dream. To be made real, it required use of the talents of men of tremendous will and tremendous ambition, since by no other force could the problems of financing and engineering and new developments be brought to a consummation.

So manifest were the advantages of the machine age, however, that the United States fearlessly, cheerfully, and, I think, rightly, accepted the bitter with the sweet. It was thought that no price was too high to pay for the advantages which we could draw from a finished industrial system. This history of the last half century is accordingly in large measure a history of a group of financial Titans, whose methods were not scrutinized with too much care, and who were honored in proportion as they produced the results, irrespective of the means they used. The financiers who pushed the railroads to the Pacific were always ruthless, often wasteful, and frequently corrupt; but they did build railroads, and we have them today.

. . . As long as we had free land; as long as population was growing by leaps and bounds; as long as our industrial plants were insufficient to supply our own needs, society chose to give the ambitious man free play and unlimited reward provided only that he produced the economic plant so much desired.

During this period of expansion, there was equal opportunity for all and the business of government was not to interfere but to assist in the development of industry. This was done at the request of businessmen themselves.

. . . Some of my friends tell me that they do not want the government in business. With this I agree; but I wonder whether they realize the implications of the past. For while it has been American doctrine that the government must not go into business in competition with private enterprises, still it has been traditional, particularly in Republican administrations, for business urgently to ask the government to put at private disposal all kinds of government assistance. The same man who tells you that he does not want to see the government interfere in business—and he means it, and has plenty of good reasons for saying so—is the first to go to Washington and ask the government for a prohibitory tariff on his product . . . Each group has sought protection from the government for its own special interests, without realizing that the function of government must be to favor no small group at the expense of its duty to protect the rights of personal freedom and of private property of all its citizens.

. . . A glance at the situation today only too clearly indicates that equality of opportunity as we have known it no longer exists. Our industrial plant is built; the problem just now is whether under existing conditions it is not overbuilt. Our last frontier has long since been reached, and there is practically no more free land. More than half of our people do not live on the farms or on lands and cannot derive a living by cultivating their own property. There is no safety valve in the form of a Western prairie to which those thrown out of work by the Eastern economic machines can go for a new start. We are not able to invite the immigration from Europe to share our endless plenty. We are now providing a drab living for our own people.

Our system of constantly rising tariffs has at last reacted against us to the point of closing our Canadian frontier on the north, our European markets on the east, many of our Latin American markets to the south, and a goodly proportion of our Pacific markets on the west, through the retaliatory tariffs of those countries.

. . . Just as freedom to farm has ceased, so also the opportunity in business has narrowed. It still is true that men can start small enterprises, trusting to native shrewdness and ability to keep abreast

119

of competitors; but area after area has been preempted altogether by the great corporations, and even in the fields which still have no great concerns, the small man starts under a handicap. The unfeeling statistics of the past three decades show that the independent businessman is running a losing race. Perhaps he is forced to the wall; perhaps he cannot command credit; perhaps he is "squeezed out," in Mr. Wilson's words, by highly organized corporate competitors, as your corner grocery man can tell you.

Recently a careful study was made of the concentration of business in the United States. It showed that our economic life was dominated by some six hundred odd corporations who controlled two-thirds of American industry. Ten million small businessmen divided the other third. More striking still, it appeared that if the process of concentration goes on at the same rate, at the end of another century we shall have all American industry controlled by a dozen corporations, and run by perhaps a hundred men. But plainly, we are steering a steady course toward economic oligarchy, if we are not there already.

Clearly, all this calls for a re-appraisal of values. A mere builder of more industrial plants, a creator of more railroad systems, and organizer of more corporations, is as likely to be a danger as a help. The day of the great promoter or the financial Titan, to whom we granted everything if only he would build, or develop, is over. Our task now is not discovery or exploitation of natural resources, or necessarily producing more goods. It is the soberer, less dramatic business of administering resources and plants already in hand, of seeking to reestablish foreign markets for our surplus production, of meeting the problem of underconsumption, of adjusting production to consumption, of distributing wealth and products more equitably, of adapting existing economic organizations to the service of the people. The day of enlightened administration has come.

Just as in older times the central government was first a haven of refuge, and then a threat, so now in a closer economic system the central and ambitious financial unit is no longer a servant of national desire, but a danger. I would draw the parallel one step farther. We did not think because national government had become a threat in the 18th century that therefore we should abandon the principle of national government. Nor today should we abandon the principle of strong economic units called corporations, merely because their power is susceptible of easy abuse. In other times we dealt with the problem of an unduly ambitious central government by modifying it gradually into a constitutional democratic government. So today we are modifying and controlling our economic units.

As I see it, the task of government in its relation to business is to assist the development of an economic declaration of rights, an economic constitutional order. This is the common task of statesman and businessman. It is the minimum requirement of a more permanently safe order of things.

Happily, the times indicate that to create such an order is not only the proper policy of government, but it is the only line of safety for our economic structures as well. We know, now, that these economic units cannot exist unless prosperity is uniform, that is, unless purchasing power is well distributed throughout every group in the nation. That is why even the most selfish of corporations for its own interest would be glad to see wages restored and unemployment ended and to bring the Western farmer back to his accustomed level of prosperity and to assure a permanent safety to both groups. That is why some enlightened industries themselves endeavor to limit the freedom of action of each man and business group within the industry in the common interest of all; why business men everywhere are asking a form of organization which will bring the scheme of things into balance, even though it may in some measure qualify the freedom of action of individual units within the business.

. . . The Declaration of Independence discusses the problem of government in terms of a contract. Government is a relation of give and take, a contract, perforce, if we would follow the thinking out of which it grew. Under such a contract rulers were accorded power, and the people consented to that power on consideration that they be accorded certain rights. The task of statesmanship has always been the re-definition of these rights in terms of a changing and growing social order. New conditions impose new requirements upon government and those who conduct government.

. . . I feel that we are coming to a view through the drift of our legislation and our public thinking in the past quarter century that private economic power is, to enlarge an old phrase, a public trust as well. I hold that continued enjoyment of that power by any individual or group must depend upon the fulfillment of that trust . . . The terms of that contract are as old as the republic, and as new as the new economic order.

Every man has a right to life; and this means that he has also a right to make a comfortable living. He may by sloth or crime decline to exercise that right; but it may not be denied him. We have no actual famine or dearth; our industrial and agricultural mechanism can produce enough and to spare. Our government formal and informal, political and economic, owes to everyone an avenue to possess himself of a portion of that plenty sufficient for his needs, through his own work.

Every man has a right to his own property, which means a right to be assured, to the fullest extent attainable, in the safety of his savings. By no other means can men carry the burdens of those parts of life which, in the nature of things, afford no chance of labor; childhood, sickness, old age. In all thought of property, this right is paramount; all other property rights must yield to it. If, in accord with this principle, we must restrict the operations of the speculator, the manipulator, even the financier, I believe we must accept the restriction as needful, not to hamper individualism but to protect it.

These two requirements must be satisfied, in the main, by the individuals who claim and hold control of the great industrial and financial combinations which dominate so large a part of our industrial life. They have undertaken to be not businessmen, but princes of property. I am not prepared to say that the system which produces them is wrong. I am very clear that they must fearlessly and competently assume the responsibility which goes with the power. So many enlightened businessmen know this that the statement would be little more than a platitude, were it not for an added implication.

This implication is, briefly, that the responsible heads of finance and industry instead of acting each for himself, must work together to achieve the common end. They must, where necessary, sacrifice this or that private advantage; and in reciprocal self-denial must seek a general advantage. It is here that formal government—political government, if you choose—comes in. Whenever in the pursuit of this objective the lone wolf, the unethical competitor, the reckless promoter, the Ishmael or Insull whose hand is against every man's, declines to join in achieving an end recognized as being for the public welfare, and threatens to drag the industry back to a state of anarchy, the government may properly be asked to apply restraint. Likewise, should the group ever use its collective power contrary to the public welfare, the government must be swift to enter and protect the public interest.

The government should assume the function of economic regulation only as a last resort, to be tried only when private initiative, inspired by high responsibility, with such assistance and balance as government can give, has finally failed. As yet there has been no final failure, because there has been no attempt; and I decline to assume that this nation is unable to meet the situation.

The final term of the high contract was for liberty and the

pursuit of happiness. We have learned a great deal of both in the past century. We know that individual liberty and individual happiness mean nothing unless both are ordered in the sense that one man's meat is not another man's poison. We know that the old "rights of personal competency," the right to read, to think, to speak, to choose and live a mode of life, must be respected at all hazards. We know that liberty to do anything which deprives others of those elemental rights is outside the protection of any compact; and that government in this regard is the maintenance of a balance, within which every individual may have a place if he will take it; in which every individual may find safety if he wishes it; in which every individual may attain such power as his ability permits, consistent with his assuming the accompanying responsibility.

. . . Faith in America, faith in our tradition of personal responsibility, faith in our institutions, faith in ourselves demand that we recognize the new terms of the old social contract. We shall fulfill them, as we fulfilled the obligation of the apparent Utopia which Jefferson imagined for us in 1776, and which Jefferson, Roosevelt and Wilson sought to bring to realization. We must do so, lest a rising tide of misery, engendered by our common failure, engulf us all. But failure is not an American habit; and in the strength of great hope we must all shoulder our common load.

## Chapter 5

## "RENDEZVOUS WITH DESTINY"

### Franklin Roosevelt Offers America a New Burst of Economic Freedom: 1936

IF FRANKLIN ROOSEVELT'S campaign speeches in 1932 were intended to end Republican rule and usher in a bold new era of activist government, his acceptance speech at the 1936 Democratic convention had an altogether different intention— to transform the very ideals of American democracy. Roosevelt's "rendezvous with destiny" speech stands the test of time as one of the most radical presidential campaign speeches to be delivered by a major party candidate in modern American history. It was FDR's own version of the Gettysburg Address: an inspired effort to present a new vision of American government and a reinterpretation of the meaning of freedom in a representative democracy.

With the country rebounding from the worst of the Great Depression, Roosevelt judged early on that the 1936 race would be a referendum on him personally and the first four years of the New Deal. That would suit the president just fine. Unemployment had dipped to 5 percent from a high of 30 percent four years earlier, as millions of Americans were employed in one of the various New Deal programs set up by FDR and his administration. Even corporate profits were on the rise. The popular Roosevelt (his approval ratings stood at above 60 percent) was at little risk of losing reelection against his uninspiring Republican opponent, Kansas governor Alf Landon.[1] But on this night, Roosevelt's electoral goals went beyond his mere political needs—he was seeking to frame the election in terms that would give him a mandate for the liberal vision of government he sought to enshrine in the country.

## A Magical Night

Roosevelt's appearance at the Democratic convention had all the trappings of a political coronation. It was a magical night, the kind one would expect to read about in a political novel rather than experience in real life. But sometimes, even in politics, life imitates art. As the crowd streamed into Philadelphia's cavernous Franklin Field, a gentle rain was falling. But at 9:30 P.M., seemingly on cue, the rain ended, the skies began to clear, and a bright half-moon poked its light through the clouds.[2] More than a hundred thousand people were now seated (to date, the largest political audience in the nation's history), eagerly anticipating the arrival of the president.

Instead of the usual political anthems, the Philadelphia Symphony Orchestra played Tchaikovsky and opera star Lily Pons serenaded the crowd.[3] There was genuine electricity in the stadium. "Something happened to that audience," wrote legendary political reporter Raymond Clapper. "It had been lifted, not to a cheap political emotional pitch, but to something finer."[4]

As Vice President Garner was at the podium accepting his renomination, there was a stir in the crowd: the president had arrived. FDR's motorcade entered the stadium to rapturous applause. Arthur Schlesinger Jr. captured the scene: "The orchestra went into 'Hail to the Chief'; spotlights, scurrying through the black sky, stabbed at the President; and the side curtains suddenly drew back, showing Roosevelt in a pool of brilliant light, a smile on his face, his hand raised high. The crowd went wild."[5]

As the president approached the stage, the elderly poet Edwin Markham came forward to greet him. Pushed by the surging crowd behind him, Markham lost his footing, and tumbled into Roosevelt's son James, who was helping the president to the podium. The brace holding FDR's leg snapped out of place and he fell over. A fast-acting Secret Service agent, who dived to the ground to break the president's fall, prevented worse injury. The president was surrounded by his entourage, so his tumble was not seen by the crowd. But his speech text was scattered across the ground. "Clean me up," he ordered, and snapped at them not to step on "those damned sheets." FDR later said "it was the most frightful few minutes of my life."[6]

As he came to the podium, Roosevelt bantered with the crowd while he tried to arrange his speech pages in proper order. He then proceeded to deliver what Roosevelt biographer Conrad Black called "one of the greatest speeches of his life" and Secretary of Interior Harold Ickes termed the "greatest political speech I have ever heard."[7]

## A Populist Call to Arms

Amazingly, the text was the product of several fathers. Roosevelt had asked two teams of speechwriters to draft his remarks. One was helmed by Raymond Moley, his primary speechwriter from the 1932 campaign, who was tasked with drawing up moderate and sober remarks. The other team, led by Sam Rosenman, was asked to come up with a more "militant bare-fisted statement."[8] As was often the case with FDR, he was his own best speechwriter, and he combined both drafts into the speech delivered in Philadelphia. But there would be acrimony first.

At a dinner the night before Roosevelt was renominated, a bitter fight ensued between the president and Moley. Rosenman later recounted that "for the first and only time in my life, I saw the President forget himself as a gentlemen." It would largely mark the end of the friendship between Roosevelt and Moley, who would eventually switch parties and become a harsh critic of the New Deal.[9]

Moley was increasingly alarmed by the president's mimicking of the populist rhetoric of Louisiana senator Huey Long, whose "Share Our Wealth" program called for the redistribution of wealth in the form of higher taxes on rich individuals and corporations. These radical policies had gained great prominence during the worst days of the Depression. But when Long was assassinated in 1935, their political influence generally died with him. Yet that didn't stop Roosevelt from playing the populist card. In his 1936 State of the Union address, Roosevelt railed against "a power seeking minority" that was pursuing nothing less than a "restoration of their selfish power." He claimed that this group, which he would later refer to as "economic royalists," would "'gang up' against the people's liberties" and if they had their way "will take the course of every autocracy of the past—power for themselves, enslavement for the public."[10]

The harshness of Roosevelt's tone is almost impossible to take seriously—he was anything but a radical, no matter what some of his conservative critics would claim. Instead, Roosevelt had a preternatural ability to understand the way America's political winds were blowing. He knew better than most that a little demagoguery could go a long way in helping Americans blow off steam without resorting to more extreme and dangerous government policies.[11] As political philosopher Isaiah Berlin would say of Roosevelt's political approach, he "was providing a vast safety valve for pent-up bitterness and indignation, and trying to prevent revolution and construct a regime which should establish greater economic equality, social justice and happiness . . . without altering the basis of freedom and democracy in his country."[12]

The increasingly populist tone of Roosevelt's rhetoric was not the only surprising element of his acceptance speech. A typical renomination address generally features a message of "stay the course" balanced by a healthy amount of credit taken for the successes of the past four years. For some presidents the latter can be tricky, but that was clearly the least of Roosevelt's problems. He simply could have walked onto the stage, recited the country's improved economic prospects, reminded Americans of Herbert Hoover and the Republican Party's policies of four years hence, and ensured himself reelection. (In fact, this approach would describe many of his speeches during the fall campaign.) Yet on this night Roosevelt took a far different and altogether more courageous route.

FDR made little effort to boast about the country's economic improvement, just briefly reminding the audience of his 1933 inaugural address by noting that "we have conquered fear." He offered no specific policies for his second term, nor did he mention his opponent, Landon, or even the Republican Party by name. Instead, his speech became a sermon, a history lesson, and a forward-looking manifesto, offering Roosevelt's unique perspective on the evolution of freedom in American society and the role that he believed government must continue to play in the lives of its citizens. Roosevelt was calling on the American people to stay the course, but it was a controversial course and one far less popular than the president himself.

Roosevelt began by noting that Philadelphia was a fitting place to gather, because the responsibility of the American people in the 1930s was to continue the revolution that had been started there 160 years before. America's founding fathers, Roosevelt reminded the audience, had taken up arms "to win freedom from the tyranny of political autocracy. That victory gave the business of governing into the hands of the average man." The result was that "political tyranny was wiped out at Philadelphia on July 4, 1776."

Yet for all the success of the American Revolution in providing political emancipation, new and unexpected economic challenges began to appear—railroads, the telegraph and radio, mass production and mass distribution. Echoing themes developed in his Commonwealth Club speech of 1932, Roosevelt argued that these new facets of modern civilization, controlled in large measure by the wealthiest of Americans, put the very freedom of the American people at risk. "Economic royalists carved new dynasties" and "the whole structure of modern life was impressed into this royal service," claimed Roosevelt, at his populist best. FDR referred to the nation's "new industrial dictatorship" and complained that "individual initiative was crushed in the cogs of a great machine"—a wonderful if somewhat overstated metaphor for Americans already dismayed by the increasing industrialization and impersonalization of modern life. In a neat rhetorical trick, Roosevelt conflated the wealthy businessman of modern capitalism with the original British royalists who sought to squelch America's political freedom.

Yet FDR was not interested simply in bashing the rich. Indeed, he went on to link the loss of economic freedom that was a result of the royalists' rise with the loss of political freedom. He said pointedly that the "political equality we once had" was meaningless in the face of economic "inequality." "For too many of us," Roosevelt said, "life was no longer free; liberty no longer real; men could no longer follow the pursuit of happiness." These words go to the very heart of what it means to be an American and of the very freedoms enshrined in the Declaration of Independence and the Constitution. From Roosevelt's perspective, the same rationale for Americans to take up arms in 1776 existed in 1936—to ensure freedom. But unlike Wilson, whose call for a New Freedom in 1912 meant returning America to the way things used to be, FDR was charting a truly original course, calling for a new burst of economic and in turn political liberty.

Just as Lincoln reconceived the founding ideals of American democracy at Gettysburg, Roosevelt, by arguing that "if the average citizen is guaranteed equal opportunity in the polling place, he must have equal opportunity in the market place," was reconceptualizing the very meaning of freedom in a modern society. As Schlesinger would say of Roosevelt's intent, "The issue here was whether democracy as a form of government could survive in industrial society."[13]

Yet the impediments standing against this shift in national priorities were well constructed. "These economic royalists complain that we seek to overthrow the institutions of America. What they really complain of is that we seek to take away their power. Our allegiance to American institutions requires the overthrow of this kind of power," argued Roosevelt.

So with these powerful forces arrayed against the American people, how were they to achieve true emancipation? How was the power of the "economic royalists" to be thwarted? In Roosevelt's conception, it was the state that must do the people's bidding. "Government in a modern civilization has certain inescapable obligations to its citizens, among which are protection of the family and the home, the establishment of a democracy of opportunity, and aid to those overtaken by disaster."

Having set up his narrative and followed through with his basic argument, Roosevelt then took what may seem like an odd, even sentimental turn. (This may also be a result of the often patchwork nature of Roosevelt's speeches.) In arguing what should guide this new conception of government's role, he offered three principles as lodestars—faith, hope, and, above all, charity.

Clearly, it was charity that in FDR's view is the most important and overriding ideal. Roosevelt's words spoke volumes:

Charity literally translated from the original means love, the love that understands, that does not merely share the wealth

131

of the giver, but in true sympathy and wisdom helps men to help themselves. We seek not merely to make government a mechanical implement, but to give it the vibrant personal character that is the very embodiment of human charity. We are poor indeed if this nation cannot afford to lift from every recess of American life the dread fear of the unemployed that they are not needed in this world. We cannot afford to accumulate a deficit in the books of human fortitude.

If Bryan put forth the idea that government had a responsibility to the working masses, if Wilson and TR conceived of a new relationship between the private and public sectors, FDR was offering the nation principles to guide the state's relationship with its own citizens—charity based on increased economic opportunity and the promise of a better and fuller life for all Americans. This was more than just a unique definition of freedom; it was a rejection of Hoover-style individualism and a fundamental reexamination of the means by which Americans could achieve the ideals of the American dream. Reading the above passage, it would hardly seem surprising that at Roosevelt's first inaugural he rested his hand on the family Bible at First Corinthians: "For now we see through a glass, darkly; but then face to face; now I know in part; but then shall I know even as also I am known. And now abideth faith, hope, charity, these three; but the greatest of these is charity."[14]

Roosevelt's approach did not necessarily have broad popular support. Political polling showed that most Americans in the 1930s considered themselves conservative (53 percent) and nearly half believed that New Deal policies had the potential to create dictatorship. Indeed, a majority of the country felt the time had come for the states to take back from the federal government the responsibility of social assistance. Yet in the face of such opposition, FDR relied largely on his own deep reservoir of popularity to carry through this call to arms.[15]

Roosevelt beseeched his fellow citizens to join him in this crusade to remake America. In some of the most beautiful and memorable words ever spoken on the campaign trail, FDR told the American people, "There is a mysterious cycle in human events. To some generations much is given. Of other generations much is expected. This generation of Americans has a rendezvous with destiny."

In his conclusion, Roosevelt laid out for his audience the true stakes of the 1936 election: "Here in America we are waging a great and successful war. It is not alone a war against want and destitution and economic demoralization. It is more than that; it is a war for the survival of democracy." And in words that echo the final lines of the Gettysburg Address, "We are fighting to save a great and precious form of government for ourselves and for the world."

Roosevelt departed the podium to deafening applause from the partisan crowd. The president stood with his family around him, and the orchestra played "Auld Lang Syne." Asking for the song to be played again, Roosevelt began to sing the words, and soon all of Franklin Field was joining in. Even after he had departed, many of the crowd stayed—no doubt in awe over the extraordinary performance they had just witnessed.[15]

As the campaign gathered steam in the fall, Roosevelt upped his rhetorical attacks. In a late October speech at New York's Madison Square Garden, he declared, "I should like to have it said of my first administration that in it the forces of selfishness and lust for power met their match. I should like to have it said of my second administration that in it these forces met their master."[17] Roosevelt reminded his highly partisan audiences that under Harding, Coolidge, and Hoover, the country for twelve years "was afflicted with hear-nothing, see-nothing, do-nothing government." He went on to warn them that "powerful influences strive today" to return to America a "doctrine" of government that believes it is at its "best" when it "is most indifferent to mankind."[18]

Roosevelt won a smashing victory in November, losing only two states to Landon and winning nearly 61 percent of the popular vote—the second highest total ever in American history. In his inaugural address in January 1937, Roosevelt drew on themes similar to those in his renomination speech. He laid out a sweeping vision of American democracy where the "one-third of a nation ill-housed, ill-clad, ill-nourished" would enjoy new opportunities driven by an activist government whose progress would be assessed not by "whether we add more to the abundance of those who have much" but by "whether we provide enough for those who have too little."[19]

With these two speeches, FDR was advancing a far more radical and invasive conception of government in the twentieth century. While eight years before, Herbert Hoover had warned against the meddling of the state in economic affairs, Roosevelt was now calling for a wholesale reconsideration of the federal government's roles and responsibilities—and arguing that if America was to be truly free, then a newly assertive and activist government must lead the way. The modern framework of the welfare state, the belief that government had a duty and responsibility to lift up those in need, the idea that economic freedom must go hand in hand with political freedom—these were notions strongly hinted at in 1932 but offered wholeheartedly for the American people's consideration in 1936. For all the public's reluctance, these were ideas they embraced then and largely continue to support today. Every American is still feeling the aftershocks of Roosevelt's clarion call for a "rendezvous with destiny." More than seventy years after those words were spoken on a July evening in Philadelphia, we are living in the America that Franklin Delano Roosevelt remade.

*Franklin D. Roosevelt Accepts the Democratic Nomination
for President, Philadelphia, June 27, 1936*

Here, and in every community throughout the land, we are met at a time of great moment to the future of the nation. It is an occasion to be dedicated to the simple and sincere expression of an attitude toward problems, the determination of which will profoundly affect America.

I come not only as a leader of a party, not only as a candidate for high office, but as one upon whom many critical hours have imposed and still impose a grave responsibility.

For the sympathy, help and confidence with which Americans have sustained me in my task I am grateful. For their loyalty I salute the members of our great party, in and out of political life in every part of the Union. I salute those of other parties, especially those in the Congress of the United States who on so many occasions have put partisanship aside. I thank the governors of the several states, their legislatures, their state and local officials who participated unselfishly and regardless of party in our efforts to achieve recovery and destroy abuses. Above all I thank the millions of Americans who have borne disaster bravely and have dared to smile through the storm.

America will not forget these recent years, will not forget that the rescue was not a mere party task. It was the concern of all of us. In our strength we rose together, rallied our energies together, applied the old rules of common sense, and together survived.

In those days we feared fear. That was why we fought fear. And today, my friends, we have won against the most dangerous of our foes. We have conquered fear.

But I cannot, with candor, tell you that all is well with the world. Clouds of suspicion, tides of ill-will and intolerance gather darkly in many places. In our own land we enjoy indeed a fullness of life greater than that of most nations. But the rush of modern civilization itself has raised for us new difficulties, new problems which must be solved if we are to preserve to the United States the political and economic freedom for which Washington and Jefferson planned and fought.

Philadelphia is a good city in which to write American history. This is fitting ground on which to reaffirm the faith of our fathers; to pledge ourselves to restore to the people a wider freedom; to give to 1936 as the founders gave to 1776—an American way of life.

That very word freedom, in itself and of necessity, suggests freedom from some restraining power. In 1776 we sought freedom from the tyranny of a political autocracy—from the eighteenth-century royalists who held special privileges from the crown. It was to perpetuate their privilege that they governed without the consent of the governed; that they denied the right of free assembly and free speech; that they restricted the worship of God; that they put the average man's property and the average man's life in pawn to the mercenaries of dynastic power; that they regimented the people.

And so it was to win freedom from the tyranny of political autocracy that the American Revolution was fought. That victory gave the business of governing into the hands of the average man, who won the right with his neighbors to make and order his own destiny through his own government. Political tyranny was wiped out at Philadelphia on July 4, 1776.

Since that struggle, however, man's inventive genius released new forces in our land which reordered the lives of our people. The age of machinery, of railroads; of steam and electricity; the telegraph and the radio; mass production, mass distribution—all of these combined to bring forward a new civilization and with it a new problem for those who sought to remain free.

For out of this modern civilization economic royalists carved new dynasties. New kingdoms were built upon concentration of control over material things. Through new uses of corporations, banks and securities, new machinery of industry and agriculture, of labor and capital—all undreamed of by the fathers—the whole structure of modern life was impressed into this royal service.

There was no place among this royalty for our many thousands of small businessmen and merchants who sought to make a worthy use of the American system of initiative and profit. They were no more free than the worker or the farmer. Even honest and progressive-minded men of wealth, aware of their obligation to their generation, could never know just where they fitted into this dynastic scheme of things.

It was natural and perhaps human that the privileged princes of these new economic dynasties, thirsting for power, reached out for control over government itself. They created a new despotism and wrapped it in the robes of legal sanction. In its service new mercenaries sought to regiment the people, their labor, and their property. And as a result the average man once more confronts the problem that faced the Minute Man.

The hours men and women worked, the wages they received, the conditions of their labor—these had passed beyond the control of the people, and were imposed by this new industrial dictatorship. The savings of the average family, the capital of the small businessmen, the investments set aside for old age—other people's money—these were tools which the new economic royalty used to dig itself in.

Those who tilled the soil no longer reaped the rewards which were their right. The small measure of their gains was decreed by men in distant cities.

Throughout the nation, opportunity was limited by monopoly. Individual initiative was crushed in the cogs of a great machine. The field open for free business was more and more restricted.

Private enterprise, indeed, became too private. It became privileged enterprise, not free enterprise.

An old English judge once said: "Necessitous men are not free men." Liberty requires opportunity to make a living—a living decent according to the standard of the time, a living which gives man not only enough to live by, but something to live for.

For too many of us the political equality we once had won was meaningless in the face of economic inequality. A small group had concentrated into their own hands an almost complete control over other people's property, other people's money, other people's labor—other people's lives. For too many of us life was no longer free; liberty no longer real; men could no longer follow the pursuit of happiness.

Against economic tyranny such as this, the American citizen could appeal only to the organized power of government. The collapse of 1929 showed up the despotism for what it was. The election of 1932 was the people's mandate to end it. Under that mandate it is being ended.

The royalists of the economic order have conceded that political freedom was the business of the government, but they have maintained that economic slavery was nobody's business. They granted that the government could protect the citizen in his right to vote, but they denied that the government could do anything to protect the citizen in his right to work and his right to live.

Today we stand committed to the proposition that freedom is no half-and-half affair. If the average citizen is guaranteed equal opportunity in the polling place, he must have equal opportunity in the market place.

These economic royalists complain that we seek to overthrow the institutions of America. What they really complain of is that we seek to take away their power. Our allegiance to American institutions requires the overthrow of this kind of power. In vain they seek to hide behind the flag and the Constitution. In their blindness they forget what the flag and the Constitution stand for. Now, as always, they stand for democracy, not tyranny; for freedom, not subjection; and against a dictatorship by mob rule and the over-privileged alike.

The brave and clear platform adopted by this convention, to which I heartily subscribe, sets forth that government in a modern civilization has certain inescapable obligations to its citizens, among which are protection of the family and the home, the establishment of a democracy of opportunity, and aid to those overtaken by disaster.

But the resolute enemy within our gates is ever ready to beat down our words unless in greater courage we will fight for them.

For more than three years we have fought for them. This convention, in every word and deed, has pledged that the fight will go on.

The defeats and victories of these years have given to us as a people a new understanding of our government and of ourselves. Never since the early days of the New England town meeting have the affairs of government been so widely discussed and so clearly appreciated. It has been brought home to us that the only effective guide for the safety of this most worldly of worlds, the greatest guide of all, is moral principle.

We do not see faith, hope, and charity as unattainable ideals, but we use them as stout supports of a nation fighting the fight for freedom in a modern civilization.

Faith—in the soundness of democracy in the midst of dictatorships.

Hope—renewed because we know so well the progress we have made.

Charity—in the true spirit of that grand old word. For charity literally translated from the original means love, the love that understands, that does not merely share the wealth of the giver, but in true sympathy and wisdom helps men to help themselves.

We seek not merely to make government a mechanical implement, but to give it the vibrant personal character that is the very embodiment of human charity.

We are poor indeed if this nation cannot afford to lift from every recess of American life the dread fear of the unemployed that they are not needed in the world. We cannot afford to accumulate a deficit in the books of human fortitude.

In the place of the palace of privilege we seek to build a temple out of faith and hope and charity.

It is a sobering thing, my friends, to be a servant of this great cause. We try in our daily work to remember that the cause belongs not to us, but to the people. The standard is not in the hands of you and me alone. It is carried by America. We seek daily to profit from experience, to learn to do better as our task proceeds.

Governments can err, presidents do make mistakes, but the immortal Dante tells us that Divine justice weighs the sins of the cold-blooded and the sins of the warm-hearted on different scales.

Better the occasional faults of a government that lives in a spirit of charity than the consistent omissions of a government frozen in the ice of its own indifference.

There is a mysterious cycle in human events. To some generations much is given. Of other generations much is expected. This generation of Americans has a rendezvous with destiny.

In this world of ours in other lands, there are some people, who, in times past, have lived and fought for freedom, and seem to have grown too weary to carry on the fight. They have sold their heritage of freedom for the illusion of a living. They have yielded their democracy.

I believe in my heart that only our success can stir their ancient hope. They begin to know that here in America we are waging a great and successful war. It is not alone a war against want and destitution and economic demoralization. It is more than that; it is a war for the survival of democracy. We are fighting to save a great and precious form of government for ourselves and for the world.

I accept the commission you have tendered me. I join with you. I am enlisted for the duration of the war.

## Chapter 6

# THE BIRTH OF A POLITICAL STEREOTYPE

### Franklin Roosevelt and Harry Truman Brand Their GOP Opponents as Heartless, Do-Nothing Isolationists: 1940–1948

L IBERAL TAX-AND-SPENDERS," "GOP isolationists," "blame America firsters," and "extremists"—these are just a few of the overarching political stereotypes that have come to define American politics in the twentieth century. Americans have become so inured to these shorthand characterizations that many of our political debates are spent either inoculating politicians from them or perpetuating them.

Political stereotypes are some of the most potent devices in the speechwriter's bag of rhetorical tricks, and any examination of politics in the twentieth century benefits from a look at such labels. Indeed, flippant political image making is nothing new in American politics. In the forty years after the Civil War, there was hardly a Republican politician who missed an opportunity to wave the so-called bloody shirt of Democratic rebellion.

In contemporary times few politicians have been more effective at tarring their opponents with the stain of political caricature than Franklin Delano Roosevelt. In the wake of the 1932 election,

Roosevelt ushered in two of the most powerful and resonant stereotypes in American political history: the heartless Republican Party as handmaiden to the wealthy and scourge of the working man, and a GOP dedicated to building walls around America and shrugging off the nation's international responsibilities. While the latter image has largely been vanquished, the former remains a millstone around the neck of the GOP and one of FDR's most lasting political legacies.

The three speeches featured in this chapter are not necessarily great oratory. Harry Truman's 1948 acceptance speech in particular is more mean-spirited than spirit-lifting. But what each of these addresses demonstrates is the extent to which powerful political stereotypes were used to brilliant effect by both Roosevelt and Truman. Paradoxically, their political success moved the Republican Party toward a more fundamentally activist political philosophy and away from isolationism, albeit reluctantly. FDR's and Truman's attacks would help to marginalize conservatism in America for nearly four decades and create a bipartisan consensus supporting the welfare state at home and internationalism overseas.

The popularity of the New Deal and the Democratic Party's identification with the workingman was a political sword that Democrats would wield against Republicans for much of the twentieth century. Four decades earlier, the Great Commoner, William Jennings Bryan, had adopted a similar philosophy. In 1896, the "idle holders of idle capital" won. In 1932, FDR routed them from the field.

While Americans weren't prepared to embrace activist government at the turn of the century, the breadlines and Hoovervilles of the 1920s changed their minds. FDR, and in turn the Democratic Party, became a hero to the working class, farmers, and African Americans who would come to form the backbone of the so-called New Deal coalition, which dominated American politics for the next thirty years. While FDR birthed this effective political approach, future politicians such as Truman, Lyndon Johnson, and other Democrats would continue utilizing it to great effect.

## THE 1940 CAMPAIGN: FDR TAKES ON THE ISOLATIONISTS

Today, Franklin Roosevelt is remembered as one of the foremost statesmen of American history. What is often forgotten, however, were his peerless skills as a partisan orator. What distinguished Roosevelt was his wily use of biting humor and a well-constructed "man of the people" persona. As he sought an unprecedented third term in 1940, FDR would put these political advantages to work, hitting the campaign trail as his Republican rival, Wendell Willkie, began gaining political traction.

Willkie's candidacy presented a tricky situation for FDR. Unlike his drab, conservative rival in 1936, Alf Landon, Roosevelt was facing a true political phenomenon. Willkie was a businessman by trade and only a recent convert to the Republican Party, but in the spring and summer of 1940 he took the GOP and the nation by storm. On May 8, Willkie's support stood at 3 percent among Republican voters.[1] By late June 1940 he was the party's nominee for president of the United States. *Time* magazine's poignant obituary of Willkie in 1944 summed up well the phenomenon of his candidacy:

Nothing in American political history could have prepared . . . for the almost religious passion that forced the Willkie candidacy over every barrier that political tricks could devise, overwhelming all precedents under the mighty chant . . . "We Want Willkie!"[2]

At a time when pro-business, laissez-faire conservatives continued to dominate the GOP, Willkie was a true moderate

Republican and a committed internationalist—at the 1924 Democratic convention he actively supported a failed plank endorsing the League of Nations—who, unlike the top Republican candidates for president (Taft, Dewey, and Vandenberg), believed America must strongly support the Allies in Europe.[3] In his speech accepting the GOP nomination he declared unabashedly, "I am glad to pledge my wholehearted support to the President" in both supplying the European allies and preparing the country's defenses. Courageously, he supported the president's call for a military draft, refusing to use the move as a political weapon against Roosevelt.[4]

Willkie's popularity, his rough-hewn and tousled midwestern image, and his strong internationalist stance made it difficult for FDR to tag his opponent with the isolationist label. However, attacking GOP congressional leaders for the same crime . . . well, that would be a bit easier.

During the closing days of the campaign, FDR set out on a whirlwind tour of New York City, where he was greeted by an estimated two million well-wishers. The day was capped by a nationally broadcast political speech at Madison Square Garden. "The Champ" was met by a rapturous welcome from twenty-two thousand Democratic partisans as more than thirty thousand listened outside on loudspeakers and another forty to fifty million Americans sat by their radios.[5] FDR began by making clear what he thought of his Republican opponents:

> I . . . brand as false the statement being made by Republican campaign orators, day after day and night after night, that the rearming of America is slow, that it is hamstrung and impeded, that it will never be able to meet threats from abroad. Those are the whisperings of appeasers.

Comparing one's opponent to Neville Chamberlain and Marshal Philippe Pétain or other famous appeasers is effective today;

in 1940 it worked even better. Willkie might have been an internationalist committed to stopping Nazism, but the same could not be said about the congressional Republicans. "For almost seven years," Roosevelt declared, "the Republican leaders in the Congress kept on saying that I was placing too *much* emphasis on national defense. And now today these men of great vision have suddenly discovered that there is a war going on in Europe and another one in Asia."

FDR repeatedly seized on what he referred to as the Republicans' "record of timidity, weakness and shortsightedness" and compared it to the governments in France and the United Kingdom that had failed to stand up to the Nazi threat. The harsh words came naturally for Roosevelt, who genuinely seemed to despise the isolationists and believed passionately that America's future lay in global engagement. In addition, the rhetorical approach was similar to one Roosevelt had taken throughout the campaign, namely, identifying his opponents with words that suggested they weren't just wrong on foreign policy but were in fact "evil" and "subversive."[6]

Repeatedly, FDR went back to the *Congressional Record* and used the words of his GOP opponents to "indict those Republican leaders out of their own mouths," branding them as isolationists and flip-floppers who were bemoaning the country's lack of military preparedness after spending the previous seven years voting against his defense policies.

Throughout the speech, FDR compared his interlocutors to circus performers. "Republican orators swing through the air," "Republican candidates began to turn new somersaults," and "they seized their trapeze with the greatest of ease, and reversed themselves in mid-air" were just some of the words FDR used to paint Republicans as a party devoid of core beliefs.

However, one rather important word did not escape FDR's lips—Willkie. Instead, FDR drew out the names of more easily attackable GOP leaders who had fought against his rearmament policies: the discredited former President Hoover, the famed isolationist senators Vandenberg and Taft. But FDR saved his greatest venom—and his rhetorical coup de grâce—for three GOP isolationist congressmen: Joe Martin, Bruce Barton, and Hamilton Fish.

Echoing the popular children's poem "Wynken, Blynken and Nod," FDR ridiculed the three men with the rhyme "Congressmen Martin, Barton and Fish."[7] But, pronounced in Roosevelt's Brahmin accent, it sounded more like "Mahtin, Bahton . . . and then Fish!"[8] The crowd laughed with delight and began chanting the names of the unfortunate triumvirate—an event that would be repeated elsewhere during the final days of the campaign. Willkie understood full well the implications of the Garden speech. "When I heard the president hang the isolationist votes of Martin, Barton and Fish on me," he later admitted, "I knew I was licked."[9]

Beyond FDR's rhetorical attack, the "Martin, Barton and Fish" speech had important policy implications. Roosevelt was struggling against the nation's historical reluctance to become more directly involved in global affairs. He needed to do more than just defeat his opponents and win reelection—he needed to destroy isolationism and make it a political liability for Republicans. Throughout the campaign FDR stressed his commitment to America's defense, his empathy with the victims of Nazi aggression, and his dismissal of the "appeasers" who were weakening America's security in the face of international peril. There were, however, limits to FDR's rhetoric. Only days before the election he told a partisan crowd in Boston that "your boys are not going to be sent into any foreign wars." It was of course one promise that Roosevelt would not be able to keep.[10]

For the GOP, however, FDR was creating a toxic and lasting political stereotype. *Heartless*, *timid*, *short-sighted*, and *isolationist* were the words that millions of Americans began to associate with the Republican Party. For all their effort to nominate a more moderate face in Willkie and later Dewey in 1944 and 1948, the political stereotype that was crystallized by the Garden speech would tarnish the GOP image for years to come.

## ROOSEVELT'S LAST CAMPAIGN: DEFENDING FALA

Four years later, as Roosevelt sought a fourth term, many political observers wondered whether the president really had his heart in the race. Some aides noted that he didn't "seem to give a damn" about the campaign.[11] New health concerns about the president were also being raised, particularly after a nationally broadcast speech in Bremerton, Washington, where he suffered an angina attack and delivered what many considered a substandard performance.

A *Washington Post* editorial the morning of his September 23 address to the Teamsters union in Washington, D.C., warned that "Roosevelt is going to have to pull his campaign out of the slough of apathy, indifference and confusion into which it has fallen."[12] His own daughter, Anna, worried that the speech could be "an awful flop."[13] But the Champ was being severely underestimated. That night he would deliver one of his greatest speeches ever.

By 1944, the GOP was making every effort to present to the voting public a more progressive image, offering support in the Republican Party platform for Social Security and the rights of union workers. Roosevelt would have none of it. "Many of the Republican leaders and Congressmen and candidates . . . would not even recognize these progressive laws if they met them in broad daylight," he claimed. FDR focused on what he called GOP "insincerity" and "inconsistency," noting, "When votes are at stake, they suddenly discover that they really love labor . . .

Now imitation may be the sincerest form of flattery—but I am afraid in this case it is the most obvious common or garden variety of fraud."

FDR again returned to the circus imagery of 1940. "We all have seen many marvelous stunts in the circus but no performing elephant could turn a hand-spring without falling flat on its back."

The albatross of the 1929 crash, the Great Depression, and the uninspired presidency of Herbert Hoover remained enormous liabilities—ones that FDR was quick to remind voters of. "You remember the closed banks and the breadlines and the starvation wages; the foreclosures of homes and farms, and the bankruptcies of business; the 'Hoovervilles,' and the young men and women of the Nation facing a hopeless, jobless future; the closed factories and mines and mills; the ruined and abandoned farms; the stalled railroads and the empty docks; the blank despair of a whole Nation—and the utter impotence of the Federal government."

While FDR drew attention to the more progressive elements in the Republican Party, he went to great pains to remind voters that they "were not able to drive the Old Guard Republicans from their entrenched positions." This was the same old guard that had brought economic ruin and, according to FDR, was still running the show for Republicans.

Yet for all of FDR's partisan attacks, he saved the best for last—and with one brief paragraph for all intents and purposes ended the 1944 race for president. After cataloging the GOP's litany of false attacks (even comparing them to the "big lie" techniques of Nazi propagandist Joseph Goebbels), Roosevelt lambasted Republicans for intimating that he had left his pet Scottish terrier, Fala, behind on an Aleutian island and at taxpayers' expense sent a naval destroyer to retrieve him.

Fala's "Scotch soul was furious," and "he has not been the same dog since," complained Roosevelt. "I am accustomed to hearing malicious falsehoods about myself," he said. "But I think

I have a right to resent, to object to libelous statements about my dog." The crowd roared in laughter. It was a brilliant parry. After all, what kind of person attacks a man's dog?

The notion that Republicans were so heartless they would go after Roosevelt's Scottish terrier only added to the negative stereotype that many Americans held about the GOP. The dig made Republicans seem petty and gave them little room for rebuttal. The press response to the speech was glowing. "The Champ had swung—a full roundhouse blow," said one newsman.[14] The *Washington Post* was even more effusive: "In form, content, delivery it had it all of the old Roosevelt wizardry. Watching him, you felt that here was the virtuoso back again at the keyboard . . . getting everything out of the instrument from the classical to a touch of boogie-woogie."[15] The impact of Roosevelt's words was summed up well by a letter received by the White House days after the speech: "Your speech should be re-broadcast as often as possible—for if it is done—the Republicans will only receive the votes of the National Manufacturers Association and American Bankers Association and those who insist on being blind, deaf, and dumb."[16]

FDR's Republican opponent, New York governor Thomas Dewey, called the address "a speech of mud-slinging, ridicule and wisecracks, which plumbed the depths of demagogy, inciting hatred and distrust."[17] There was certainly a ring of truth to Dewey's comments, but it would make little difference on Election Day, as FDR won another term as president.

## TRUMAN DEFEATS DEWEY

Within six months, however, FDR would be gone and the untested Harry S Truman became president. FDR bequeathed his successor a host of international and domestic challenges, but from a political perspective Truman was operating from a position of great strength. Due to Roosevelt's political and rhetorical genius, the Republican Party was still seen by millions of Americans in a negative light and the preponderance of public opinion was on the side of the Democrats. It was a reservoir of goodwill that Truman would desperately need three years later.

Today, Harry Truman is venerated as the kind of no-nonsense, plain-speaking politician that seems so rare in American politics. Yet as president, he was one of the more unpopular men ever to occupy the White House. In the run-up to the 1948 election, few thought he had any chance of winning reelection—particularly his lackluster opponent, Thomas Dewey.

Truman wasn't going to win running a positive campaign. He was simply too unpopular, and many Americans believed the time had come for change in Washington. Facing the prospect of being the first Democrat to lose a national election in twenty years, he had little choice but to adopt a scorched-earth policy against the "do-nothing Republican Congress," falling back on the political stereotypes, constructed by Roosevelt, that made so many Americans mistrust Republican leaders.

As the party began to gather in Philadelphia to nominate Truman, it felt to many like a funereal gathering.[18] Alternative candidates were trumpeted, debates over civil rights rent the party, and few if any of the gathered delegates truly believed the seemingly formidable Republicans could be defeated.

Truman and the Democrats had little in their favor except the abiding belief among millions of working-class Americans that the Democratic Party was *their* party. The seventy-year-old Kentucky senator Alben Barkley, an unabashed New Dealer, started the ball rolling on the first night declaring, "I am not an expert on cobwebs, but if my memory does not betray me, when the Democratic Party took over the Government of the United States sixteen years ago, even the spiders were so weak from starvation that they could not weave a cobweb in any department of the

Government in Washington."[19] These caustic words, which combined images of privation with GOP inaction, helped propel Barkley to the number two place on the Democratic ticket as Truman's running mate.

The excitement of Barkley's opening remarks was tempered by the party's growing fissures over race, dramatized by the adoption of a progressive plank on civil rights into the party platform. The fractious debate pushed Truman's acceptance speech to 2:00 A.M., so those Americans able to watch the proceedings on television were likely sound asleep when Truman in his white double-breasted suit strode to the podium. Eschewing written remarks, Truman chose to speak extemporaneously using an outline prepared in part by legendary FDR speechwriter Samuel Rosenman.[20]

He began by telling the sleepy delegates in no uncertain terms, "Senator Barkley and I will win this election and make these Republicans like it. Don't you forget that! We will do that because they are wrong and we are right." Truman ripped the bark off his opponents. "The people know that the Democratic Party is the people's party," he told the delegates. The Republican Party, on the other hand, "favors the privileged few and not the common everyday man."

The irony of the election was that in most respects the Republican standard-bearer had come around to the Democrats' thinking. The GOP platform, which Dewey willingly endorsed, called for expanding Social Security and increasing funding for public housing, and it embraced a generally activist approach to government. Unfortunately for Dewey, the leadership of the Republican-led Eightieth Congress still wasn't on board. In his acceptance speech, Truman threw the political equivalent of a Hail Mary pass, calling the GOP's bluff by demanding a special session of Congress and daring the opposition party to pass its own platform. Congress demurred, playing exactly into Truman's hands and further magnifying the dominant, negative political image of Republicans.

Truman's incendiary acceptance speech was a harbinger of the rhetoric to come. His whistle-stop stump speeches featured some of the harshest attacks ever unleashed by a sitting president. These were not grand policy speeches filled with inspiring words or a hopeful vision of the future. Instead, they were small, mean-spirited speeches, and as the campaign heated up, they became increasingly spiteful. In their unabashed attacks against eastern moneyed elites, Truman's speeches evoked Bryan's ferocious 1896 rhetoric. According to campaign historian Zachary Karabell, "It was a campaign of us and them, of anger and bitterness, of the haves and have-nots. Truman fought to lead the country for another four years, and to achieve that victory he was willing to sow dissension, stir up fear, and slander his opponents."[21]

In Detroit, he said that the "reactionary" who backed the Republican Party had "a calculating machine where his heart ought to be."[22] In Iowa, he repeatedly called the Republicans "gluttons of privilege," warned that their victory would lead to "a return of the Wall Street economic dictatorship," and claimed that the "record of the Republican 80th Congress is one long attack on the welfare of the farmer." In Denver, he said the Republican Party was "controlled by silent and cunning men who have a dangerous lust for power and privilege" and were "puppets of big business." In Fresno, California, he accused the local Republican congressman of doing "everything he could possibly could to cut the throats of the farmer and the laboring man."[23] In Utah, he spoke of his opponents as "bloodsuckers who have offices in Wall Street."[24] In New Jersey, he reminded voters that "in 1920 to 1932, they had complete control of the government. Look what they did to it."[25]

In Chicago, Truman speculated that Dewey and the Republicans could be budding fascists. Even worse, he intimated the existence of darker forces and compared the current situation in America to that of pre-1933 Germany: "when a few men get control of the economy of the nation, they find a front man to run the country for them ... so they [wealthy German manufacturers, bankers, and landowners] put money and influence behind Adolf Hitler. We know the rest of the story."[26] Besides being historically dubious, these broadsides were unprecedented attacks for a sitting president to make, but Truman was undaunted. In all, Truman delivered 275 speeches and traveled more than twenty-two thousand miles spreading his message of GOP iniquity.[27] Everywhere Truman went on the campaign trail he railed at the "special interests" and "powerful lobbies" who controlled the Republican Party, and portrayed Democrats as the only bulwark against economic deprivation. Truman even attacked his own audiences for their apathy in congressional elections two years before, telling a Labor Day crowd in Detroit's Cadillac Square that "if you stay at home, as you did in 1946, and keep these reactionaries in power, you will deserve every blow you get."[28]

When Truman said, as he repeatedly did, that Democrats were the party of the people, it struck a chord with millions of working-class Americans—and accurately reflected his own worldview. Truman's rhetoric was deeply influenced by the prairie populism that came from being a child of the Midwest, a former farmer and haberdasher from Independence, Missouri. It was of little surprise that the key to Truman's victory came from the farmers of the fly-over states.

## A DAMNING PARTISAN LEGACY

As we all know, in the end, Truman's words at the Philadelphia convention proved prophetic. He indeed won the election and in the process pulled the greatest upset in American political history. But the country would pay a heavy price for Truman's take-no-prisoners approach—a heightened sense of partisanship and anger among Republicans that would help to shape political divisions in the country for the next several decades.

Republicans were outraged by Truman's campaign, believing that he had used vicious attacks to steal an election that after sixteen years in opposition was rightfully theirs. They did not take the loss well. Their embrace of Senator Joe McCarthy's anti-Communist appeals was, in part, a result of lingering resentment and anger toward an administration that they felt had attacked them unfairly.[29] After all, from their perspective, demagoguery on the issue of Communist subversion wasn't much different from the incendiary charges that Truman launched against the GOP.[30] Historian David Fromkin would later argue that Truman's defeat of Dewey had significant and often negative consequences for American foreign policy in the Cold War era: "Much of the anti-Communist hysteria whipped up by frustrated Republican losses of the 1948 elections in an effort to discredit the Truman Administration . . . might have been avoided had the Republicans won." Certainly, incessant GOP attacks against Democrats for losing China and not demonstrating sufficient vigilance in confronting the Soviet Union and Communism never would have occurred if Dewey had won the presidency.[31]

But more significantly, the loss created a general sense of soul-searching in the Republican Party. Dewey persuasively argued that the GOP could not be expected to win a national election in America if they were seen to "oppose farm price supports, unemployment insurance, old age benefits, slum clearance, and other social programs."[32] He was clearly correct. If there was any direct result of the 1948 race, it was that Republicans had little choice but to willingly embrace much of the Democrats' domestic policies. While Dewey had tried this approach in 1948, the liability of a stubborn GOP Congress was too much for him to overcome. It would take another twenty years for Republicans to move beyond the heartless, isolationist, and overall negative image of their party. In the meantime, the battle between the moderate and conservative wings of the party would continue unabated.

For Democrats, 1948 was the sweetest victory. But it wouldn't last. Truman's win would serve as a high-water mark of sorts—the party would never again enjoy the same level of sustained political and ideological dominance in American politics. At a time when the party needed to craft fresh messages and reach out to new suburban voters and those inclined to support a step back from the activist policies of the New Deal, Democrats returned to the usual hobbyhorse of GOP malevolence. As Truman said in his acceptance speech, "The battle lines of 1948 are the same as they were in 1932." At least, that was how Truman ran the campaign, falling back on the political coalition and more specifically the stereotypes that his predecessor had so deeply ingrained in America's national discourse. It was small wonder that Walter Lippmann would later comment, "It can be said with much justice that of all Roosevelt's electoral triumphs this one in 1948 is the most impressive."[33]

Faced with electoral defeat, Truman made a Hobbesian choice and decided demagoguery was the most effective arrow in his quiver. But it hardly provided the party with a long-term platform to continue its electoral dominance. Truman's approach might have worked in 1948, but as he and the party were soon to discover, there are limits to the effectiveness of political stereotyping.

*Franklin D. Roosevelt Uses the Trio of Martin, Barton, and Fish to Brand Republicans as Isolationists, New York, October 28, 1940*

Tonight, for the second time, I take up the public duty—the far from disagreeable duty—of answering major campaign falsifications with facts.

Last week in Philadelphia, which is supposed to be the City of Brotherly Love, but isn't always, I nailed the falsehood about some fanciful secret treaties to dry on the barn door. I nailed that falsehood and other falsehoods the way when I was a boy up in Dutchess County we used to nail up the skins of foxes and weasels. And, incidentally, I think it was a kinsman of mine, about thirty years ago, who invented the term, "weasel words."

Tonight I am going to nail up the falsifications that have to do with our relations with the rest of the world and with the building up of our Army, our Navy and our air defense. It is a very dangerous thing to distort facts about things like that, because if repeated over and over again, it is apt to create a sense of fear and doubt in the minds of some of the American people.

I now brand as false the statement being made by Republican campaign orators, day after day and night after night, that the rearming of America is slow, that it is hamstrung and impeded, that it will never be able to meet threats from abroad. Those are the whisperings of appeasers.

That particular misstatement has a history. It came into the world last June, just about the time of the Republican National Convention. Before that, the responsible Republican leaders had been singing an entirely different song. For almost seven years the Republican leaders in the Congress kept on saying that I was placing too *much* emphasis on national defense.

And now today these men of great vision have suddenly

discovered that there is a war going on in Europe and another one in Asia. And so, now, always with their eyes on the good old ballot box, they are charging that we have placed too *little* emphasis on national defense.

But, unlike them, the printed pages of the Congressional Record cannot be changed or suppressed at election time. And based on that permanent record of their speeches and their votes, I make this assertion—that if the Republican leaders had been in control of the Congress of the United States during the past seven years, the important measures for our defense would not now be law; and the Army and Navy of the United States would still be in almost the same condition in which I found them in 1933.

Remember, I am making those charges against the responsible political leadership of the Republican Party. But there are millions—millions and millions—of patriotic Republicans who have at all times been in sympathy with the efforts of this Administration to arm the nation adequately for purposes of defense.

. . . As early as 1933 the storm was gathering in Europe and in Asia. Year by year I reported the warnings of danger from our listening posts in foreign lands. But I was only called "an alarmist" by the Republican leadership, and by the great majority of the Republican newspapers of the country.

Year by year I asked for more and more defense appropriations. In addition, I allocated hundreds of millions of dollars for defense work from relief funds. The C.C.C. [Civilian Conservation Corps] helped, the Public Works helped—as was understood by the Congress when the money was voted by them.

Today our Navy is at a peak of efficiency and fighting strength. Ship for ship, man for man, it is as powerful and efficient as any single navy that ever sailed the seas in history. But it is not as powerful as combinations of other navies that might be put together in an attack upon us. Our Army and our air forces are now at the highest level that they have ever been in peacetime. But in the light of existing dangers they are not great enough for the absolute safety of America at home.

While this great, constructive work was going forward, the Republican leaders were definitely and beyond peradventure of doubt trying to block our efforts toward national defense. They not only voted against these efforts; but they stated time and again through the years that they were unnecessary and extravagant, that our armed strength was sufficient for any emergency.

I propose now to indict these Republican leaders out of their own mouths—these leaders who now disparage our defenses—with what they themselves said in the days before this election year, about how adequate our defenses already were.

Listen to this for instance:

"The facts are that we have the largest and most powerful Navy we ever had, except for two years after the World War, and the greatest air forces we ever had and a match for any nation."

Now, who do you suppose made that statement a little over two years ago? It was not I. It was not even a member of this Administration. It was the ranking Republican member of the House Committee on Foreign Affairs, Republican leader, Hamilton Fish.

And now listen to the only living ex-President of the United States. He said in that same year, two years ago:

We shall be expending nine hundred million dollars more than any nation on earth. We are leading in the arms race.

And now listen to Republican leader Senator Vandenberg, also speaking at that time. He said that our defense expenditures had already brought us "an incomparably efficient Navy"; and he said further, "I rise in opposition to this super-super Navy bill. I do not believe it is justified by any conclusive demonstration of national necessity."

And now listen to what Republican leader Senator Taft—the runner-up for the Republican Presidential nomination this year—said this past February, 1940:

"The increase of the Army and Navy over the tremendous appropriations of the current year seems to be unnecessary if we are
concerned solely with defense."

There is the record on that; the permanent crystal clear record.
Until the present political campaign opened, Republican leaders,
in and out of the Congress shouted from the housetops that our
defenses were fully adequate.

Today they proclaim that this Administration has starved our
armed forces, that our Navy is anemic, our Army puny, our air
forces piteously weak.

Yes, it is a remarkable somersault.

I wonder if the election could have something to do with it.
And this seems to be what they would have called "logic" when I
was at school: If the Republican leaders were telling the truth in
1938 and 1939, then—out of their own mouths—they stand convicted of inconsistency today. And, as we used to say, per contra,
if they are telling the truth today, they stand convicted of inconsistency in 1938 and 1939.

The simple truth is that the Republican Party, through its leadership, played politics with defense, the defense of the United
States, in 1938 and 1939. And they are playing politics with the
national security of America today.

That same group would still control their party in Congress at
the next session. It is the Congress which passes the laws of the
United States. The record of those Republican leaders shows
what a slim chance the cause of strong defense would have, if they
were in control.

Not only in their statements but in their votes is written their
record of sabotage of this Administration's continual efforts to increase our defenses to meet the dangers that loomed ever larger
and larger upon the horizon.

For example, deeply concerned over what was happening in Europe, I asked the Congress in January, 1938, for a naval expansion

of twenty per cent—forty-six additional ships and nine hundred and fifty new planes.

What did the Republican leaders do when they had this chance to increase our national defense almost three years ago? You would think from their present barrage of verbal pyrotechnics, that they rushed in to pass that bill, or that they even demanded a larger expansion of the Navy.

But, ah my friends, they were not in a national campaign for votes then.

In those days they were trying to build up a different kind of political fence.

In those days they thought that the way to win votes was by representing this Administration as extravagant in national defense, indeed as hysterical, and as manufacturing panics and inventing foreign dangers.

But now, in the serious days of 1940, all is changed! Not only because they are serious days, but because they are election days as well.

On the radio these Republican orators swing through the air with the greatest of ease; but the American people are not voting this year for the best trapeze performer.

The plain fact is that when that naval bill I was speaking about was submitted to the Congress, the Republican leaders jumped in to fight it.

Who were they? There was the present Republican candidate for Vice President, Senator McNary. There were Senator Vandenberg and Senator Nye. And there was the man who would be the Chairman of the House Committee on Foreign Affairs, Congressman Fish.

. . . I say that the Republican leaders played politics with defense in 1938 and 1939. I say that they are playing politics with our national security today.

. . . The Republican campaign orators and leaders are all now yelling "me too" on help to Britain. But this fall they had their chance to vote to give aid to Britain and other democracies—and they turned it down.

This chance came when I recommended that the Congress repeal the embargo on the shipment of armaments and munitions to nations at war, and permit such shipment on a "cash-and-carry basis." It is only because of the repeal of the embargo law that we have been able to sell planes and ships and guns and munitions to victims of aggression.

But how did the Republicans vote on the repeal of that embargo?

In the Senate the Republicans voted fourteen to six against it. In the House the Republicans voted one hundred and forty to nineteen against it.

The Act was passed by Democratic votes but it was over the opposition of the Republican leaders. And just to name a few, the following Republican leaders, among many others, voted against the Act: Senators McNary, Vandenberg, Nye and Johnson; now wait, a perfectly beautiful rhythm—Congressmen Martin, Barton and Fish.

Now, at the eleventh hour, they have discovered what we knew all along—that overseas success in warding off invasion by dictatorship forces means safety to the United States. It means also continued independence to those smaller nations which still retain their independence. And it means the restoration of sovereignty to those smaller nations which have temporarily lost it. As we know, one of the keystones of American policy is the recognition of the right of small nations to survive and prosper.

Great Britain and a lot of other nations would never have received one ounce of help from us—if the decision had been left to Martin, Barton and Fish.

And, finally, let me come down to something that happened two months ago.

In the Senate there was an amendment to permit the United States Government to prevent profiteering or unpatriotic obstruction by any corporation in defense work . . .

The bill was adopted all right—by Democratic votes. But the opposing vote of those eight Republican leaders showed what would happen if the National Government were turned over to their control. For their vote said, in effect, that they put money rights ahead of human lives—to say nothing of national security.

You and I, and the overwhelming majority of Americans, will never stand for that.

Outside the halls of Congress eminent Republican candidates began to turn new somersaults. At first they denounced the bill; then, when public opinion rose up to demand it, they seized their trapeze with the greatest of ease, and reversed themselves in mid-air.

This record of Republican leadership—a record of timidity, of weakness, of short-sightedness—is as bad in international as in military affairs.

It is the same record of timidity, of weakness, of short-sightedness which they showed in domestic affairs when they were in control before 1933.

But the Republican leaders' memories seem to have been short, in this, as in some other matters. And by the way—who was it said that an elephant never forgets?

It is the same record of timidity, of weakness and of short-sightedness that governed the policy of the confused, reactionary governments in France and England before the war.

That fact was discovered too late in France.

It was discovered just in time in England.

Pray God that, having discovered it, we won't forget it either.

For eight years our main concern, as you know and as the nation knows, has been to look for peace and the preservation of peace.

. . . I am asking the American people to support a continuance of this type of affirmative, realistic fight for peace. The alternative is to risk the future of the country in the hands of those with this record of timidity, weakness and short-sightedness or to risk it in the inexperienced hands of those who in these perilous days are willing recklessly to imply that our boys are already on their way to the transports.

This affirmative search for peace calls for clear vision. It is necessary to mobilize resources, minds and skills, and every active force for peace in all the world.

We have steadily sought to keep mobilized the greatest force of all—religious faith, devotion to God.

. . . Shadows, however, are still heavy over the faith and the hope of mankind.

We—who walk in the ways of peace and freedom and light—have seen the tragedies enacted in one free land after another.

We have not been blind to the causes or the consequences of these tragedies.

We guard ourselves against all evils—spiritual as well as material—which may beset us. We guard against the forces of anti-Christian aggression, which may attack us from without, and the forces of ignorance and fear which may corrupt us from within.

We go forward with firm faith. And we shall continue to go forward in peace.

## *Franklin D. Roosevelt Defends the Honor of His Scottish Terrier, Fala, Washington, D.C., September 23, 1944*

Well, here we are together again—after four years—and what years they have been! You know, I am actually four years older, which is a fact that seems to annoy some people. In fact, in the mathematical field there are millions of Americans who are more than eleven years older than when we started in to clear up the mess that was dumped in our laps in 1933.

We all know that certain people who make it a practice to depreciate the accomplishments of labor—who even attack labor as unpatriotic—they keep this up usually for three years and six months in a row. But then, for some strange reason they change their tune—every four years—just before election day. When votes are at stake, they suddenly discover that they really love labor and that they are anxious to protect labor from its old friends.

I got quite a laugh, for example—and I am sure that you did—when I read this plank in the Republican platform adopted at their National Convention in Chicago last July: "The Republican Party accepts the purposes of the National Labor Relations Act, the Wage and Hour Act, the Social Security Act and all other Federal statutes designed to promote and protect the welfare of American working men and women, and we promise a fair and just administration of these laws."

You know, many of the Republican leaders and Congressmen and candidates, who shouted enthusiastic approval of that plank in that Convention Hall would not even recognize these progressive laws if they met them in broad daylight. Indeed, they have personally spent years of effort and energy—and much money—in fighting every one of those laws in the Congress, and in the press, and in the courts, ever since this Administration began to advocate them and enact them into legislation. That is a fair example of their insincerity and of their inconsistency.

The whole purpose of Republican oratory these days seems to be to switch labels. The object is to persuade the American people that the Democratic Party was responsible for the 1929 crash and the depression, and that the Republican Party was responsible for all social progress under the New Deal.

Now, imitation may be the sincerest form of flattery—but I am afraid that in this case it is the most obvious common or garden variety of fraud.

Of course, it is perfectly true that there are enlightened, liberal elements in the Republican Party, and they have fought hard and honorably to bring the Party up to date and to get it in step with the forward march of American progress. But these liberal elements were not able to drive the Old Guard Republicans from their entrenched positions.

Can the Old Guard pass itself off as the New Deal?

I think not.

We have all seen many marvelous stunts in the circus but no performing elephant could turn a hand-spring without falling flat on his back.

. . . What the Republican leaders are now saying in effect is this: "Oh, just forget what we used to say, we have changed our minds now—we have been reading the public opinion polls about these things and now we know what the American people want." And they say: "Don't leave the task of making the peace to those old men who first urged it and who have already laid the foundations for it, and who have had to fight all of us inch by inch during the last five years to do it. Why, just turn it all over to us. We'll do it so skillfully—that we won't lose a single isolationist vote or a single isolationist campaign contribution."

I think there is one thing that you know: I am too old for that. I cannot talk out of both sides of my mouth at the same time.

The government welcomes all sincere supporters of the cause of effective world collaboration in the making of a lasting peace. Millions of Republicans all over the Nation are with us—and have been with us—in our unshakable determination to build the solid structure of peace. And they too will resent this campaign talk by those who first woke up to the facts of international life a few short months ago when they began to study the polls of public opinion.

. . . Words come easily, but they do not change the record. You are, most of you, old enough to remember what things were like for labor in 1932.

You remember the closed banks and the breadlines and the starvation wages; the foreclosures of homes and farms, and the bankruptcies of business; the "Hoovervilles," and the young men and women of the Nation facing a hopeless, jobless future; the closed factories and mines and mills; the ruined and abandoned farms; the stalled railroads and the empty docks; the blank despair of a whole Nation—and the utter impotence of the Federal Government.

You remember the long, hard road, with its gains and its setbacks, which we have traveled together ever since those days.

Now there are some politicians who do not remember that far back, and there are some who remember but find it convenient to forget. No, the record is not to be washed away that easily.

The opposition in this year has already imported into this campaign a very interesting thing, because it is foreign. They have imported the propaganda technique invented by the dictators abroad. Remember, a number of years ago, there was a book, *Mein Kampf*, written by Hitler himself. The technique was all set out in Hitler's book—and it was copied by the aggressors of Italy and Japan. According to that technique, you should never use a small falsehood; always a big one, for its very fantastic nature would make it more credible—if only you keep repeating it over and over and over again.

Well, let us take some simple illustrations that come to mind. For example, although I rubbed my eyes when I read it, we have been told that it was not a Republican depression, but a Democratic depression from which this Nation was saved in 1933—that this Administration—this one today—is responsible for all the suffering and misery that the history books and the American people have always thought had been brought about during the twelve ill-fated years when the Republican party was in power.

Now, there is an old and somewhat lugubrious adage which says: "Never speak of rope in the house of a man who has been hanged." In the same way, if I were a Republican leader speaking to a mixed audience, the last word in the whole dictionary that I think I would use is that word "depression."

. . . But perhaps the most ridiculous of these campaign falsifications is the one that this Administration failed to prepare for the war that was coming. I doubt whether even Goebbels would have tried that one. For even he would never have dared hope that the voters of America had already forgotten that many of the Republican leaders in the Congress and outside the Congress tried to thwart and block nearly every attempt that this Administration made to warn our people and to arm our Nation . . . Many of those very same leaders . . . would be in control of the machinery of the Congress and of the Republican Party, in the event of a Republican victory this fall.

These Republican leaders have not been content with attacks on me, or my wife, or on my sons. No, not content with that, they now include my little dog, Fala. Well, of course, I don't resent attacks, and my family doesn't resent attacks, but Fala *does* resent them. You know, Fala is Scotch, and being a Scottie, as soon as he learned that the Republican fiction writers in Congress and out had concocted a story that I had left him behind on the Aleutian Islands and had sent a destroyer back to find him—at a cost to the taxpayers of two or three, or eight or twenty million dollars—his Scotch soul was furious. He has not been the same dog since. I am accustomed to hearing malicious falsehoods about myself—such as that old, worm-eaten chestnut that I have represented myself as indispensable. But I think I have a right to resent, to object to libelous statements about my dog.

Well, I think we all recognize the old technique. The people of this country know the past too well to be deceived into forgetting. Too much is at stake to forget. There are tasks ahead of us which we must now complete with the same will and the same skill and intelligence and devotion that have already led us so far along the road to victory.

There is the task of finishing victoriously this most terrible of all wars as speedily as possible and with the least cost in lives.

There is the task of setting up international machinery to assure that the peace, once established, will not again be broken.

And there is the task that we face here at home—the task of reconverting our economy from the purposes of war to the purposes of peace.

. . . The victory of the American people and their allies in this war will be far more than a victory against Fascism and reaction and the dead hand of despotism of the past. The victory of the American people and their allies in this war will be a victory for democracy. It will constitute such an affirmation of the strength and power and vitality of government by the people as history has never before witnessed.

And so, my friends, we have had affirmation of the vitality of democratic government behind us, that demonstration of its resilience and its capacity for decision and for action—we have that knowledge of our own strength and power—we move forward with God's help to the greatest epoch of free achievement by free men that the world has ever known.

## Harry S Truman Takes on the "Do-Nothing" Eightieth Congress in Accepting the Democratic Nomination for President, Philadelphia, July 14, 1948

I can't tell you how very much I appreciate the honor which you have just conferred upon me. I shall continue to try to deserve it.

I accept the nomination.

. . . Senator Barkley and I will win this election and make these Republicans like it—don't you forget that!

We will do that because they are wrong and we are right, and I will prove it to you in just a few minutes.

This convention met to express the will and reaffirm the beliefs of the Democratic Party. There have been differences of opinion, and that is the democratic way. Those differences have been settled by a majority vote, as they should be.

Now it is time for us to get together and beat the common enemy. And that is up to you.

We have been working together for victory in a great cause. Victory has become a habit of our party. It has been elected four times in succession, and I am convinced it will be elected a fifth time next November.

The reason is that the people know that the Democratic Party is the people's party, and the Republican Party is the party of special interest, and it always has been, always will be.

The record of the Democratic Party is written in the accomplishments of the last sixteen years. I don't need to repeat them.

. . . Confidence and security have been brought to the people by the Democratic Party. Farm income has increased from less than $2½ billion in 1932 to more than $18 billion in 1947. Never in the world were the farmers of any republic or any kingdom or any other country as prosperous as the farmers of the United States; and if they don't do their duty by the Democratic Party, they are the most ungrateful people in the world!

Wages and salaries in this country have increased from $29 billion in 1933 to more than $128 billion in 1947. That's labor, and labor never had but one friend in politics, and that is the Democratic Party and Franklin D. Roosevelt.

And I say to labor what I have said to the farmers: they are the most ungrateful people in the world if they pass the Democratic Party by this year.

The total national income has increased from less than $40 billion in 1933 to $203 billion in 1947, the greatest in all the history of the world. These benefits have been spread to all the people, because it is the business of the Democratic Party to see that the people get a fair share of these things.

This last, worst, 80th Congress proved just the opposite for the Republicans.

The record on foreign policy of the Democratic Party is that the United States has been turned away permanently from isolationism, and we have converted the greatest and best of the Republicans to our viewpoint on that subject.

The United States has to accept its full responsibility for leadership in international affairs. We have been the backers and the people who organized and started the United Nations, first started under that great Democratic president Woodrow Wilson as the League of Nations. The League was sabotaged by the Republicans in 1920. And we must see that the United Nations continues as a strong and growing body, so we can have everlasting peace in the world.

We have removed trade barriers in the world, which is the best asset we can have for peace. Those trade barriers must not be put back into operation again.

We have started the foreign aid program, which means the recovery of Europe and China and the Far East. We instituted the program for Greece and Turkey, and I will say to you that all these things were done in a cooperative and bipartisan manner . . .

As I have said time and time again, foreign policy should be the policy of the whole nation and not the policy of one party or the other. Partisanship should stop at the water's edge; and I shall continue to preach that through this whole campaign.

I would like to say a word or two now on what I think the Republican philosophy is; and I will speak from actions and from history and from experience.

The situation in 1932 was due to the policies of the Republican Party control of the government of the United States. The Republican Party, as I said a while ago, favors the privileged few and not the common everyday man. Ever since its inception, that party has been under the control of special privilege; and they have completely proved it in the 80th Congress. They proved it by the things they did to the people and not for them. They proved it by the things they failed to do . . .

Time and time again I recommended extension of price control . . . I asked for that extension in September 1945, in November 1945, in a Message on the State of the Union in 1946; and that price control legislation did not come to my desk until June 30, 1946, on the day on which it was supposed to expire. And it was such a rotten bill that I couldn't sign it. And 30 days after that, they sent me one just as bad. I had to sign it, because they quit and went home.

They said, when OPA [Office of Price Administration] died, that prices would adjust themselves for the benefit of the country. They have been adjusting themselves all right! They have gone all the way off the chart in adjusting themselves, at the expense of the consumer and for the benefit of the people that hold the goods.

I called a special session of the Congress in November 1947 . . . and I set out a 10-point program for the welfare and benefit of this country—among other things, standby controls. I got nothing. Congress has still done nothing.

. . . In the field of labor we needed moderate legislation to promote labor-management harmony, but Congress passed instead that so-called Taft-Hartley Act, which has disrupted labor-management relations and will cause strife and bitterness for years to come if it is not repealed, and the Democratic platform says it ought to be repealed.

On the Labor Department, the Republican platform of 1944 said, if they were in power, that they would build up a strong Labor Department. They have simply torn it up. Only one bureau is left that is functioning, and they cut the appropriation of that so it can hardly function.

I recommended an increase in the minimum wage. What did I get? Nothing. Absolutely nothing.

I suggested that the schools in this country are crowded, teachers underpaid, and that there is a shortage of teachers . . . I urged Congress to provide $300 million to aid the states in the present educational crisis. Congress did nothing about it. Time and again I have recommended improvements in the Social Security law, including extending protection to those not now covered, and increasing the amount of benefits, to reduce the eligibility age of women from sixty-five to sixty years. Congress studied the matter for two years, but couldn't find the time to extend or increase the benefits. But they did find time to take Social Security benefits away from 750,000 people, and they passed that over my veto.

I have repeatedly asked the Congress to pass a health program. The Nation suffers from lack of medical care. That situation can be remedied anytime the Congress wants to act upon it.

Everybody knows that I recommended to the Congress the civil rights program. I did that because I believed it to be my duty under the Constitution. Some of the members of my own party disagree with me violently on this matter. But they stand up and do it openly! People can tell where they stand. But the Republicans all professed to be for these measures. But Congress failed to act . . .

Now, everybody likes to have low taxes, but we must reduce the national debt in times of prosperity. And when tax relief can be given, it ought to go to those who need it most, and not those who need it least, as this Republican rich-man's tax bill did when they passed it over my veto on the third try.

The first one of these was so rotten that they couldn't even stomach it themselves. They finally did send one that was somewhat improved, but it still helps the rich and sticks a knife into the back of the poor.

Now the Republicans came here a few weeks ago, and they wrote a platform . . . and that platform had a lot of promises and statements of what the Republican Party is for and what they would do if they were in power. They promised to do in that platform a lot of things I have been asking them to do that they have refused to do when they had the power.

The Republican platform cries about cruelly high prices. I have been trying to get them to do something about high prices ever since they met the first time.

Now listen! This is equally bad and as cynical. The Republican platform comes out for slum clearance and low-rental housing. I have been trying to get them to pass that housing bill ever since they met the first time, and it is still resting in the Rules Committee, that bill.

The Republican platform favors educational opportunity and promotion of education. I have been trying to get Congress to do something about that ever since they came there, and that bill is at rest in the House of Representatives.

The Republican platform is for extending and increasing Social Security benefits. Think of that! Increasing Social Security benefits! Yet when they had the opportunity, they took 750,000 off the Social Security rolls!

I wonder if they think they can fool the people of the United States with such poppycock as that!

There is a long list of these promises in that Republican platform . . . I have discussed a number of these failures of the Republican 80th Congress. Every one of them is important. Two of
them are of major concern to nearly every American family. They
failed to do anything about high prices; they failed to do anything
about housing.

My duty as president requires that I use every means within my
power to get the laws the people need on matters of such importance and urgency.

I am therefore calling this Congress back into session July 26th.

On the 26th day of July, which out in Missouri we call Turnip
Day, I am going to call Congress back and ask them to pass laws
to halt rising prices, to meet the housing crisis—which they are
saying they are for in their platform.

At the same time I shall ask them to act upon other vitally
needed measures such as aid to education, which they say they are
for; a national health program; civil rights legislation, which they
say they are for; an increase in the minimum wage, which I doubt
very much they are for; extension of the Social Security coverage
and increased benefits, which they say they are for . . .

Now, my friends, if there is any reality behind that Republican
platform, we ought to get some action from a short session of the
80th Congress. They can do this job in fifteen days, if they want
to do it. They will still have time to go out and run for office.

They are going to try to dodge their responsibility. They are
going to drag all the red herrings they can across this campaign,
but I am here to say that Senator Barkley and I are not going to let
them get away with it.

Now, what that worst, 80th Congress does in this special
session will be the test. The American people will not decide by
listening to mere words, or by reading a mere platform. They will
decide on the record, the record as it has been written. And in the
records is the stark truth, that the battle lines of 1948 are the same

as they were in 1932, when the nation lay prostrate and helpless as a result of Republican misrule and inaction.

In 1932 we were attacking the citadel of special privilege and greed. We were fighting to drive the money changers from the temple. Today, in 1948, we are now the defenders of the stronghold of democracy and of equal opportunity, the haven of the ordinary people of this land and not of the favored classes or the powerful few. The battle cry is just the same now as it was in 1932, and I paraphrase the words of Franklin D. Roosevelt as he issued the challenge, in accepting nomination in Chicago: "This is more than a political call to arms. Give me your help, not to win votes alone, but to win in this new crusade to keep America secure and safe for its own people."

Now, my friends, with the help of God and the wholehearted push which you can put behind this campaign, we can save this country from a continuation of the 80th Congress and from misrule from now on.

I must have your help. You must get in and push, and win this election. The country can't afford another Republican Congress.

## Chapter 7

# "THE BRIGHT SUNSHINE OF HUMAN RIGHTS"

## Hubert Humphrey Upholds the Cause of Civil Rights at the Democratic National Convention: 1948

JUST AS THE Democrats and President Harry Truman were pulling off one of the most unexpected and extraordinary upsets in American political history, the seeds of the party's downturn were being planted at its national convention in Philadelphia. No single issue would do more to rend the Democratic Party throughout the 1960s, '70s, and '80s than the issue of race. Franklin Roosevelt had built a grand political coalition (the New Deal coalition) on a shaky foundation—white southerners, urban ethnic voters, farmers, and African Americans. It was a coalition that would not survive the eventual demand for equal rights from America's black population. Though that struggle would not take true form until the 1960s, the first shot was fired in Philadelphia, in 1948, by Hubert Humphrey.

To be sure, the potency of the race issue was not lost on Franklin Roosevelt. Just as he had earlier marginalized the isolationists and laissez-faire conservatives, FDR intended to do the same with Jim Crow. During the 1944 presidential campaign FDR made clear his intentions to the segregationist South: "The right to vote must be open to our citizens irrespective of race, color, or creed—without tax or artificial restriction of any kind. The sooner we get to that basis of political equality, the better it will be for the country as a whole."[1]

FDR did not live to see this dream realized, and by 1948, the party was facing the possibility of crushing defeat in November. Most Democrats weren't interested in pushing the race issue and further imperiling the party's already meager chances on Election Day. Truman, was facing dissension from both sides—southerners who felt that his civil rights program, announced in February, went too far, and northern liberals who felt that it didn't go far enough. Divisions in the party were threatening to shatter the New Deal coalition.

His own personal support for civil rights notwithstanding, Truman, along with the party's Platform Committee, was content simply to endorse the same civil rights plank that had appeared in the 1944 platform and leave the issue at that, for fear of sparking a southern walkout at the convention. But an increasingly loud faction of Democrats, led by the Americans for Democratic Action (ADA), would hear none of it. The ADA demanded that the issue be brought to the convention floor, and proposed a minority civil rights plank that would endorse Truman's own civil rights program, namely, opposition to poll taxes, support for anti-lynching and fair employment laws, and integration of the military.[2]

## STANDING UP FOR CIVIL RIGHTS

Hubert Humphrey, the mayor of Minneapolis and the Democratic candidate for Senate in Minnesota, was a vocal civil rights supporter and quickly became the leader and the voice of the pro-civil-rights faction. Humphrey had warned repeatedly that if the Democrats didn't act, the Republicans would reclaim their historical role as defender of equal rights (after all, it was the GOP, under the leadership of Abraham Lincoln, that had freed the slaves). He derided the proposed civil rights plank as a "sellout to states rights" and argued that the party had a historical responsibility to take a stand in support of those whose rights were being suppressed.[3]

Humphrey was the logical choice to plead the liberal case on the convention floor. He had already developed local renown as an extraordinary speaker—reportedly tapes of his speeches were passed around by Minnesotans like bootlegged concerts.[4] Former congressman Andrew Biemiller, one of the founders of the ADA, told Humphrey that only if he spoke to the convention would the minority plank have any chance of passing.[5] Humphrey was torn both by his concern that the ADA's effort would spoil the party's chances in November, and fear for his own political future. Truman advisers made clear to the young mayor that if the civil rights issue split the party and helped elect Dewey, he would be finished in Democratic politics.[6]

Until 5:00 A.M. the ADA group (meeting in a University of Pennsylvania fraternity house) argued over the best way to proceed. When it was suggested that the ADA plank be tied directly to Truman's own program for civil rights, by commending the president for his "courageous stand" on the issue, Humphrey was finally convinced and announced that he would speak to the convention that very afternoon. According to Joseph Rauh Jr., one of the founders of the ADA, "the cheer at the fraternity house could have been heard at Convention Hall blocks away."[7]

With only ten hours to draft remarks in support of the minority plank, Humphrey began furiously writing, even dictating notes to his secretary while he was in the shower. As he bounded to the stage, wearing a large yellow Truman pin and looking exhausted from the night's backroom jockeying, Humphrey prepared to deliver a speech that would not only shape his political career but transform the political destiny of the Democratic Party.[8]

In an impassioned address Humphrey exhorted the Democratic Party to take a progressive and activist approach to civil rights. Invoking the names of Roosevelt, Truman, and Jefferson, Humphrey argued that fighting for racial equality was fundamental to the party's ethos. He boldly and provocatively asserted that while "other political parties may have talked more about civil rights . . . the Democratic Party has surely done more about civil rights."

Knowing that he could not win the debate on purely political grounds, Humphrey instead imbued his speech with a healthy dose of morality and religious fervor, describing a "spiritual crisis" in the country and the need for Democrats to adopt a "morally sound position" on civil rights. At a time when many were claiming that a more forthright position on racial issues would bring serious political costs, Humphrey was raising the bar, arguing that Democrats had a responsibility that went beyond such crass considerations. That meant not accepting any half measures. As Humphrey passionately told the audience: "There will be no hedging, and there will be no watering down of the instruments and the princip[le]s of the civil-rights program."

Further, Humphrey cast the fight in the broadest terms possible (in some respects foreshadowing the approach taken by Martin Luther King Jr. fifteen years later), arguing that every American had a stake in the question of civil rights. While the assembled delegates were all Democrats, Humphrey argued that they had a higher responsibility. "We're here as Americans," he told the convention, "We're here as the believers in the princip[le] and the ideology of democracy." At a time when the world "was being challenged by the world of slavery," if America was to be "a leader in the free world," there could be no "double standard." Humphrey argued that "our demands for democratic practices in other lands will be no more effective than the guarantee of those practices in our own country."

Everyone in America was affected by the question of race, but clearly some more than others, and Humphrey saved his strongest words for the southern delegates in the convention hall. "To those who say that we are rushing this issue of civil rights, I say to them we are 172 years too late. To those who say that this civil-rights program is an infringement on states' rights, I say this: The time has arrived in America for the Democratic Party to get out of the shadow of states' rights and to walk forthrightly into the bright sunshine of human rights."

The casting of light and dark imagery, the use of antithesis argument, the evoking of American history to both uplift and shame his audience—all of these rhetorical tools came together in one truly brilliant and memorable line. Not since the closing words of the "Cross of Gold" speech did a sentence uttered at a national convention have a more sustained impact than these few words.[9]

Humphrey concluded his remarks by evoking the Great Emancipator himself, Abraham Lincoln, telling the delegates, "For the whole two billion members of the human family, our land is now, more than ever before, the last best hope on earth." It's hard to imagine Humphrey was unaware of the particular salience of Lincoln to the events taking place in Philadelphia in the summer of 1948. The last phrase was taken from his 1862 message to Congress, and it is instructive to reexamine the words that preceded and followed it four score and six years before:

In giving freedom to the slave, we assure freedom to the free—honorable alike in what we give, and what we preserve. We shall nobly save, or meanly lose, the last best hope of earth. Other means may succeed; this could not fail. The way is plain, peaceful, generous, just—a way which, if followed, the world will forever applaud, and God must forever bless.

In fittingly Lincolnesque language, Humphrey offered the assembled delegates and the millions of Americans listening at home a stirring vision of American destiny: "We shall beg[i]n here the fuller and richer realization of that hope—that promise of a land where all men are truly free and equal, and each man uses his freedom and equality wisely well."

## THE SOUTH WALKS OUT

The delegates erupted in applause, staging a ten-minute-long demonstration in support of Humphrey.[10] A vote that earlier had seemed doomed now swung hugely in the liberals' favor. At the same time, however, the speech fully exposed the growing fissures between the southern bloc of the party and its more liberal northern wing. The reaction from southern delegates was swift. When the convention later reconvened, Handy Ellis from the Alabama delegation announced that because of the civil rights platform adopted, "we cannot with honor further participate in the proceedings of this Convention . . . we bid you good-bye." With that, Ellis and the other twelve members of the Alabama delegation and all the delegates from Mississippi turned and walked from the hall, accompanied by catcalls and taunts.[11]

Two weeks later, southern Democrats assembled in Birmingham, Alabama, to get their revenge on a party they felt had abandoned them. There, behind the leadership of South Carolina governor Strom Thurmond, they launched an independent third-party campaign, under the banner of the States' Rights Democratic Party, or, as they were more popularly known, the Dixiecrats. Thurmond did his best to cast the party's break as a philosophical issue of states' rights and not a question of race. But the convention in Alabama would feature some of the most virulent racists the South had to offer, and Thurmond's efforts at moderation were belied by his own words when he accepted the party's nomination for president:

"There's not enough troops in the Army to force the southern people to break down segregation and admit the Negro race into our theaters, into our swimming pools, into schools and into our homes."[12]

Thurmond would end up taking four southern states from Truman's column, but only in those states where the Dixiecrat candidate was listed on the ballot as the Democratic nominee for president instead of Truman. The rest of the region stayed solidly Democratic. While many believed that the exiting of southern Democrats would doom President Harry Truman's chances in November, the passage of the civil rights plank was in fact partly responsible for his improbable win. African American voters turned out in droves for the president, helping solidify for generations to come the party's support from this crucial voting bloc. In addition, many northern liberals who were flirting with Henry Wallace's candidacy on the Progressive Party ticket returned to the Democratic fold because of its newfound toughness on the civil rights question.

However, while the party would embrace Humphrey's message in 1948, racial fissures would, in time, divide the party from the "Solid South," contributing to the gradual decline of the Democratic coalition over the next four decades. Future Democrats were simply unable to craft a political strategy to make up for the loss of the South's electoral votes. The result was that the question of civil rights, launched by Humphrey's stirring words, would in time drive a wedge through the party. Even worse for Democrats, the issue would eventually alienate the party's most solid constituencies, union members and white ethnic voters, the so-called Reagan Democrats.

But, in the end, the speech played an essential role in furthering the cause of equal rights in America. For the first time a major political party had debated at its national convention the status of African Americans and the continuing stain of segregation on the country—and civil rights had won. Had Humphrey not taken the courageous step of delivering his memorable remarks in Philadelphia, this long-overdue debate within the Democratic Party would have been further delayed.[13] For African Americans, the Humphrey speech and the resulting shift by the Democratic Party on civil rights would begin a slow and steady process that would culminate sixteen years later, with a southern president signing the landmark Civil Rights Act of 1964, finally taking the nation "forthrightly into the bright sunshine of human rights."

*Hubert Humphrey Debates the Civil Rights Plank in the
Democratic Party Platform, Philadelphia, July 14, 1948*

Mr. Chairman, fellow Democrats, fellow Americans:

I realize that in speaking in behalf of the minority report on civil
rights . . . I'm dealing with a charged issue—with an issue which
has been confused by emotionalism on all sides of the fence. I realize that there are here today friends and colleagues of mine, many
of them, who feel just as deeply and keenly as I do about this issue
and who are yet in complete disagreement with me.

My respect and admiration for these men and their views was
great when I came to this convention. It is now far greater because of the sincerity, the courtesy, and the forthrightness with
which many of them have argued in our prolonged discussions in
the platform committee.

Because of this very great respect—and because of my profound belief that we have a challenging task to do here—because
good conscience, decent morality, demands it—I feel I must rise
at this time to support a report—the minority report—a report
that spells out our democracy, a report that the people of this
country can and will understand, and a report that they will enthusiastically acclaim on the great issue of civil rights.

Now let me say this at the outset: that this proposal is made for
no single region. Our proposal is made for no single class, for no
single racial or religious group in mind. All of the regions of this
country, all of the states have shared in our precious heritage of
American freedom. All the states and all the regions have seen at
least some of the infringements of that freedom . . . all people,
white and black, all groups, all racial groups have been the victims
at time[s] in this nation of . . . vicious discrimination.

The masterly statement of our keynote speaker, the distinguished United States Senator from Kentucky, Alben Barkley,

made that point with great force. Speaking of the founder of our Party, Thomas Jefferson, he said this:

"He did not proclaim that all the white, or the black, or the red, or the yellow men are equal; that all Christian or Jewish men are equal; that all Protestant and Catholic men are equal; that all rich and poor men are equal; that all good and bad men are equal. What he declared was that all men are equal; and the equality which he proclaimed was the equality in the right to enjoy the blessings of free government in which they may participate and to which they have given their support."

Now these words of Senator Barkley's are appropriate to this convention of the oldest, the most truly progressive political party in America. From the time of Thomas Jefferson, the time when that immortal American doctrine of individual rights, under just and fairly administered laws, the Democratic Party has tried hard to secure expanding freedoms for all citizens. Oh, yes, I know, other political parties may have talked more about civil rights, but the Democratic Party has surely done more about civil rights.

We have made great progress in every part of this country. We've made great progress in the South; we've made it in the West, in the North, and in the East. But we must now focus the direction of that progress towards the realization of a full program of civil rights to all. This convention must set out more specifically the direction in which our Party efforts are to go.

We can be proud that we can be guided by the courageous trail blazing of two great Democratic Presidents. We can be proud of the fact that our great and beloved immortal leader Franklin Roosevelt gave us guidance. And we can be proud of the fact that Harry Truman has had the courage to give to the people of America the new emancipation proclamation.

It seems to me that the Democratic Party needs to make definite pledges of the kinds suggested in the minority report, to maintain the trust and the confidence placed in it by the people of all races and all sections of this country. Sure, we're here as Democrats. But my good friends, we're here as Americans; we're here as the believers in the princip[le] and the ideology of democracy, and I firmly believe that as men concerned with our country's future, we must specify in our platform the guarantees which we have mentioned in the minority report.

Yes, this is far more than a Party matter. Every citizen in this country has a stake in the emergence of the United States as a leader in the free world. That world is being challenged by the world of slavery. For us to play our part effectively, we must be in a morally sound position. We can't use a double standard . . . for measuring our own and other people's policies. Our demands for democratic practices in other lands will be no more effective than the guarantee of those practices in our own country.

Friends, delegates, I do not believe that there can be any compromise on the guarantees of the civil rights which we have mentioned in the minority report. In spite of my desire for unanimous agreement on the entire platform . . . there are some matters which I think must be stated clearly and without qualification . . . There will be no hedging, and there will be no watering down— if you please—of the instruments and the princip[le]s of the civil-rights program.

To those who say that we are rushing this issue of civil rights, I say to them we are 172 years late. To those who say that this civil-rights program is an infringement on states' rights, I say this: The time has arrived in America for the Democratic Party to get out of the shadows of states' rights and to walk forthrightly into the bright sunshine of human rights. People—human beings— this is the issue of the 20th century. People of all kinds—all sorts of people—and these people are looking to America for leadership, and they're looking to America for precept and example.

My good friends, my fellow Democrats, I ask you for a calm consideration of our historic opportunity. Let us do forget the evil passions and the blindness of the past. In these times of world economic, political, and spiritual—above all spiritual crisis, we cannot and we must not turn from the path so plainly before us. That path has already led us through many valleys of the shadow of death. And now is the time to recall those who were left on that path of American freedom.

For all of us here, for the millions who have sent us, for the whole two billion members of the human family, our land is now, more than ever before, the last best hope on earth. And I know that we can, and I know that we shall beg[i]n here the fuller and richer realization of that hope—that promise of a land where all men are truly free and equal, and each man uses his freedom and equality wisely well.

My good friends, I ask my Party, I ask the Democratic Party, to march down the high road of progressive democracy. I ask this convention to say in unmistakable terms that we proudly hail, and we courageously support, our President and leader Harry Truman in his great fight for civil rights in America!

*Chapter 8*

# "LET'S TALK SENSE TO THE AMERICAN PEOPLE"

## Adlai Stevenson Redefines American Patriotism: 1952

I N THE GRAND sweep of American campaign speechwriting, no
presidential candidate delivered oratory more memorable, more
challenging, or more consistently extraordinary than Adlai Stevenson. His speeches were a moving combination of self-deprecation,
soaring eloquence, and inspiring vision that few presidential candidates have reached or even aspired to. Stevenson was an unsuccessful politician (he won only one election) but at a time when
Democrats needed a burst of energy, he brought a sense of humility, courage, and sacrifice to the campaign trail. Though some were
turned off by Stevenson's "egghead" demeanor, millions of others
were energized by Stevenson's call to arms. His candor and commitment to idealism in politics would form the intellectual backbone of the Democratic Party throughout the 1960s.

Stevenson was surely one of the more rhetorically prolific candidates to run for president. A modern presidential candidate generally repeats the same words over and over again until he can
practically recite them in his sleep. But Stevenson refused to deliver the same speech twice and offered new remarks almost
everywhere he went on the campaign trail. It certainly allowed

him to put together a stirring collection of campaign speeches, but it was hell on the speechwriters.[1]

Politics did not naturally course through Stevenson's blood. He didn't seek his first elected office until he reached the age of forty-eight, when he ran for governor of Illinois in 1948. Moreover, Stevenson had a unique perspective on political campaigns. In the introduction to a collection of his 1952 campaign speeches he wrote, "Believing utterly in democracy and the collective reason of properly informed people, I have always thought that political campaigns for offices of great responsibility are both an opportunity and an obligation to talk sensibly and truthfully about public questions and their full implications."[2] On the campaign trail, Stevenson would be true to his word.

## TALKING SENSE

Stevenson made every effort possible *not* to be the Democratic Party's nominee for president in 1952. Even after being asked directly by President Harry Truman to accept the nomination, he told the president that he wasn't interested. The fact that an endorsement from the deeply unpopular Truman was not exactly the brass ring might also have explained his reticence.

But with no obvious candidate in the Democratic field, a movement to draft Stevenson took on a life of its own. Truman had announced in March his intention not to seek reelection. Senators Estes Kefauver, from Tennessee, and Richard Russell, of Georgia, had entered the Democratic primaries, but neither energized the party's rank and file. When the Democratic delegates gathered in Chicago, there was no front-runner or even an assumed nominee. It was, in effect, an open convention, but for many delegates the reluctant Stevenson seemed the best candidate for the top nod.

Stevenson's opening speech to the convention would spark the momentum of his candidacy. Traditionally, welcoming speeches at national conventions are not terribly memorable, particularly those delivered at noon on a Monday afternoon. But Stevenson's speech was highly anticipated and the hall was packed with backers. As he was introduced, a spontaneous and unorganized demonstration of support for Stevenson broke out. For at least ten minutes, the delegates cheered, waved banners, and screamed, "We want Stevenson."[3]

The governor delivered an address that featured not only his typical eloquence but also pointed political attack and a clarion call for national sacrifice. Stevenson was quick to remind his audience of "the greatest era of economic and social progress in our history," particularly in comparison to "the depths of shattering national misery" that came as a result of "Republican rule."[4]

But this was not a speech of mere New Deal platitudes. Stevenson told the delegates that the American people had come to expect much from Democratic leadership, and the party must deliver on those expectations. "They see in us relentless determination to stand fast against the barbarian at the gate, to cultivate allies with a decent respect for the opinion of others, to patiently explore every misty path to peace and security which is the only certainty of lower taxes and a better life."[5]

He told Democrats that this legacy of success and responsibility of leadership must inform their efforts going forward—but they must offer the American people more. "A great record of past achievement is not enough. There can be no complacency, perhaps for years to come. We dare not just look back to great yesterdays. We must look forward to great tomorrows." As was Stevenson's way, he was also doling out a healthy dose of castor oil: "What America needs and the world wants is not bombast, abuse and double talk, but a sober message of firm faith and confidence."[6]

Stevenson was not interested in resuming Truman's divisive

1948 campaign. He told his advisers it was not his intention to run against the memory of Herbert Hoover, as Roosevelt, Truman and countless Democratic officeholders had done in every election since 1932.[7] At a time when Democrats were deeply unpopular and the party had fallen victim to the ossification and corruption that so often come when one party is in power for too many years, Stevenson sought to give Democrats a new sense of political meaning and inspiration.

Stevenson's speech (which was interrupted twenty-seven times by applause) united the party behind his candidacy.[8] Days later, as he accepted the party's nomination for president, Stevenson would take his message of national sacrifice and political probity even further. After telling the audience with typical Stevenson humility that he would have preferred "a stronger, a wiser, a better man" to be taking on the responsibilities of party leadership, he nonetheless reminded Democrats that "more important than winning the election is governing the nation . . . Better we lose this election than mislead the people; and better we lose than misgovern the people."[9]

"The ordeal of the twentieth century—the bloodiest, most turbulent era of the Christian age—is far from over," Stevenson sternly warned. "Sacrifice, patience, understanding and implacable purpose may be our lot for years to come. Let's face it." And then, in the speech's most stirring passage—the words that would come to define his campaign—he said, "Let's talk sense to the American people. Let's tell them the truth, that there are no gains without pains, that we are now on the eve of great decisions, not easy decisions, like resistance when you are attacked, but a long, patient, costly struggle, which alone can assure triumph over the great enemies of man—war, poverty and tyranny."[10] Arthur Schlesinger Jr., the Harvard history professor, presidential biographer, and Pulitzer Prize winner who would later join Stevenson's staff as a speechwriter, called the speech a "brilliant literary document, complex and carefully wrought in its composition, bearing the imprint of a highly individual, complicated, sensitive and distinguished personality."[11]

Ironically, Stevenson benefited from the fact that few thought GOP nominee Dwight Eisenhower could be beaten in 1952. Even some Democrats believed that if the two-party system was to be maintained, Republicans *needed* to win in November and embrace the responsibility of national leadership. With little chance of victory, Stevenson could be his own man, giving him enormous leeway in eschewing traditional political considerations.

## THE ELKS CLUB GATHERS

It was a leeway that he would consistently take advantage of over the next three and a half months. It helped that Stevenson's speechwriting team was likely the most impressive group of writers ever put to work on behalf of a presidential candidate. They worked out of a local Elks Club in Springfield, Illinois, hence earning the title "Elks Club Group." Considering Stevenson's insistence on always delivering fresh material on the campaign trail, the Elks had their work cut out for them.

At the head of the group was Schlesinger, who made it his goal to ensure that the candidate's speeches were both "simple and militant," and not "complex and philosophic," all the while remaining true to the party's New Deal legacy. It was a difficult exercise in a campaign that seemed to go out of its way to court southern voters and Republican moderates and "talk sense" to traditional Democratic constituencies.[12]

Joining him was a steady stream of writers, including the Harvard economist John Kenneth Galbraith, Stevenson biographer John Barlow Martin, future secretary of labor Willard Wirtz, and a host of others. The conduit between Stevenson and the Elks

Club Group (Stevenson almost never spoke directly to the writers) was his longtime friend and adviser Carl McGowan, who would often rewrite speech drafts.

It wasn't accidental that Stevenson kept himself at arm's length from the Elks—he wanted people to believe that he had written all of his own speeches. Stevenson was proud of his writing skills and once confided in a friend that his most preferred profession would have been that of a writer.[13] While Stevenson was generally happy to share credit on most issues, speechwriting was different. When it was suggested that others wrote his words, he became furious; he even had a break with his close friend Bill Atwood when Atwood hinted that he wrote one of Stevenson's speeches.[14]

The writers generally received little more guidance than a cryptic sentence or two from McGowan. As for feedback, there wasn't much of that either. But in their many hours together in the cramped confines of the Elks Club, Stevenson's writers spent hours doing what speechwriters do: parsing words, editing texts, talking politics, drinking lots of coffee, smoking too many cigarettes, and not getting enough sleep.

But above all, they produced wondrous rhetoric. Amazingly, for the greatness of the two speeches that Stevenson delivered at the convention, they were neither the best that Stevenson would deliver in 1952 nor the most pointed and direct. Stevenson's best speech would come on August 27, 1952, in remarks to the American Legion in New York City.

## REDEFINING PATRIOTISM

The American Legion, as one of the foremost veterans' groups in America, has become a regular stop in presidential politics. In the days before Stevenson spoke to the group, Eisenhower had delivered a controversial speech advocating a policy of "liberation" on behalf of captive Eastern European nations trapped under the Soviet Union's thumb. It was an incendiary and admittedly dangerous message, but one that played well with a group that had already passed resolutions calling for the removal of Secretary of State Dean Acheson as well as improved relations with Franco's fascist government in Spain.[15]

Stevenson was never going to match this type of heated rhetoric, and he wasn't about to try. Stevenson turned to one of his most prominent speechwriters, Pulitzer Prize–winning poet and writer Archibald MacLeish, and asked him to draft remarks based on "the idea of Americans first and veterans second."[16] In a follow-up note he made clear his intentions for the speech:

> I get so sick of the everlasting appeals to the cupidity and prejudice of every group which characterize our political campaigns. There is something finer in people; they know that they owe something too. I should like to try, at least, to appeal to their sense of obligation as well as their avarice.[17]

MacLeish would produce a first draft—one that was rewritten by other members of the Elks Club and Stevenson himself. In the end, five writers would weigh in on the speech, but inspired by a mere few words of guidance from the candidate, MacLeish conceived a speech that is among the most courageous ever to emanate from the campaign trail.

Stevenson began by sounding his usual tone of self-deprecation, noting his "lowly" military career as an apprentice seaman. Stevenson was always going to be at a disadvantage on security and military matters in comparison to Eisenhower. But at the same time he was no shrinking violet on security issues. He was a strong Cold Warrior and gave no quarter to Communism or, more particularly, Communists in America's ranks. "Communism is abhorrent," Stevenson declared. "It is strangulation of the individual; it is death for the soul. Americans who have surrendered to this misbegotten idol have surrendered their right to our trust. And there can be no secure place for them in our public life."

Certainly, Stevenson could have continued in this vein, offering the usual campaign-season platitudes about the proud legacy of the Legion and the need for vigilant anti-Communism. But he was far more interested in focusing on the responsibility that came with American power and in particular the question of "patriotism in the context of our times." At a time when individuals such as Joe McCarthy were defining patriotism via scurrilous anti-Communist attacks, it was a gutsy effort. But if he was truly going to "talk sense" to the American people, here was his chance.

According to Stevenson, patriotism entailed something greater than the small-minded politics of McCarthy. "I venture to suggest that what we mean is a sense of national responsibility which will enable America to remain master of her power . . . a patriotism which is not short, frenzied outbursts of emotion, but the tranquil and steady dedication of a lifetime."

"Patriotism," Stevenson would argue, "means putting country before self." To prove his point, the candidate put the Legion on notice that he would not kowtow to their specific interests. "I should tell you—my fellow Legionnaires—as I would tell all other organized groups, that I intend to resist pressure from veterans, too, if I think their demands are excessive or in conflict with the public interest . . . After all, we are Americans first and veterans second." This was amazing language, but it was indicative of his honest and unabashed approach to public discourse on the campaign trail.

In the fall of 1952, Stevenson argued that the most serious issue facing the country was those who would use "patriotism as a club for attacking other Americans." Stevenson was of course referring to McCarthy, who was twisting the very nature of patriotism in American society (although Stevenson was unafraid to take on the "self-styled patriot who thinks that a Negro, a Jew, a Catholic, or a Japanese-American is less an American than he"). His remarks sought to reestablish the link between patriotism and freedom.

Freedom of the mind, my friends, has served America well. The vigor of our political life, our capacity for change, our cultural, scientific and industrial achievements, all derive from free inquiry, from the free mind—from the imagination, re-sourcefulness and daring of men who are not afraid of new ideas. Most all of us favor free enterprise for business. Let us also favor free enterprise for the mind.

At a time when McCarthy was seemingly able to operate with impunity—even Eisenhower refused the opportunity to attack the Wisconsin senator—Stevenson was not cowed. "The tragedy of our day is the climate of fear in which we live, and fear breeds repression. Too often sinister threats to the Bill of Rights, to free-dom of the mind, are concealed under the patriotic cloak of anti-communism," said Stevenson.

While he attacked the intolerance and personal invective that had, in his mind, come to wrongly define patriotism, Stevenson also offered an affirmative, hopeful message. Stevenson asserted that love of country had become "more than a virtue," indeed "a neces-sity" and "a condition of survival" in perilous times. However, by Stevenson's interpretation, that love must be based on a positive notion of patriotism, a love of the qualities that make America great. "When an American says he loves his country, he means not only that he loves the New England hills, the prairies glistening in the sun, the wide and rising plains, the great mountains, and the sea. He means that he loves an inner air, an inner light in which free-dom lives and in which a man can draw the breath of self-respect."

And then, in the speech's most poignant moment, he reminded the Legionnaires, "Men who have offered their lives for their country know that patriotism is not the fear of something; it is the love of something. Patriotism with us is not the hatred of Russia; it is the love of this Republic and of the ideal of liberty of man and mind in which it was born, and to which this Republic is dedicated."

The response from the right was predictably harsh. Vice presidential nominee Richard Nixon, whom Stevenson personally loathed, claimed that the governor had "made light of the menace of communism." But the generally conservative American Legion didn't agree. They gave the Democratic nominee a rousing response. The *Washington Post* praised Stevenson not only for recognizing "that in 1952 weakness in the free world would be a prelude to annihilation" but also for arguing that "repression and intolerance" are "part of the weakness we must avoid."[18] McGowan would later call the speech "the best day of the campaign," and Stevenson biographer Porter McKeever described it as "a landmark in American political discourse."[19]

Unfortunately, the high-mindedness would not continue. In October, Nixon would intimate that Stevenson, Acheson, and even President Truman were "traitors" to proud American traditions. Worse, in Stevenson's mind, General Eisenhower failed to condemn McCarthy, even after he began attacking Ike's mentor General George Marshall and blaming him for the "loss of China." Marshall had made Eisenhower's career, and no man was more responsible for his meteoric rise through the military. Yet at a campaign appearance in Wisconsin on October 2, 1952, Eisenhower appeared with McCarthy and said nothing about McCarthy's increasingly unhinged attacks—even though a passage in his prepared remarks strenuously defended Marshall. It was a shameful episode and one that Stevenson never forgave. After October 2, Stevenson would refer to Eisenhower as "the general" and never again as "my distinguished opponent."[20]

A month later, the general would swamp the governor, winning the presidency in a landslide. But as the American Legion speech demonstrated, Stevenson had run a campaign to be proud of. It was not one without faults. Too much attention was paid to speeches and Stevenson's unrelenting candor on the campaign trail, which undoubtedly began to rub a few Americans the wrong way. However, no matter the campaign Stevenson ran, the enormous popularity of Eisenhower, combined with the desire for change in Washington, was likely far too much to overcome.

Nonetheless, the impact of Stevenson's run would be felt for years to come. As McKeever said of the campaign, "In the end, it was not the number of votes he received but the voters he aroused that was significant. They were the young, the idealistic, the emerging postwar generation groping for a just and better America. He was the promise of what politics might be, and a call to enter political life."[21]

At a time when American politics seemed so small and divisive in comparison to the great issues that were at stake both at home and abroad, Stevenson raised the bar and showed a generation of Americans that public service could be greater and purer than the disgusting excesses of McCarthyism.

Richard Goodwin, who later would write speeches for Presidents Kennedy and Johnson, would say that upon hearing Stevenson as a college senior, "my tiny world seemed suddenly to widen." Stevenson's words, said Goodwin, "were the words of sacrifice, but the music sang of meaning and purpose to a young man . . . He told an entire generation there was room for intelligence and idealism in public life, that politics was not just a way to live but a way to live greatly, that each of must share in the passions of the age."[22] Indeed, it is difficult to imagine that future Democratic leaders and in particular John F. Kennedy were not influenced by Stevenson's words. Eight years later, at the 1960 convention, Schlesinger would write that "no one in Los Angeles sounded like Harry Truman; all the contenders, even Johnson, were speaking in the spirit and often in the idiom of Stevenson, and none more so than Kennedy." Kennedy was, in his mind, "the heir and executor of the Stevenson revolution"—a fact that neither man, with their frosty relationship, ever would be inclined to admit.[23]

Above all, Stevenson proved that even in the crucible of the campaign trail and even in the face of defeat, great oratory can create a reality of its own—maybe not in votes, but certainly in inspiring Americans to pursue greatness.

## Adlai Stevenson Speaks to the American Legion, New York, August 25, 1952

I have attended too many conventions not to know how you are all beginning to feel here on the afternoon of your third day. You work hard at Legion business and then devote the balance of your time to the museums, art galleries, concerts and other cultural monuments of New York. And of course you have to listen to speeches too! I console myself with the thought that this punishment, while cruel, is not unusual.

I have no claim, as many of you do, to the honored title of old soldier. Nor have I risen to high rank in the armed services . . .

My own military career was brief. It was also lowly. An Apprentice Seaman in a naval training unit was not, as some of you may also recall, exactly a powerful command position in World War One.

My experience thus provided me with a very special view— what could be called a worm's-eye view—of the service. In 1918 I doubt if there was anything more wormlike than an Apprentice Seaman . . .

After the first war, many Americans lost sight of the fact that only the strong can be free. Many mistook an ominous lull for permanent peace. In those days the American Legion knew, however, that he who is not prepared today is less so tomorrow, and that only a society which could fight for survival could survive.

The Legion's fight to awaken America to the need for military preparedness is now largely won. We have made great advances in understanding the problem of national security in the modern world. We no longer think in terms of American resources alone. For the most part we now understand the need for a great international system of security, and we have taken the lead in building it.

We have joined our strength with that of others—and we have

done so in self-protection. We seek no dominion over any other nation—and the whole free world knows it! If there are those behind the Iron Curtain who don't know it, it is because their masters don't want them to know it.

I am not sure that, historically, there has been another powerful nation that has been trusted as the United States is trusted today. It is something new under the sun when the proudest nations on earth have not only accepted American leadership in the common defense effort, but have also welcomed our troops and bases on their territory . . .

Yet, all is not perfect. There are still vital interests which we and our allies are not militarily prepared to defend.

Some of us are reluctant to admit that security cannot be won cheaply by some clever diplomatic maneuver or by propaganda.

We have not yet really faced up to the problem of defending our cities against the rapidly growing threat of Soviet air power . . .

And many only partly understand or are loath to acknowledge that the costs of waging the cold war are but a fraction of the costs of hot war.

So there remain important tasks for us. I believe in a strong national defense, and I believe that we must press forward to improve our position and not waver or hesitate in this interval when the scales are so precariously balanced.

While I think it is true that today the fight for preparedness is going well, there are other and even more difficult tasks that we dare not neglect.

The United States has very large power in the world today. And the partner of power—the corollary—is responsibility. It is our high task to use our power with a sure hand and a steady touch—with the self-restraint that goes with confident strength. The purpose of our power must never be lost in the fact of our power—and the purpose, I take it, is the promotion of freedom, justice and peace in the world.

We talk a great deal about patriotism. What do we mean by patriotism in the context of our times? I venture to suggest that what we mean is a sense of national responsibility which will enable America to remain master of her power—to walk with it in serenity and wisdom, with self-respect and with the respect of all mankind; a patriotism that puts country ahead of self; a patriotism which is not short, frenzied outbursts of emotion, but the tranquil and steady dedication of a lifetime. The dedication of a lifetime—these are words that are easy to utter, but this is a mighty assignment. For it is often easier to fight for principles than to live up to them.

Patriotism, I have said, means putting country before self. This is no abstract phrase, and unhappily, we find some things in American life today of which we cannot be proud.

Consider the groups who seek to identify their special interests with the general welfare. I find it sobering to think that their pressure might one day be focused on me. I have resisted them before and I hope the Almighty will give me the strength to do so again and again. And I should tell you—my fellow Legionnaires—as I would tell all other organized groups, that I intend to resist pressures from veterans, too, if I think their demands are excessive or in conflict with the public interest, which must always be the paramount interest.

Let me suggest, incidentally, that we are rapidly becoming a nation of veterans. If we were all to claim a special reward for our service, beyond that to which specific disability or sacrifice has created a just claim, who would be left to pay the bill? After all, we are Americans first and veterans second, and the best maxim for any administration is still Jefferson's: "Equal rights for all, special privileges for none."

True patriotism it seems to me, is based on tolerance and a large measure of humility.

There are men among us who use "patriotism" as a club for attacking other Americans. What can we say for the self-styled patriot who thinks that a Negro, a Jew, a Catholic or a Japanese-American is less an American than he? That betrays the deepest article of our faith, the belief in individual liberty and equality which has always been the heart and soul of the American idea.

What can we say for the man who proclaims himself a patriot—and then for political or personal reasons attacks the patriotism of faithful public servants? I give you, as a shocking example, the attacks which have been made on the loyalty and the motives of our great wartime Chief of Staff, General Marshall. To me this is the type of "patriotism" which is, in Dr. Johnson's phrase, "the last refuge of scoundrels."

The anatomy of patriotism is complex. But surely intolerance and public irresponsibility cannot be cloaked in the shining armor of rectitude and righteousness. Nor can the denial of the right to hold ideas that are different—the freedom of man to think as he pleases. To strike freedom of the mind with the fist of patriotism is an old and an ugly subtlety.

And the freedom of the mind, my friends, has served America well. The vigor of our political life, our capacity for change, our cultural, scientific and industrial achievements, all derive from free inquiry, from the free mind—from the imagination, resourcefulness and daring of men who are not afraid of new ideas.

Most all of us favor free enterprise for business. Let us also favor free enterprise for the mind. For, in the last analysis, we would fight to the death to protect it. Why is it, then, that we are sometimes slow to detect, or are indifferent to, the dangers that beset it?

Many of the threats to our cherished freedoms in these anxious, troubled times arise, it seems to me, from a healthy apprehension about the communist menace within our country. Communism is abhorrent. It is strangulation of the individual; it is death for the soul. Americans who have surrendered to this misbegotten idol have surrendered their right to our trust. And there can be no secure place for them in our public life. Yet, as I have said before, we must take care not to burn down the barn to kill the rats. All of us, and especially patriotic organizations of enormous influence like the American Legion, must be vigilant in protecting our birthright from its too zealous friends while protecting it from its evil enemies.

The tragedy of our day is the climate of fear in which we live, and fear breeds repression. Too often sinister threats to the Bill of Rights, to freedom of the mind, are concealed under the patriotic cloak of anti-communism.

I could add, from my own experience, that it is never necessary to call a man a communist to make political capital. Those of us who have undertaken to practice the ancient but imperfect art of government will always make enough mistakes to keep our critics well supplied with ammunition. There is no need for poison gas.

. . . Let me now, in my concluding words, inquire with you how we may affirm our patriotism in the troubled yet hopeful years that are ahead.

The central concern of the American Legion—the ideal which holds it together—the vitality which animates it—is patriotism. And those voices which we have heard most clearly and which are best remembered in our public life have always had the accent of patriotism.

It was always accounted a virtue in a man to love his country. With us it is now something more than a virtue. It is a necessity, a condition of survival. When an American says he loves his country, he means not only that he loves the New England hills, the prairies glistening in the sun, the wide and rising plains, the great mountains, and the sea. He means that he loves an inner air, an inner light in which freedom lives and in which a man can draw the breath of self-respect.

Men who have offered their lives for their country know that patriotism is not the fear of something; it is the love of something. Patriotism with us is not the hatred of Russia; it is the love of this

Republic and of the ideal of liberty of man and mind in which it was born, and to which this Republic is dedicated.

With this patriotism—patriotism in its large and wholesome meaning—America can master its power and turn it to the noble cause of peace. We can maintain military power without militarism; political power without oppression; and moral power without compulsion or complacency.

The road we travel is long, but at the end lies the grail of peace. And in the valley of peace we see the faint outlines of a new world, fertile and strong. It's odd that one of the keys to abundance should have been handed to civilization on a platter of destruction. But the power of the atom to work evil gives only the merest hint of its power for good.

I believe that man stands on the eve of his greatest day. I know, too, that that day is not a gift but a prize; that we shall not reach it until we have won it.

Legionnaires are united by memories of wars. Therefore, no group is more devoted to peace. I say to you now that there is work to be done, that the difficulties and dangers that beset our path at home and abroad are incalculable. There is sweat and sacrifice; there is much of patience and quiet persistence in our horoscope. Perhaps the goal is not even for us to see in our lifetime.

But we are embarked on a great adventure. Let us proclaim our faith in the future of man. Of good heart and good cheer, faithful to ourselves and our traditions, we can lift the cause of freedom, the cause of men so high no power on earth can tear it down. We can pluck this flower, safety, from this nettle, danger. Living, speaking, like men—like Americans—we can lead the way to our rendezvous in a happy, peaceful world.

Thank you—and forgive me for imposing on you so long.

*Chapter 9*

# THE CHECKERS SPEECH

Vice Presidential Nominee Richard Nixon Saves
His Place on the Republican Ticket and Launches
a Technological Revolution: 1952

IN AMERICAN POLITICAL history, no individual garnered
more votes and held an executive branch position longer than
Richard Milhous Nixon. From the years 1952 to 1972, in only
one election did the American people not have the opportunity to
cast a ballot for him.

Yet Nixon's vast impact on American politics and society almost
never happened. The nationally televised address, known popularly
as the Checkers speech, that Nixon gave on September 23, 1952,
saved his place on the 1952 GOP presidential ticket. Without this
speech, Richard Nixon might have been nothing more than a foot-
note in the annals of American history.

The Checkers speech is legendary, but it's hardly great oratory.
It was a speech that worked effectively "in a living room but not
in a lecture hall," says Kathleen Hall Jamieson.[1] In fact, it holds
dubious legitimacy in a collection of great presidential campaign
speeches, because it probably did more than any other utterance
by an American politician to undermine the role of speechwriting
in our nation's politics.

The Checkers speech is often cited as a seminal moment in American history, and it's not an undeserved recognition—but it was not because of the power of Nixon's metaphors, the insight of his political analysis, or the stirring nature of his rhetoric. Instead, the speech changed the way we think about our elected leaders. It demonstrated the ability of television to not only humanize candidates but also transform their interaction with voters. It was one of the first uses of television in a presidential campaign, and certainly among the most effective. But above all, it brought into clear relief the role of image making in American politics and heralded the slow transformation of speechwriting from oratory to image creation and maintenance. Great words would continue to be spoken after Checkers, but the relationship between politicians and voters would be forever transformed.

## A SECRET FUND

In 1952, Richard Nixon was a rising star in the Republican Party. A one-term senator from California, he had been tapped by Dwight Eisenhower as the party's vice presidential nominee. It was a meteoric rise for the thirty-nine-year-old Nixon, who had been in public office for only six years. Yet in September, it all threatened to come crashing down. A story in the *New York Post* alleged that Nixon had maintained a private fund of $18,000, supported by influential California backers. The implication of the "secret fund" revelation was that Nixon received money from wealthy backers in return for political favors, yet there was little evidence to suggest that the fund was illegal or unethical, or that those who donated to it ever influenced Nixon. At first, Nixon thought little of the story and assumed it would blow over (he tried to explain it away in part by blaming Communists and political opponents).[2] But the charges had the potential to be devastating.

Accusations of corruption in the Truman administration had been one of Ike's key campaign themes, so having an allegedly corrupt politician on the GOP ticket ran the risk of taking the wind out of the Republicans sails. "Nixon has got to be clean as a hound's tooth," Ike told reporters.[3] When the influential Republican newspaper the *New York Herald Tribune* published an editorial calling on the VP nominee to withdraw, Nixon found himself on the razor's edge. The *Herald Tribune* was the voice of the Eastern establishment, making the editorial akin to an order from the old general himself to get off the ticket.[4] Other papers soon followed suit in urging Nixon to go quietly into the night.[5]

Nixon now faced a terrible choice: go against every fiber of his being and leave the ticket or stay on and defy Eisenhower. Ironically, it was his wife, Pat, who helped to stiffen Nixon's spine. She told him in no uncertain terms that if "you . . . do not fight back but simply crawl away, you will destroy yourself. Your life will be marred forever."[6] His resolve slackened over the days to come, but Pat's never did. "You have to fight it all the way to the end, no matter what happens," she told him.[7] Nixon wasn't going anywhere; he refused to step down.

It was former GOP nominee Thomas Dewey who first broached the idea of a national address. But it was Eisenhower who delivered the message directly. When the two men spoke for the first time during the crisis, Eisenhower told Nixon to go on television and "tell them everything there is to tell, everything you can remember since the day you entered public life. Tell them about any money you have ever received."[8] Yet Ike still refused to commit to keeping him on the ticket even if he performed well, forcing a frustrated Nixon to peevishly tell the legendary figure that it was time "to shit or get off the pot."[9] Nixon prepared to go on national television before what was at the time the largest audience ever to hear a political speech, not knowing if even the best performance would save his skin.[10]

As if the pressure on Nixon were not great enough, a mere hour before he was to speak, Dewey called again. He reported the outcome of a meeting of Eisenhower's advisers, who decided that at the end of the broadcast, Nixon should submit his resignation from the ticket. Nixon was stunned, but he regained his composure enough to tell Dewey that, like the rest of the nation, he'd have to watch the speech to see what he did. But Nixon gave one inkling of what was to come: he furiously told Dewey to remind Ike and his advisers, "I know something about politics too."[11] Nixon forbade his staff from showing a copy of the speech to either Eisenhower or the reporters covering him. He didn't want advance press coverage to influence the viewing audience.[12] The final outcome would depend on how well Nixon convinced the American people, Eisenhower, and the national press corps that he deserved to stay.[13]

## "We're Gonna Keep It"

As Nixon prepared to leave his hotel for the broadcast studio, it had the feel of a man walking the plank. The Dewey call had shredded Nixon's already fragile psyche. With only minutes to go before the broadcast, he turned to Pat in the dressing room and told her he wasn't sure he could go through with it. "Of course you can," she sternly responded.[14]

Pat knew her husband. Nixon later recounted the calm that came over him as he began to speak:

All the tension suddenly went out of me . . . I was calm and confident. Despite the lack of sleep or even of rest over the past six days, despite the abuse to which I had subjected my nerves and body—some way, somehow in a moment of great crisis a man calls up resources of physical, mental, and emotional power he never realized he had. This I was now able to do, because the hours and days of preparations had been for this one moment and I put into it everything I had. I know what I wanted to say, and I said it from the heart.[15]

Ironically, for a figure who had shown an extraordinary level of disobedience to his boss, Nixon did exactly as his running mate suggested. He discussed his personal finances in excruciating detail, offering specifics about the cost of his home, his insurance policies, his salary, and so on. For all her encouragement, Pat hated the speech. "Why do we have to tell people how little we have and how much we owe?" she plaintively asked.[16]

At the outset, Nixon pledged to lay out the facts and answer the question of whether it was "morally" appropriate to maintain such a fund—yet he pretty much did neither. He proposed three criteria by which to judge his behavior: whether he personally profited, whether the fund was secret, and whether any of the contributors received special favors. Of course, those are legalistic questions, not issues of right and wrong. Moreover, he used the judgments of outside auditors and lawyers to assess the appropriateness of the fund, again avoiding the subject of moral culpability. Next, by laying out his personal finances, he presented himself as a man of humble origins, once again changing the subject away from the issue of whether the fund he maintained with the assistance of private and anonymous donors was morally improper.

But of course, the facts of the case were secondary to the image that Nixon was seeking to project. Nixon presented himself as a child of "modest circumstances" who worked in his family's grocery store to help make ends meet. He had been accused of operating an illegal slush fund from wealthy benefactors, but according to Nixon, he and his wife, Pat, were facing financial challenges "like so many of the young couples who may be listening to us." He told the audience that Pat didn't have a mink coat, but instead a "respectable Republican cloth coat," though of course "she'd look good in anything." Nixon even cited Abraham Lincoln and his paean to ordinary Americans: "God must have loved the common people—he made so many of them." (Nixon used the line after phoning his college English and history teachers and asking for help with appropriate Lincoln quotes.)[17]

Then, in the speech's most maudlin and notorious moment, he told the audience of a gift he had received from one supporter in Texas—"a little cocker spaniel dog" that Nixon's daughter Tricia named Checkers. "And you know, the kids love the dog and I just want to say this right now, that regardless of what they say about it, we're gonna keep it." The use of the dog was reminiscent of FDR's Fala speech—once again, all is fair in love, war, and politics, but let's keep the dogs out of it.

As was his nature, Nixon hardly eschewed partisanship in the speech. He took his Democratic rival for vice president, John Sparkman, to task for putting his own wife on his Senate payroll. He attacked the Democratic nominee, Adlai Stevenson, for having a similar fund and urged him to fully reveal the donors, hinting darkly that if he did otherwise, "there is a doubt that will be raised . . . and if they don't it will be an admission that they have something to hide."

Of course, by calling for full disclosure of the candidates' finances, he was implicitly including his running mate, Eisenhower, who was far from squeaky clean in that department. The point was not lost on Eisenhower, who as he listened to his putative running mate jabbed a pencil into a pad of paper at the words "something to hide." Nixon was playing to all his key audiences: the public, the newspaper editorial boards, and above all his patron, Eisenhower.[18]

Now feeling confident, Nixon stood up from the desk where he had been sitting and deepened his counterattack. He linked the stories about the personal fund to attacks launched against him for the espionage investigation of Alger Hiss, as if to insinuate that

those who were after Nixon wanted to prevent him from exposing Communist infiltration in the U.S. government—or maybe
were Communists themselves.

In the end, though, the basic issue was not Communism but
Nixon's character. Knowing now what we do about Richard
Nixon, it's difficult to read the Checkers speech and not come
away amused or even appalled. The image cultivated runs so
counter to the Watergate-era image of "Tricky Dick." Yet in
1952 Nixon presented himself as a simple and dedicated public
servant who was struggling financially to raise a family. His was a
lifestyle that seemed frugal and even humble.[19]

For years, the Democrats had won election after election by casting themselves as the defenders of the workingman. But here was
Richard Nixon fighting on Democratic turf, portraying himself as
an "ordinary American." As Robert Ruark, a Scripps-Howard
columnist, would say of Nixon's performance, "This came closer to
humanizing the Republican Party than anything that has happened
in my memory . . . Tuesday night the nation saw a little man,
squirming his way out of dilemma and laying bare his most-private
hopes, fears and liabilities. This time the common man was a Republican, for a change."[20]

Moreover, Nixon made specific and excellent use of the new
medium of television. He generally spoke off the cuff, looking
only occasionally at his script, and made frequent eye contact with
the camera. Making the presentation in a mock living room, with
his adoring wife nearby, further humanized Nixon. As a result, his
remarks seemed more casual and conversational than a formal
address.

At the end, Nixon ignored Dewey's pre-speech admonition
and instead asked the audience to send letters and telegrams to the
Republican National Committee (RNC) as to whether he should
stay. "Whatever their decision is, I will abide by it," said Nixon,
effectively taking the call out of Eisenhower's hands and putting it

in the people's. As Nixon said these words, Eisenhower jabbed his pencil against the pad again—but this time he did it so hard that the lead broke off with "an audible crack" that could be heard by all those present.[21] Eisenhower was no dummy; he knew he'd been outmaneuvered.

## THE PEOPLE HAVE THEIR SAY

Back in Los Angeles, Nixon was beside himself as the speech ended. Time had run out on the broadcast before he'd given the address to which people should send telegrams of support. He threw his speaking notes on the floor and declared the whole exercise a "flop."[22]

It was anything but. The response was overwhelming. Western Union reported that it had never received as many wires as it did that evening. Using a hundred volunteers, it took the RNC a month just to open and sort all the mail it received. Telegrams ran 200 to 1 in favor of Nixon; letters and postcards were 74 to 1.[23] According to one study of the responses, they told a compelling story: "As evidenced by listener responses, Nixon was perceived as embodying the ideals of honesty, sincerity, trustworthiness, love of family and of the common man. They saw him as a man who shared their own feelings, thought as they thought, and valued what they valued . . . they seemed to say 'We trust him; we believe in him because he is one of us.'"[24] Now that's an effective speech.

Editorial boards, particularly those with Republican leanings, were effusive in their praise. The *New York Journal American* said his performance was "simply magnificent." The *Detroit Free Press* called Nixon "a personality of deep sincerity."[25] The *St. Paul Pioneer Press* called him "a clean and true American."[26] In terms of "dramatic impact," an editorialist in the *Los Angeles Times* compared the speech favorably to King Edward VIII's abdication of the throne.[27]

Others, however, were not so kind. The *New York Post*, which had broken the story, called the event "a private soap opera" and complained that "Nixon promised to tell all. He pledged a full and detailed accounting of what he had done with the money raised for him. No such accounting was contained in his speech."[27] A somewhat overwrought Walter Lippmann was harsher, calling it the "most demeaning experience my country has ever had to bear."[29]

Countless others watched the speech and were disgusted by Nixon's treacly performance. For many Americans it was the moment that turned them into lifelong Nixon haters.[30]

But in the end, only one audience really mattered—Dwight Eisenhower. There was no way he'd be able to resist the overwhelming public support for Nixon. Two days later Ike welcomed Nixon back to the campaign trail in West Virginia with a clasp on the shoulder and a "You're my boy."[31] He announced that day that Nixon would stay on the ticket.

For Nixon personally, the speech had an equally dramatic and some might argue devastating effect. He would later write of the Checkers speech, "This speech was to be the most important of my life. I felt now that it was my battle alone. I had been deserted by so many I had thought were friends, but who panicked in battle when the first shot was fired."[32] It would not be difficult to imagine him using the same words to describe his mind-set during Watergate. The man-against-the-world paranoia that later would come to define Nixon's worldview was no doubt formed in part by the extraordinary sense of isolation he must have felt in the run-up to the Checkers speech.

In the end, Nixon and Eisenhower would romp to victory in November. But eight years later, when his turn came at the top of the ticket, television would be Nixon's downfall. It is the ultimate irony that the first American politician to effectively use television as a communication medium would be so badly upended by it. During his legendary presidential debates with John F. Kennedy in 1960, Nixon's sallow and less than polished appearance would doom his candidacy.

In the fall of 1952, Nixon's only goal was to keep his political future alive. Little did he know he'd help launch a technological and political revolution that would transform the way Americans choose their elected leaders.

*Richard Nixon Defends His "Secret Fund" in a Televised Address to the Nation, Los Angeles September 23, 1952*

My Fellow Americans, I come before you tonight as a candidate for the Vice Presidency and as a man whose honesty and integrity have been questioned.

The usual political thing to do when charges are made against you is to either ignore them or to deny them without giving details.

I believe we've had enough of that in the United States, particularly with the present Administration in Washington, D.C. To me the office of the Vice Presidency of the United States is a great office, and I feel that the people have got to have confidence in the integrity of the men who run for that office and who might obtain it.

I have a theory, too, that the best and only answer to a smear or to an honest misunderstanding of the facts is to tell the truth. And that's why I'm here tonight. I want to tell you my side of the case.

I am sure that you have read the charge and you've heard it that I, Senator Nixon, took $18,000 from a group of my supporters.

Now, was that wrong? And let me say that it was wrong—I'm saying, incidentally, that it was wrong and not just illegal. Because it isn't a question of whether it was legal or illegal, that isn't enough. The question is, was it morally wrong?

I say that it was morally wrong if any of that $18,000 went to Senator Nixon for my personal use. I say that it was morally wrong if it was secretly given and secretly handled. And I say that it was morally wrong if any of the contributors got special favors for the contributions that they made.

And now to answer those questions let me say this:

Not one cent of the $18,000 or any other money of that type ever went to me for my personal use. Every penny of it was used to pay for political expenses that I did not think should be charged to the taxpayers of the United States.

It was not a secret fund. As a matter of fact, when I was on "Meet the Press," some of you may have seen it last Sunday—Peter Edson came up to me after the program and he said, "Dick, what about this fund we hear about?" And I said, Well, there's no secret about it. Go out and see Dana Smith, who was the administrator of the fund. And I gave him his address, and I said that you will find that the purpose of the fund simply was to defray political expenses that I did not feel should be charged to the Government.

And third, let me point out, and I want to make this particularly clear, that no contributor to this fund, no contributor to any of my campaign, has ever received any consideration that he would not have received as an ordinary constituent.

I just don't believe in that and I can say that never, while I have been in the Senate of the United States, as far as the people that contributed to this fund are concerned, have I made a telephone call for them to an agency, or have I gone down to an agency in their behalf. And the records will show that, the records which are in the hands of the Administration.

But then some of you will say and rightly, "Well, what did you use the fund for, Senator? Why did you have to have it?"

Let me tell you in just a word how a Senate office operates. First of all, a Senator gets $15,000 a year in salary. He gets enough money to pay for one trip a year, a round trip that is, for himself and his family between his home and Washington, D.C.

And then he gets an allowance to handle the people that work in his office, to handle his mail. And the allowance for my State of California is enough to hire thirteen people.

And let me say, incidentally, that that allowance is not paid to the Senator—it's paid directly to the individuals that the Senator puts on his payroll, that all of these people and all of these allowances are for strictly official business. Business, for example, when a constituent writes in and wants you to go down to the Veterans Administration and get some information about his GI policy. Items of that type, for example.

But there are other expenses which are not covered by the Government. And I think I can best discuss those expenses by asking you some questions. Do you think that when I or any other Senator makes a political speech, has it printed, should charge the printing of that speech and the mailing of that speech to the taxpayers?

Do you think, for example, when I or any other Senator makes a trip to his home state to make a purely political speech that the cost of that trip should be charged to the taxpayers?

Do you think when a Senator makes political broadcasts or political television broadcasts, radio or television, that the expense of those broadcasts should be charged to the taxpayers?

Well, I know what your answer is. The same answer that audiences give me whenever I discuss this particular problem. The answer is "no." The taxpayers shouldn't be required to finance items which are not official business but which are primarily political business.

But then the question arises, you say, "Well, how do you pay for these and how can you do it legally?"

And there are several ways that it can be done, incidentally, and that it is done legally in the United States Senate and in the Congress.

The first way is to be a rich man. I don't happen to be a rich man so I couldn't use that.

Another way that is used is to put your wife on the payroll. Let me say, incidentally, my opponent, my opposite number for the Vice Presidency on the Democratic ticket, does have his wife on the payroll. And has had her on his payroll for the ten years—the past ten years.

Now just let me say this. That's his business and I'm not critical of him for doing that. You will have to pass judgment on that particular point. But I have never done that for this reason. I have found that there are so many deserving stenographers and secretaries in Washington that needed the work that I just didn't feel it was right to put my wife on the payroll.

My wife's sitting over here. She's a wonderful stenographer. She used to teach stenography and she used to teach shorthand in high school. That was when I met her. And I can tell you folks that she's worked many hours at night and many hours on Saturdays and Sundays in my office and she's done a fine job. And I'm proud to say tonight that in the six years I've been in the House and the Senate of the United States, Pat Nixon has never been on the Government payroll.

There are other ways that these finances can be taken care of. Some who are lawyers, and I happen to be a lawyer, continue to practice law. But I haven't been able to do that. I'm so far away from California that I've been so busy with my Senatorial work that I have not engaged in any legal practice.

And also as far as law practice is concerned, it seemed to me that the relationship between an attorney and the client was so personal that you couldn't possibly represent a man as an attorney and then have an unbiased view when he presented his case to you in the event that he had one before Government.

And so I felt that the best way to handle these necessary political expenses of getting my message to the American people and the speeches I made, the speeches that I had printed, for the most part concerned this one message—of exposing this Administration, the communism in it, the corruption in it—the only way that I could do that was to accept the aid which people in my home state of California who contributed to my campaign and who continued to make these contributions after I was elected were glad to make.

And let me say I am proud of the fact that not one of them has ever asked me for a special favor. I'm proud of the fact that not one of them has ever asked me to vote on a bill other than as my own conscience would dictate. And I am proud of the fact that the taxpayers by subterfuge or otherwise have never paid one dime for expenses which I thought were political and shouldn't be charged to the taxpayers.

Let me say, incidentally, that some of you may say, "Well, that's all right, Senator; that's your explanation, but have you got any proof?"

And I'd like to tell you this evening that just an hour ago we received an independent audit of this entire fund.

I suggested to Gov. Sherman Adams, who is the chief of staff of the Dwight Eisenhower campaign, that an independent audit and legal report be obtained. And I have that audit here in my hand.

It's an audit made by the Price, Waterhouse & Co. firm, and the legal opinion by Gibson, Dunn & Crutcher, lawyers in Los Angeles, the biggest law firm and incidentally one of the best ones in Los Angeles.

I'm proud to be able to report to you tonight that this audit and this legal opinion is being forwarded to General Eisenhower. And I'd like to read to you the opinion that was prepared by Gibson, Dunn & Crutcher and based on all the pertinent laws and statutes, together with the audit report prepared by the certified public accountants.

"It is our conclusion that Senator Nixon did not obtain any financial gain from the collection and disbursement of the fund by Dana Smith; that Senator Nixon did not violate any Federal or state law by reason of the operation of the fund; and that neither the portion of the fund paid by Dana Smith directly to third persons nor the portion paid to Senator Nixon to reimburse him for designated office expenses constituted income to the Senator which was either reportable or taxable as income under applicable tax laws. (signed) Gibson, Dunn & Crutcher by Alma H. Conway."

Now that, my friends, is not Nixon speaking, but that's an independent audit which was requested because I want the American people to know all the facts and I'm not afraid of having independent people go in and check the facts, and that is exactly what they did.

But then I realize that there are still some who may say, and rightfully so, and let me say that I recognize that some will continue to smear regardless of what the truth may be, but that there has been understandably some honest misunderstanding on this matter, and there are some that will say: "Well, maybe you were able, Senator, to fake this thing. How can we believe what you say? After all, is there a possibility that maybe you got some sums in cash? Is there a possibility that you may have feathered your own nest?"

And so now what I am going to do—and incidentally this is unprecedented in the history of American politics—I am going at this time to give to this television and radio audience a complete financial history; everything I've earned; everything I've spent; everything I owe. And I want you to know the facts. I'll have to start early.

I was born in 1913. Our family was one of modest circumstances and most of my early life was spent in a store out in East Whittier. It was a grocery store—one of those family enterprises. The only reason we were able to make it go was because my mother and dad had five boys and we all worked in the store.

I worked my way through college and to a great extent through law school. And then, in 1940, probably the best thing that ever happened to me happened. I married Pat—sitting over here. We had a rather difficult time after we were married, like so many of the young couples who may be listening to us. I practiced law; she continued to teach school. I went into the service.

Let me say that my service record was not a particularly unusual one. I went to the South Pacific. I guess I'm entitled to a couple of battle stars. I got a couple of letters of commendation but I was just there when the bombs were falling and then I returned. I returned to the United States and in 1946 I ran for the Congress.

When we came out of the war, Pat and I—Pat during the war had worked as a stenographer and in a bank and as an economist for a Government agency—and when we came out the total of our savings from both my law practice, her teaching and all the time that I was in the war—the total for that entire period was just a little less than $10,000. Every cent of that, incidentally, was in Government bonds.

Well that's where we start when I go into politics. Now what have I earned since I went into politics? Well here it is—I jotted it down, let me read the notes. First of all I've had my salary as a Congressman and as a Senator. Second, I have received a total in this past six years of $1,600 from estates which were in my law firm at the time that I severed my connection with it.

And, incidentally, as I said before, I have not engaged in any legal practice and have not accepted any fees from business that came into the firm after I went into politics. I have made an average of approximately $1,500 a year from non-political speaking engagements and lectures. And then, fortunately, we've inherited a little money. Pat sold her interest in her father's estate for $3,000 and I inherited $1,500 from my grandfather.

We live rather modestly. For four years we lived in an apartment in Park Fairfax, in Alexandria, Va. The rent was $80 a month. And we saved for the time that we could buy a house.

Now, that was what we took in. What did we do with this money? What do we have today to show for it? This will surprise you, because it is so little, I suppose, as standards generally go, of people in public life. First of all, we've got a house in Washington which cost $41,000 and on which we owe $20,000.

We have a house in Whittier, Calif., which cost $13,000 and on which we owe $3,000. My folks are living there at the present time.

I have just $4,000 in life insurance, plus my G.I. policy which I've never been able to convert and which will run out in two years. I have no life insurance whatever on Pat. I have no life in-surance on our two youngsters, Patricia and Julie. I own a 1950 Oldsmobile car. We have our furniture. We have no stocks and bonds of any type. We have no interest of any kind, direct or in-direct, in any business.

Now, that's what we have. What do we owe? Well, in addi-tion to the mortgage, the $20,000 mortgage on the house in Washington, the $10,000 one on the house in Whittier, I owe $4,500 to the Riggs Bank in Washington, D.C., with interest 4½ per cent.

I owe $3,500 to my parents and the interest on that loan which I pay regularly, because it's the part of the savings they made through the years they were working so hard, I pay regularly 4 per cent interest. And then I have a $500 loan which I have on my life insurance.

Well, that's about it. That's what we have and that's what we owe. It isn't very much but Pat and I have the satisfaction that every dime that we've got is honestly ours. I should say this—that Pat doesn't have a mink coat. But she does have a respectable Re-publican cloth coat. And I always tell her that she'd look good in anything.

One other thing I probably should tell you, because if I don't they'll probably be saying this about me too, we did get something—a gift—after the election. A man down in Texas heard Pat on the radio mention the fact that our two youngsters would like to have a dog. And, believe it or not, the day before we left on this campaign trip we got a message from Union Station in Baltimore saying they had a package for us. We went down to get it. You know what it was.

It was a little cocker spaniel dog in a crate that he sent all the way from Texas. Black and white spotted. And our little girl—Tricia, the 6-year-old—named it Checkers. And you know the kids love the dog and I just want to say this right now, that regardless of what they say about it, we're gonna keep it.

It isn't easy to come before a nation-wide audience and air your life as I've done. But I want to say some things before I conclude that I think most of you will agree on. Mr. Mitchell, the chairman of the Democratic National Committee, made the statement that if a man couldn't afford to be in the United States Senate he shouldn't run for the Senate.

And I just want to make my position clear. I don't agree with Mr. Mitchell when he says that only a rich man should serve his Government in the United States Senate or in the Congress.

I don't believe that represents the thinking of the Democratic party, and I know that it doesn't represent the thinking of the Republican party.

I believe that it's fine that a man like Governor Stevenson who inherited a fortune from his father can run for President. But I also feel that it's essential in this country of ours that a man of modest means can also run for President. Because, you know, remember Abraham Lincoln, you remember what he said: 'God must have loved the common people—he made so many of them.'

And now I'm going to suggest some courses of conduct.

First of all, you have read in the papers about other funds now. Mr. Stevenson, apparently, had a couple. One of them in which a group of business people paid and helped to supplement the salaries of state employes [sic]. Here is where the money went directly into their pockets.

And I think that what Mr. Stevenson should do should be to come before the American people as I have, give the names of the people that have contributed to that fund; give the names of the people who put this money into their pockets at the same time that they were receiving money from their state government, and see what favors, if any, they gave out for that.

I don't condemn Mr. Stevenson for what he did. But until the facts are in there is a doubt that will be raised.

And as far as Mr. Sparkman is concerned, I would suggest the same thing. He's had his wife on the payroll. I don't condemn him for that. But I think that he should come before the American people and indicate what outside sources of income he has had.

I would suggest that under the circumstances both Mr. Sparkman and Mr. Stevenson should come before the American people as I have and make a complete financial statement as to their financial history. And if they don't it will be an admission that they have something to hide. And I think you will agree with me.

Because folks, remember, a man that's to be President of the United States, a man that's to be Vice President of the United States must have the confidence of all the people. And that's why I'm doing what I'm doing, and that's why I suggest that Mr. Stevenson and Mr. Sparkman since they are under attack should do what they are doing.

Now, let me say this: I know that this is not the last of the smears. In spite of my explanation tonight other smears will be made; others have been made in the past. And the purpose of the smears, I know, is this—to silence me, to make me let up.

Well, they just don't know who they're dealing with. I'm going to tell you this: I remember in the dark days of the Hiss case some of the same columnists, some of the same radio commentators who are attacking me now and misrepresenting my position were violently opposing me at the time I was after Alger Hiss.

But I continued the fight because I knew I was right. And I can say to this great television and radio audience that I have no apologies to the American people for my part in putting Alger Hiss where he is today.

And as far as this is concerned, I intend to continue the fight.

Why do I feel so deeply? Why do I feel that in spite of the smears, the misunderstandings, the necessities for a man to come up here and bare his soul as I have? Why is it necessary for me to continue this fight?

And I want to tell you why. Because, you see, I love my country. And I think my country is in danger. And I think that the only man that can save America at this time is the man that's running for President on my ticket—Dwight Eisenhower.

You say, "Why do I think it is in danger?" and I say look at the record. Seven years of the Truman-Acheson Administration and what's happened? Six hundred million people lost to the Communists, and a war in Korea in which we have lost 117,000 American casualties.

And I say to all of you that a policy that results in a loss of 600,000,000 to the Communists and a war which cost us 117,000 American casualties isn't good enough for America.

And I say that those in the State Department that made the mistakes which caused that war and which resulted in those losses should be kicked out of the State Department just as fast as we get 'em out of there.

And let me say that I know Mr. Stevenson won't do that. Because he defends the Truman policy and I know that Dwight Eisenhower will do that, and that he will give America the leadership that it needs.

Take the problem of corruption. You've read about the mess in Washington. Mr. Stevenson can't clean it up because he was picked by the man, Truman, under whose Administration the mess was made. You wouldn't trust a man who made the mess to clean it up—that's Truman. And by the same token you can't trust the man who was picked by the man that made the mess to clean it up—and that's Stevenson.

And so I say, Eisenhower, who owes nothing to Truman, nothing to the big city bosses, he is the man that can clean up the mess in Washington.

Take communism. I say that as far as that subject is concerned, the danger is great to America. In the Hiss case they got the secrets which enabled them to break the American secret State Department code. They got secrets in the atomic bomb case which enabled them to get the secret of the atomic bomb, five years before they would have gotten it by their own devices.

And I say that any man who called the Alger Hiss case a "red herring" isn't fit to be President of the United States. I say that a man who like Mr. Stevenson has pooh-poohed and ridiculed the Communist threat in the United States—he said that they are phantoms among ourselves; he's accused us that have attempted to expose the Communists of looking for Communists in the Bureau of Fisheries and Wildlife—I say that a man who says that isn't qualified to be President of the United States.

And I say that the only man who can lead us in this fight to rid the Government of both those who are Communists and those who have corrupted this Government is Eisenhower, because Eisenhower, you can be sure, recognizes the problem and he knows how to deal with it.

Now let me say that, finally, this evening I want to read to you just briefly excerpts from a letter which I received, a letter which, after all this is over, no one can take away from me. It reads as follows:

"Dear Senator Nixon,

"Since I'm only 19 years of age I can't vote in this Presidential election but believe me if I could you and General Eisenhower would certainly get my vote. My husband is in the Fleet Marines in Korea. He's a corpsman on the front lines and we have a two-month-old son he's never seen. And I feel confident that with great Americans like you and General Eisenhower in the White House, lonely Americans like myself will be united with their loved ones now in Korea.

"I only pray to God that you won't be too late. Enclosed is a small check to help you in your campaign. Living on $85 a month [it] is all I can afford at present. But let me know what else I can do."

Folks, it's a check for $10, and it's one that I will never cash.

And just let me say this. We hear a lot about prosperity these days but I say, why can't we have prosperity built on peace rather than prosperity built on war? Why can't we have prosperity and an honest government in Washington, D.C., at the same time. Believe me, we can. And Eisenhower is the man that can lead this crusade to bring us that kind of prosperity.

And now, finally, I know that you wonder whether or not I am going to stay on the Republican ticket or resign.

Let me say this: I don't believe that I ought to quit because I am not a quitter. And, incidentally, Pat's not a quitter. After all, her name was Patricia Ryan and she was born on St. Patrick's Day, and you know the Irish never quit.

But the decision, my friends, is not mine. I would do nothing that would harm the possibilities of Dwight Eisenhower to become President of the United States. And for that reason I am submitting to the Republican National Committee tonight through this television broadcast the decision which it is theirs to make.

Let them decide whether my position on the ticket will help or hurt. And I am going to ask you to help them decide. Wire and write the Republican National Committee whether you think I should stay on or whether I should get off. And whatever their decision is, I will abide by it.

But just let me say this last word. Regardless of what happens I'm going to continue this fight. I'm going to campaign up and down America until we drive the crooks and the Communists and those that defend them out of Washington. And remember, folks, Eisenhower is a great man. Believe me. He's a great man. And a vote for Eisenhower is a vote for what's good for America.

## Chapter 10

## "I SHALL GO TO KOREA"

### Dwight D. Eisenhower Vanquishes
### the Isolationists: 1952

B Y THE FALL of 1952, there were few individuals as revered in the United States as General Dwight D. Eisenhower. The hero of Normandy, Ike had continued his service to the nation as supreme commander of NATO. Not surprisingly, both Democrats and Republicans had tried to bring Eisenhower into their respective camps to run for president. But Ike's core beliefs had less to do with party labels and more with his commitment to internationalism and U.S. global leadership at the dawn of the Cold War. Maintaining America's global responsibilities was the touchstone that motivated Ike's political career. To realize that goal, Eisenhower would have to run as a Republican and set an internationalist course for not only the Republican Party but also the country. The race for the White House in 1952 would give him just that opportunity.

For more than a generation, the Republican Party had been in thrall to its isolationist wing. Though the party continued to nominate palatable moderates such as Thomas Dewey and Wendell Willkie, in Congress the isolationists held sway—consistently voting against President Roosevelt's rearmament

strategy and counseling non-intervention on the brink of World
War II.

By 1952 the party was still controlled by leaders such as Robert
Taft, "Mr. Republican," a committed isolationist and the likely
GOP presidential nominee, who even after the tumult of World
War II wanted to see America pull back from its global responsibilities. To Eisenhower, leaders such as Taft were anathema to his
own worldview. Eisenhower simply didn't believe that Taft was
up to the job of president in a time when America's global leadership was crucial in the fight against Communism. In February
1951 a secret meeting was brokered between the two men at
which Taft's sparse knowledge of foreign affairs was evident. The
general later said of his erstwhile opponent that he was "a very
stupid man" with "no intellectual ability, nor any comprehension
of the issues of the world."[1]

While some still hold strong to the notion that Eisenhower was
drafted for the Republican nomination and did little of his own
politicking, it seems clear today that Ike actively sought the presidency. In the years leading up to the 1952 election, Ike gave repeated addresses that cultivated his image as "a warrior for peace,
a devotee of freedom, an apostle of cooperation, and a man of
deep humility who represented the aspirations of a war-weary
generation."[2] Yet the purpose was one born as much out of sacrifice as it was naked political expediency.

The evidence is substantial that Ike was motivated to run because of his devotion to "duty, honor and country" rather than his
own personal political ambitions.[3] As he told friends, "Anybody is
a damn fool if he actually seeks to be President."[4]


## THE COMMUNIST THREAT

At the GOP convention in July 1952 Eisenhower bested Taft to
win the party's nomination. But defeating the isolationists was

only the first part of Ike's challenge. The second was to bring the vanquished Taft supporters, the party's rabid anti-Communists, and the internationalists into a political coalition. Ike would use Communism and the war in Korea to accomplish this political high-wire balancing act.

At the outset of the campaign, Ike's comments on foreign policy issues and anti-Communism in general were relatively moderate in tone. It was a far cry from the more bellicose attitudes of many in the GOP who were constantly and aggressively attacking the lame-duck Truman and his administration for not only its failure at home but also its "capitulation" to the Communists in China.

But as the campaign heated up, Eisenhower could tell where the political winds were blowing, and his words began to take a similarly heated tone. He strongly attacked the Democrats—and in particular the familiar Republican target of Secretary of State Dean Acheson—for their stewardship of American foreign policy. He also began employing more virulent anti-Communist rhetoric, openly endorsing the GOP attack line that Democrats had "lost China" and more implicitly supporting the notion of "sell-out" to the Soviets at Yalta in 1945—a key Republican talking point.

In August, Eisenhower went before the American Legion and pledged a policy of "liberation" for Eastern Europe to free these captive nations from Communist domination. This was tough and even dangerous rhetoric that led many to argue Eisenhower was risking war with the Soviets.

But it wasn't until late September that Eisenhower began to utilize the incendiary words of the far right in attacking Democrats for underestimating the Red threat both at home and abroad. In October, during an infamous campaign trip to Wisconsin, where Ike omitted words from his prepared text condemning Senator Joseph McCarthy, he sounded a harshly anti-Communist tone, warning of "contamination in some degree of virtually every department, every agency, every bureau, every section of our Government."[5] His language represented a new and aggressive attack from a politician who not only exuded moderation and stability but also was deeply respected by most Americans. Columnist Ernest K. Lindley would write of Eisenhower, "I have never before heard a presidential candidate say quite so much which sounded so little like himself." [6] Yet Ike was now a politician who needed to mollify the anti-Communist and isolationist wings of his own party—and also put his Democratic opponent on the defensive.

However, by linking himself so closely with the anti-Democratic rhetoric of those on the extreme right, Eisenhower was helping cultivate the new partisan divide that was emerging between the two parties over the best means for confronting Communism. His comments gave credibility to more hard-edged Republicans, particularly Ike's running mate, Richard Nixon. For many Americans, the type of talk that Eisenhower was employing didn't seem unusual—they had been getting it from Republican politicians for several years. But to hear such talk from "the General" was something else altogether.

## EISENHOWER TALKS ABOUT KOREA

Not surprisingly, no other issue would come to dominate the 1952 election as significantly as the Korean War, which began in June 1950 and by the eve of Election Day in 1952 saw American and Chinese troops battling along the Thirty-eighth Parallel. By the time Ike had resigned from the military in June 1952 to run for president, more than twenty thousand Americans had died in the conflict and the war was at a standstill, with neither side able to score a clear military advantage.

Growing voter anxiety over the Korean situation demanded that Eisenhower speak more explicitly about the issue. (By late October more than half of the electorate cited the war as their number one concern.[7]) A speech in Detroit a mere week before the election would give the general just such an opportunity. According to Emmet Hughes, Eisenhower's speechwriter, "The origin of the speech was simple and inexorable in political logic . . . It rose from the need to say something affirmative on the sharpest issue of the day—*without* engaging in frivolous assurances and *without* binding a future administration to policies or actions fashioned in mid-campaign by any distorting temptations of domestic politics."[8]

Hughes was articulating an approach that would come to fundamentally define campaign trail rhetoric on questions of foreign policy. Politicians do not want to be tied down to campaign-driven foreign policy positions, preferring to maintain maximum flexibility should they win the White House. (Eisenhower's running mate, Richard Nixon, would use this approach brilliantly vis-à-vis Vietnam during his 1968 presidential campaign.) Ike wanted to reassure the American people that he would bring peace, but how . . . well, that was something that he would hold off deciding until he became president. At the Masonic Temple in Detroit on October 24, 1952, Eisenhower would follow Hughes's counsel, giving Americans not a policy road map but instead a pledge—and a commitment to peace.

Ike brought to the speechwriting process an unusually high level of experience. When stationed in the Philippines, Eisenhower had served as the military speechwriter for General Douglas MacArthur. While Eisenhower was not a stirring rhetorician, Hughes believed that Ike had a rare facility with the written word: "The man whose own sense of syntax, as displayed over years of presidential press conferences, would invite smiles and jokes, possessed, nonetheless, a remarkably quick and exacting faculty for editing."[9] Throughout his campaign speeches, Ike consistently avoided inexactitude and imprecision—he was a man who wanted no ambiguity in his addresses, but direct, forthright language.

Indeed, he barely edited the "Korea" speech, changing only the phrasing of his declaration "I shall go to Korea" so that it stood out more emphatically."[10]

Such an approach is obvious in Eisenhower's address at Detroit's Masonic Temple. His oratory was nowhere near as eloquent as that of his opponent, Adlai Stevenson. Instead, the speech was a virtual prosecutor's brief. Eisenhower laid out the "facts" to the electorate, making a persuasive case for Democratic failure in Korea. "It was never inevitable, it was never inescapable . . . The Korean War—more perhaps than any other war in history—simply and swiftly followed the collapse of our political defenses . . . we failed to read and to outwit the totalitarian mind," Eisenhower argued. Such an attack had deep, symbolic ramifications. If Democrats were unable to outwit the North Koreans, how could they stand toe-to-toe with the much larger and significant Soviet threat? The message was clear: Democrats failed to understand either the true nature of the enemy or the challenges that America was facing.[11]

In his precise style Eisenhower depicted in excruciating and often devastating detail the Truman administration's miscues in Korea. He noted the many warnings from the military as well as Republican lawmakers that the withdrawal of American troops from the Korean peninsula would lead to the invasion and occupation of the South. Finally, he referred to Acheson's disastrous "defense perimeter" comment, which had conspicuously left Korea out of the zone of American military responsibility. The litany of missteps and missed opportunities cited by Eisenhower was overwhelming and difficult for any Democrat to rebut:

The responsibility for this record cannot be dodged or evaded. Even if not a single Republican leader had warned so clearly against the coming disaster, the responsibility for the fateful political decisions would still rest wholly with the men charged with making those decisions—in the Department of State and in the White House. They cannot escape that responsibility now or ever.

But Eisenhower went beyond simply harping on Democratic failure, laying out a number of proposals for ending the war (albeit all lacking in detail or specificity). One of these, however, would captivate the American people and convince them of Eisenhower's sincerity about ending the war—the simple pledge "I shall go to Korea." When he spoke the words in Detroit, the crowd "stood up and cheered in a way few American political meetings have heard."[12] Thunderous applause arose outside the hall as well, as the campaign had set up outdoor speakers to handle the overflow crowd. Traveling reporters quickly understood the ramifications of Ike's comments: an Associated Press reporter, upon hearing Eisenhower's pledge packed up his things, left the press train, and declared the election over.[13]

The combination of Eisenhower's deep reservoir of public respect on military matters, the litany of the Truman administration's failures in Korea, and the desire among the American people for an end to the war would prove electrifying.

In fact, it is because of these five words that this speech is considered "one of the most effective campaign speeches of modern times."[14] But Eisenhower would take the message a step further by presenting the American people with a stark choice, one that hardly could be taken lightly: "In rendering their verdict, the people must judge with courage and with wisdom. For—at this date—any faltering in America's leadership is a capital offense against freedom. In this trial, my testimony, of a personal kind, is quite simple. A soldier all my life, I have enlisted in the greatest cause of my life—the cause of peace."

Even though Eisenhower's rhetoric was taking on martial tones, he still understood the need to leave his audience with a hopeful message for the future—something that more extreme Republicans seemed incapable of providing.

Finally, Ike would present the American people with a rallying point for the challenges to come. "I do not believe it a presumption for me to call the effort of all who have enlisted with me—a crusade. I use that word only to signify two facts. First: We are united and devoted to a just cause of the purest meaning to all humankind. Second: We know that—for all the might of our effort—victory can come only with the gift of God's help. In this spirit—humble servants of a proud ideal—we do soberly say: This is a crusade."

While it is likely that Eisenhower would have won the election even without the Detroit speech, after twenty years of Democratic rule and Truman's unlikely victory four years earlier, nothing could ever be taken for granted.

But Eisenhower's speech resonated for far longer than the ten days leading up to Election Day, 1952. While most remember Eisenhower's pledge to go to Korea, the campaign's most lasting legacy was its ability to bring the internationalist and hawkish wings of the Republican Party together. At the same time Eisenhower was aligning himself with the language of the more radical anti-Communist wing of the Republican Party he still maintained his well-earned credibility as a moderate and above all a safe leader who could be trusted on national security affairs. Throughout the late stages of the 1952 campaign, Eisenhower figured out how to straddle both sides of that fence. In short, he was cobbling together a GOP coalition that would give him the flexibility he needed to govern the nation effectively and chart a more internationalist direction for American foreign policy. Moreover, by staking out the middle ground, and championing muscular internationalism, Eisenhower's subsequent victory would ensure that the isolationists would never again hold sway in the Republican Party.

In the end, this would be one of Eisenhower's great legacies: the embrace in both parties of the nation's emerging global responsibilities. While Democrats and Republicans would spend much of the Cold War arguing over who was tougher against the Communist threat (with the GOP generally winning), a bipartisan and internationalist foreign policy consensus was put into place— one that would dominate American politics for the next half century and help win the Cold War.

## Dwight D. Eisenhower Addresses the Korean Crisis at the Masonic Temple, Detroit, October 24, 1952

In this anxious autumn for America, one fact looms above all others in our people's mind. One tragedy challenges all men dedicated to the work of peace. One word shouts denial to those who foolishly pretend that ours is not a nation at war. This fact, this tragedy, this word is: Korea.

A small country—Korea has been, for more than two years, the battleground for the costliest foreign war our nation has fought, excepting the two world wars. It shall been the burial ground for 20,000 American dead. It has been another historic field of honor for the valor and skill and tenacity of American soldiers.

All these things it has been—and yet one thing more. It has been a symbol—a telling symbol—of the foreign policy of our nation.

It has been a sign—a warning sign—of the way the administration has conducted our world affairs.

It has been a measure—a damning measure—of the quality of leadership we have been given.

Tonight I am going to talk about our foreign policy and of its supreme symbol—the Korean War. I am not going to give you elaborate generalizations—but hard, tough facts. I am going to state the unvarnished truth.

What, then, are the plain facts?

The biggest fact about the Korean War is this: it was never inevitable, it was never inescapable. No fantastic fiat of history decreed that little South Korea—in the summer of 1950—would fatally tempt Communist aggressors as their easiest victim. No demonic destiny decreed that America had to be bled this way in order to keep South Korea free and to keep freedom itself self-respecting.

We are not mute prisoners of history. That is a doctrine for totalitarians. It is no creed for free men.

There is a Korean War—and we are fighting it—for the simplest of reasons: because free leadership failed to check and to turn back Communist ambition before it savagely attacked us. The Korean War—more perhaps than any other war in history—simply and swiftly followed the collapse of our political defenses. There is no other reason than this: we failed to read and to outwit the totalitarian mind.

I know something of this totalitarian mind. Through the years of World War II, I carried a heavy burden of decision in the free world's crusade against the tyranny then threatening us all. Month after month, year after year, I had to search out and to weigh the strengths and weaknesses of an enemy driven by the lust to rule the great globe itself.

World War II should have taught us all one lesson. The lesson is this: to vacillate, to hesitate—to appease even by merely betraying unsteady purpose—is to feed a dictator's appetite for conquest and to invite war itself.

That lesson—which should have firmly guided every great decision of our leadership through these later years—was ignored in the development of the administration's policies for Asia since the end of World War II. Because it was ignored, the record of these policies is a record of appalling failure.

The record of failure dates back—with red-letter folly—at least to September of 1947. It was then that General Albert Wedemeyer—returned from a Presidential mission to the Far East—submitted to the President this warning: "The withdrawal of American military forces from Korea would result in the occupation of South Korea by either Soviet troops or, as seems more likely, by the Korean military units trained under Soviet auspices in North Korea."

That warning and his entire report were disregarded and suppressed by the administration.

The terrible record of these years reaches its dramatic climax in a series of unforgettable scenes on Capitol Hill in June of 1949. By then the decision to complete withdrawal of American forces from Korea—despite menacing signs from the North—had been drawn up by the Department of State . . . [The Secretary of State] and his aides faced a group of Republican Congressmen both skeptical and fearful.

What followed was historic and decisive.

. . . First: Republican Congressman John Lodge of Connecticut asked "(Do) you feel that the Korean Government is able to fill the vacuum caused by the withdrawal of the occupation forces?"

The administration answered: "Definitely."

Second: A very different estimate of the risk involved came from Republican Congressman Walter Judd of Minnesota. He warned: "I think the thing necessary to give security to Korea at this stage of the game is the presence of a small American force and the knowledge (on the Soviet side) that attack upon it would bring trouble with us." "I am convinced," Representative Judd continued, "that if we keep even a battalion there, they are not going to move. And if the battalion is not there"—listen now to his warning—"the chances are they will move within a year."

What a tragedy that the administration shrugged off that so accurate warning!

Third: The Secretary of State was asked if he agreed that the South Koreans alone—and I quote—"will be able to defend themselves against any attack from the northern half of the country." To this the Secretary answered briskly: "We share that same view. Yes, sir."

Rarely in Congressional testimony has so much misinformation been compressed so efficiently into so few words.

. . . Finally: This remarkable scene of the summer of 1949 ends with a memorable document. The Minority Report of five Republican members of the House Foreign Affairs Committee on July 26, 1949, submitted this solemn warning.

. . . "It is reliably reported that Soviet troops, attached to the

North Korean puppet armies, are in position of command as well as acting as advisors. This development may well presage the launching of a full-scale military drive across the 38th Parallel. Our forces have been withdrawn from South Korea at the very instant when logic and common sense both demanded no retreat from the realities of the situation." The report continues: "Already along the 38th Parallel aggression is speaking with the too-familiar voices of howitzers and cannons. Our position is untenable and indefensible. The House should be aware of these facts."

These words of eloquent, reasoned warning were spoken eleven months before the Korean War broke.

Behind these words was a fervent, desperate appeal. That appeal was addressed to the administration. It begged at least some firm statement of American intention that might deter the foreseen attack.

What was the administration answer to that appeal?

The first answer was silence—stubborn, sullen silence for six months.

Then, suddenly, came speech—a high government official at long last speaking out on Asia. It was now January of 1950. What did he say? He said, "The United States Government will not provide military aid or advice to Chinese forces on Formosa."

Then, one week later, the Secretary of State announced his famous "defense perimeter"—publicly advising our enemies that, so far as nations outside this perimeter were concerned, "no person can guarantee these areas against military attack." Under these circumstances, it was cold comfort to the nations outside this perimeter to be reminded that they could appeal to the United Nations.

These nations, of course, included Korea. The armies of Communism, thus informed, began their big build-up. Six months later they were ready to strike across the 38th Parallel. They struck on June 25, 1950.

On that day, the record of political and diplomatic failure of this administration was completed and sealed.

The responsibility for this record cannot be dodged or evaded. Even if not a single Republican leader had warned so clearly against the coming disaster, the responsibility for the fateful political decisions would still rest wholly with the men charged with making those decisions—in the Department of State and in the White House. They cannot escape that responsibility now or ever.

When the enemy struck, on that June day of 1950, what did America do? It did what it always has done in all its times of peril. It appealed to the heroism of its youth. This appeal was utterly right and utterly inescapable. It was inescapable not only because this was the only way to defend the idea of collective freedom against savage aggression. That appeal was inescapable because there was now in the plight into which we had stumbled no other way to save honor and self-respect.

The answer to that appeal has been what any American knew it would be. It has been sheer valor—valor on all the Korean mountain-sides that, each day, bear fresh scars of new graves.

Now—in this anxious autumn—from these heroic men there comes back an answering appeal. It is no whine, no whimpering plea. It is a question that addresses itself to simple reason. It asks: Where do we go from here? When comes the end? Is there an end?

. . . To these questions there are two false answers—both equally false. The first would be any answer that dishonestly pledged an end to war in Korea by any imminent, exact date. Such a pledge would brand its speaker as a deceiver.

The second and equally false answer declares that nothing can be done to speed a secure peace. It dares to tell us that we, the strongest nation in the history of freedom, can only wait—and wait—and wait. Such a statement brands its speaker as a defeatist.

My answer—candid and complete—is this:

The first task of a new administration will be to review and re-examine every course of action open to us with one goal in view: to bring the Korean War to an early and honorable end. This is my pledge to the American people.

For this task a wholly new administration is necessary. The reason for this is simple. The old administration cannot be expected to repair what it failed to prevent.

Where will a new administration begin?

It will begin with its President taking a simple, firm resolution. The resolution will be: to [forgo] the diversions of politics and to concentrate on the job of ending the Korean War—until that job is honorably done.

That job requires a personal trip to Korea.

I shall make that trip. Only in that way could I learn how best to serve the American people in the cause of peace.

I shall go to Korea.

That is my second pledge to the American people.

Carefully, then, this new administration, unfettered by past decisions and inherited mistakes, can review every factor—military, political and psychological—to be mobilized in speeding a just peace.

Progress along at least two lines can instantly begin. We can—first—step up the program of training and arming the South Korean forces. Manifestly, under the circumstances of today, United Nations forces cannot abandon that unhappy land. But just as troops of the Republic of Korea covet and deserve the honor of defending their frontiers, so should we give them maximum assistance to insure their ability to do so.

. . . We must carefully weigh all interrelated courses of action. We will, of course, constantly confer with associated free nations of Asia and with the cooperating members of the United Nations. Thus we could bring into being a practical plan for world peace.

That is my third pledge to you.

As the next administration goes to work for peace, we must be guided at every instant by that lesson I spoke of earlier . . . To vacillate, to appease, to placate is only to invite war—vaster war—bloodier war. In the words of the late Senator Vandenberg,* appeasement is not the road to peace; it is only surrender on the installment plan.

I will always reject appeasement.

And that is my fourth pledge to you.

A nation's foreign policy is a much graver matter than rustling papers and bustling conferences. It is much more than diplomatic decisions and trade treaties and military arrangements.

A foreign policy is the face and voice of a whole people. It is all that the world sees and hears and understands about a single nation. It expresses the character and the faith and the will of that nation. In this, a nation is like any individual of our personal acquaintance; the simplest gesture can betray hesitation or weakness, the merest inflection of voice can reveal doubt or fear.

It is in this deep sense that our foreign policy has faltered and failed.

For a democracy, a great election, such as this, signifies a most solemn trial. It is the time when—to the bewilderment of all tyrants—the people sit in judgment upon the leaders. It is the time when these leaders are summoned before the bar of public decision. There they must give evidence both to justify their actions and explain their intentions.

In the great trial of this election, the judges—the people—must not be deceived into believing that the choice is between isolationism and internationalism. That is a debate of the dead past. The vast majority of Americans of both parties know that to keep

---

*This refers to Senator Arthur Vandenberg, Republican from Michigan, who "converted" from isolationism to internationalism and was one of the architects of America's Cold War foreign policy consensus.

their own nation free, they bear a majestic responsibility for freedom through all the world. As practical people, Americans also know the critical necessity of unimpaired access to raw materials on other continents for our own economic and military strength.

Today the choice—the real choice—lies between policies that assume that responsibility awkwardly and fearfully—and policies that accept that responsibility with sure purpose and firm will. The choice is between foresight and blindness, between doing and apologizing, between planning and improvising.

In rendering their verdict, the people must judge with courage and with wisdom. For—at this date—any faltering in America's leadership is a capital offense against freedom. In this trial, my testimony, of a personal kind, is quite simple. A soldier all my life, I have enlisted in the greatest cause of my life—the cause of peace.

I do not believe it a presumption for me to call the effort of all who have enlisted with me—a crusade.

I use that word only to signify two facts. First: We are united and devoted to a just cause of the purest meaning to all humankind. Second: We know that—for all the might of our effort—victory can come only with the gift of God's help.

In this spirit—humble servants of a proud ideal—we do soberly say: This is a crusade.

# Chapter 11

## THE NEW FRONTIER

### John F. Kennedy Challenges a Generation of Americans: 1960

MANY OF THE speeches in this collection focus on a singular question: what is the role of the government in the lives of the American people? In 1960, John F. Kennedy turned that concept on its head, instead posing the rhetorical question: what is the role of the American people in the life of their nation and their government?

This idea, captured in Kennedy's acceptance speech at the 1960 Democratic convention and even more famously followed up in his inaugural address, presented the American people with a clear choice for the future—and offered a political philosophy that representead a sea change from what many Americans, including Kennedy, saw as the "bland, vapid, self-satisfied, banal society" of the 1950s.[1]

In his acceptance speech, John Kennedy did not offer empty promises. Instead, he beseeched the American people to join him in confronting the grave challenges facing the nation at the dawn of the 1960s. Kennedy was unabashedly explicit on this point: "The New Frontier of which I speak is not a set of promises, it is a set of challenges. It sums up not what I intend to offer the

American people, but what I intend to ask of them. It appeals to their pride, not to their pocketbook—it holds out the promise of more sacrifice instead of more security." Kennedy made no grand promises to his audience (one would be hard pressed to identify any specific policy agenda or plan of action for a Kennedy presidency in this speech); rather, he belittled those who would offer the American people nothing more than a "golden future." And he bemoaned the fact that "too many Americans have lost their way, their will, and their sense of historic purpose."

During the campaign of 1960 there was a growing sense in America that the nation was facing a true crisis of confidence. There was a belief that America had become too enamored with materialism and newfound domestic tranquility to face the grave challenges of inequality at home and the Communist threat overseas. Kennedy's goal was, above all, to right the national ship and prepare the country for the great challenges that lay ahead. To accomplish his goal, he fell back on familiar terrain.

## THE SPIRIT OF THE AMERICAN FRONTIER

The greatest political speeches generally evoke the powerful imagery of American folklore, political tradition, and national exceptionalism. Throughout American history national leaders have wrapped themselves in the iconic imagery of great national events, revered political figures, or founding American myths. Kennedy took this approach in 1960 by casting his acceptance speech in the deeply rooted concept of the American frontier. Standing in the windswept Los Angeles Coliseum at the edge of the great North American landmass that American pioneers had conquered and settled, JFK drew upon the powerful and mythic image of opportunity and promise that the frontier has always evoked in the nation's political culture.

In the early days of the republic, the frontier was a literal place, the great unsettled and untamed world beyond the original thirteen colonies. At the turn of the century, Frederick Jackson Turner had argued in his seminal "The Significance of the Frontier in American History" that once this land was settled, the nation began to seek not only a new "frontier" but also the opportunity to live up to the ideal of the frontiersman—the rugged individual who, armed with nothing more than a six-gun and the fundamental spirit of American ingenuity, had tamed the great North American continent. Turner's "frontier thesis" would become the defining political image for generations of progressive and liberal candidates.[2]

While many would invoke this image, few would do it as effectively as Kennedy. At a time when he was asking Americans to give more of themselves, it was a natural and resonant rhetorical trope.

Kennedy noted that all Americans must play a role in helping fight what he would later call the "long, twilight struggle" of tyranny, poverty, disease and war. "The pioneers of old gave up their safety, their comfort and sometimes their lives to build a new world here in the West. They were not the captives of their own doubts, the prisoners of their own price tags. Their motto was not 'every man for himself'—but 'all for the common cause.'" Of the American people, Kennedy asked the same.

The future president challenged the American people to be true to that rich American legacy and make a clear choice, "not merely between two men or two parties, but between the public interest and private comfort—between national greatness and national decline—between the fresh air of progress and the stale, dank atmosphere of 'normalcy'—between determined dedication and creeping mediocrity." His evocation of Harding's "return to normalcy" was a none too subtle swipe at those who believed America could maintain the status quo.

For those not alive in the 1960s, it may sometimes seem difficult to understand the absolute veneration many felt for John F. Kennedy. He was to a large extent a president of tragically unfulfilled promise. His foreign policy record was mixed, from the extraordinary (defusing the Cuban missile crisis) to the desultory (the disastrous Bay of Pigs invasion, his underwhelming performance at the Vienna summit with Soviet premier Nikita Khrushchev, and expanded U.S. involvement in Vietnam). His domestic record, while stronger, saw foot-dragging on the issue of civil rights.

But, like few presidents in American history, Kennedy understood the power of the bully pulpit. He challenged his audiences, he openly spoke of sacrifice in the name of patriotism, and he was willing to confront unpleasant untruths and seemingly intractable challenges. As he said at the opening of his acceptance speech, "The times are too grave, the challenge too urgent, and the stakes too high—to permit the customary passions of political debate." Recognizing the need to bring the country together, Kennedy largely eschewed any significant policy discussion, believing that to do so would risk dividing the nation between those who supported Democratic policies and those who did not. Kennedy felt that unity in facing great national challenges was too great a goal to take the chance of becoming mired in the specific details of fiscal, education, or health care policy.[3]

More directly, Kennedy was speaking to a new generation of leaders and citizens. These were not the baby boomers of today but the so-called greatest generation, which had ensured America's victory against the challenge of fascism during World War II. "All over the world, particularly in the newer nations, young men are coming to power—men who are not bound by the traditions of the past—men who are not blinded by the old fears and hates and rivalries—young men who can cast off the old slogans and delusions and suspicions."

With direct allusions to Gettysburg and the words of Lincoln, Kennedy imparted to his audience a message that the challenges

America faced in the 1960s were as significant as any the nation had ever faced. "It would be easier to shrink back from that frontier, to look to the safe mediocrity of the past, to be lulled by good intentions and high rhetoric—and those who prefer that course should not cast their votes for me regardless of party." It is difficult to imagine a candidate today speaking words such as these to the American people. As the legendary James "Scotty" Reston said of the young nominee, "He has not taken the easy or the traditional way."[4]

## Preaching Sacrifice

To be sure, the New Frontier speech was not JFK's best. His opening attacks on his Republican opponent, Richard Nixon, though couched largely in terms of Nixon's timidity of vision and his devotion to the status quo, detracted from the high-minded nature of the speech's main themes. Due to exhaustion from the convention, not to mention his chronically bad back, Kennedy read the speech quickly, undermining his usually polished delivery. Moreover, while the image of the New Frontier was original, the main themes of the speech were not. Kennedy had and would continue to preach the message of sacrifice throughout the campaign. Repeatedly he would tell audiences, "It is time to get this country moving again," "In a dangerous time we need to be told what we must do if we are going to maintain our freedom," and "It is our obligation and our privilege to be the defenders of the gate in a time of maximum danger. If we fail freedom fails . . . Has any people since Athens had a comparable responsibility and opportunity?"[5] In the famous debates with Vice President Nixon he asked, "Are we as strong as we must be if we're going to maintain our independence, and if we're going to maintain and hold out the hand of friendship . . . to those who look to us for survival?"[6] And Kennedy did not spare himself, noting at one point, "In 1960 we must elect a President who will lead the people—who will risk, if he must, his popularity for his responsibility."[7]

In virtually every campaign appearance Kennedy found the opportunity to invoke the Cold War in reminding his countrymen of the need for vigilance in confronting the Soviet threat.[8] Rarely before or since has America been a witness to a politician who was so candid with his audiences, so confident in the power of his challenging campaign message, and so sure that Americans would respond affirmatively.

The idea of patriotic sacrifice and determination in the face of grave foreign threats was not new to Kennedy—it had long been a part of his basic political philosophy. In 1940's *Why England Slept* he spoke of the need to "make long-sustained sacrifices" to preserve democracy. In his introduction to *Profiles in Courage* he wrote, "We expect individuals to sacrifice their private interests to permit the national good to progress."[9]

Indeed, the time Kennedy spent in England in the 1930s fundamentally shaped his political ideology and instilled in him the belief that Americans must be prepared to give of themselves in the name of freedom. JFK was strongly influenced by his rhetorical and political hero, Winston Churchill, who throughout the interwar years warned of the rising Nazi menace and was harshly critical of Great Britain's failure to prepare accordingly. Kennedy believed that America was acting in a similar manner to Britain during the 1930s—what Churchill would call the "Locust Years"— in its indifference to the Communist threat.

In November 1959, in a direct allusion to Churchill, Kennedy delivered remarks at the Wisconsin Democratic Party annual convention entitled "The Years the Locusts Have Eaten" in which he bemoaned America's taking of the "easy way" while the Soviet Union was working hard to surpass the United States. In the New Frontier speech he quoted Churchill's legendary "Finest Hour" address, delivered after the fall of France in 1940. Regularly on the campaign trail he alluded to Churchill's prewar warnings about the Nazi threat and argued that America faced a similar challenge. It's little wonder that British prime minister Harold Macmillan would later say of Kennedy's 1960 campaign that he ran "on the Churchill ticket."[10]

While some would later complain that the "missile gap" with the Soviets, of which Kennedy warned, turned out to be nonexistent, he was not alone in believing that the country was at risk of being surpassed by the Soviets. Indeed, the reluctance of the Eisenhower administration to share intelligence information debunking the gap would only serve to bolster Kennedy's thinking on the matter. Obviously the political benefit of attacking Nixon and the Republicans on national security was not lost on JFK and his advisers, but it would be incorrect to suggest that Kennedy did not believe the threat was real. He almost certainly did.[11]

It has become familiar hyperbole to say that Kennedy's New Frontier shaped a generation. Like much of the mythology around JFK, this is certainly an exaggeration. But at the same time there is little question that the spirit of sacrifice, which defined Kennedy's campaign message, would in some measure shape the political direction of the decade and beyond. Tragically, of course, Kennedy would not live to see his words come to fruition. Nonetheless, the concept of the New Frontier and the notion of American patriotism that it embodied would propel millions of Americans to look at their nation, and their responsibility to it, in a whole new light.

## *John F. Kennedy Accepts the Democratic Nomination for President, Los Angeles, July 14, 1960*

With a deep sense of duty and high resolve, I accept your nomination.

I accept it with a full and grateful heart—without reservation—and with only one obligation—the obligation to devote every effort of body, mind and spirit to lead our Party back to victory and our Nation back to greatness.

I am grateful too, that you have provided me with such an eloquent statement of our Party's platform. Pledges which are made so eloquently are made to be kept. "The Rights of Man"—the civil and economic rights essential to the human dignity of all men—are indeed our goal and our first principles. This is a Platform on which I can run with enthusiasm and conviction.

. . . I am fully aware of the fact that the Democratic Party, by nominating someone of my faith, has taken on what many regard as a new and hazardous risk—new, at least since 1928. But I look at it this way: the Democratic Party has once again placed its confidence in the American people, and in their ability to render a free, fair judgment—to uphold the Constitution and my oath of office—and to reject any kind of religious pressure or obligation that might directly or indirectly interfere with my conduct of the Presidency in the national interest. My record of fourteen years supporting public education—supporting complete separation of church and state—and resisting pressure from any source on any issue should be clear by now to everyone.

I hope that no American, considering the really critical issues facing this country, will waste his franchise by voting either for me or against me solely on account of my religious affiliation. It is not relevant. I want to stress, what some other political or religious leader may have said on this subject. It is not relevant what abuses may have existed in other countries or in other times. It is not relevant what pressures, if any, might conceivably be brought to bear on me. I am telling you now what you are entitled to know: that my decisions on any public policy will be my own—as an American, a Democrat and a free man.

Under any circumstances, however, the victory we seek in November will not be easy. We all know that in our hearts. We recognize the power of the forces that will be aligned against us. We know they will invoke the name of Abraham Lincoln on behalf of their candidate—despite the fact that the political career of their candidate has often seemed to show charity toward none and malice for all.

. . . But we are not merely running against Mr. Nixon. Our task is not merely one of itemizing Republican failures. Nor is that wholly necessary. For the families forced from the farm will know how to vote without our telling them. The unemployed miners and textile workers will know how to vote. The old people without medical care—the families without a decent home—the parents of children without adequate food or schools—they all know that it's time for a change.

But I think the American people expect more from us than cries of indignation and attack. The times are too grave, the challenge too urgent, and the stakes too high—to permit the customary passions of political debate. We are not here to curse the darkness, but to light the candle that can guide us through that darkness to a safe and sane future. As Winston Churchill said on taking office some twenty years ago: if we open a quarrel between the present and the past, we shall be in danger of losing the future.

Today our concern must be with the future. For the world is changing. The old era is ending. The old ways will not do.

Abroad, the balance of power is shifting. There are new and more terrible weapons—new and uncertain nations—new pressures of population and deprivation. One-third of the world, it has been said, may be free—but one-third is the victim of cruel repression—and the other one-third is rocked by the pangs of poverty, hunger and envy. More energy is released by the awakening of these new nations then by the fission of the atom itself. Meanwhile, Communist influence has penetrated further into Asia, stood astride the Middle East and now festers some ninety miles off the coast of Florida.

. . . The world has been close to war before—but now man, who has survived all previous threats to his existence, has taken into his mortal hands the power to exterminate the entire species some seven times over.

Here, at home, the changing face of the future is equally revolutionary. The New Deal and the Fair Deal were bold measures for their generations—but this is a new generation.

A technological revolution on the farm has led us to an output explosion—but we have not yet learned how to harness that explosion usefully, while protecting our farmers' right to full parity income.

An urban population explosion has crowded our schools, cluttered up our suburbs, and increased the squalor of our slums.

A peaceful revolution for human rights—demanding an end to racial discrimination in all parts of our community life—has strained at the leashes imposed by timid executive leadership.

A medical revolution has extended the life of our elder citizens without providing the dignity and security those later years deserve. And a revolution of automation finds machines replacing men in the mines and mills of America, without replacing their incomes or their training or their needs to pay the family doctor, grocer and landlord.

There has also been a change—a slippage—in our intellectual and moral strength. Seven lean years of drought and famine have withered a field of ideas. Blight has descended on our regulatory agencies—and a dry rot, beginning in Washington, is seeping into every corner of America—in the payola mentality, the expense account way of life, the confusion between what is legal and what is right. Too many Americans have lost their way, their will, and their sense of historic purpose.

It is a time, in short, for a new generation of leadership—new men to cope with new problems and new opportunities.

All over the world, particularly in the newer nations, young men are coming to power—men who are not bound by the traditions of the past—men who are not blinded by the old fears and hates and rivalries—young men who can cast off the old slogans and delusions and suspicions.

The Republican nominee-to-be, of course, is also a young man. But his approach is as old as McKinley. His party is the party of the past. His speeches are generalities from Poor Richard's Almanac. Their platform, made up of left-over Democratic planks, has the courage of our old convictions. Their pledge is a pledge to the status quo—and today there can be no status quo.

For I stand tonight facing west on what was once the last frontier. From the lands that stretch three thousand miles behind me, the pioneers of old gave up their safety, their comfort and sometimes their lives to build a new world here in the West. They were not the captives of their own doubts, the prisoners of their own price tags. Their motto was not "every man for himself"—but "all for the common cause." They were determined to make that new world strong and free, to overcome its hazards and its hardships, to conquer the enemies that threatened from without and within.

Today some would say that those struggles are all over—that all the horizons have been explored—that all the battles have been won—that there is no longer an American frontier.

But I trust that no one in this vast assemblage will agree with those sentiments. For the problems are not all solved and the battles are not all won—and we stand today on the edge of a New

Frontier—the frontier of the 1960's—a frontier of unknown opportunities and perils—a frontier of unfulfilled hopes and threats.

Woodrow Wilson's New Freedom promised our nation a new political and economic framework. Franklin Roosevelt's New Deal promised security and succor to those in need. But the New Frontier of which I speak is not a set of promises—it is a set of challenges. It sums up not what I intend to offer the American people, but what I intend to ask of them. It appeals to their pride, not to their pocketbook—it holds out the promise of more sacrifice instead of more security.

But I tell you the New Frontier is here, whether we seek it or not. Beyond that frontier are the uncharted areas of science and space, unsolved problems of peace and war, unconquered pockets of ignorance and prejudice, unanswered questions of poverty and surplus. It would be easier to shrink back from that frontier, to look to the safe mediocrity of the past, to be lulled by good intentions and high rhetoric—and those who prefer that course should not cast their votes for me, regardless of party.

But I believe the times demand new invention, innovation, imagination, decision. I am asking each of you to be pioneers on that New Frontier. My call is to the young in heart, regardless of age—to all who respond to the Scriptural call: "Be strong and of a good courage; be not afraid, neither be thou dismayed."

For courage—not complacency—is our need today—leadership—not salesmanship. And the only valid test of leadership is the ability to lead, and lead vigorously. A tired nation, said David Lloyd George, is a Tory nation—and the United States today cannot afford to be either tired or Tory.

There may be those who wish to hear more—more promises to this group or that—more harsh rhetoric about the men in the Kremlin—more assurances of a golden future, where taxes are always low and subsidies ever high. But my promises are in the platform you have adopted—our ends will not be won by rhetoric and we can have faith in the future only if we have faith in our-selves.

For the harsh facts of the matter are that we stand on this frontier at a turning-point in history. We must prove all over again whether this nation—or any nation so conceived—can long endure—whether our society—with its freedom of choice, its breadth of opportunity, its range of alternatives—can compete with the single-minded advance of the Communist system.

Can a nation organized and governed such as ours endure? That is the real question. Have we the nerve and the will? Can we carry through in an age where we will witness not only new breakthroughs in weapons of destruction—but also a race for mas-tery of the sky and the rain, the ocean and the tides, the far side of space and the inside of men's minds?

Are we up to the task—are we equal to the challenge? Are we willing to match the Russian sacrifice of the present for the future—or must we sacrifice our future in order to enjoy the present?

That is the question of the New Frontier. That is the choice our nation must make—a choice that lies not merely between two men or two parties, but between the public interest and pri-vate comfort—between national greatness and national decline—between the fresh air of progress and the stale, dank atmosphere of "normalcy"—between determined dedication and creeping mediocrity.

All mankind waits upon our decision. A whole world looks to see what we will do. We cannot fail their trust, we cannot fail to try.

It has been a long road from that first snowy day in New Hampshire to this crowded convention city. Now begins another long journey, taking me into your cities and homes all over America. Give me your help, your hand, your voice, your vote. Recall with me the words of Isaiah: "They that wait upon the

Lord shall renew their strength; they shall mount up with wings as eagles; they shall run and not be weary."

As we face the coming challenge, we too shall wait upon the Lord, and ask that he renew our strength. Then shall we be equal to the test. Then shall we not be weary. And then we shall prevail.

Thank you.

## Chapter 12

# GETTING RELIGION ON THE CAMPAIGN TRAIL

## John F. Kennedy Upholds the Notion of Religious Tolerance: 1960

FOR THE FIRST 136 years of American presidential history, three characteristics defined America's presidential nominees: they were white, they were male, and they were Protestant. In 1928, New York governor Al Smith, who was Catholic, changed all that, becoming the first non-Protestant to be nominated for president. But, as is the case for many trailblazers, his was a Pyrrhic victory. He suffered humiliation and defeat as he was buried under an avalanche of lurid, conspiratorial, and hate-filled anti-Catholic attacks.

In 1960, Massachusetts senator John F. Kennedy would fare far better, in part because he took a different tack than Smith and confronted his intolerant opponents directly, arguing that by the basic notion of American fairness he should not be disqualified for the White House simply because of his Catholic faith. Instead of defending Church doctrine or his own religious views, Kennedy upheld his strongly held belief in the separation of church and state and argued that his religion was a matter of private, not public, concern.

In the process, he delivered what many consider one of the best campaign speeches in U.S. political history. It is certainly among the most effective. To modern readers, its vigilant defense of the separation of church and state and the privacy of one's faith will likely seem quaint. The discussion of one's religious beliefs has become such an integral part of modern American politics that the speech Kennedy delivered to rave reviews in 1960 would probably cost him the White House today.

## THE "CATHOLIC ISSUE"

Throughout Kennedy's run for the White House in 1960 the so-called religious issue dogged his campaign. The familiar argument that Catholics could not reject clerical authority was regularly launched against Kennedy. These attacks were due largely to ignorance of Catholic traditions and faith, but there was also a strong undercurrent of old-fashioned religious bigotry at play. After the beating Smith took in 1928, many Democrats were fearful that the same innuendos and deep-seated fears of the Catholic Church would sink Kennedy's presidential chances. Yet throughout the Democratic primaries Kennedy continued to prove that these fears were misplaced.

In Wisconsin, Kennedy's Catholicism was front and center. Two days before the primary election, the *Milwaukee Journal* amazingly listed the state's voter breakdown in three columns: Democrats, Republicans, and Catholics. Nonetheless, Kennedy won easily—although not with the landslide that some had predicted. Making matters worse, in six of the state's ten districts that JFK won, there were a particularly high number of Catholic voters, leading some to argue that Kennedy had won only because of high Catholic turnout, a feat that likely would not be replicated elsewhere on the campaign trail.[1]

JFK's opponent in the primaries, Hubert Humphrey, who had

initially pledged to drop out if he couldn't win in Wisconsin (which bordered his home state of Minnesota), stayed in the race and staked his candidacy on West Virginia, with its heavily Protestant population. Many argued that a poor showing by Kennedy would imperil his chances of winning the nomination. In an effort to confront the religious issue head-on, JFK went before the American Society of Newspaper Editors on April 21, 1960, and provided his first full views on the question of religion in government. Kennedy argued for complete separation of church and state and made it clear that "I do not speak for the Catholic Church on issues of public policy, and no one in the church speaks for me."[2]

Whether it was his fervent defense of his ability to be both a good Catholic *and* a good American or his tireless campaigning, the result in West Virginia was even better than he could have hoped for—a smashing 61 percent to 39 percent victory and Humphrey's withdrawal from the race.

## KENNEDY DEFENDS HIS FAITH

Kennedy might have been led to believe that with his win in the Democratic primaries the religious issue would finally be put to bed. Clearly his Catholicism did not dissuade Democrats from making him the party's standard-bearer in 1960. While his advisers considered the possibility that at some point they would have to make a statement on Kennedy's religion, they assumed it would more likely come at the end of the campaign. But in the first week of September, a new group—and a new crisis—appeared. The National Conference of Citizens for Religious Freedom, consisting of approximately 150 Protestant clergymen, (almost all of whom were Republicans) and led by one of the country's most widely read ministers, Dr. Norman Vincent Peale, publicly declared that Kennedy's religious faith should be an issue of debate in the campaign.[3]

The group alleged that Kennedy would be unable to free himself from the Church's "determined efforts to breach the wall of separation of church and state."[4] One minister intimated that Kennedy was "like Khrushchev" and "a captive of a system."[5] Peale himself was overheard warning that with Kennedy's possible election, "our American culture is at stake."[6] Apparently the irony of the group's name and its apparent objective was lost on the participants.

It would be impossible for the Kennedy campaign to allow this latest anti-Catholic salvo to go unanswered. Theodore Sorensen, Kennedy's speechwriter, would later say that the campaign believed the religious issue was the single biggest obstacle to winning the White House.[7] He confided to a friend in the days before the speech, "We can win or lose this election right there in Houston on Monday night."[8] Such attacks from a spokesman as prominent as Peale threatened to legitimatize anti-Catholic rhetoric that up to that point had been confined in the popular press to "backwoods Bible-thumpers."[9] Plus Kennedy seemed to be itching for the fight: "I'm getting tired of these people who think I want to replace the gold at Fort Knox with a supply of holy water," he said.[10]

Kennedy had been asked to speak to the Houston Ministerial Association on September 12, and he accepted the invitation. According to Sorensen, the candidate was not one to openly discuss his religious views. Kennedy was "neither self-conscious nor superior about his religion but simply accepted it as part of his life . . . not once in eleven years—despite all our discussions of church-state affairs—did he ever disclose his personal views on man's relation to God."[11] A quote often attributed to his wife, Jacqueline, provides a more cynical take: "I think it is unfair for Jack to be opposed because he is a Catholic. After all, he's such a poor Catholic."[12]

This tone of ambivalence toward his personal faith comes

across in the Houston speech. Speaking in subdued, even somber tones, Kennedy stated at the outset that the country should be talking about the "spread of Communist influence" or the "hungry children I saw in West Virginia," not his Catholic faith. But since the "religious issue" had continued to rear its head, he wearily noted, "it is apparently necessary for me to state once again—not what kind of church I believe in, for that should be important only to me—but what kind of America I believe in." With these words Kennedy made it clear he was not about to get into an ecclesiastical debate or even one about his personal faith.

Kennedy's rhetorical intention was clear: to shift the debate away from piety to his vision about the "kind of America" he believed in. In this sense, JFK was firmly implanting his comments into a larger argument about the proper role of religion in American society. In Kennedy's America there were no "religious test oaths." There was complete separation of church and state, "where no Catholic prelate would tell the President—should he be Catholic—how to act, and no Protestant minister would tell his parishioners for whom to vote." The beliefs of the president were "his own private affair, neither imposed upon him by the nation, nor imposed by the nation upon him as a condition to holding that office." There would be, according to Kennedy, no official religion, and no religious group would be able "to impose its will" on either the "general populace or the public acts of its officials." Finally, Kennedy sketched out a vision of America "where religious intolerance will someday end, where all men and all churches are treated as equals."

Of course, these words had the effect of hoisting the Protestant ministers by their own petard. After all, what was the difference between the Pope telling a president how to vote and a Protestant minister telling his followers to vote against a candidate because of his religious beliefs? It was the same sort of meddling in political affairs by what should be a non-political man of faith. What's worse, Peale's group was hiding behind the notion of promoting religious freedom when in reality they were imposing their very own religious litmus test.

What is today most striking about Kennedy's remarks is their impersonal manner. There is a nonsectarian element to this speech—JFK's religious faith seemed to be secondary to his patriotic faith. Kennedy made it clear that he believed the separation between church and state must be absolute. (Indeed, some Catholic figures would privately grumble about the rhetorical separation Kennedy made between one's religion and one's public life.) He noted his position against appointing an American ambassador to the Vatican, and his opposition to both aid for parochial schools and boycotts of public schools (which he pointedly noted he attended as a youngster). He even asserted that he would resign his office rather than violate either his conscience or the national interest—assigning equal weight to both. In the speech's most memorable sentence, and in a further example of Kennedy's long-standing appreciation for antithesis phrasing, he declared, "I am not the Catholic candidate for President. I am the Democratic Party's candidate for President who happens also to be a Catholic." Again, his religion seemed secondary to his more important status as a nominee for president.

Kennedy matched his vision of America with his own heroic record of military service. "This is the kind of America I fought for in the South Pacific, and the kind my brother died for in Europe. No one suggested then that we might have a divided loyalty, that we did not believe in liberty, or that we belonged to a disloyal group that threatened . . . 'the freedoms for which our forefathers died.'"

By highlighting his war record and the tragic death of his brother Joe and then counterposing those to the malicious accusations launched against him, Kennedy turned the tables on his opponents. Apparently, Kennedy argued, it was appropriate for a

Catholic to sacrifice his life in defense of his country, but when he sought national office his loyalty to the nation could be openly questioned. This was a brilliant rhetorical tool for exposing the inconsistency in those who would impose a religious test on any politician. No longer was the issue one of Kennedy's religion; rather, it was the intolerance of his critics.

But Kennedy wisely didn't use just his own war record; he fell back on American and in particular Texas mythology, namely, the Alamo. He noted that alongside Bowie and Crockett were men named Fuentes, McCafferty, Bailey, Badillo, and Carey, and "no one knows whether they were Catholics or not. For there was no religious test there at the Alamo."

Kennedy asserted that the nation's forefathers died for this type of religious anonymity, which stemmed from their singular identity as Americans. This powerful notion formed the backdrop for his final peroration: "If this election is decided on the basis that 40 million Americans lost their chance of being President on the day they were baptized, then it is the whole nation that will be the loser . . . in the eyes of history, and in the eyes of our own people."

In the end, Kennedy firmly rooted the speech in a very basic and profound American ideal: the fundamental notion of opportunity that is part and parcel of the American dream. Using this standard and a simple plea for fairness, JFK argued that he should be judged not by his religion but by his political and policy views. He told the audience that "if I should lose on the real issues, I shall return to my seat in the Senate, satisfied that I'd tried my best and was fairly judged." His was a powerful plea for equal opportunity and tolerance of religious diversity.

At the conclusion of the speech, which was broadcast live across Texas, came possibly the event's most dramatic moment, as Kennedy was peppered with skeptical questions from the assembled ministers. The contrast between Kennedy's smooth and humble demeanor and the accusatory, even picayune interrogatories from the hostile audience only strengthened the public response, engendering greater sympathy for Kennedy. The hostility of the crowd was clear to most observers—not once during Kennedy's remarks was he interrupted by applause.

The speech's impact was indeed electrifying. Videos of Kennedy's remarks were distributed around the country, particularly in heavily Catholic urban areas. These tapes became the key advertising tool for the campaign. Sorensen, in his traditionally understated manner, remarked later that the speech may have made "some converts to his candidacy."[13] Speaker of the House Sam Rayburn was a bit more effusive: "As we say in my part of Texas, he ate 'em blood raw."[14]

The editorial response was even more overwhelming. The *New York Times* praised Kennedy and echoed the Democratic candidate's own words: "No American will be doing his duty if he votes against him because he is a Catholic, exactly as no American will be doing his duty if he votes for him because he is Catholic."[15] The *Washington Post* chimed in, "We do not see what more he could do or say to satisfy the doubters."[16] Most tellingly, the group headed by Peale called the speech "the most complete, unequivocal and reassuring statement which could be expected of any person in his position."[17] The Protestant ministers clearly had been put on the defensive by Kennedy's presentation. After the speech it would become nearly impossible to directly attack a presidential candidate over questions of his religious faith.[18]

To this day, it's impossible to fully judge the political impact of the Houston speech. There is no doubt that the address was crucial in rallying heavily Catholic northeastern and midwestern states. In addition, Kennedy strengthened his identification with ethnic minority voters in the North. While Roosevelt had initially brought these folks into the Democratic coalition, it was Kennedy's 1960 presidential campaign that helped seal the deal.

Though they may have been Protestant, many of these ethnic minorities saw Kennedy as a kindred soul—a fellow outsider in 1960s America.[19]

Of course, at the same time, Kennedy's razor-thin margin of victory was far less than his own staff had assumed, lending credence to the notion that anti-Catholic fear and bias cut into his final vote totals. Kennedy would become the first man elected to the White House without winning a majority of Protestant votes.

In the end, of course, Kennedy did win. A once sacrosanct taboo in American politics had been broken, and it was a testament, in part, to Kennedy's stirring words. As Theodore White said of the speech, "He had for the first time more fully and explicitly than any other thinker of his faith defined the personal doctrine of a modern Catholic in a democratic society."[20] With the Houston speech, Kennedy had exposed the un-American nature of anti-religious bigotry, and never again would a Catholic presidential candidate be put under such harsh scrutiny. Forty-four years later, when John Kerry sought the White House, his Catholicism was barely even remarked upon—a much-delayed victory for religious tolerance and acceptance in America.

## John F. Kennedy Addresses the Houston Ministerial Association, September 12, 1960

While the so-called religious issue is necessarily and properly the chief topic here tonight, I want to emphasize from the outset that I believe that we have far more critical issues in the 1960 campaign; the spread of Communist influence, until it now festers only 90 miles from the coast of Florida—the humiliating treatment of our President and Vice President by those who no longer respect our power—the hungry children I saw in West Virginia, the old people who cannot pay their doctors bills, the families forced to give up their farms—an America with too many slums, with too few schools, and too late to the moon and outer space. These are the real issues which should decide this campaign. And they are not religious issues—for war and hunger and ignorance and despair know no religious barrier.

But because I am a Catholic, and no Catholic has ever been elected President, the real issues in this campaign have been obscured—perhaps deliberately, in some quarters less responsible than this. So it is apparently necessary for me to state once again— not what kind of church I believe in, for that should be important only to me—but what kind of America I believe in.

I believe in an America where the separation of church and state is absolute; where no Catholic prelate would tell the President—should he be Catholic—how to act, and no Protestant minister would tell his parishioners for whom to vote; where no church or church school is granted any public funds or political preference, and where no man is denied public office merely because his religion differs from the President who might appoint him, or the people who might elect him.

I believe in an America that is officially neither Catholic, Protestant nor Jewish; where no public official either requests or accept instructions on public policy from the Pope, the National

Council of Churches or any other ecclesiastical source; where no religious body seeks to impose its will directly or indirectly upon the general populace or the public acts of its officials, and where religious liberty is so indivisible that an act against one church is treated as an act against all.

For while this year it may be a Catholic against whom the finger of suspicion is pointed, in other years it has been—and may someday be again—a Jew, or a Quaker, or a Unitarian, or a Baptist. It was Virginia's harassment of Baptist preachers, for example, that led to Jefferson's statute of religious freedom. Today, I may be the victim, but tomorrow it may be you—until the whole fabric of our harmonious society is ripped apart at a time of great national peril.

Finally, I believe in an America where religious intolerance will someday end, where all men and all churches are treated as equals, where every man has the same right to attend or not to attend the church of his choice, where there is no Catholic vote, no anti-Catholic vote, no bloc voting of any kind, and where Catholics, Protestants and Jews, at both the lay and the pastoral levels, will refrain from those attitudes of disdain and division which have so often marred their works in the past, and promote instead the American ideal of brotherhood.

That is the kind of America in which I believe. And it represents the kind of Presidency in which I believe, a great office that must be neither humbled by making it the instrument of any religious group nor tarnished by arbitrarily withholding it—its occupancy from the members of any one religious group. I believe in a President whose views on religion are his own private affair, neither imposed by him upon the nation, nor imposed by the nation upon him as a condition to holding that office.

I would not look with favor upon a President working to subvert the first amendment's guarantees of religious liberty; nor would our system of checks and balances permit him to do so.

And neither do I look with favor upon those who would work to subvert Article VI of the Constitution by requiring a religious test, even by indirection. For if they disagree with that safeguard, they should be openly working to repeal it.

I want a Chief Executive whose public acts are responsible to all and obligated to none, who can attend any ceremony, service, or dinner his office may appropriately require of him to fulfill; and whose fulfillment of his Presidential office is not limited or conditioned by any religious oath, ritual, or obligation.

This is the kind of America I believe in—and this is the kind of America I fought for in the South Pacific, and the kind my brother died for in Europe. No one suggested then that we might have a divided loyalty, that we did not believe in liberty, or that we belonged to a disloyal group that threatened—I quote—"the freedoms for which our forefathers died."

And in fact this is the kind of America for which our forefathers did die when they fled here to escape religious test oaths that denied office to members of less favored churches—when they fought for the Constitution, the Bill of Rights, the Virginia Statute of Religious Freedom—and when they fought at the shrine I visited today, the Alamo. For side by side with Bowie and Crockett died Fuentes, and McCafferty, and Bailey, and Badillo, and Carey—but no one knows whether they were Catholics or not. For there was no religious test there.

I ask you tonight to follow in that tradition—to judge me on the basis of 14 years in the Congress, on my declared stands against an Ambassador to the Vatican, against unconstitutional aid to parochial schools, and against any boycott of the public schools—which I attended myself. And instead of doing this, do not judge me on the basis of these pamphlets and publications we all have seen that carefully select quotations out of context from the statements of Catholic church leaders, usually in other countries, frequently in other centuries, and rarely relevant to any situation here. And always omitting, of course, the statement of the American Bishops in 1948 which strongly endorsed Church-State separation, and which more nearly reflects the views of almost every American Catholic.

I do not consider these other quotations binding upon my public acts. Why should you?

But let me say, with respect to other countries, that I am wholly opposed to the State being used by any religious group, Catholic or Protestant, to compel, prohibit, or prosecute the free exercise of any other religion. And that goes for any persecution, at any time, by anyone, in any country. And I hope that you and I condemn with equal fervor those nations which deny their Presidency to Protestants, and those which deny it to Catholics. And rather than cite the misdeeds of those who differ, I would also cite the record of the Catholic Church in such nations as France and Ireland, and the independence of such statesmen as De Gaulle and Adenauer.

But let me stress again that these are my views.

For contrary to common newspaper usage, I am not the Catholic candidate for President.

I am the Democratic Party's candidate for President who happens also to be a Catholic.

I do not speak for my church on public matters; and the church does not speak for me.

Whatever issue may come before me as President, if I should be elected, on birth control, divorce, censorship, gambling or any other subject, I will make my decision in accordance with these views—in accordance with what my conscience tells me to be in the national interest, and without regard to outside religious pressure or dictates. And no power or threat of punishment could cause me to decide otherwise.

But if the time should ever come—and I do not concede any conflict to be remotely possible—when my office would require me to either violate my conscience or violate the national interest, then I would resign the office; and I hope any conscientious public servant would do likewise.

But I do not intend to apologize for these views to my critics of either Catholic or Protestant faith; nor do I intend to disavow either my views or my church in order to win this election.

If I should lose on the real issues, I shall return to my seat in the Senate, satisfied that I'd tried my best and was fairly judged.

But if this election is decided on the basis that 40 million Americans lost their chance of being President on the day they were baptized, then it is the whole nation that will be the loser, in the eyes of Catholics and non-Catholics around the world, in the eyes of history, and in the eyes of our own people.

But if, on the other hand, I should win this election, then I shall devote every effort of mind and spirit to fulfilling the oath of the Presidency—practically identical, I might add, with the oath I have taken for 14 years in the Congress. For without reservation, I can, "solemnly swear that I will faithfully execute the office of President of the United States, and will to the best of my ability preserve, protect, and defend the Constitution—so help me God."

## Chapter 13

## THE CONSERVATIVE MOMENT

### Senator Barry Goldwater Defends Extremism in the Pursuit of Liberty: 1964

S AN FRANCISCO'S COW PALACE was in an ugly mood on July
13, 1964. Days earlier, in a pitched battle for the soul of the
Republican Party, conservatives led by Arizona senator Barry Goldwater had vanquished the moderate Rockefeller Republicans—and
they were in no mood for reconciliation.

The conservatives exulted in victory, openly mocking the moderates. Black delegates fared no better, as they were spat on and
cursed at by some of the crowd. Jackie Robinson, an observer on
the convention floor, later said, "I now believe I know how it felt
to be a Jew in Hitler's Germany."[1] When the runner-up, New
York governor Nelson Rockefeller, spoke against rising extremism
in the party, he was interrupted twenty-two times with catcalls and
boos.[2] Platform planks repudiating the John Birch Society and other
extremist groups as well as resolutions reinforcing the party's historic support for civil rights were soundly rejected. The invective
started from the top of the ticket. When asked to accept a phone
call from Rockefeller conceding the nomination, Goldwater an-
grily responded, "I don't want to talk to that son-of-a-bitch."[3]

The conservative victory in San Francisco was three decades in the making, born out of years of frustration as the party consistently nominated "acceptable" moderate candidates from Willkie to Dewey to Eisenhower. Conservatives wanted to offer the American people "a choice not an echo" by nominating a true ideological conservative. Though Goldwater hardly dominated the Republican primaries, losing badly in New Hampshire and Oregon and winning uncontested victories elsewhere, the organizing skills of his supporters and divisions among moderate candidates, including Rockefeller, Philadelphia governor William Scranton, and 1960 vice presidential nominee Henry Cabot Lodge, smoothed the path for the Arizona senator. As political journalist Richard Rovere would note, the goal of Goldwater's acolytes was not to bring the party together but instead "a total ideological victory and the total destruction of their critics. They wished to punish as well as to prevail."[4]

Goldwater's subsequent take-no-prisoners acceptance speech at the GOP convention represented a seismic change in the political philosophy of the Republican Party. The conservatives utterly rejected the postwar liberal consensus of confronting Communism abroad and maintaining the modern welfare state at home. Goldwater called for the rollback of Communism through military means if necessary and dramatically scaling back growing federal power at home. It is a speech and political call to arms that continues to resonate to this day.

Looking back, it is difficult to accurately reflect the fear that Barry Goldwater instilled in millions of Americans. This was the campaign of the legendary "Daisy" television ad, which none too subtly hinted at the possibility of nuclear Armageddon if Goldwater were to win in November. Charges of fascism and extremism were regularly hurled at the candidate, and magazine articles hinted that Goldwater was mentally unstable.[5] In a survey of twelve thousand psychiatrists, only a tiny minority, 657, considered Goldwater fit to serve as president.[6]

Goldwater did little to contradict these assertions. He joked about sawing the Eastern Seaboard off from the United States and letting it float out to sea. He called for Social Security to be made voluntary, attacked federal aid for education, and mused about lobbing nuclear weapons into the men's room at the Kremlin. Goldwater pretty much opposed every major government program since the dawn of the New Deal.[7] According to a Harris poll taken on the eve of the GOP convention, a majority of the American people disagreed with Goldwater on eight of the ten issues offered in the survey. Not since Hoover had a presidential candidate been so fundamentally out of touch with the American people.[8]

Any opportunity Goldwater would have to moderate his image would come in San Francisco. A unifying address would contradict his toxic image, forcing Americans to reexamine him and offering him a fighting chance in November. Goldwater's chief speechwriter, Karl Hess, drafted just such a set of conciliatory remarks. But Barry Goldwater wasn't interested in moderation. Denison Kitchel, a close Goldwater friend and longtime adviser, and William Baroody Jr., the founder of the conservative American Enterprise Institute, took over the speechwriting process and drafted a set of remarks that more accurately reflected Goldwater's attitude toward his vanquished opponents. Goldwater's objective as he prepared to step to the podium at the Cow Palace was to chart a new and more conservative course for the Republican Party and make a "historic break" with the moderation of the past.[9] From Goldwater's perspective, to then make a peace offering to Rockefeller and the moderates was both "politically illogical" and "personally contradictory."[10] In the end, Goldwater was in his own words "not a philosopher" but instead "a salesman trying to sell the conservative view of government."[11]

There was also a personal element at play as well. Goldwater was not the type of politician to take a slight lying down. The "libs," as Goldwater called the moderates, had, in his view, attacked him mercilessly. This was his chance to hit back—and hit back hard. An anecdote from Goldwater's autobiography provides some insight into the siege mentality of the candidate and his advisers. While preparing his remarks, the campaign received word that a new Opinion Research poll gave President Johnson a sixty-point lead in the national ballot. Goldwater turned to Hess and said, "Instead of writing an acceptance speech, we should be putting together a rejection speech and tell them all to go to hell." In the end, that's pretty much what he did.[12]

## THE CONSCIENCE OF A CONSERVATIVE

Introduced by former vice president Richard Nixon to a raucous crowd, Goldwater cut an uncompromising figure behind his distinctive and old-fashioned black-rimmed glasses. The speech he would deliver was very much in tune with his stern, unemotional visage. Indeed, Goldwater showed little excitement as he prepared to deliver remarks that were among the most ideologically focused of any given by a major presidential candidate.

On paper, his opening sentence sounded resolute: "From this moment, united and determined, we will go forward together, dedicated to the ultimate and undeniable greatness of the whole man. Together we will win." But in the audio of the speech, Goldwater's tone belied the insistence of his language. His monotone delivery makes it hard to believe that Goldwater was truly convinced he could win in November.

However, as Goldwater delved into the heart of his speech—and the cause of conservatism—he became more impassioned. Suddenly, Goldwater's language was focused and active; it practically crackles off the page. Goldwater took a rhetorical straight line to accomplish what many politicians seek to do in a circuitous route. He made it clear that the American people had an unambiguous choice in the 1964 election between freedom and tyranny—tyranny not only from the Soviet Union but at home as well from what he denounced as the "swampland" and "dead-end streets" of "collectivism." On these words his voice rose, and the insistence of his tone made the firmness of his commitment clear.

In a nifty bit of repetition Goldwater asserted what was ultimately at stake in the 1964 election and what must be the mission of all Republicans: in "every action," "every word," "every breath," and "every heartbeat," the aim must be "freedom." In all, Goldwater used the words *free*, *freedom*, or *liberty* approximately forty times in the speech.[13] Goldwater consistently used the rhetorical device of repetition to drive home his point. His opponents did not simply talk; they "talked and talked and talked and talked." They did not simply fail; they "failed and failed and failed."

Goldwater dramatically linked the threat of Communism with the cause of freedom. In one of the speech's many memorable phrases, he asserted, "We must make clear that until its goals of conquest are absolutely renounced and its relations with all nations tempered, Communism and the governments it now controls are enemies of every man on earth who is or wants to be free."

There was no ambiguity here and no room for compromise—only by actively and directly confronting Communism could America truly achieve freedom. Goldwater created a straw man out of his opponents' moderation and lack of vigilance in confronting this threat. He lamented the abundant "failures" of Democratic presidents in Berlin, Laos, Cuba, and Vietnam: "Failures proclaim lost leadership, obscure purpose, weakening wills and the risk of inciting our sworn enemies to new aggression and to new excesses," Goldwater declared. America was at risk, he intimated, not because of the enemies that are arrayed against it but because of the weakness of its leaders' political will in the face of that threat.

Weakness—and, even more directly, the appearance of weakness—was seemingly the greatest bogeyman for Goldwater. He told the assembled delegates that the nation must "dispel the foggy thinking which avoids hard decisions in the delusion that a world of conflict will somehow mysteriously resolve itself into a world of harmony, if we just don't rock the boat or irritate the forces of aggression—and this is hogwash." He reminded the audience, in a stentorian voice, "that only the strong can remain free; that only the strong can keep the peace."

But under Democratic rule, Goldwater argued, the nation had allowed its strength to be sapped. America's "strength to deter war has been stilled, and even gone into a planned decline," said Goldwater. "It has been during Democratic years," he gravely declared, "that we have weakly stumbled into conflicts, timidly refusing to draw our own lines against aggression, deceitfully refusing to tell even our own people of our full participation and tragically letting our finest men die on battlefields unmarked by purpose, unmarked by pride or the prospect of victory."

To be sure, Goldwater did more than harp on what he saw as failure. He made a concerted effort to stake out a clear vision of a Goldwater presidency—a foreign policy committed to open commerce, aggressive anti-Communism, and a domestic policy that limited the federal government to "only those needed and constitutionally sanctioned tasks which cannot otherwise be performed." He even evoked Martin Luther King Jr.'s "I Have a Dream" speech with his repeated use of the phrase "I can see" as he spoke of this future of freedom.

But while he lambasted his Democratic opponents, Goldwater's speech was less an attack on them than a broadside against the moderate voices in his party. Rockefeller supporters who might have hoped for an olive branch were presented instead with epithets. He made it clear that Republicanism must not be "made fuzzy and futile by unthinking and stupid labels." Even after extolling the "balance," "diversity," and "creative differences" of Republicans and quoting Lincoln's admonition about "discordant" elements in the party, he nonetheless told his audience, "This Republican party is a party for free men. Not for blind followers and not for conformists." So much for conciliation or compromise with moderate Republicans: either you were with the conservatives or you were against them.

And then in the speech's coup de grace—one of the most memorable moments in the history of American political speechmaking—Goldwater gravely intoned that "extremism in the defense of liberty is no vice," and that "moderation in the pursuit of justice is no virtue."★ The words shook the convention—literally. Delegates began frantically shaking the struts holding up ABC's broadcast booth, and the roars from the crowd could be heard outside the hall.[14] Later, Goldwater would complain that the line was widely misinterpreted by the media and his critics. It was not an attack on moderates, he said, but simply a statement that "there was nothing wrong in being strong in the defense of freedom and no particular good in being weak toward justice."[15] While such an interpretation is certainly believable, it speaks volumes about the political tin ear of Goldwater and his advisers. It should hardly seem surprising that the moderates had a different takeaway from the line.

Though Goldwater said the address was "the best speech I ever made," the national reaction was immediate and overwhelmingly negative.[16] Nixon called the speech "childish" and said after hearing it he felt "almost physically sick."[17] Scranton, Lodge, and Rockefeller, respectively, labeled it "dangerous," "irresponsible," and "frightening."[18] Eisenhower called it an "offense to the whole

---

★Although many have ascribed this phrase to Cicero or Burke, it was, according to Goldwater speechwriter Harry Jaffa, an allusion to Thomas Paine's *Rights of Man*: "A thing moderately good is not so good as it ought to be. Moderation in temper is always a virtue; but moderation in principle is always a vice."

American system." Liberal California governor Pat Brown said the speech "had the stench of fascism."[19] The *New York Times* accused the GOP standard-bearer of reducing "a once great party to the status of an ugly, angry, frustrated faction."[20] The *Washington Post* said, "If a party so committed were to gain public office in this country there would be nothing left for us to do but pray."[21]

There really is no nice way to say it: Goldwater's speech was an unmitigated political disaster. Democrats sought to present the Arizona senator as a radical extremist, and he embraced this toxic image. What's worse, instead of presenting Americans with an accessible or unifying message for the future, he brusquely dismissed those who did not share his extreme views. It was reminiscent of Bryan's harshly divisive rhetoric sixty-eight years earlier. As the NBC political reporter Edwin Newman understatedly summed it up, "Senator Goldwater's speech tonight did not bring into the fold those who were inclined to be outside before."[22]

## GOLDWATER VERSUS THE GREAT SOCIETY

The fears engendered by Goldwater's extreme tone were easily exploited by President Johnson and his supporters. Instead of having an important national debate about activist government in the 1960s, the country debated Goldwater's mental acuity as Lyndon Johnson was given a virtual political free pass.

Earlier that spring, LBJ had laid out a utopian vision for where he planned to take America in the 1960s. Launching his own political revolution, no less seminal than the one jump-started in San Francisco, Johnson challenged the American people to use the nation's vast political wealth "to enrich and elevate our national life, and to advance the quality of our American civilization."[23]

At the University of Michigan commencement on May 22, 1964, he told the assembled graduates, "For in your time we have the opportunity to move not only toward the rich society and the powerful society, but upward to the Great Society."[24] This vision of the future was as ambitious as the one charted by LBJ's hero Franklin Delano Roosevelt in the New Deal:

> The Great Society is a place where every child can find knowledge to enrich his mind and to enlarge his talents. It is a place where leisure is a welcome chance to build and reflect, not a feared cause of boredom and restlessness. It is a place where the city of man serves not only the needs of the body and the demands of commerce but the desire for beauty and the hunger for community. It is a place where man can renew contact with nature. It is a place which honors creation for its own sake and for what it adds to the understanding of the race. It is a place where men are more concerned with the quality of their goals than the quantity of their goods. But most of all, the Great Society is not a safe harbor, a resting place, a final objective, a finished work. It is a challenge constantly renewed, beckoning us toward a destiny where the meaning of our lives matches the marvelous products of our labor.[25]

These words represented a significant shift in the role of government in the lives of the American people. Yet the country spent little time debating the full implications of these changes. Polls showed that more than half of Americans were either "unhappy" or "indifferent" about President Johnson's domestic policies. In fact, public opinion ratings of the administration were far lower then Johnson's standing in national polls against Goldwater.[26]

LBJ traveled the country preaching a message of national reconciliation and activist government, and millions of Americans who were wary of his grandiose vision would nonetheless enthusiastically cast their ballot for the president because they were so deeply fearful of his opponent. The famed columnist James

"Scotty" Reston described the dilemma many Americans felt: "It would be difficult to underestimate the number of people who are going to vote for the President next week with a profound sense of uneasiness, not because he has removed their doubts or convinced or exalted them, but simply because he is the only alternative to Goldwater."[27] It was little wonder, what with the president asking Americans, "Which man's thumb you want to be close to that button, what man you want to reach over and pick up that receiver on that hot line when they say, 'Moscow is calling'?"[28]

But it was more than just fear that did in Goldwater. Conservatives had long believed that most Americans sympathized with their worldview, and if given a clear choice on Election Day, they would choose the conservative alternative. There was some basis for the argument—in fact, a poll in the fall of 1964 showed that most Americans self-identified as "ideologically" conservative.[29] But in 1964, after more than three decades of New Deal–style liberalism, the electorate tempered its conservative outlook with an embrace of government activism. Americans might have sympathized with Goldwater when he talked about individualism or basic American values, but they were aghast when he advocated making Social Security voluntary or doing away with the essential elements of the liberal welfare state. The American people still expected their government to provide a basic social safety net, and they were not ready for the hard-edged ideological fervor that drove Goldwater-style conservatism.

## LOSING THE BATTLE, WINNING THE WAR

On Election Day Goldwater was swamped, suffering the single worst defeat in American political history. LBJ viewed his overwhelming victory as an endorsement of the Great Society and his vision for America. It wasn't. Within two years, the steady decline of the Democratic Party would begin as the Great Society, Johnson's overreaching, and the corrosive effects of the Vietnam War would help bring Republicans back to power.

That, of course, is the great irony of Goldwater and this speech. Since 1964, virtually every Republican presidential nominee has borrowed heavily (though not exclusively) from Goldwater's message of smaller government at home and exporting freedom abroad. Within four years, the rhetoric of Goldwater and his supporters—which seemed so out of bounds in 1964—would become a fundamental part of the GOP's political strategy.[30] It informed Nixon's attacks on Democratic weakness and failure in 1968. It was the virtual basis of Ronald Reagan's campaign message. And the similarities between the Cow Palace speech and George W. Bush's 2004 renomination speech and inaugural address are unmistakable.

For all the negative elements of Goldwater's speech, there was something to his conservative message that struck a chord with millions of Americans. As Reston would describe the phenomenon, "Mr. Goldwater touches the deep feeling of regret in American life: regret over the loss of simplicity and fidelity; regret over the loss of the frontier spirit of pugnacious individuality; regret, in sort, over the loss of America's innocent and idealistic youth . . . Somehow, along the way, all these frustrations have been transferred into political terms and the true Republican believer, not the extremists in the party, but many of the most moderate and responsible Republicans . . . have come to identify the Democrats with everything from the decline of individual responsibility, to unemployment, racial tension, international confusion, and juvenile delinquency."[31] Goldwater's rhetoric was too hawkish in 1964, but his conservative politics and that of his supporters reflected a growing political movement in America that would fully flower in just a few short years.

Perhaps most ominously, Goldwater's speech demonstrated the

power of the civil rights issue in promoting GOP-style conservatism. Many had speculated that a growing white backlash against the civil rights movement combined with growing radicalism in the African American community would provide a boost to Goldwater's campaign. After all, on the campaign trail, Goldwater railed against the civil rights bill and was one of only eight senators to vote against it (though it went unmentioned in his acceptance speech). But unlike Alabama governor George Wallace or his ilk, few accused Goldwater of being a racist. Indeed, Goldwater failed to take advantage of the opportunity "to play the race card."[32] He instead cloaked his opposition to the bill in an attack on the overweening power of the state that he believed the legislation would herald.

But there was a lesson in the strong support that Goldwater received from some white voters. Without his opposition to the civil rights bill, he never would have won all five of the Deep South states—the first Republican to do so since Reconstruction. Implicitly, Goldwater's campaign linked political conservatism with opposition to civil rights legislation—an approach that George Wallace had already been using on the campaign trail. In fact, it was an approach that a generation of Republican office seekers would utilize in appealing to white voters who feared racial integration and yet weren't inclined to support politicians who took openly racist positions. By the time the white backlash fully developed several years later, the conservative movement was in perfect position to take advantage.

In the end, the power and single-mindedness of the conservative message would eventually wipe out the moderate wing of the party. With the exception of Gerald Ford (a sitting president who barely fended off the conservative challenge from Ronald Reagan), never again would the party nominate a candidate who was not ideologically conservative or at the very least paid lip service to conservative priorities.

As counterintuitive as it may seem, by shifting the ideological direction of the party at a time when the country was beginning to reject New Deal–style government and turn against the civil rights movement, Goldwater's blistering 1964 convention speech actually may have been the most successful speech in American political history. As conservative commentator George Will would later muse, Barry Goldwater won in 1964—it just took sixteen years to count the votes.

## Barry Goldwater Accepts the Republican Nomination for President, San Francisco, July 13, 1964

From this moment, united and determined, we will go forward together dedicated to the ultimate and undeniable greatness of the whole man. Together we will win.

... My fellow Republicans, our cause is too great for any man to feel worthy of it. Our task would be too great for any man did he not have with him the heart and the hands of this great Republican Party. And I promise you tonight that every fibre of my being is consecrated to our cause, that nothing shall be lacking from the struggle that can be brought to it by enthusiasm, by devotion and plain hard work.

In this world no person, no party can guarantee anything, but what we can do and what we shall do is to deserve victory and victory will be ours. The Good Lord raised this mighty Republic to be a home for the brave and to flourish as the land of the free—not to stagnate in the swampland of collectivism, not to cringe before the bully of Communism.

Now my fellow Americans, the tide has been running against freedom. Our people have followed false prophets. We must, and we shall, return to proven ways—not because they are old, but because they are true.

We must, and we shall, set the tide running again in the cause of freedom. And this party, with its every action, every word, every breath and every heartbeat, has but a single resolve, and that is freedom. Freedom made orderly for this nation by our constitutional government. Freedom under a government limited by laws of nature and of nature's God. Freedom balanced so that order lacking liberty will not become the slavery of the prison cell; balanced so that liberty lacking order will not become the license of the mob and of the jungle.

Now, we Americans understand freedom, we have earned it; we have lived for it, and we have died for it. This nation and its people are freedom's models in a searching world. We can be freedom's missionaries in a doubting world.

But, ladies and gentlemen, first we must renew freedom's mission in our own hearts and in our own homes.

During four futile years the Administration which we shall replace has distorted and lost that faith. It has talked and talked and talked and talked the words of freedom, but it has failed and failed and failed in the works of freedom.

Now failure cements the wall of shame in Berlin; failures blot the sands of shame at the Bay of Pigs; failures marked the slow death of freedom in Laos; failures infest the jungles of Vietnam; and failures haunt the houses of our once great alliances and undermine the greatest bulwark ever erected by free nations, the NATO community.

Failures proclaim lost leadership, obscure purpose, weakening wills and the risk of inciting our sworn enemies to new aggressions and to new excesses.

And because of this Administration we are tonight a world divided. We are a nation becalmed. We have lost the brisk pace of diversity and the genius of individual creativity. We are plodding along at a pace set by centralized planning, red tape, rules without responsibility and regimentation without recourse.

Rather than useful jobs in our country, people have been offered bureaucratic make-work, rather than moral leadership, they have been given bread and circuses; they have been given spectacles, and, yes, they've even been given scandals.

Tonight there is violence in our streets, corruption in our highest offices, aimlessness among our youth, anxiety among our elderly, and there's a virtual despair among the many who look beyond material success toward the inner meaning of their lives. And where examples of morality should be set, the opposite is seen. Small men seeking great wealth or power have too often and too long turned even the highest levels of public service into mere personal opportunity.

Now, certainly simple honesty is not too much to demand of men in government. We find it in most. Republicans demand it from everyone. They demand it from everyone no matter how exalted or protected his position might be.

The growing menace in our country tonight, to personal safety, to life, to limb and property, in homes, in churches, on the playgrounds and places of business, particularly in our great cities, is the mounting concern or should be, of every thoughtful citizen in the United States. Security from domestic violence, no less than from foreign aggression, is the most elementary and fundamental purpose of any government, and a government that cannot fulfill this purpose is one that cannot long command the loyalty of its citizens.

History shows us, demonstrates that nothing, nothing prepares the way for tyranny more than the failure of public officials to keep the streets from bullies and marauders.

Now we Republicans see all this as more—much more—than the result of mere political differences, or mere political mistakes. We see this as the result of a fundamentally and absolutely wrong view of man, his nature and his destiny.

Those who seek to live your lives for you, to take your liberties in return for relieving you of yours; those who elevate the state and downgrade the citizen, must see ultimately a world in which earthly power can be substituted for Divine Will. And this nation was founded upon the rejection of that notion and upon the acceptance of God as the author of freedom.

Now those who seek absolute power, even though they seek it to do what they regard as good, are simply demanding the right to enforce their own version of heaven on earth, and let me remind you, they are the very ones who always create the most hellish tyranny.

Absolute power does corrupt, and those who seek it must be suspect and must be opposed. Their mistaken course stems from false notions, ladies and gentlemen, of equality. Equality, rightly understood as our founding fathers understood it, leads to liberty and to the emancipation of creative differences; wrongly understood, as it has been so tragically in our time, it leads first to conformity and then to despotism.

Fellow Republicans, it is the cause of Republicanism to resist concentrations of power, private or public, which enforce such conformity and inflict such despotism.

It is the cause of Republicanism to insure that power remains in the hands of the people—and, so help us God, that is exactly what a Republican President will do with the help of a Republican Congress.

It is further the cause of Republicanism to restore a clear understanding of the tyranny of man over man in the world at large. It is our cause to dispel the foggy thinking which avoids hard decisions in the delusion that a world of conflict will somehow mysteriously resolve itself into a world of harmony, if we just don't rock the boat or irritate the forces of aggression—and this is hogwash.

It is, further, the cause of Republicanism to remind ourselves, and the world, that only the strong can remain free; that only the strong can keep the peace.

Now I needn't remind you, or my fellow Americans regardless of party, that Republicans have shouldered this hard responsibility and marched in this cause before. It was Republican leadership under Dwight Eisenhower that kept the peace, and passed along to this Administration the mightiest arsenal for defense the world has ever known.

And I needn't remind you that it was the strength and the unbelievable will of the Eisenhower years that kept the peace by using our strength, by using it in the Formosa Strait, and in Lebanon, and by showing it courageously at all times.

It was during those Republican years that the thrust of Communist imperialism was blunted. It was during those years of Republican leadership that this world moved closer not to war but closer to peace than at any other time in the last three decades.

And I needn't remind you, but I will, that it's been during Democratic years that our strength to deter war has been stilled and even gone into a planned decline. It has been during Democratic years that we have weakly stumbled into conflicts, timidly refusing to draw our own lines against aggression, deceitfully refusing to tell even our own people of our full participation and tragically letting our finest men die on battlefields unmarked by purpose, unmarked by pride or the prospect of victory.

Yesterday it was Korea; tonight it is Vietnam. Make no bones of this. Don't try to sweep this under the rug. We are at war in Vietnam. And yet the President, who is the Commander in Chief of our forces, refuses to say . . . whether or not the objective over there is victory, and his Secretary of Defense continues to mislead and misinform the American people, and enough of it has gone by.

And I needn't remind you, but I will, it has been during Democratic years that a billion persons were cast into Communist captivity and their fate cynically sealed.

Today in our beloved country we have an Administration which seems eager to deal with Communism in every coin known—from gold to wheat; from consulates to confidence, and even human freedom itself.

Now the Republican cause demands that we brand Communism as the principal disturber of peace in the world today. Indeed, we should brand it as the only significant disturber of the peace. And we must make clear that until its goals of conquest are absolutely renounced and its relations with all nations tempered, Communism and the governments it now controls are enemies of every man on earth who is or wants to be free.

Now, we here in America can keep the peace only if we remain vigilant, and only if we remain strong. Only if we keep our eyes open and keep our guard up can we prevent war. And I want to make this abundantly clear—I don't intend to let peace or freedom be torn from our grasp because of lack of strength, or lack of will—and that I promise you Americans.

I believe that we must look beyond the defense of freedom today to its extension tomorrow. I believe that the Communism which boasts it will bury us will instead give way to the forces of freedom. And I can see in the distant and yet recognizable future the outlines of a world worthy of our dedication, our every risk, our every effort, our every sacrifice along the way. Yes, a world that will redeem the suffering of those who will be liberated from tyranny.

I can see, and I suggest that all thoughtful men must contemplate, the flowering of an Atlantic civilization, the whole world of Europe reunified and free, trading openly across its borders, communicating openly across the world.

This is a goal far, far more meaningful than a moon shot. It's a truly inspiring goal for all free men to set for themselves during the latter half of the twentieth century. I can see and all free men must thrill to the events of this Atlantic civilization joined by its great ocean highway to the United States. What a destiny! What a destiny can be ours to stand as a great central pillar linking Europe, the Americas, and the venerable and vital peoples and cultures of the Pacific.

I can see a day when all the Americas—North and South—will be linked in a mighty system—a system in which the errors and misunderstandings of the past will be submerged one by one in a rising tide of prosperity and interdependence.

We know that the misunderstandings of centuries are not to be wiped away in a day or wiped away in an hour. But we pledge, we pledge that human sympathy—what our neighbors to the South call an attitude of sympatico—no less than enlightened self-interest will be our guide.

And I can see this Atlantic civilization galvanizing and guiding emergent nations everywhere. Now I know this freedom is not the fruit of every soil. I know that our own freedom was achieved through centuries by unremitting efforts by brave and wise men. And I know that the road to freedom is a long and a challenging road, and I know also that some men may walk away from it, that some men resist challenge, accepting the false security of governmental paternalism.

And I pledge that the America I envision in the years ahead will extend its hand in help, in teaching and in cultivation so that all new nations will be at least encouraged to go our way; so that they will not wander down the dark alleys of tyranny or to the dead-end streets of collectivism.

My fellow Republicans, we do no man a service by hiding freedom's light under a bushel of mistaken humility. I seek an America proud of its past, proud of its ways, proud of its dreams and determined actively to proclaim them. But our example to the world must, like charity, begin at home.

In our vision of a good and decent future, free and peaceful, there must be room for the liberation of the energy and the talent of the individual, otherwise our vision is blind at the outset.

We must assure a society here which, while never abandoning the needy or forsaking the helpless, nurtures incentives and opportunity for the creative and the productive.

We must know the whole good is the product of many single contributions.

And I cherish the day when our children once again will restore as heroes the sort of men and women who, unafraid and undaunted, pursue the truth, strive to cure disease, subdue and make fruitful our natural environment, and produce the inventive engines of production, science and technology.

This nation, whose creative people have enhanced this entire span of history, should again thrive upon the greatness of all those things which we—as individual citizens—can and should do.

During Republican years, this again will be a nation of men and women, of families proud of their role, jealous of their responsibilities, unlimited in their aspirations—a nation where all who can will be self-reliant.

We Republicans see in our constitutional form of government the great framework which assures the orderly but dynamic fulfillment of the whole man, and we see the whole man as the great reason for instituting orderly government in the first place.

We see in private property and in economy based upon and fostering private property the one way to make government a durable ally of the whole man rather than his determined enemy. We see in the sanctity of private property the only durable foundation for constitutional government in a free society.

And beyond that we see in a cherished diversity of ways, diversity of thoughts, of motives, and accomplishments. We don't seek to lead anyone's life for him. We only seek to secure his rights, guarantee him opportunity to strive with government performing only those needed and constitutionally sanctioned tasks which cannot otherwise be performed.

We Republicans seek a government that attends to its inherent responsibilities of maintaining a stable monetary and fiscal climate, encouraging a free and a competitive economy and enforcing law and order.

Thus do we seek inventiveness, diversity, and creativity within a stable order, for we Republicans define government's role where needed at many, many levels, preferably through the one closest to the people involved: our towns and our cities, then our counties, then our states then our regional contacts and only then the national government.

That, let me remind you, is the land of liberty built by

decentralized power. On it also we must have balance between the branches of government at every level.

Balance, diversity, creative difference—these are the elements of Republican equation. Republicans agree, heartily, to disagree on many, many of their applications. But we have never disagreed on the basic fundamental issues of why you and I are Republicans.

This is a party—this Republican Party is a party for free men. Not for blind followers and not for conformists. Back in 1858 Abraham Lincoln said this of the Republican Party . . . "It was composed of strained, discordant, and even hostile elements." . . . Yet all of these elements agreed on one paramount objective: to arrest the progress of slavery, and place it in the course of ultimate extinction.

Today, as then, but more urgently and more broadly than then, the task of preserving and enlarging freedom at home and safeguarding it from the forces of tyranny abroad is great enough to challenge all our resources and to require all our strength.

Anyone who joins us in all sincerity we welcome. Those who do not care for our cause, we don't expect to enter our ranks in any case. And let our Republicanism, so focused and so dedicated, not be made fuzzy and futile by unthinking and stupid labels.

I would remind you that extremism in the defense of liberty is no vice! And let me remind you also that moderation in the pursuit of justice is no virtue!

By the beauty of the very system we Republicans are pledged to restore and revitalize, the beauty of this Federal system of ours is in its reconciliation of diversity with unity. We must not see malice in honest differences of opinion, and no matter how great, so long as they are not inconsistent with the pledges we have given to each other in and through our Constitution.

Our Republican cause is not to level out the world or make its people conform in computer-regimented sameness. Our Republican cause is to free our people and light the way for liberty throughout the world. Ours is a very human cause for very humane goals. This party, its good people, and its unquestionable devotion to freedom will not fulfill the purposes of this campaign which we launch here now until our cause has won the day, inspired the world, and shown the way to a tomorrow worthy of all our yesteryears.

. . . I accept your nomination with humbleness, with pride, and you and I are going to fight for the goodness of our land. Thank you.

*Chapter 14*

# THE "FORGOTTEN AMERICANS" AND THE POLITICS OF FEAR

George Wallace and Richard Nixon Use Civil Rights to Undermine Activist Government: 1964–1968

I F THE FIRST half century of American presidential politics was focused largely on economic issues, the second half would feature an ongoing and often divisive debate about the issue of race and the fundamental question of what role government should play in furthering the civil rights of all Americans.

Throughout the 1960s few politicians more pungently captured the nation's turbulent and often conflicted mood on racial issues than Alabama governor and four-time presidential candidate George Wallace. Today Wallace is generally viewed in simplistic terms: racist, segregationist, demagogue. While all these labels are fairly applied, they don't do full justice to Wallace's abundant strengths as a politician and his ability to reflect the uncertainty and fear of the American electorate in the 1960s. The speeches he delivered during his 1964 and 1968 presidential campaigns are masterly examples of political demagoguery—but they were more than racist appeals. They would become the rhetorical template for a generation of conservative attacks on government.

## WALLACE HEADS NORTH

Wallace's first foray into national politics came in 1964, and it was in some respects the most influential, as it would help set an ideological tone for racial politics in the 1960s. Wallace first became a national figure when at his 1963 inauguration he theatrically thumbed his nose at the civil rights movement, declaring, "Segregation now, segregation tomorrow, segregation forever." Five months later his famous "stand in the schoolhouse door" to prevent integration of the University of Alabama garnered him even more attention. Still, few believed that an Alabama segregationist could translate his narrow appeal outside the confines of the South. But George Wallace would soon prove "that water flows both ways."[1]

It would be unfair and intellectually dishonest to suggest, as some Democrats did, that every person who voted for George Wallace was a racist. But it would be equally dishonest to deny that fear among middle-class whites of rising black power and its perceived relationship to growing crime rates, national disorder, and diminishing economic security that paved the way for Wallace's political ascendancy. It was small wonder that in 1968, when Wallace ran for president as a third-party candidate, he did best in those white communities abutting predominately black neighborhoods.[2]

Wallace never directly attacked black people. In his campaign speeches he would go to great pains to tell his audience that he'd never made a racist speech in his life.[3] Yet it would take a fool not to recognize that race fueled Wallace's rise. A Harris poll in July 1964 found that 58 percent of whites were concerned that blacks might "take over" their job; 43 percent feared blacks moving into their neighborhood.[4] As one Alabama politician would say of Wallace, "He can use all the other issues—law and order, running your own schools, protecting property rights—and never mention race. But people will know he's telling them, 'A nigger's trying to get your job, trying to move into your neighborhood.'"[5]

Wisconsin was the first state where Wallace ventured onto the national stage, entering the Democratic primary for president. On the surface it was a terrible place to begin his campaign. Though it had elected Joseph McCarthy to the U.S. Senate, the state was liberal, was heavily unionized, and had only a small black minority. However, by 1964 Wallace had already begun broadening his segregationist rhetoric by attacking the growing power and influence of the federal government and so-called bearded bureaucrats in Washington who couldn't park their bicycles straight.

His angry rhetoric struck a chord with white voters in Wisconsin, where he won just over a third of the Democratic primary vote.[6] Soon after, in Indiana 30 percent of primary voters would support the Alabama governor.[7] But the biggest shock would come in Maryland, where Wallace scored a stunning 43 percent of the vote. Wallace won 90 percent of white voters in the state's Eastern Shore and sixteen of twenty-three counties in the state. If not for a huge turnout among African Americans, Wallace likely would have won a clear majority.[8] Many shrugged off Wallace's strong performance, but these numbers were the clear sign of a burgeoning political revolt and a historic realignment.

Caught up by his image as a segregationist and racist, many Americans missed the larger significance of Wallace's candidacy and his extraordinary ability to play so skillfully on the fears and passions of his audience.[9] Fear of change was a strong motivator for many Wallace supporters, as was their growing sense of alienation from the America they saw on their TV screens. Wallace was a master of playing the "politics of powerlessness."[10] As biographer Dan Carter says of Wallace, "His genius was his ability to voice his listeners' sense of betrayal—of victimhood—and to refocus their anger."[11] In Wallace's rhetoric, we see the attack lines that have become so familiar to millions of Americans who came of age in the 1970s, '80s, and '90s.

For many Wallace supporters, the "civil rights agitators" and "anti-war demonstrators" were indicative of the nation's faltering moral compass. It wasn't just crime—it was a general coarsening in social mores and a breakdown of public order as reflected by rising divorce rates, growing numbers of out-of-wedlock pregnancies, increasing availability of pornography and drugs, and diminishing respect for once sacred institutions, as dramatized by the Supreme Court decision to end prayer in the nation's schools.[12]

Wallace and many of his supporters were embittered by the perceived slights from the cultural elite of America as personified by these larger societal shifts. As he would say at a political rally in 1966, "When the liberals and intellectuals say the people don't have any sense, they talkin' about us people."[13] As an "outsider" himself, Wallace understood the rising sense of grievance that millions of Americans felt: the palpable feeling that American society and culture were becoming less in tune with their values. Music was edgier, teenagers were more rebellious, movies were more risqué. This burgeoning cultural revolution was unsettling for many and bred further alienation and a sense of isolation, which Wallace's us-versus-them rhetoric reflected. As has often been the case with neo-fascist or authoritarian political movements, Wallace's words gave comfort to those who saw the world changing around them—and not necessarily for the better.[14]

## "THE BEST BRUSH-ARBOR REVIVALIST IN SOUTH ALABAMA"

Rarely would Wallace capture the angry and uncertain mood of Americans as effectively as he did on July 4, 1964, in a speech at the Southeast Fairgrounds in Atlanta, Georgia. Coming the day after President Johnson signed the landmark civil rights bill,

"Wallace was," according to Wayne Greenhaw of the *Alabama Journal*, "at his speech-making best. He would later repeat the style and form countless times, but he would never be better. He had his audience humming with him like the best brush-arbor revivalist in south Alabama."[15] Written by his key speechwriter, Asa Carter, who was also a member of the Ku Klux Klan, the speech was infused with the spirit of paranoia and fear that defined so much of Wallace's public rhetoric.

George Wallace was not what one would call an inspirational politician. His advisers used to stand among the audience when Wallace spoke, making note of the phrases that garnered the largest applause. Soon Wallace's speeches would include only the lines guaranteed to receive the best audience response.[16] This was not a man looking to write poetry on the stump. But when it came to understanding and reflecting his audience and playing directly on their greatest fears, few did it better than George Wallace.

The best political speeches often invoke the image of a political straw man, whether it was FDR's triumvirate of "Martin, Barton and Fish" or Truman's "do-nothing Congress." In Atlanta, Wallace's straw men were the "liberal left-wing press" and the "pinknik" social engineers in Washington, D.C.

"A left-wing monster has risen up in this nation," warned Wallace. "It has invaded the government. It has invaded the news media. It has invaded the leadership of many of our churches. It has invaded every phase and aspect of the life of freedom-loving people."

Few institutions would be smeared by Wallace's rhetorical abuse as harshly as the "arrogant, contemptuous, highhanded, and literal despots" of the liberal judiciary (a form of tyranny worse than King George III, Wallace alleged). It was the unelected judiciary, claimed Wallace, that was most responsible for the steady undermining of the basic civil rights of ordinary (i.e., white) Americans. After a number of controversial rulings on civil rights, in support of criminal defendants, and against school prayer, judges were an easy target for Wallace's rhetorical bomb throwing.

Wallace's attacks on the federal judiciary were so strong that at times they verged into the realm of delusion. He argued that the courts "don't like our form of government" and were actively seeking to "establish a better one."

How were they to achieve this goal? Wallace had an answer: "overthrow our existing form, destroy the democratic institutions created by the people, change the outlook, religion, and philosophy, and bring the whole area of human thought, aspiration, action and organization, under the absolute control of the court. Their decisions reveal this to be the goal of the liberal element on the court which is in a majority at present." As unhinged as these comments may seem, Wallace went even further, claiming that if Americans wanted to predict the decisions of the court, they could find the answers in "the Communist Manifesto."

One can try to be polite about such assertions, but in all honesty, they are insanely paranoid and completely divorced from reality. Wallace's supercharged and unhinged rhetoric might have been what historian Richard Hofstadter had in mind when he wrote these words in his seminal essay "The Paranoid Style in American Politics": "The paranoid spokesman sees the fate of conspiracy in apocalyptic terms—he traffics in the birth and death of whole worlds, whole political orders, whole systems of human values."[17]

In the same vein, Wallace claimed that the liberal leviathan comprising the courts, the media, and the bureaucrats in Washington was waging an assault on honest and law-abiding Americans. "It consists of many various and powerful interests," claimed Wallace. "But it has combined into one massive drive and is held together by the cohesive power of the emotion, setting forth civil rights as supreme to all."

Next came the payoff for his already angry and energized

audience, which of course rejected the primacy of the civil rights issue: "In reality, it is a drive to destroy the rights of private property, to destroy the freedom and liberty of you and me." This was the essence of Wallace's appeal—the campaign to provide civil rights to African Americans was in fact a direct assault on the rights of white Americans. In Wisconsin he reassured his audience that a vote for him was not a vote for segregation, but instead "a vote for the right to run your schools, your business, your lives as you and you alone see fit."[18] Now, who could argue with that?

What was so effective about Wallace's rhetoric was his ability to conflate the civil rights movement with a larger struggle for freedom against tyranny—not freedom from racial oppression for blacks, but freedom for all Americans from the oppression of "an all powerful central government." Again, there is virtually no discussion of race, only of the affronts to hardworking Americans. As Wallace liked to say, "you know who the biggest bigots in the world are—they're the ones who call others bigots."[19] Wallace claimed that civil rights legislation would "destroy individual freedom and liberty" in America, and he presented himself as the only true bulwark against "liberal left-wing dogma," "the continuing trend toward a socialist state," and the slow erosion of Americans' "rights and liberties." Wallace reassured his audience that they weren't racist—they were simply defending their own civil rights and fighting for freedom.

These overarching themes, which were so incendiary in 1964, would eventually become standard discourse in American politics. Not only would they define Wallace's four runs for the White House, but they helped to turn government in America into a four-letter word. By painting a picture of an overzealous and elitist federal government all too willing to sacrifice middle-class Americans for the larger societal goal of integration and black empowerment, Wallace's populist rhetoric helped breed the nation's growing mistrust and cynicism toward its elected leaders. His impact on changing the perspectives of millions of Americans toward their government is incalculable. While once the notion of an activist role for government was seen as a positive by America's working class, Wallace's unrequited attacks convinced many white Americans that the further expansion of federal power would infringe on their freedom. This changed conception of government combined with Wallace's simple populist attacks on elite federal bureaucrats would pave the way for the conservative Republican movement that would transform American politics over the next four decades.

Those who followed in Wallace's footsteps understood the importance of cloaking their attacks in language that was a bit more judicious. The Alabama governor was at his core a bomb thrower. While many Americans may have been sympathetic to Wallace's rhetoric, there were millions who simply could not in good faith cast a ballot for a man who was clearly a racist and who expounded a political view that was at times so clearly unbalanced. It was a point well understood by Richard Nixon as he sought the White House in 1968.

That so many loyal Democrats in Wisconsin, Indiana, and Maryland would vote for Wallace in the spring of 1964 was an unmistakable sign that appeals to racial fear could serve as political gold for the right messenger. In 1968, Richard Nixon returned from the depths of his past political failures to become exactly that messenger.

## THE NEW NIXON

After the 1968 race for the White House, the writer Joe McGinnis published a seminal examination of Richard's Nixon election campaign, titled *The Selling of the President, 1968*. The book charted the way that Nixon used highly choreographed events and a slick, Madison Avenue–driven marketing approach to convince voters that he was in fact "the new Nixon"—and the best man to unify the country.

In his acceptance speech at the 1968 Republican convention, Nixon used this new approach brilliantly, sounding a masterful tone of political illusion and evasiveness by adapting Wallace's appeal to white racism all the while casting himself as the voice of America's silent majority and "forgotten" Americans. Nixon figured out how to use coded racist language while at the same time avoiding Wallace's "redneck poltergeist" image.[20] As one observer of Nixon's campaign would later note, both Wallace and Nixon were angling for the same fish, but while Wallace "baited his hook with good old Southern country blood-red crawlers," Nixon preferred "a dry fly."[21]

This sort of image making on Nixon's part was by no means unusual. In fact, if one wants to pinpoint the exact moment when political speechwriting began to decisively turn the corner from stirring oratory to poll-driven image making, Nixon's 1968 acceptance speech is a good place to start. To be sure, this is a great speech at times, poignant and even poetic, particularly in its closing peroration, which for the first time brought a directly autobiographical element to the campaign trail. Nonetheless, it's a speech based almost exclusively on platitudes and "oratory so evenhanded as to be meaningless."[22]

Nixon didn't even bother with specific policy promises, but instead pledged action of an indeterminate nature. "And so tonight I do not promise the millennium in the morning. I don't promise that we can eradicate poverty, and end discrimination, eliminate all danger of wars in the space of four, or even eight years. But, I do promise action—a new policy for peace abroad; a new policy for peace and progress and justice at home."

There is no better metaphor for Nixon's 1968 campaign than his position on the most pressing issue of the campaign—Vietnam. Nixon refused to get into specifics, instead claiming to have a secret plan for peace, but rest assured, he told his audience, that the first objective "our next Administration will be to bring an honorable end to the war in Vietnam." On crime, he bemoaned "the loan sharks and the numbers racketeers," the "filth peddlers and the narcotics peddlers," and the "cities enveloped in smoke and flame" and "sirens in the night," and proposed a decidedly underwhelming solution—the appointment of a new attorney general.[23]

It's certainly not unusual for a presidential candidate running against an incumbent party to focus more on what's wrong in the country rather than what's right. But rarely has the pendulum swung so far in one direction. By playing on the growing fears of the American people about rising crime (an image generally associated with Democrats), Nixon offered something the other side seemingly couldn't deliver—a return to order. It was hardly surprising that Nixon's most effective campaign ad was one that showed a middle-aged white woman walking on a city street as an announcer dismayingly recited the increases in violent crime over the past several years.[24]

Contrasting America's crime-ridden cities and the young antiwar demonstrators with "the forgotten Americans, the nonshouters, the non-demonstrators," Nixon presented himself as the defender of basic American values. Though he cast himself as a believer in the "principle of civil rights," he also echoed one of Wallace's key rhetorical premises, namely, defining safety and security as the most important civil right and making the "forgotten Americans" into America's real victims. For millions of white Americans who felt threatened by urban race riots, for those concerned about racial integration, and for those who were increasingly making an implicit link between the War on Poverty, rising crime rates, and the nation's black underclass, it was a resonant message.

The idea of "forgotten Americans" was not an original political concept. In 1932, during his campaign for the presidency,

Franklin Roosevelt spoke movingly about the "forgotten man at the bottom of the economic pyramid" and pledged that a Democratic administration would focus on minimizing the economic plight of these individuals. The "forgotten man" became symbolic of the Democratic Party's attention to the workingman and its sacrosanct political position as the "party of the people." But just as he had cast himself in the guise of the common man in the Checkers speech, Nixon was seeking to replicate that effort sixteen years later by arguing that Democrats had forgotten exactly those they had once pledged never to forsake. Indeed, Nixon's evocation of the "forgotten man" predated even Checkers, finding its way into his first political campaign, when he ran for Congress in 1946.[25]

Nixon would subtly take this argument a step further by arguing that the activist government, which Democrats had built to relieve the suffering of the "forgotten man," was now being directed along racial lines and against the interests of white Americans:

> For the past five years we have been deluged by government programs for the unemployed; programs for the cities; programs for the poor. And we have reaped from these programs an ugly harvest of frustration, violence and failure across the land. And now our opponents will be offering more of the same—more billions for government jobs, government housing, government welfare. I say it is time to quit pouring billions of dollars into programs that have failed in the United States of America.

To his image as the defender of forgotten Americans, Nixon added his own political straw man to the mix—the notion of failed and exuberant government programs, the implicit image of "frustrated" and "violent" unemployed poor inner-city residents (i.e., the black underclass), and the explicit message that if Democrats were elected, the American people could expect more of the same. It's a straw man not that dissimilar to the one presented by Wallace—just done in a far more nuanced manner.

Building to his stirring conclusion, Nixon even co-opted King's "I Have a Dream" speech with his refrain "I see a day . . ." followed by a vision of the future with images of an America at peace, secure, prosperous, and above all hopeful for the future.

Finally, in the speech's peroration Nixon poignantly cast himself as the product of a humble upbringing who through the guidance of a loving family and hard work was able to reach the heights of political power. This image, which drew upon powerful American mythology, was almost identical to the one Nixon used in his Checkers speech of 1952. The promise of the American dream has always been a powerful and moving concept, and at a time when millions of Americans felt the country was falling apart around them, it was one they pined to embrace.

## CRAFTING THE NEW REPUBLICAN MAJORITY

At the same time Nixon was implicitly tarring the Democrats as the party of welfare, higher taxes, government largesse, and national weakness, he was casting the once feared Republican Party of Goldwater, Hoover, and the "old Nixon" as the new "people's party": a defender of basic values, of law and order, and of personal responsibility. In *Nixon Agonistes*, Garry Wills's brilliant examination of Nixon's complicated psyche, the author highlights the effect of Nixon's words on his audience: "He knew that 1968 was a time when those who had succeeded felt somehow cheated . . . They had worked and earned, not only for money or material things, but for a spiritual goal . . . And now the kids, the sophisticates, the 'effete snobs' were denying them that honor. Nixon came to reassure such men, to tell them he believed in them, he had not forgotten, he was one of them."[26]

Yet, for all of Nixon's obvious efforts at image making, there is, if one looks closely, a real substantive policy agenda buried in the platitudes. In 1968, Americans desperately wanted order and, to quote Harding, a "return to normalcy." Frankly, considering the tumultuous events of the year, could anyone really blame them? They wanted to feel safe in their neighborhoods. They wanted to be reassured that fear of rising black power didn't make them racists. Most of all, they wanted their government to move away from the whirlwind of Great Society legislation and return to its most fundamental responsibility—providing Americans with basic security and order.

Nixon's acceptance speech reflected that desire. As Mary McGrory, the legendary political reporter for the *Washington Post*, would say of his campaign, "Nixon does not seek to lead public opinion but to follow it."[27] If 1932 offered an endorsement of bold experimentation and 1960 a sense of shared national sacrifice, in the 1968 race Nixon, better than any other candidate, spoke to the American people's desire for a cooling-off period and a step back from the precipice of racial and increasingly generational division. It was a passionless campaign for the White House, but as Theodore White would put it, "Passion was the very emotion [Nixonians] sought to avoid—passion had ruined the party in 1964, passion ravaged the nation in 1968."[28]

The 1968 election wasn't an endorsement of conservative government (that would come later). As president, Nixon consistently straddled the fence between slowing down more invasive integration efforts and continuing government support for black empowerment. Nixon did not shrink government, à la Barry Goldwater. If anything, he expanded it. Government agencies such as OSHA and the EPA, which are today conservative bogeyman, took root under Nixon. To be sure, Nixon's victory was barely an endorsement of the Republican Party. He had gained the support of only 43 percent of the electorate, and while Republicans made gains in the House and Senate, Democrats continued to hold strong majorities in both houses.

However, others who followed in Nixon's footsteps would take the central rhetorical themes of his campaign and use them to push for a far more aggressive style of conservative politics—a style that would spark the party's resurgence over the next several decades while at the same intensifying the nation's already raw racial, social, and cultural divisions. The attacks on government would intensify, and confidence in the nation's governing institutions would continue to erode. The seed of a new conservative-driven and divisive form of populist politics, birthed by George Wallace, midwifed by Richard Nixon, and given full growth by Ronald Reagan and George W. Bush, was planted in the words and ideas contained in these two speeches.

## *George Wallace Calls for "Freedom" from Civil Rights Legislation, Atlanta, July 4, 1964*

We come here today in deference to the memory of those stalwart patriots who on July 4, 1776, pledged their lives, their fortunes, and their sacred honor to establish and defend the proposition that governments are created by the people, empowered by the people, derive their just powers from the consent of the people, and must forever remain subservient to the will of the people.

Today, 188 years later, we celebrate that occasion and find inspiration and determination and courage to preserve and protect the great principles of freedom enunciated in the Declaration of Independence.

It is therefore a cruel irony that the President of the United States has only yesterday signed into law the most monstrous piece of legislation ever enacted by the United States Congress.

It is a fraud, a sham, and a hoax.

This bill will live in infamy. To sign it into law at any time is tragic. To do so upon the eve of the celebration of our independence insults the intelligence of the American people.

It dishonors the memory of countless thousands of our dead who offered up their very lives in defense of principles which this bill destroys.

Never before in the history of this nation have so many human and property rights been destroyed by a single enactment of the Congress. It is an act of tyranny. It is the assassin's knife stuck in the back of liberty.

With this assassin's knife and a blackjack in the hand of the Federal force-cult, the left-wing liberals will try to force us back into bondage. Bondage to a tyranny more brutal than that imposed by the British monarchy which claimed power to rule over the lives of our forefathers under sanction of the Divine Right of kings.

Today, this tyranny is imposed by the central government which claims the right to rule over our lives under sanction of the omnipotent black-robed despots who sit on the bench of the United States Supreme Court.

This bill is fraudulent in intent, in design, and in execution. It is misnamed. Each and every provision is mistitled. It was rammed through the Congress on the wave of ballyhoo, promotions, and publicity stunts reminiscent of P. T. Barnum.

It was enacted in an atmosphere of pressure, intimidation, and even cowardice, as demonstrated by the refusal of the United States Senate to adopt an amendment to submit the bill to a vote of the people.

To illustrate the fraud—it is not a civil rights bill. It is a Federal Penal Code. It creates Federal crimes which would take volumes to list and years to tabulate because it affects the lives of 192 million American citizens. Every person in every walk and station of life and every aspect of our daily lives becomes subject to the criminal provisions of this bill.

It threatens our freedom of speech, of assembly, or association, and makes the exercise of these Freedoms a Federal crime under certain conditions.

It affects our political rights, our right to trial by jury, our right to the full use and enjoyment of our private property, the freedom from search and seizure of our private property and possessions, the freedom from harassment by Federal police and, in short, all the rights of individuals inherent in a society of free men.

Ministers, lawyers, teachers, newspapers, and every private citizen must guard his speech and watch his actions to avoid the deliberately imposed booby traps put into this bill. It is designed to make Federal crimes of our customs, beliefs, and traditions. Therefore, under the fantastic powers of the Federal judiciary to punish for contempt of court and under their fantastic powers to regulate our most intimate aspects of our lives by injunction, every American citizen is in jeopardy and must stand guard against these despots.

Yet there are those who call this a good bill.

. . . It was left-wing radicals who led the fight in the Senate for the so-called civil rights bill now about to enslave our nation.

We find Senator Hubert Humphrey telling the people of the United States that "non-violent" demonstrations would continue to serve a good purpose through a "long, busy and constructive summer." Yet this same Senator told the people of this country that passage of this monstrous bill would ease tensions and stop demonstrations. This is the same Senator who suggested . . . that the President call the fifty state Governors together to work out ways and means to enforce this rotten measure.

There is no need for him to call on me. I am not about to be a party to anything having to do with the law that is going to destroy individual freedom and liberty in this country.

I am having nothing to do with enforcing a law that will destroy our free enterprise system.

I am having nothing to do with enforcing a law that will destroy neighborhood schools.

I am having nothing to do with enforcing a law that will destroy the rights of private property.

I am having nothing to do with enforcing a law that destroys your right—and my right—to choose my neighbors—or to sell my house to whomever I choose.

I am having nothing to do with enforcing a law that destroys the labor seniority system.

I am having nothing to do with this so-called civil rights bill. The liberal left-wingers have passed it. Now let them employ some pinknik social engineers in Washington, D.C., to figure out what to do with it.

. . . But I am not here to talk about the separate provisions of the Federal Penal Code. I am here to talk about principles which have been overthrown by the enactment of this bill. The principles that you and I hold dear. The principles for which our forefathers fought and died to establish and to defend. The principles for which we came here to rededicate ourselves.

But before I get into that, let me point out one important fact. It would have been impossible for the American people to have been deceived by the sponsors of this bill had there been a responsible American press to tell the people exactly what the bill contained. If they had had the integrity and the guts to tell the truth, this bill would never have been enacted.

Whoever heard of truth put to the worst in free and open encounter? We couldn't get the truth to the American people. You and I know that that's extremely difficult to do where our newspapers are owned by out-of-state interests. Newspapers which are run and operated by left-wing liberals, Communist sympathizers, and members of the Americans for Democratic Action and other Communist front organizations with high sounding names.

However, we will not be intimidated by the vultures of the liberal left-wing press. We will not be deceived by their lies and distortions of truth. We will not be swayed by their brutal attacks upon the character and reputation of any honest citizen who dares stand up and fight for liberty.

. . . As I have said before, that Federal Penal Code could never have been enacted into law if we had had a responsible press who was willing to tell the American people the truth about what it actually provides. Nor would we have had a bill had it not been for the United States Supreme Court.

Now on the subject of the court let me make it clear that I am not attacking any member of the United States Supreme Court as an individual. However, I do attack their decisions, I question their intelligence, their common sense and their judgment, I consider the Federal judiciary system to be the greatest single threat to individual freedom and liberty in the United States today, and I'm going to take off the gloves in talking about these people.

There is only one word to describe the Federal judiciary today. That word is "lousy."

They assert more power than claimed by King George III, more power than Hitler, Mussolini, or Khrushchev ever had. They assert the power to declare unconstitutional our very thoughts. To create for us a system of moral and ethical values. To outlaw and declare unconstitutional, illegal, and immoral the customs, traditions, and beliefs of the people, and furthermore they assert the authority to enforce their decrees in all these subjects upon the American people without their consent.

. . . The court today, just as in 1776, is deaf to the voices of the people and their repeated entreaties: they have become arrogant, contemptuous, highhanded, and literal despots.

It has been said that power corrupts and absolute power corrupts absolutely. There was never greater evidence as to the proof of this statement than in the example of the present Federal judiciary.

I want to touch upon just a few of the acts of tyranny which have been sanctioned by the United States Supreme Court and compare these acts with the acts of tyranny enumerated in the Declaration of Independence.

The colonists objected most strenuously to the imposition of taxes upon the people without their consent.

Today, the Federal judiciary asserts the same tyrannical power to levy taxes in Prince Edward County, Virginia, and without the consent of the people. Not only that, but they insist upon the power to tell the people for what purposes their money must be spent.

. . . Today we have actually witnessed the invasion of the State of Arkansas, Mississippi, and Alabama by the armed forces of the United States and maintained in the state against the will of the people and without consent of state legislatures.

It is a form of tyranny worse than that of King George III who had sent mercenaries against the colonies because today the Federal Judicial tyrants have sanctioned the use of brother against brother and father against son by federalizing the National Guard.

In 1776 the colonists also complained that the monarch ". . . Has incited domestic insurrections against us . . ."

Today we have absolute proof that the Federal Department of Justice has planned, supervised, financed and protected acts of insurrection in the southern states, resulting in vandalism, property damage, personal injury, and staggering expense to states.

In 1776 it was charged that the monarchy had asserted power to ". . . Dissolve representative houses and to punish . . . For opposing with manly firmness his invasions of the rights of the people . . ."

Today, the Federal judiciary asserts the power not only to dissolve state legislatures but to create them and to dissolve all state laws and state judicial decrees, and to punish a state governor by trial without jury ". . . For opposing with manly firmness his invasions of the rights of the people . . ."

The colonists also listed as acts of tyranny: ". . . The erection of a multitude of new offices and sent hither swarms of officers to harass our people and to eat out their substance . . .";

. . . "For depriving us in many cases, of the benefits of trial by jury . . . For taking away our charters, abolishing our most valuable laws, and altering fundamentally [the] form of our government; for suspending our own legislatures and declaring themselves invested with power to legislate for us in all cases whatsoever."

The United States Supreme Court is guilty of each and every one of these acts of tyranny.

THE "FORGOTTEN AMERICANS"

Therefore, I echo the sentiments of our forefathers who declared: "a prince, whose character is thus marked by every act which may define a tyrant, is unfit to be the ruler of a free people"

Ladies and Gentlemen, I have listed only a few of the many acts of tyranny which have been committed or specifically sanctioned by the United States Supreme Court.

. . . It is perfectly obvious from the left-wing liberal press and from the left-wing law journals that what the court is saying behind all the jargon is that they don't like our form of government.

They think they can establish a better one. In order to do so it is necessary that they overthrow our existing form, destroy the democratic institutions created by the people, change the outlook, religion, and philosophy, and bring the whole area of human thought, aspiration, action and organization, under the absolute control of the court. Their decisions reveal this to be the goal of the liberal element on the court which is in a majority at present.

It has reached the point where one may no longer look to judicial decisions to determine what the court may do. However, it is possible to predict with accuracy the nature of the opinions to be rendered. One may find the answer in the Communist Manifesto.

The Communists are dedicated to the overthrow of our form of government. They are dedicated to the destruction of the concept of private property. They are dedicated to the object of destroying religion as the basis of moral and ethical values.

. . . I do not call the members of the United States Supreme Court Communists. But I do say, and I submit for your judgment the fact that every single decision of the court in the past ten years which related in any way to each of these objectives has been decided against freedom and in favor of tyranny.

A politician must stand on his record. Let the court stand on its record.

The record reveals, for the past number of years, that the chief, if not the only beneficiaries of the present court's rulings, have been duly and lawfully convicted criminals, Communists, atheists, and clients of vociferous left-wing minority groups.

You can't convict a Communist in our Federal court system. Neither can you convict one of being a Communist in Russia, China, or Cuba. The point is that the United States Supreme Court refuses to recognize the Communist conspiracy and their intent to "bury us."

Let us look at the record further with respect to the court's contribution to the destruction of the concept of God and the abolition of religion.

The Federal court rules that your children shall not be permitted to read the bible in our public school systems.

Let me tell you this, though. We still read the bible in Alabama schools and as long as I am governor we will continue to read the bible no matter what the Supreme Court says.

Federal courts will not convict a "demonstrator" invading and destroying private property. But the Federal courts rule you cannot say a simple "God is great, God is good, we thank Thee for our food," in kindergartens supported by public funds.

Now, let us examine the manner in which the court has continuously chipped away at the concept of private property. It is contended by the left-wing liberals that private property is merely a legal fiction. That one has no inherent right to own and possess property.

The courts have restricted and limited the right of acquisition of property in life and have decreed its disposition in death and have ruthlessly set aside the wills of the dead in order to attain social ends decreed by the court. The court has substituted its judgment for that of the testator based on social theory.

. . . They assert the right to convert a private place of business into a public place of business without the consent of the owner and without compensation to him.

. . . Let us take a look at the attitude of the court with respect to the control of the private resources of the nation and the allocation of the productive capacity of the nation.

The Supreme Court decisions have sanctioned enactment of the civil rights bill.

What this bill actually does is to empower the United States government to reallocate the entire productive capacity of the agricultural economy covered by quotas and acreage allotments of various types on the basis of race, creed, color and national origin.

. . . The power is there. I am not in the least impressed by the protestations that the government will use this power with benevolent discretion.

We know that this bill authorizes the President of the United States to allocate all defense productive capacity of this country on the basis of race, creed, or color.

It does not matter in the least that he will make such allocations with restraint. The fact is that it is possible with a politically dominated agency to punish and to bankrupt and destroy any business that deals with the Federal government if it does not bow to the wishes and demands of the president of the United States.

All of us know what the court has done to capture the minds of our children.

The Federal judiciary has asserted the authority to prescribe regulations with respect to the management, operation, and control of our local schools. The second Brown decision in the infamous school segregation case authorized Federal district courts to supervise such matters as teacher hiring, firing, promotion, the expenditure of local funds, both administratively and for capital improvements, additions, and renovations, the location of new schools, the drawing of school boundaries, busing and transportation of school children, and, believe it or not, it has asserted the right in the Federal judiciary to pass judgment upon the curricula adopted in local public schools.

. . . In ruling after ruling, the Supreme Court has overstepped its constitutional authority. While appearing to protect the people's interest, it has in reality become a judicial tyrant.

It's the old pattern. The people always have some champion whom they set over them. And nurse into greatness. This, and no other, is the foot from which a tyrant springs, after first appearing as a protector.

This is another way of saying that the people never give up their liberties and their freedom. But under some delusion. But yet there is hope.

There is yet a spirit of resistance in this country which will not be oppressed. And it is awakening. And I am sure there is an abundance of good sense in this country which cannot be deceived.

I have personal knowledge of this. Thirty-four percent of the Wisconsin Democrats supported the beliefs you and I uphold and expound.

Thirty percent of the Democrats in Indiana join us in fighting this grab for executive power by those now in control in Washington.

And, listen to this, forty-three percent of the Democrats in Maryland, practically in view of the nation's capital, believe as you and I believe.

So, let me say to you today. Take heart. Millions of Americans believe just as we in this great region of the United States believe.

I shall never forget last spring as I stood in the midst of a great throng of South Milwaukee supporters at one of the greatest political rallies I have ever witnessed.

A fine-looking man grabbed my hand and said:

"Governor, I've never been south of South Milwaukee, but I am a Southerner!" Of course, he was saying he believed in the principles and philosophy of the southern people . . . Of you here today and the people of my state of Alabama.

He was right.

Being a southerner is no longer geographic. It's a philosophy and an attitude.

One destined to be a national philosophy—embraced by millions of Americans—which shall assume the mantle of leadership and steady a governmental structure in these days of crises.

Certainly I am a candidate for President of the United States.

If the left-wingers do not think I am serious—let them consider this.

I am going to take our fight to the people—the court of public opinion—where truth and common sense will eventually prevail.

. . . Conservatives of this nation constitute the balance of power in presidential elections.

I am a conservative.

. . . I welcome a fight between our philosophy and the liberal left-wing dogma which now threatens to engulf every man, woman, and child in the United States.

. . . The American people have been pushed around long enough and that they, like you and I, are fed up with the continuing trend toward a socialist state which now subjects the individual to the dictates of an all-powerful central government.

. . . I want to remain free. I want your children and mine and our prosperity to be unencumbered by the manipulations of a soulless state.

I intend to fight for a positive, affirmative program to restore constitutional government and to stop the senseless bloodletting now being performed on the body of liberty by those who lead us willingly and dangerously close to a totalitarian central government.

In our nation, man has always been sovereign and the state has been his servant. This philosophy has made the United States the greatest free nation in history.

This freedom was not a gift. It was won by work, by sweat, by tears, by war, by whatever it took to be—and to remain free.

Are we today less resolute, less determined and courageous than our fathers and our grandfathers?

. . . We are not unmindful and careless of our future. We will not stand aside while our conscientious convictions tell us that a dictatorial Supreme Court has taken away our rights and our liberties.

We will not stand idly by while the Supreme Court continues to invade the prerogatives left rightfully to the states by the constitution.

We must not be misled by left-wing incompetent news media that day after day feed us a diet of fantasy telling us we are bigots, racists and hate-mongers to oppose the destruction of the constitution and our nation.

A left-wing monster has risen up in this nation. It has invaded the government. It has invaded the news media. It has invaded the leadership of many of our churches. It has invaded every phase and aspect of the life of freedom-loving people.

It consists of many and various and powerful interests, but it has combined into one massive drive and is held together by the cohesive power of the emotion, setting forth civil rights as supreme to all.

But, in reality, it is a drive to destroy the rights of private property, to destroy the freedom and liberty of you and me.

. . . Politically evil men have combined and arranged themselves against us. The good people of this nation must now associate themselves together, else we will fall one by one, an unpitied sacrifice in a struggle which threatens to engulf the entire nation.

We can win. We can control the election of the president in November.

Our object must be our country, our whole country and nothing but our country.

. . . We are not going to change anything by sitting on our hands hoping that things will change for the better. Those who cherish individual freedom have a job to do.

First, let us let it be known that we intend to take the offensive and carry our fight for freedom across this nation. We will wield the power that is ours—the power of the people.

Let it be known that we will no longer tolerate the boot of tyranny. We will no longer hide our heads in the sand. We will reschool our thoughts in the lessons our forefathers knew so well.

We must destroy the power to dictate, to forbid, to require, to demand, to distribute, to edict, and to judge what is best and enforce that will of judgment upon free citizens.

We must revitalize a government founded in this nation on faith in God.

I ask that you join with me and that together, we give an active and courageous leadership to the millions of people throughout this nation who look with hope and faith to our fight to preserve our constitutional system of government with its guarantees of liberty and justice for all within the framework of our priceless freedoms.

## Richard Nixon Speaks to the "Forgotten Majority" in Accepting the Republican Party's Nomination for President, Miami, August 8, 1968

Mr. Chairman, delegates to this convention, my fellow Americans.

Sixteen years ago I stood before this Convention to accept your nomination as the running mate of one of the greatest Americans of our time—or of any time—Dwight D. Eisenhower.

Eight years ago, I had the highest honor of accepting your nomination for President of the United States. Tonight, I again proudly accept that nomination for President of the United States.

But I have news for you. This time there is a difference.

This time we are going to win.

. . . We are going to win because this great Convention has demonstrated to the nation that the Republican Party has the leadership, the platform and the purpose that America needs . . . After a period of forty years when power has gone from the cities and the states to the government in Washington, D.C., it's time to have power go back from Washington to the states and to the cities of this country all over America.

We are going to win because at a time that America cries out for the unity that this Administration has destroyed, the Republican Party—after a spirited contest for its nomination—for President and for Vice President stands united before the nation tonight.

. . . My fellow Americans, most important—we are going to win because our cause is right.

We make history tonight—not for ourselves but for the ages. The choice we make in 1968 will determine not only the future of America but the future of peace and freedom in the world for the last third of the Twentieth Century. And the question that we answer tonight: can America meet this great challenge?

For a few moments, let us look at America, let us listen to America to find the answer to that question.

As we look at America, we see cities enveloped in smoke and flame. We hear sirens in the night. We see Americans dying on distant battlefields abroad. We see Americans hating each other; fighting each other; killing each other at home.

And as we see and hear these things, millions of Americans cry out in anguish. Did we come all this way for this? Did American boys die in Normandy, and Korea, and in Valley Forge for this?

Listen to the answer to those questions.

It is another voice. It is the quiet voice in the tumult and the shouting. It is the voice of the great majority of Americans, the forgotten Americans—the non-shouters; the non-demonstrators. They are not racists or sick; they are not guilty of the crime that plagues the land. They are black and they are white—they're native born and foreign born—they're young and they're old.

They work in America's factories. They run America's businesses. They serve in government. They provide most of the soldiers who died to keep us free. They give drive to the spirit of America. They give lift to the American Dream. They give steel to the backbone of America. They are good people, they are decent people; they work, and they save, and they pay their taxes, and they care.

Like Theodore Roosevelt, they know that this country will not be a good place for any of us to live in unless it is a good place for all of us to live in.

This I say to you tonight is the real voice of America. In this year 1968, this is the message it will broadcast to America and to the world.

Let's never forget that despite her faults, America is a great nation. And America is great because her people are great.

With Winston Churchill, we say: "We have not journeyed all this way across the centuries, across the oceans, across the mountains, across the prairies because we are made of sugar candy."

America is in trouble today not because her people have failed but because her leaders have failed. And what America needs are leaders to match the greatness of her people.

And this great group of Americans, the forgotten Americans, and others know that the great question Americans must answer by their votes in November is this: Whether we shall continue for four more years the policies of the last five years.

And this is their answer and this is my answer to that question. When the strongest nation in the world can be tied down for four years in a war in Vietnam with no end in sight; when the richest nation in the world can't manage its own economy; when the nation with the greatest tradition of the rule of law is plagued by unprecedented lawlessness; when a nation that has been known for a century for equality of opportunity is torn by unprecedented racial violence; and when the President of the United States cannot travel abroad or to any major city at home without fear of a hostile demonstration—then it's time for new leadership for the United States of America.

My fellow Americans, tonight I accept the challenge and the commitment to provide that new leadership for America. And I ask you to accept it with me.

And let us accept this challenge not as a grim duty but as an exciting adventure in which we are privileged to help a great nation realize its destiny. And let us begin by committing ourselves to the truth—to see it like it is, and tell it like it is—to find the truth, to speak the truth, and to live the truth—that's what we will do.

We've had enough of big promises and little action. The time has come for honest government in the United States of America.

And so tonight I do not promise the millennium in the morning. I don't promise that we can eradicate poverty, and end discrimination, eliminate all danger of war in the space of four, or even eight years. But, I do promise action—a new policy for peace abroad; a new policy for peace and progress and justice at home.

Look at our problems abroad. Do you realize that we face the stark truth that we are worse off in every area of the world tonight than we were when President Eisenhower left office eight years ago. That's the record. And there is only one answer to such a record of failure and that is a complete housecleaning of those responsible for the failures of that record. The answer is a complete re-appraisal of America's policies in every section of the world.

We shall begin with Vietnam.

We all hope in this room that there is a chance that current negotiations may bring an honorable end to that war. And we will say nothing during this campaign that might destroy that chance.

But if the war is not ended when the people choose in November, the choice will be clear. Here it is. For four years this Administration has had at its disposal the greatest military and economic advantage that one nation has ever had over another in any war in history. For four years, America's fighting men have set a record for courage and sacrifice unsurpassed in our history. For four years, this Administration has had the support of the Loyal Opposition for the objective of seeking an honorable end to the struggle.

Never has so much military and economic and diplomatic power been used so ineffectively. And if after all of this time and all of this sacrifice and all of this support there is still no end in sight, then I say the time has come for the American people to turn to new leadership—not tied to the mistakes and the policies of the past. That is what we offer to America.

And I pledge to you tonight that the first priority foreign policy objective of our next Administration will be to bring an honorable end to the war in Vietnam. We shall not stop there—we need a policy to prevent more Vietnams.

All of America's peace-keeping institutions and all of America's foreign commitments must be re-appraised. Over the past twenty-five years, America has provided more than one-hundred and fifty billion dollars in foreign aid to nations abroad.

In Korea and now again in Vietnam, the United States furnished most of the money, most of the arms; most of the men to help the people of those countries defend themselves against aggression.

Now we are a rich country. We are a strong nation. We are a populous nation. But there are two hundred million Americans and there are two billion people that live in the Free World.

And I say the time has come for other nations in the Free World to bear their fair share of the burden of defending peace and freedom around this world. What I call for is not a new isolationism. It is a new internationalism in which America enlists its allies and its friends around the world in those struggles in which their interest is as great as ours.

And now to the leaders of the Communist world, we say: After an era of confrontation, the time has come for an era of negotiation.

Where the world's super powers are concerned, there is no acceptable alternative to peaceful negotiation. Because this will be a period of negotiation, we shall restore the strength of America so that we shall always negotiate from strength and never from weakness.

And as we seek peace through negotiation, let our goals be made clear: We do not seek domination over any other country. We believe deeply in our ideas, but we believe they should travel on their own power and not on the power of our arms. We shall never be belligerent but we shall be as firm in defending our system as they are in expanding theirs.

We believe this should be an era of peaceful competition, not only in the productivity of our factories but in the quality of our ideas.

We extend the hand of friendship to all people, to the Russian people, to the Chinese people, to all people in the world.

And we shall work toward the goal of an open world—open skies, open cities, open hearts, open minds.

The next eight years, my friends, this period in which we are entering, I think we will have the greatest opportunity for world peace but also face the greatest danger of world war of any time in our history.

I believe we must have peace. I believe that we can have peace, but I do not underestimate the difficulty of this task. Because you see the art of preserving peace is greater than that of waging war and much more demanding. But I am proud to have served in an Administration which ended one war and kept the nation out of other wars for eight years. And it is that kind of experience and it is that kind of leadership that America needs today, and that we will give to America with your help.

And as we commit to new policies for America tonight, let us make one further pledge: For five years hardly a day has gone by when we haven't read or heard a report of the American flag being spit on; an embassy being stoned; a library being burned; or an ambassador being insulted some place in the world. And each incident reduced respect for the United States until the ultimate insult inevitably occurred.

And I say to you tonight that when respect for the United States of America falls so low that a fourth-rate military power, like North Korea, will seize an American naval vessel on the high seas, it is time for new leadership to restore respect for the United States of America.

My friends, America is a great nation.

And it is time we started to act like a great nation around the world. It is ironic to note when we were a small nation—weak militarily and poor economically—America was respected. And the reason was that America stood for something more powerful than military strength or economic wealth.

The American Revolution was a shining example of freedom in action which caught the imagination of the world.

Today, too often, America is an example to be avoided and not followed.

A nation that can't keep the peace at home won't be trusted to keep the peace abroad. A President who isn't treated with respect at home will not be treated with respect abroad. A nation which can't manage its own economy can't tell others how to manage theirs. If we are to restore prestige and respect for America abroad, the place to begin is at home in the United States of America.

My friends, we live in an age of revolution in America and in the world. And to find the answers to our problems, let us turn to a revolution, a revolution that will never grow old. The world's greatest continuing revolution, the American Revolution.

The American Revolution was and is dedicated to progress, but our founders recognized that the first requisite of progress is order. Now, there is no quarrel between progress and order—because neither can exist without the other.

So let us have order in America—not the order that suppresses dissent and discourages change but the order which guarantees the right to dissent and provides the basis for peaceful change.

And tonight, it is time for some honest talk about the problem of order in the United States.

Let us always respect, as I do, our courts and those who serve on them. But let us also recognize that some of our courts in their decisions have gone too far in weakening the peace forces as against the criminal forces in this country and we must act to restore that balance.

Let those who have the responsibility to enforce our laws and our judges who have the responsibility to interpret them be dedicated to the great principles of civil rights.

But let them also recognize that the first civil right of every American is to be free from domestic violence, and that right must be guaranteed in this country.

And if we are to restore order and respect for law in this country there is one place we are going to begin. We are going to have a new Attorney General of the United States of America.

I pledge to you that our new Attorney General will be directed by the President of the United States to launch a war against organized crime in this country. I pledge to you that the new Attorney General of the United States will be an active belligerent against the loan sharks and the numbers racketeers that rob the urban poor in our cities. I pledge to you that the new Attorney General will open a new front against the filth peddlers and the narcotics peddlers who are corrupting the lives of the children of this country.

Because, my friends, let this message come through clear from what I say tonight. Time is running out for the merchants of crime and corruption in American society.

The wave of crime is not going to be the wave of the future in the United States of America.

We shall re-establish freedom from fear in America so that America can take the lead in re-establishing freedom from fear in the world.

And to those who say that law and order is the code word for racism, there and here is a reply: Our goal is justice for every American. If we are to have respect for law in America, we must have laws that deserve respect.

Just as we cannot have progress without order, we cannot have order without progress, and so, as we commit to order tonight, let us commit to progress.

And this brings me to the clearest choice among the great issues of this campaign.

For the past five years we have been deluged by government programs for the unemployed; programs for the cities; programs for the poor. And we have reaped from these programs an ugly harvest of frustration, violence and failure across the land. And now our opponents will be offering more of the same—more billions for government jobs, government housing, government welfare. I say it is time to quit pouring billions of dollars into programs that have failed in the United States of America.

To put it bluntly, we are on the wrong road—and it's time to take a new road, to progress.

Again, we turn to the American Revolution for our answer.

The war on poverty didn't begin five years ago in this country. It began when this country began. It's been the most successful war on poverty in the history of nations. There is more wealth in America today, more broadly shared, than in any nation in the world.

We are a great nation. And we must never forget how we became great. America is a great nation today not because of what government did for people—but because of what people did for themselves over a hundred-ninety years in this country.

So it is time to apply the lessons of the American Revolution to our present problem.

Let us increase the wealth of America so that we can provide more generously for the aged; and for the needy; and for all those who cannot help themselves.

But for those who are able to help themselves—what we need are not more millions on welfare rolls—but more millions on payrolls in the United States of America.

Instead of government jobs, and government housing, and government welfare, let government use its tax and credit policies to enlist in this battle the greatest engine of progress ever developed in the history of man—American private enterprise.

Let us enlist in this great cause the millions of Americans in volunteer organizations who will bring a dedication to this task that no amount of money could ever buy. And let us build bridges, my friends, build bridges to human dignity across that gulf that separates black America from white America.

Black Americans, no more than white Americans, they do not want more government programs which perpetuate dependency. They don't want to be a colony in a nation.

They want the pride, and the self-respect, and the dignity that can only come if they have an equal chance to own their own homes, to own their own businesses, to be managers and executives as well as workers, to have a piece of the action in the exciting ventures of private enterprise.

I pledge to you tonight that we shall have new programs which will provide that equal chance.

We make great history tonight.

We do not fire a shot heard 'round the world but we shall light the lamp of hope in millions of homes across this land in which there is no hope today.

And that great light shining out from America will again become a beacon of hope for all those in the world who seek freedom and opportunity.

My fellow Americans, I believe that historians will recall that 1968 marked the beginning of the American generation in world history.

Just to be alive in America, just to be alive at this time is an experience unparalleled in history. Here is where the action is. Think.

Thirty-two years from now most Americans living today will celebrate a new year that comes once in a thousand years. Eight years from now, in the second term of the next President, we will celebrate the 200th anniversary of the American Revolution.

And by our decision in this election, we, all of us here, all of you listening on television and radio, we will determine what kind of nation America will be on its 200th birthday; we will determine what kind of a world America will live in the year 2000.

This is the kind of a day I see for America on that glorious Fourth—eight years from now.

I see a day when Americans are once again proud of their flag. When once again at home and abroad, it is honored as the world's greatest symbol of liberty and justice.

I see a day when the President of the United States is respected and his office is honored because it is worthy of respect and worthy of honor.

I see a day when every child in this land, regardless of his background, has a chance for the best education our wisdom and schools can provide, and an equal chance to go just as high as his talents will take him.

I see a day when life in rural America attracts people to the country, rather than driving them away.

I see a day when we can look back on massive breakthroughs in solving the problems of slums and pollution and traffic which are choking our cities to death.

I see a day when our senior citizens and millions of others can plan for the future with the assurance that their government is not going to rob them of their savings by destroying the value of their dollars.

I see a day when we will again have freedom from fear in America and freedom from fear in the world.

I see a day when our nation is at peace and the world is at peace and everyone on earth—those who hope, those who aspire, those who crave liberty—will look to America as the shining example of hopes realized and dreams achieved.

My fellow Americans, this is the cause I ask you to vote for. This is the cause I ask you to work for. This is the cause I ask you to commit to—not just for victory in November but beyond that to a new Administration.

Because the time when one man or a few leaders could save America is gone. We need tonight nothing less than the total commitment and the total mobilization of the American people if we are to succeed.

Government can pass laws. But respect for law can come only from people who take the law into their hearts and their minds—and not into their hands.

Government can provide opportunity. But opportunity means nothing unless people are prepared to seize it. A President can ask for reconciliation in the racial conflict that divides Americans. But reconciliation comes only from the hearts of people.

And tonight, therefore, as we make this commitment, let us look into our hearts and let us look down into the faces of our children. Is there anything in the world that should stand in their way? None of the old hatreds mean anything when we look down into the faces of our children. In their faces is our hope, our love, and our courage.

Tonight, I see the face of a child.

He lives in a great city. He is black. Or he is white. He is Mexican, Italian, Polish. None of that matters. What matters, he's an American child.

That child in that great city is more important than any politician's promise. He is America. He is a poet. He is a scientist, he is a great teacher, he is a proud craftsman. He is everything we ever hoped to be and everything we dare to dream to be.

He sleeps the sleep of childhood and he dreams the dreams of a child. And yet when he awakens, he awakens to a living nightmare of poverty, neglect and despair. He fails in school. He ends up on welfare. For him the American system is one that feeds his stomach and starves his soul. It breaks his heart. And in the end it may take his life on some distant battlefield. To millions of children in this rich land, this is their prospect of the future.

But this is only part of what I see in America.

I see another child tonight.

He hears the train go by at night and he dreams of far away places where he'd like to go. It seems like an impossible dream. But he is helped on his journey through life.

A father who had to go to work before he finished the sixth grade, sacrificed everything he had so that his sons could go to college. A gentle, Quaker mother, with a passionate concern for peace, quietly wept when he went to war but she understood why he had to go. A great teacher, a remarkable football coach, an inspirational minister encouraged him on his way. A courageous wife and loyal children stood by him in victory and also defeat. And in his chosen profession of politics, first there were scores, then hundreds, then thousands, and finally millions worked for his success.

And tonight he stands before you—nominated for President of the United States of America.

You can see why I believe so deeply in the American Dream.

For most of us the American Revolution has been won; the American Dream has come true.

And what I ask you to do tonight is to help me make that dream come true for millions to whom it's an impossible dream today.

One hundred and eight years ago, the newly elected President of the United States, Abraham Lincoln, left Springfield, Illinois, never to return again. He spoke to his friends gathered at the railroad station. Listen to his words:

"Today I leave you. I go to assume a greater task than devolved on General Washington. The great God which helped him must help me. Without that great assistance, I will surely fail. With it, I cannot fail."

Abraham Lincoln lost his life but he did not fail.

The next President of the United States will face challenges which in some ways will be greater than those of Washington or Lincoln. Because for the first time in our nation's history, an American President will face not only the problem of restoring peace abroad but of restoring peace at home.

Without God's help and your help, we will surely fail; but with God's help and your help, we shall surely succeed.

My fellow Americans, the long dark night for America is about to end.

The time has come for us to leave the valley of despair and climb the mountain so that we may see the glory of the dawn—a new day for America, and a new dawn for peace and freedom in the world.

## Chapter 15

## AMERICA "COME HOME"

Hubert Humphrey, George McGovern, and the Rise of
the Doves in the Democratic Party: 1968–1972

O N ELECTION DAY 1968 the Democratic Party experienced
a reversal of fortune unlike any before seen in American
politics. Four years before, Lyndon Johnson had won the greatest
victory in American electoral history, with more than six out of ten
Americans casting a ballot for him. In 1968, only four out of
ten Americans voted for Hubert Humphrey. The party's growing
divisions and its increasing alienation from the New Deal coalition, Democrats' once unassailable political base, placed the party's
national electoral dominance in growing peril.

While race represented a genuine cleavage in the party, the divisions among Democrats on national security and foreign policy
would prove, over the long term, to be equally destructive. Fairly
or unfairly, the image of Democrats as feckless and weak on military matters was born out of the tumult of 1968; the rise of the
antiwar wing of the party, the candidacies of Eugene McCarthy
and Robert Kennedy, and the image of Vietnam War demonstrators scuffling with police at the Democratic National Convention
in Chicago. It would further take root with the ascendancy of the
liberal George McGovern and his call at the party's 1972 national

convention for America to "come home." To this day, few political stereotypes have done more damage to a political party than the twinned images of national security weakness and the Democratic Party.

## THE FLIGHT OF THE DOVES

Ironically, it was Democrats who had pioneered the use of campaign attacks on national security weakness. John F. Kennedy used the presence of a so-called missile gap with the Soviet Union to defeat his GOP opponent, Richard Nixon, in 1960. Before then, Roosevelt and Truman had consistently hung the isolationist label around the necks of Republicans. As these examples demonstrate, on the campaign trail foreign affairs often are more about perception rather than specific policy choices. Thus in 1968, the ascension of foreign policy doves within the Democratic Party would create a political opening for Republicans—one they would continue to take advantage of for nearly four decades.

Led by Minnesota senator Eugene McCarthy's insurgent campaign for the Democratic nomination and later Senator Robert Kennedy's entry into the race, the antiwar wing of the party had helped to drive President Lyndon Johnson from the White House in late March 1968. In one of the most dramatic moments in American political history, LBJ had gone on live television to tell the country of his plans for peace in Vietnam. But the policy element of the speech was overshadowed by Johnson's stunning conclusion: "I shall not seek, and I will not accept, the nomination of my party for another term as your President." It was an announcement so shocking and unexpected that some Americans (including my father) leaped out of their seats at the news.

But the doves were not content simply to force Johnson out of power: they were seeking nothing less than to reorient the party's approach to international affairs. They argued that the time had come for a reexamination of America's global responsibilities and the reliance on military solutions for achieving foreign policy objectives. A defensible position, for sure, but from a political perspective it stood in stark contrast to the views of many Americans.

One of the great misunderstood elements of the antiwar movement is the extent to which it did *not* reflect public opinion on the Vietnam War. When Eugene McCarthy scored 40 percent of the vote in the New Hampshire primary it represented the dissatisfaction of both those who opposed the war *and* those who were supportive. Exit polls indicated not only were the majority of voters in the state unaware of McCarthy's position on the war but 60 percent of his supporters believed Johnson's Vietnam policies were failing because "he was not being aggressive enough." In fact, nearly one in five McCarthy voters ended up supporting George Wallace in the general election.[1]

For millions of Americans, the counterculture antiwar movement had become a reflection of all that they detested about the changes occurring in American society. To the committed anti-Communists in organized labor and the old-time Democratic urban machines, the antiwar marchers were part of the problem. In July 1968, when delegates gathered inside the Democratic convention in Chicago, tens of thousands of demonstrators gathered outside the convention hall. Increasingly, Americans (and, in fact, many lifelong Democrats) were not making much of a distinction between the two groups. The full-scale riots that ensued in Chicago laid bare the growing divisions not only in the Democratic coalition but also in American society. Mayor Richard J. Daley's police force did more than just keep order; they aggressively attacked and beat demonstrators in what was later termed a "police riot." Yet most Americans were none too bothered. In fact, only 21 percent of those polled felt that the Chicago police used "excessive force," and a majority of Americans supported the police actions.[2]

The riots in Chicago capped off what had been a tumultuous and tragic primary campaign. Robert Kennedy had been gunned down at the Ambassador Hotel in Los Angeles after winning the California primary. McCarthy's candidacy and South Dakota senator George McGovern's late entry into the race under a peace banner were unable to bring together the disparate wings of the party. Instead, Democrats turned to Vice President Hubert Humphrey as the party nominee.

The antiwar forces in the party were outraged by the pick. Humphrey remained a supporter of—and, as far as the demonstrators were concerned, an embodiment of—the administration's Vietnam policy. On the campaign trail, they made Humphrey's life a living hell. Wherever the vice president went, he was met by angry hecklers who denounced him in the harshest of terms. "Dump the Hump," "Stop the War," and even "Sieg Heil" were just some of the catcalls he heard. Making matters worse, a September 27 poll showed Humphrey mired in the high twenties, only seven points ahead of the insurgent campaign of George Wallace.[3]

Scheduled to speak in Salt Lake City on September 30, 1968, Humphrey decided that a bold stroke was needed in order to take back the political advantage and pacify the antiwar wing of the party. He would call for a halt to the bombing of North Vietnam in an effort to spur ongoing peace talks in Paris. Of course, as any speechwriter will tell you, staking out a position is one thing, finding the right words to articulate it is something else altogether. Writing Humphrey's Salt Lake City speech was a tortured experience, as drafts were passed around, dismissed, and reedited in the days leading up to the address. It was an apt metaphor for Democratic disarray on Vietnam.

George Ball, who had resigned as U.S. Ambassador to the United Nations to become Humphrey's key foreign policy adviser, helped write the initial draft, a long speech about America's global responsibilities with a brief mention of Vietnam at the end.

Larry O'Brien, Humphrey's campaign manager, called it an "abomination."[4]

The campaign went back to the drawing board as Ted Van Dyk, the vice president's speechwriter, broke out a scuttled draft from months earlier that contained a "virtually unconditional pledge" to cease bombing against North Vietnam. The candidate and speechwriter spent much of a Sunday afternoon editing the text. Most of Humphrey's top advisers were happy with the newest draft—until word came back from peace negotiators in Paris that they were not convinced they could accept Humphrey's statement. Wanting to avoid the appearance of undercutting the peace talks—which had become Nixon's entire rationale for saying nothing about the war—Humphrey began to reconsider how far he should go.[5]

The candidate flew to Utah as the internal debates continued. Until 4:30 A.M., Humphrey and his top advisers argued over just the right words, with his political people telling him that he couldn't win without a halt to the bombing and his foreign policy advisers recommending a more conditional approach. Unable to fully separate himself from the president and state a clear path forward for achieving peace, he took the middle road, calling for an end to the bombing of North Vietnam conditioned on evidence of Communist goodwill. O'Brien was furious at the result, saying it was "not worth a damn," but it was as far as Humphrey was willing to go.[6] President Johnson wasn't much happier; when Humphrey informed him of the speech's content, he groused, "Hubert, you give that speech, and you'll be screwed."[7]

The crux of Humphrey's address were the few lines that focused on the issue at the forefront of the antiwar agenda—stopping the bombing of North Vietnam.

As President, I would stop the bombing of the North as an acceptable risk for peace because I believe it could lead to success in the negotiations and thereby shorten the war. This would be the best protection for our troops. In weighing that risk—and before taking action—I would place key importance on evidence—direct or indirect—by deed or word—of Communist willingness to restore the demilitarized Zone between North and South Vietnam. Now if the Government of North Vietnam were to show bad faith, I would reserve the right to resume the bombing.

Theodore White said of the Salt Lake City speech, it "will go down in history as no great document of diplomacy."[8] In fact, upon close examination it was difficult to tell how Humphrey's "new approach" significantly differed from that of the Johnson White House. It was the *image* of a change in policy that seemed to matter most. Eschewing the vice presidential seal and being introduced as the Democratic candidate for president, as opposed to a member of the Johnson administration, were calculated efforts to demonstrate to the American people that Hubert Humphrey was his own man, even if the reality seemed to indicate otherwise. Humphrey's aides went out of their way to suggest that the candidate had broken with the president and was siding now with the antiwar faction of the party. According to the *New York Times*, "Mr. Humphrey was pictured by some members of his entourage as having committed himself irrevocably to a bombing halt. They viewed his qualifications as 'window-dressing' necessary to domestic and international political realities."[9]

The effect was galvanizing: the liberal wing of the party saw Humphrey's shift as a significant step forward. Humphrey was now seen as the "peace nominee." Letters supporting the vice president—and, even more important, cash—poured into the Democratic National Committee. The hecklers disappeared. Instead, Humphrey was greeted by signs reading IF YOU MEAN IT, WE'RE WITH YOU. McCarthy, who had once refused to endorse

Humphrey, now tepidly offered his support, as did the liberal Americans for Democratic Action, which the vice president had helped found.

Humphrey's tepid move to the left was part and parcel of a larger shift happening within the Democratic Party. While Democrats, under the leadership of President Harry Truman, had led the way in aggressively fighting Communism and laying the underpinning for the Cold War, the party was increasingly beginning to question its internationalist positions. Gene McCarthy, who became the political voice of the antiwar movement, had a mere decade earlier been a committed anti-Communist. By 1968 he was questioning the very notion of American engagement in the world, the validity of the "military industrial complex," and the country's prominent role as "the world's judge and the world's policeman."[10] His tough words were the first such criticisms of Cold War orthodoxy by a major party candidate since the dawn of the Cold War.[11] There was a growing sense among the liberal wing of the party that a fundamental reassessment of the country's position in the world was needed. Moreover, liberals were openly and vigorously questioning the efficacy of military means in achieving America's foreign policy objectives, as foreshadowed by a statement, little-remarked at the time, near the back of Humphrey's speech:

> As President, I would undertake a new strategy for peace in this world, based not on American omnipotence, but on American leadership, not only military and economic, but moral. That new strategy for peace would emphasize working through the United Nations, strengthening and maintaining our key alliances for mutual security, particularly including NATO, supporting international peacekeeping machinery and working with other nations to build new institutions and instruments for cooperation.

Later in the speech Humphrey emphasized a desire to reduce military expenditures "systematically among all countries of the world." This new focus on international institutions and away from harder-edged security issues would increasingly reflect the mind-set of Democrats—at the same time that Republicans were becoming more martially toned in their support for the military and voicing the need for a new aggressive front in confronting the Soviet Union. Ironically, these more aggressive Republicans did not include Richard Nixon, who in his 1968 acceptance speech pledged "an era of negotiations" after "an era of confrontations." It was conservatives such as Ronald Reagan who would take up the mantle of strident anti-Communism."

In the end, of course, even the support of the antiwar wing of the party would not be enough to save Humphrey, who lost by less than one percentage point in the popular vote but was swamped in the Electoral College. Four years after Johnson's resounding victory over Goldwater, it represented an overwhelming repudiation of the Democratic Party and the beginning of a genuine political realignment in the country.

Humphrey's defeat created great opportunities for the liberal wing of the party, which used the momentum from 1968 to make their claim for the leadership of the Democratic Party. They would find their standard-bearer in the person of South Dakota senator George McGovern, the party's candidate in the 1972 campaign for the White House. After a series of misfortunes and tragedies derailed the candidacies of the initial front-runner, Edmund Muskie, as well as Humphrey, Massachusetts senator Ted Kennedy, and George Wallace, McGovern emerged as the nominee, on the strength of a formidable grassroots organization. Washington senator Henry "Scoop" Jackson, a long-standing New Deal Democrat, ran on a moderate platform blasting those in the party who "were running down America" and were unwilling to acknowledge the genuine concerns among millions of Americans about rising crime rates. For his troubles, Jackson was labeled a "warmonger" and "racist" by the left and did pitifully in primary voting.[12]

McGovern was one of the party's more liberal candidates at a time when the country was becoming more and more conservative on both racial issues and national security. It was a fact laid bare in the spring of 1972. As the campaign season was heating up, President Nixon announced, as a last-ditch effort to bring resolution at the Paris peace talks, his intention to escalate bombing and mine North Vietnam's Haiphong port. The response from Democrats was predictable. McGovern called it "a flirtation with World War III"; Muskie accused Nixon of "jeopardizing the major security interests of the United States"; even Congressman Ed Koch called the president "an international lawbreaker." It was hard to find any Democrat willing to support the president's policy. Yet the American people took a very different perspective, with public opinion polls showing nearly two thirds of Americans supporting the escalation—this at the same time that other polls showed Americans pushing for an end to the war. Americans, in the parlance of Nixon, wanted "peace with honor"; the Democrats just wanted to get out.[13]

With McGovern calling for immediate withdrawal of all American troops from Vietnam—as opposed to the gradual withdrawal advocated and implemented by Nixon—the contrast between the two parties could not have have been greater. Not only were Democrats increasingly seen as out of touch with mainstream America on issues of racial integration, but on foreign policy they were further and further out of sync with the electorate, which, while tired of war in Southeast Asia, was not willing to embrace the steps being advocated by Democrats—even if these steps may have seemed correct and proper, both at the time and in retrospect.

## A Mess in Miami

The scene at the Democratic convention in Miami, with every imaginable liberal interest group flexing their political muscle, did little to help McGovern's chances. When the candidate finally delivered his acceptance speech, it came at three in the morning, long after most Americans had gone to bed. By the time McGovern mounted the stage to speak, the convention's viewing audience had dropped from more than 17 million to a mere 3.6 million.[14] While many of his fellow countrymen missed the live speech, the message of this evocative, at times poetic, even evangelical speech would be repeated continuously on the campaign trail—and for many would come to define the Democratic Party at the dawn of the 1970s. (Though famed historian and former presidential speechwriter Arthur Schlesinger Jr. would pen an initial draft of the remarks, the speech was written largely by McGovern himself.)[15]

On domestic policy, the speech evoked the politics of the New Deal, once again pitting Democrats, as the party of the people, versus Republicans, as the party of big business and the wealthy. Amazingly, there was only one sentence in the entire speech about crime, even though this was an issue that was front and center in the minds of millions of Americans.

International affairs is where McGovern staked out the most controversial territory. McGovern's political rise had been nourished on his antiwar credentials, and he did not disappoint his supporters, as he pledged that "within 90 days of my inauguration, every American soldier and every American prisoner will be out of the jungle and out of their cells and then home in America where they belong."

But McGovern's focus on foreign affairs went beyond Southeast Asia and bordered on isolationism. "This is also the time to turn away from excessive preoccupation overseas to the rebuilding of our own nation. America must be restored to a proper role in the world," said McGovern. The irony here is rich. McGovern's words were remarkably similar to those spoken by Nixon in 1968, who called for "a new internationalism in which America enlists its allies and its friends around the world in those struggles in which their interest is as great as ours." The problem for Democrats was one of perception and the increasingly negative image of the party on national security matters. As a Cold Warrior, Nixon could get away with such a conciliatory tone. As an antiwar Democrat, McGovern could not.

McGovern also offered a new definition of U.S. national security that featured a decidedly domestic tone, arguing that "for 30 years we have been so absorbed with fear and danger from abroad that we have permitted our own house to fall into disarray." McGovern asserted that national security and strength must encompass "schools for our children as well as silos for our missiles"; "the health of our families as much as the size of our bombs"; "the safety of our streets, and the condition of our cities, and not just the engines of war."

He concluded his remarks by poetically and repetitiously asking America to "come home" from, among other things, "military spending so wasteful that it weakens our nation."

There was none of the tough-talking, bear-any-burden rhetoric of Kennedy's "New Frontier," no Wilsonian proclamation that America must be a beacon to the world. And one can only imagine what Roosevelt and Truman might have had to say about McGovern's new approach to foreign affairs. The speech was a shot across the bow of the postwar bipartisan consensus on containing and fighting Communism. It was one thing to speak of withdrawal from Vietnam, but in McGovern's words there was no sense of "honor" or the notion that America had sacrificed its young men for a noble cause.

McGovern's call for America to "come home" would provide rich fodder for Republican claims of Democratic weakness on national security. As Nixon's speechwriter Pat Buchanan said, the Democrats' message could be summarized as "weakness abroad" and "permissiveness at home."[16] McGovern's speech represented a seismic shift from the party's previously hawkish stance on foreign policy to a national security strategy based more on human rights and less on military strength. (It is a shift that would become even more pronounced during the presidency of Jimmy Carter.) Those who were outside the Democratic convention in Chicago in 1968 were now inside the hall, running the show.

The Democrats' weakened image on foreign policy would prove disastrous from both political and policy perspectives. While Bill Clinton in 1992 was able to tackle the party's harmful image on welfare, taxes, and crime, among others, the party's negative stain on foreign affairs has remained far more difficult to wash off. Is it any wonder that in the spring of 2004, an unnamed senior Bush administration figure was quoted in the *Wall Street Journal* as saying of Democratic nominee John Kerry's opposition to the war in Iraq that "it's never stopped being 1968" for Democrats?[17] A better description of the Democratic Party's political vulnerability on national security is harder to imagine. It's hardly a surprise that in every election since 1968 in which foreign affairs has played a key role, Democrats have lost.

The move of the Democrats to the left on foreign affairs would provide the political impetus for a muscular conservative political movement oriented toward more aggressively confronting the Soviet Union and relying more slavishly on the use of military force. While Democrats were increasingly casting a jaundiced eye toward the military, Republicans were embracing a more hawkish foreign policy stance with little fear of negative political repercussions. If any one issue would come to define the difference between the two parties after 1972, it would be foreign policy and national security. It is a divide that remains crucial to understanding American politics in the twenty-first century.

## Hubert Humphrey Breaks with President Johnson and Calls for a Conditional Bombing Halt in Vietnam, Salt Lake City, September 30, 1968

Tonight I want to share with you my thoughts as a citizen and a candidate for President of the United States. I want to tell you what I think about great issues which I believe face this nation.

I want to talk with you about Vietnam, and about another great issue in the search for peace in the world—the issue of stopping the threat of nuclear war.

. . . For the past several weeks, I have tried to tell you what was in my heart and on my mind.

But sometimes that message has been drowned out by the voices of protesters and demonstrators.

I shall not let the violence and disorder of a noisy few deny me the right to speak or to destroy the orderly democratic process.

. . . When I accepted the Democratic party's nomination and platform, I said that the first reality that confronted this nation was the need for peace in Vietnam.

I have pledged that my first priority as President shall be to end the war and obtain an honorable peace.

. . . 112 days from now, there will be a President, a new Administration, and new advisers.

If there is no peace by then, it must be their responsibility to make a complete reassessment of the situation in Vietnam—to see where we stand and to judge what we must do.

As I said in my acceptance speech: The policies of tomorrow need not be limited by the policies of yesterday.

We must look to the future. For neither vindication nor repudiation of our role in Vietnam will bring peace or be worthy of our country.

. . . The end of the war is not yet in sight. But our chances for peace are far better today than they were a year or even a month ago.

On March 31, the war took on an entirely new dimension. On that date President Johnson by one courageous act removed the threat of bombing from 90 per cent of the people, and 78 per cent of the land area, of North Vietnam.

On that date President Johnson sacrificed his own political career in order to bring negotiations that could lead to peace.

Until that time, the struggle was only on the battlefield.

Now our negotiators are face to face across the table with negotiators from North Vietnam.

A process has been set in course. And lest that process be set back, our perseverance at the conference table must be great as our courage has been in the war.

There have been other changes during these past few months.

. . . While we have stood with our allies in Vietnam, several things have happened.

Other nations of Southeast Asia—given the time we have bought for them—have strengthened themselves . . . have begun to work together . . . and are far more able to protect themselves against any future subversion or aggression.

In South Vietnam itself, a constitution has been written, elections have been stepped up, and the South Vietnamese Army has increased its size and capacity, and improved its equipment, training and performance—just as the Korean Army did during the latter stages of the Korean War.

So, in sharp contrast to a few months ago—we see peace negotiations going on.

We see a stronger Southeast Asia.

We see a stronger South Vietnam.

Those are the new circumstances which a new President will face in January.

In light of those circumstances—and assuming no marked change in the present situation—how would I proceed as President?

Let me make clear what I would not do.

I would not undertake a unilateral withdrawal.

To withdraw would not only jeopardize the independence of South Vietnam and the safety of other Southeast Asian nations. It would make meaningless the sacrifices we have already made. It would be an open invitation to more violence, more aggression, more instability.

It would, at this time of tension in Europe, cast doubt on the integrity of our word under treaty and alliance.

Peace would not be served by weakness or withdrawal.

Nor would I escalate the level of violence in either North or South Vietnam. We must seek to de-escalate.

The platform of my party says that the President should take reasonable risks to find peace in Vietnam. I shall do so.

North Vietnam, according to its own statements and those of others, has said it will proceed to prompt and good faith negotiations, if we stop the present limited bombing of the North.

We must always think of the protection of our troops.

As President, I would stop the bombing of the North as an acceptable risk for peace because I believe it could lead to success in the negotiations and thereby shorten the war. This would be the best protection for our troops. In weighing that risk—and before taking action—I would place key importance on evidence—direct or indirect—by deed or word—of Communist willingness to restore the demilitarized zone between North and South Vietnam.

Now if the Government of North Vietnam were to show bad faith, I would reserve the right to resume the bombing.

Now secondly, I would take the risk that South Vietnamese

would meet the responsibilities they say they are now ready to assume in their own self-defense.

I would move, in other words, toward de-Americanization of the war.

I would sit down with the leaders of South Vietnam to set a specific timetable by which American forces could be systematically reduced while South Vietnamese forces took over more and more of the burden.

The schedule must be a realistic one—one that would not weaken the over-all Allied defense posture. I am convinced such action would be as much in South Vietnam's interest as in ours.

What I am proposing is that it should be basic to our policy in Vietnam that the South Vietnamese take over more and more of the defense of their own country.

That would be an immediate objective of the Humphrey-Muskie Administration as I sought to end the war.

If the South Vietnamese Army maintains its present rate of improvement, I believe this will be possible next year—without endangering either our remaining troops or the safety of South Vietnam.

I do not say this lightly. I have studied this matter carefully.

Third, I would propose once more an immediate cease-fire—with United Nations or other international supervision and supervised withdrawal of all foreign forces from South Vietnam.

American troops are fighting in numbers in South Vietnam today only because North Vietnamese forces were sent to impose Hanoi's will on the South Vietnamese people by aggression.

We can agree to bring home our forces from South Vietnam, if the North Vietnamese agree to bring theirs home at the same time.

External forces assisting both sides could and should leave at the same time, and should not be replaced.

The ultimate key to an honorable solution must be free elections in South Vietnam—with all people, including members of the National Liberation Front and other dissident groups, able to participate in those elections if they were willing to abide by peaceful processes.

That, too, would mean some risk.

But I have never feared the risk of one man, one vote. I say: let the people speak. And accept their judgment, whatever it is.

The Government of South Vietnam should not be imposed by force from Hanoi or by pressure from Washington. It should be freely chosen by all the South Vietnamese people . . .

Those are the risks I would take for peace.

I do not believe any of these risks would jeopardize our security or be contrary to our national interest.

There is, of course, no guarantee that all these things could be successfully done.

Certainly, none of them could be done if North Vietnam were to show bad faith.

But I believe there is a good chance these steps could be undertaken with safety for our men in Vietnam.

As President, I would be dedicated to carrying them out—as I would be dedicated to urging the Government of South Vietnam to expedite all political, economic and social reforms essential to broadening popular participation including high priority to land reform, more attention to the suffering of refugees, and constant Government pressure against inflation and corruption.

I believe all of these steps could lead to an honorable and lasting settlement, serving both our own national interest and the interests of the independent nations of Southeast Asia.

We have learned a lesson from Vietnam.

The lesson is not that we should turn our backs on Southeast Asia, or on other nations or peoples in less familiar parts of the world neighborhood.

The lesson is, rather, that we should carefully define our goals and priorities. And within those goals and priorities, that we should formulate policies which will fit new American guidelines.

Applying the lesson of Vietnam, I would insist as President that we review other commitments made in other times, that we carefully decide what is and is not in our national interest.

. . . Let me be clear: I do not counsel withdrawal from the world.

I do not swerve from international responsibility.

I only say that, as President, I would undertake a new strategy for peace in this world, based not on American omnipotence, but on American leadership, not only military and economic but moral.

That new strategy for peace would emphasize working through the United Nations, strengthening and maintaining our key alliances for mutual security, particularly including NATO, supporting international peacekeeping machinery, and working with other nations to build new institutions and instruments for cooperation.

In a troubled and dangerous world we should seek not to march alone, but to lead in such a way that others will wish to join us.

Even as we seek peace in Vietnam, we must for our own security and well-being seek to halt and turn back the costly and even more dangerous arms race.

Five nations now have nuclear bombs.

The United States and the Soviet Union already possess enough weapons to burn and destroy every human being on this earth.

Unless we stop the arms race, unless we stop 15 to 20 more nations from getting nuclear bombs and nuclear bomb technology within the next few years, this generation may be the last. For 20 years we have lived under the constant threat that some irresponsible action or even some great miscalculation could blow us all up in the wink of an eye.

There is danger that we have become so used to the idea that we no longer think it abnormal—forgetting that our whole world structure depends for its stability on the precarious architecture of what Winston Churchill called the "balance of terror." This is no longer an adequate safeguard for peace.

. . . If I am President, I shall take the initiative to find the way—under carefully safeguarded, mutually acceptable international inspection—to reduce arms budgets and military expenditures systematically among all countries of the world.

Our country's military budget this year is $80 billion.

It is an investment we have to make under existing circumstances. It protects our freedom.

But if we can work with other nations so that we can all reduce our military expenditures together, with proper safeguards and inspection, then it will be a great day for humanity.

All of us will have moved further away from self-destruction. And all of us will have billions of dollars with which to help people live better lives.

. . . On the great issues of Vietnam, of the arms race and of human rights in America, I have clear differences with Mr. Nixon and Mr. Wallace.

I call on both of these men to join me in open debate before the American people.

Let us put our ideas before the people. Let us offer ourselves for their judgment—as men and as leaders. Let us appear together—in front of the same audiences or on the same television screens, and at the same time—to give the people a choice.

We must not let a President be elected by the size of his advertising budget.

We cannot let a President be elected without having met the issues before the people.

I am willing to put myself, my programs, my capacity for leadership, before the American people for their judgment.

I ask the Republican nominee and the third-party candidate to do the same.

I ask, before Election Day, that we be heard together as you have heard me alone tonight.

I appeal to the people—as citizens of a nation whose compassion and sense of decency and fair play have made it what Lincoln called "the last best hope on earth."

I appeal to you as a person who wants his children to grow up in that kind of country.

I appeal to you to express and vote your hopes and not your hates.

I intend, in these five weeks, to wage a vigorous, tireless and forthright campaign for the Presidency. I shall not spare myself, or those who will stand with me.

I have prepared myself. I know the problems facing this nation. I do not shrink from these problems. I challenge them. They were made by men. I believe they can be solved by men.

If you will give me your confidence and support, together we shall build a better America.

## George McGovern Accepts the Democratic Nomination for President and Asks America to "Come Home," Miami Beach, July 14, 1972

Tonight I accept your nomination with a full and grateful heart . . . My nomination is all the more precious in that it is a gift of the most open political process in all of our political history.

It is the sweet harvest of the work of tens of thousands of tireless volunteers, young and old alike, funded by literally hundreds of thousands of small contributors in every part of this nation.

Those who lingered on the brink of despair only a short time ago have been brought into this campaign, heart, hand, head and soul, and I have been the beneficiary of the most remarkable political organization in the history of this country.

It is an organization that gives dramatic proof to the power of love and to a faith that can literally move mountains.

As Yeats put it, "Count where man's glory most begins and ends, and say: My glory was I had such friends."

This is the people's nomination and next January we will restore the government to the people of this country.

I believe that American politics will never be quite the same again.

We are entering a new period of important and hopeful change in America, a period comparable to those eras that unleashed such remarkable ferment in the period of Jefferson and Jackson and Roosevelt.

Let the opposition collect their $10 million in secret money from the privileged few and let us find one million ordinary Americans who will contribute $25 each to this campaign, a Million Member Club with members who will not expect special favors for themselves but a better land for us all.

In the literature and music of our children we are told, to

everything there is a season and a time to every purpose under heaven. And for America, the time has come at last.

This is the time for truth, not falsehood. In a Democratic nation, no one likes to say that his inspiration came from secret arrangements by closed doors, but in the sense that is how my candidacy began. I am here as your candidate tonight in large part because during four administrations of both parties, a terrible war has been chartered behind closed doors.

I want those doors opened and I want that war closed. And I make these pledges above all others: the doors of government will be opened, and that war will be closed.

Truth is a habit of integrity, not a strategy of politics, and if we nurture the habit of truth in this campaign, we will continue to be truthful once we are in the White House.

Let us say to Americans, as Woodrow Wilson said in his first campaign of 1912, "Let me inside the government and I will tell you what is going on there."

Wilson believed, and I believe, that the destiny of America is always safer in the hands of the people than in the conference rooms of any elite.

So let us give our—let us give your country the chance to elect a government that will seek and speak the truth, for this is the time for the truth in the life of this country.

And this is also a time, not for death, but for life. In 1968 many Americans thought they were voting to bring our sons home from Vietnam in peace, and since then 20,000 of our sons have come home in coffins.

I have no secret plan for peace. I have a public plan. And as one whose heart has ached for the past ten years over the agony of Vietnam, I will halt the senseless bombing of Indochina on Inaugural Day.

There will be no more Asian children running ablaze from bombed-out schools. There will be no more talk of bombing the dikes or the cities of the North.

And within 90 days of my inauguration, every American soldier and every American prisoner will be out of the jungle and out of their cells and then home in America where they belong.

And then let us resolve that never again will we send the precious young blood of this country to die trying to prop up a corrupt military dictatorship abroad.

This is also the time to turn away from excessive preoccupation overseas to the rebuilding of our own nation. America must be restored to her proper role in the world. But we can do that only through the recovery of confidence in ourselves.

. . . Now, in the months ahead I deeply covet the help of every Democrat, of every Republican, of every Independent who wants this country to be the great and good land that it can be. This is going to be a national campaign, carried to every part of the nation—North, South, East and West. We are not conceding a single state to Richard Nixon.

. . . Now, to anyone is this hall or beyond who doubts the ability of Democrats to join together in common cause, I say never underestimate the power of Richard Nixon to bring harmony to Democratic ranks. He is the unwitting unifier and the fundamental issue of this national campaign, and all of us are going to help him redeem a pledge he made ten years ago—that next year you won't have Richard Nixon to kick around any more.

We have had our fury and our frustrations in these past months and at this Convention, but frankly, I welcome the contrast with the smug and dull and empty event which will doubtless take place here in Miami next month.

We chose this struggle, we reformed our Party, and we let the people in. So we stand today not as a collection of backroom strategies, not as a tool of ITT or any other special interest. So let our opposite stand on the status quo while we seek to refresh the American spirit.

I believe that the greatest contribution America can now make to our fellow mortals is to heal our own great but very deeply troubled land. We must respond—we must respond to that ancient command: "Physician, heal thyself."

Now, it is necessary in an age of nuclear power and hostile forces that we be militarily strong. America must never become a second-rate nation. As one who has tasted the bitter fruits of our weakness before Pearl Harbor in 1941, I give you my pledge that if I become the President of the United States, America will keep its defenses alert and fully sufficient to meet any danger.

We will do that not only for ourselves, but for those who deserve and need the shield of our strength—our old allies in Europe and elsewhere, including the people of Israel who will always have our help to hold their Promised Land.

Yet I believe that every man and woman in this Convention Hall knows that for 30 years we have been so absorbed with fear and danger from abroad that we have permitted our own house to fall into disarray.

We must now show that peace and prosperity can exist side by side. Indeed, each now depends on the existence of the other. National strength includes the credibility of our system in the eyes of our own people as well as the credibility of our deterrent in the eyes of others abroad.

National security includes schools for our children as well as silos for our missiles.

It includes the health of our families as much as the size of our bombs, the safety of our streets, and the condition of our cities, and not just the engines of war.

If we some day choke on the pollution of our own air, there will be little consolation in leaving behind a dying continent ringed with steel.

So while protecting ourselves abroad, let us form a more perfect union here at home. And this is the time for that task.

We must also make this a time of justice and jobs for all our people. For more than three and a half years we have tolerated stagnation and a rising level of joblessness, with more than five million of our best workers unemployed at this very moment. Surely, this is the most false and wasteful economics of all.

Our deep need is not for idleness but for new housing and hospitals, for facilities to combat pollution and take us home from work, for better products able to compete on vigorous world markets.

The highest single domestic priority of the next administration will be to ensure that every American able to work has a job to do.

That job guarantee will and must depend on a reinvigorated private economy, freed at last from the uncertainties and burdens of war, but it is our firm commitment that whatever employment the private sector does not provide, the Federal government will either stimulate or provide itself.

Whatever it takes, this country is going back to work. America cannot exist with most of our people working and paying taxes to support too many others mired in a demeaning and hopeless welfare mess.

Therefore, we intend to begin by putting millions back to work and after that is done, we will assure to those unable to work an income fully adequate to a decent life.

Now beyond this, a program to put America back to work demands that work be properly rewarded. That means the end of a system of economic controls in which labor is depressed, but prices and corporate profit run sky-high.

It means a system of national health insurance so that a worker can afford decent health care for himself and his family.

It means real enforcement of the laws so that the drug racketeers are put behind bars and our streets are once again safe for our families.

And above all, above all, honest work must be rewarded by a fair and just tax system.

The tax system today does not reward hard work: it penalizes it. Inherited or invested wealth frequently multiplies itself while paying no taxes at all. But wages on the assembly line or in farming the land, these hard-earned dollars are taxed to the very last penny.

There is a depletion allowance for oil wells, but no depletion for the farmer who feeds us, or the worker who serves as all.

The administration tells us that we should not discuss tax reform in an election year. They would prefer to keep all discussion of the tax laws in closed rooms where the administration, its powerful friends, and their paid lobbyists, can turn every effort at reform into a new loophole for the rich and powerful.

But an election year is the people's year to speak, and this year, the people are going to ensure that the tax system is changed so that work is rewarded and so that those who derive the highest benefits will pay their fair share rather than slipping through the loopholes at the expense of the rest of us.

So let us stand for justice and jobs and against special privilege.

And this is the time to stand for those things that are close to the American spirit. We are not content with things as they are. We reject the view of those who say, "America—love it or leave it." We reply, "Let us change it so we may love it the more."

And this is the time. It is the time for this land to become again a witness to the world for what is just and noble in human affairs. It is time to live more with faith and less with fear, with an abiding confidence that can sweep away the strongest barriers between us and teach us that we are truly brothers and sisters.

So join with me in this campaign. Lend Senator Eagleton* and me your strength and your support, and together we will call America home to the ideals that nourished us from the very beginning.

---

*McGovern's running mate, Missouri senator Thomas Eagleton, who would later leave the ticket after reports surfaced that he had undergone shock treatment for depression.

From secrecy and deception in high places; come home, America

From military spending so wasteful that it weakens our nation; come home, America.

From the entrenchment of special privileges and tax favoritism; from the waste of idle lands to the joy of useful labor; from the prejudice based on race and sex; from the loneliness of the aging poor and the despair of the neglected sick—come home, America.

Come home to the affirmation that we have a dream. Come home to the conviction that we can move our country forward.

Come home to the belief that we can seek a newer world, and let us be joyful in that homecoming, for this "is your land, this land is my land—from California to New York island, from the redwood forest to the gulf stream waters—this land was made for you and me."

So let us close on this note: May God grant each one of us the wisdom to cherish this good land and to meet the great challenge that beckons us home.

And now is the time to meet that challenge.

Good night, and Godspeed to you all.

## Chapter 16

# THE TRIUMPH OF CONSERVATISM

Ronald Reagan Gives Birth to the Conservative
Ascendancy and the Politics of Optimism: 1980

WILLIAM HOWARD TAFT once said of the American people that if given a choice between a conservative candidate
and a reformist candidate, they will almost always choose the conservative. While there is some truth to Taft's words, the history of
presidential campaigns in the twentieth century demonstrates that
Taft was as bad a prognosticator as he was a dieter. America certainly has had a long dalliance with conservatism, but in the four
decades after Herbert Hoover was forced from the White House,
the American people consistently and overwhelmingly rejected
conservative political candidates at the national ballot box. In the
election of 1980, that would all begin to change.

In 1964, conservatives seized control of the Republican Party,
on the presidential level, for the first time since the age of Coolidge and Hoover. The catastrophic loss suffered by their standard-
bearer, Barry Goldwater, suggested that they had blown their
opportunity to seize the reins of national power. But the obituar-
ies offered to conservatives in the wake of Goldwater's defeat
were premature, to say the least.

Instead of buckling under, conservatives chose a different

approach. They began working more feverishly at the grassroots level, winning state and local races and building up their base of support in the party. In 1976, they barely missed the chance to derail the nomination of Gerald Ford. In 1978, a number of "New Right" conservative leaders were elected to Congress (including later Speaker of the House Newt Gingrich), and in California, Proposition 13 was passed, capping property taxes across the state and heralding the first step in a larger national "taxpayer revolt." By 1980, the conservatives had taken over the Republican Party from within—and their timing could not have been better. The American people's growing distaste with activist government, a growing lack of confidence in national Democrats, a crippling energy crisis and economic dislocation at home combined with humiliation abroad would provide them with the best opportunity in nearly three generations to seize national power.[1]

The political stars were aligned in the conservatives' favor—but the true difference in 1980 would be Ronald Reagan's accessible brand of political conservatism. Goldwater had presented his conservative message in the rhetoric of divisiveness, dogmatism, and pessimism; Reagan wrapped his conservativism in the language of national greatness, the inherent optimism of the American dream, age-old American notions of individual responsibility, and above all, the desire of the electorate to once again feel proud about their nation.

## MALAISE

In the summer of 1980, national pride was in short supply in the United States, and affection for the nation's commander in chief was practically nonexistent. In 1976, former Georgia governor Jimmy Carter had won the presidency on a simple but potent political message: "I will never lie to you." In the wake of Watergate and the excesses of Vietnam, these words resonated deeply with the American people. An outsider to Washington, candidate Carter found the right words to appeal to the American people. But as president, his tune was seemingly always off-key. This was never more true than on July 15, 1979, when he delivered the infamous "malaise" speech.

Looking back on it today, the "malaise" speech qualifies as one of the more truly bizarre episodes in modern presidential history. Carter had been scheduled to deliver a nationally televised speech to the country on July 5, laying out his response to the nation's ongoing energy crisis. But at the last minute he abruptly cancelled the address and left Washington for the presidential retreat of Camp David and what he called a "domestic summit." Theodore White laid out the surreal scene: "What followed is difficult to describe in believable terms: The President's closest advisers were about to gather to discuss the spirit and faith of a questioning nation. In the court of almost any other contemporary sovereign, the attempt would be material for comedy."[2]

For more than a week, the nation's highest elected leader went into seclusion as a steady stream of political and religious leaders, business executives, academics, and notable liberal thinkers traveled to the Catoctin Mountains in Maryland to discuss the despondent mood that had overtaken the country. The seclusion was broken only by presidential trips to small towns in Pennsylvania and West Virginia so that the president could receive insight from "ordinary citizens."

After more than ten days of retreat, Carter returned to Washington prepared to tell the American people of his deliberations. From his desk in the Oval Office, he delivered a speech that was unlike any other ever given by a sitting president. It was a message not of policy or politics, but one of spirit and faith. Carter told the American people that the nation was suffering from a "crisis that strikes at the very heart and soul of our national will." Carter went on to assess the challenges facing America:

We can see this crisis in the growing doubt about the meaning of our own lives and in the loss of unity of purpose for our nation. The erosion of our confidence in the future is threatening to destroy the social and political fabric of America . . . Our people are losing their faith, not only in government itself but in the ability as citizens to serve as the ultimate rulers and shapers of our democracy . . . In a nation that was proud of hard work, strong families, close-knit communities, and our faith in God, too many of us now to tend to worship self-indulgence and consumption . . . But we've discovered that owning things and consuming things does not satisfy our longing for meaning. We've learned that piling up material goods cannot fill the emptiness of lives which have no confidence or purpose.[3]

Carter spent the last third of the speech laying out his new energy policy, but it was Carter's spiritual diagnosis that drew the greatest attention. Media and political reaction was mixed. Some thought the presidential address was a courageous attempt to speak frankly to the American people about the challenges facing the country. Carter's Democratic rival, Massachusetts senator Ted Kennedy, thought the speech was an abdication of presidential leadership and a reprehensible effort to blame the American people for the nation's problems. After all, for most Americans the greatest problem in the country was the people who were running it.

In the days after the speech Carter's poll numbers shot up. Mail poured into the White House in support of the president's message For a brief moment, it seemed that Carter might have turned around his presidency. But days later, the White House demonstrated its incompetence once again by demanding the resignation of the entire cabinet. Carter was trying to show the nation that he was indeed a bold and decisive leader, but the move had the exact opposite effect, sending the dollar into a tailspin and raising fresh doubts about Carter's leadership. A month after the speech, a Gallup poll showed that 84 percent of Americans thought the country was on the wrong track and 67 percent believed the United States was in "deep and serious trouble." Carter's approval rating plummeted as well, dropping to 19 percent in September 1979.[4]

Four months later, when Iranian students seized the U.S. embassy in Tehran and took dozens of American diplomats hostage, America's malaise would only worsen. Here was a superpower being humiliated by a bunch of college students and a bearded religious cleric. The sense of frustration and national impotence was palpable.

Yet Carter had put his finger on what was truly ailing the nation. Americans *were* worried about the future. Polls showed that they increasingly believed that the country's best days had passed and that their children's future would be worse than their own. Their faith in America was being tested. But instead of telling Americans to rise to the challenge and persevere in the face of intractable problems, Carter was focusing almost exclusively on the nation's ills and ignoring the uplifting message that Americans needed and wanted to hear. He had diagnosed the nation's malady but failed to provide any sort of cure. Carter wasn't giving the electorate a road map for righting the nation's affairs and he was failing to provide decisive leadership in taking the country out of its national funk. Ronald Reagan, who said of the address, "People who talk about an age of limits are really talking about their own limitations, not America's," would not make the same mistake.[5]

## REAGAN'S CONSERVATIVE POPULISM

For more than sixteen years Reagan had been preaching the gospel of conservatism. In many respects, Reagan's acceptance speech at the 1980 Republican convention in Detroit was nothing new—he had been giving some variation of that speech for nearly two decades. Reagan's rise to political fame came in 1964 when on the eve of the presidential election he delivered a nationally broadcast address titled "A Time to Choose" that laid out the conservative manifesto. The impact was electrifying, and it propelled Reagan to national prominence. It was, according to famed *Washington Post* correspondent David Broder, the most extraordinary political debut since that of William Jennings Bryan. The speech, which of course did little to change the final results of the race, nonetheless showed the power of a conservative message delivered in language that was both accessible and hopeful.

Two years later Reagan would defeat the liberal stalwart Pat Brown in the California gubernatorial election. In 1968 his name would be bandied around as a possible presidential nominee. In 1976 he came within a hairsbreadth of unseating the incumbent, President Gerald Ford, for the Republican nomination. By the eve of the 1980 election Reagan was the face of the conservative movement, having traveled the country delivering more than 125 speeches in the two years before he announced his candidacy.[6]

While many Americans had been sympathetic to Barry Goldwater's conservative message, they found the messenger frightening and too extreme for the nation's highest office. The same could be said for George Wallace and his ad hominem attacks on the federal government and the growing federal bureaucracy. For all of the nation's inherent conservatism, of which Taft spoke, modern conservatives were generally associated with naysaying, contrarianism, and opposition to even the most meager effort to assist Americans in need. Conservatives had "played the national scold for 40 years" and paid a heavy political price.[7] Since the days of Roosevelt it was an image that countless Democratic politicians had perpetuated. It seemingly had become easier for conservative

Republicans to say what they were opposed to, rather than what they supported. Pessimism had become the movement's defining trait—but Reagan was the exception.

Reagan smoothed the rough edges of conservatism. Where Goldwater was insistent, unrelenting, and ideologically single-minded, Reagan's brand of conservatism was welcoming and above all optimistic. Where Goldwater announced a virtual declaration of war on the moderate wing of the GOP, Reagan spoke of his desire to unify the country and "renew the American spirit and sense of purpose." While Goldwater declared war on the federal government and wanted to dismantle its key functions in a slash-and-burn manner, Reagan wanted to reduce its size and return to the notion that government's responsibility was to serve the people, not the other way around. As one campaign observer would note about Reagan way back in 1968, "He is Goldwater mutton, dressed up as lamb."[8] Reagan's politics were simple: a commitment to smaller national government and the ingenuity of the American people, combined with tough-minded anti-Communism and an inherent belief in the goodness of America. As his campaign manager Stuart Spencer would later say of Reagan, "I see less change in him than any political figure I have ever known. He has a set of values and everything stems from those values."[9] Reagan's vision of American potential and greatness touched a patriotic chord that had been long dormant in America. When repeated on the campaign trail, it brought not cynical guffaws but instead applause and often tears.[10]

In the face of Carter's "crisis of confidence," Republicans were offering the American people a hopeful vision for the future. The tables had been turned—Democrats were now seen as the party of pessimism and diminished expectations, mired in the past glories of the New Deal and oblivious to the challenges of America in the 1980s. Republicans were the ones evoking the spirit of America's most basic values.

## REPUBLICANS CHANGE THEIR STRIPES

The decision to hold the party convention in Detroit, long a stronghold of labor and Democrats, was symbolic of the change in direction for Republicans. Conservatives were reaching out directly to the blue-collar voters who had shunned them for so long. The unexpected appearance on the convention stage of Benjamin Hooks, the head of the NAACP, and Henry Kissinger, architect of détente and the avowed enemy of the conservative wing of the GOP (and a frequent Reagan punching bag in his 1976 primary campaign for the White House), would have been unimaginable in 1964, but in 1980 the two were met with polite if indifferent applause.[11]

Nevada senator Paul Laxalt, in his nominating speech, praised Reagan's record as governor of California in raising assistance levels for higher education, increasing aid to those "truly" in need, protecting the environment, and even improving mental health facilities.[12] Finally, in an effort to bring the party together, Reagan selected the moderate George H. W. Bush as his vice presidential nominee, outraging many conservatives.

Certainly, some would argue that Republicans were simply covering up their more objectionable policies in the guise of an optimistic message. When Gerald Ford would suggest that Reagan was offering only simple solutions to complex policy challenges, the charge had more than a kernel of truth.[13] Yet, at the same time, Reagan was crafting an aspirational political message that spoke to the American people's greatest hopes for their nation. In 1980, people wanted a leader who would take them out of the doldrums, and it was on this point that Reagan focused his acceptance speech as he called for a "rebirth of the American tradition of leadership":

The major issue of this campaign is the direct political, personal and moral responsibility of Democratic Party leadership—in the White House and in Congress—for this unprecedented calamity which has befallen us . . . They say that the United States has had its day in the sun; that our nation has passed its zenith. They expect you to tell your children that the American people no longer have the will to cope with their problems; that the future will be one of sacrifice and few opportunities.

My fellow citizens, I utterly reject that view. The American people, the most generous on earth, who created the highest standard of living, are not going to accept the notion that we can only make a better world for others by moving backwards ourselves . . . the American people deserve better from those to whom they entrust our nation's highest offices.

"Family, work, neighborhood, peace and freedom" became the watchwords of Reagan's conservative message as he pledged to the nation a "national crusade to make America great again." The return to these American values was, at is essence, the root of Reagan's political appeal.

Reagan went on to describe a litany of President Carter's foreign policy embarrassments, from America's diminished reputation in the world to the ongoing saga of the Iranian hostage crisis. Decrying "four more years of weakness, indecision, mediocrity and incompetence," Reagan asked the assembled delegates, "Is the United States stronger and more respected now than it was three-and-a-half years ago?" The answer was clearly no, and Reagan declared that his victory in November would stand as "proof" that the America had "renewed our resolve to preserve world peace and freedom. This nation will once again be strong enough to do that." Reagan's words portended a new approach to foreign policy in which the United States would more aggressively confront not only the Soviet Union but also the spread of Communism.

Reagan presented his call to arms as the next logical step in America's advancement. Beginning with Plymouth Rock and the Mayflower Compact, alluding to the Revolutionary War and the Gettysburg Address, he asked the audience, "Isn't it once again time to renew our compact of freedom; to pledge to each other all that is best in our lives; all that gives meaning to them—for the sake of this; our beloved and blessed land? Together, let us make this a new beginning." This was language that was reflective of the progress narrative of American nationalism, and what America wanted to hear, particularly at a time when the current president was talking about limitations in the national spirit.

Reagan would go on to quote Roosevelt's "rendezvous with destiny" and echo Thomas Paine, declaring, "The time is now, my fellow Americans, to recapture our destiny, to take it into our own hands." Reagan was firmly planting his message of political renewal in America's founding ideals and values, creating a logical progression from the great advances of American democracy to the present day. But while earlier leaders had usually spoken of a new burst of freedom accompanied by an expanded role for the federal government, Reagan was taking the opposite approach—calling instead for a fundamental reappraisal of the role of government in the lives of the American people.

While Carter wanted to preserve the welfare state that Roosevelt, Truman, and Johnson had constructed over more than four decades, Reagan sought to fundamentally weaken it. The government, he argued, had become too large, too wasteful, too intrusive in the workings of the free market, and too out of touch with the values of the American people.

Reagan pledged to "put an end to the notion that the American taxpayer exists to fund the federal government." "The federal government," he declared, "exists to serve the American people. On January 20th, we are going to re-establish that truth." Reagan told the nation that he would "restore to the federal government the capacity to do the people's work without dominating their lives. I pledge to you a government that will not only work well, but wisely; its ability to act tempered by prudence and its willingness to do good balanced by the knowledge that government is never more dangerous than when our desire to have it help us blinds us to its great power to harm us."

Earlier conservatives' railings against "big government" hadn't resonated among a populace that still viewed government activism in a positive light. But by 1980, Reagan's call for smaller government, fiscal responsibility, and decreased regulation resounded deeply with a populace increasingly suspicious and resentful of the government. In fact, by extolling individual liberties, individual responsibility, and economic opportunity, the policy solutions advocated by conservatives, such as across-the-board tax cuts to work requirements for welfare recipients and later school choice initiatives, were fundamentally aimed at addressing the greatest concerns that Americans had about the perceived failures of the federal government.[14]

In 1980, half the electorate characterized government as "too powerful"; only a mere 15 percent thought it was "not too strong." It was the highest anti-government sentiment since the question had been first asked in 1964. But thanks to George Wallace and Richard Nixon, this antipathy toward big government also had a healthy racial component. A look inside the polls showed that Americans were not upset with everything government did, such as Social Security, anti-crime initiatives, or programs to improve educational opportunity; they were upset about welfare, public housing, and other programs geared toward helping poor minority populations. The dismay with which mainly white Americans viewed these programs more than outweighed their positive view of the federal government's other responsibilities. It was small wonder that on the campaign trail Reagan would attack Cadillac-driving "welfare mothers" or that he would open his campaign for president on a platform of states' rights at the Neshoba County Fair in the town of Philadelphia, Mississippi, where three civil rights workers had been killed in 1964. Reagan clearly understood the link between government activism and racial suspicion.

While the evolving views of the American people may have been complex, one thing was clear: not since Goldwater and before him Hoover had the country faced such a stark choice between two differing approaches to the role of government in their lives.

Yet at the same time, Reagan was not giving the American people the clear choice that so many on the right would have preferred. Americans wanted change, but like his hero Roosevelt, Reagan seemed to understand that he could push only so far. When in 1964 Goldwater had talked of making Social Security voluntary, Reagan committed to supporting and maintaining the integrity of Social Security, long a bugaboo of the conservative right. Though the party platform had refused to support the Equal Rights Amendment, Reagan made a point of trying to heal the wounds by pledging to work with the nation's governors in "eliminat[ing] discrimination against women." Finally, Reagan also recognized that traditionally Democratic constituencies would not be so easily convinced to turn their back on activist government. That's why at the end of the speech he pulled out his trump card, quoting the standard-bearer of the New Deal:

The time is now to redeem promises once made to the American people by another candidate, in another time and another place. He said, "For three long years I have been going up and down this country preaching that government—federal, state, and local—costs too much. I shall not stop that preaching. As an immediate program of action, we must abolish useless offices.

We must eliminate unnecessary functions of government, . . .
we must consolidate subdivisions of government and, like the
private citizen, give up luxuries which we can no longer afford" . . . So said Franklin Delano Roosevelt in his acceptance
speech to the Democratic National Convention in July 1932.

It was a brilliant rhetorical trick, linking Reagan's conservative
politics with the icon of liberalism and using Roosevelt's words to
highlight the incompetence and profligate behavior of the modern Democratic Party. Much of the convention crowd was stunned.
For many Republicans the name Roosevelt, the architect of the
New Deal and the modern welfare state, was still a four-letter
word. But for Reagan, who had grown up a New Deal Democrat
and who still spoke in the idioms of that era, the allusions to Roosevelt came naturally and were the key to his political appeal.
While other conservative politicians were, in a sense, trying to
convert Democrats to their cause, Reagan could fairly argue that
he had once been one of them—a New Deal Democrat whose
party had "deserted" him. When Reagan spoke the words of national renewal and greatness à la Roosevelt, it was not some foreign language, it was his mother tongue.[15]

In the end, Reagan's rhetorical approach along with his soothing portrayal of age-old American values reassured the millions of
Americans who were still suspicious about conservatism. This
speech would help convince them that nothing Reagan said was
truly out of the mainstream of American political thought. Just as
millions of Americans had questioned whether John F. Kennedy
had the gravitas to be president, many raised the same questions
about Reagan. After all, the man was an actor, and he adhered to
a political ideology that had long been discredited. But like the
best political oration (such as Kennedy's New Frontier speech),
Reagan's words rose to the occasion.

This was a speech of great reverence, befitting a would-be

president.[16] Throughout the general election, Carter would attack Reagan unmercifully, portraying him as a warmonger, an anachronism, and most shamelessly, a racist. But for many of the Americans who saw Reagan's speech in Detroit, Carter's attacks would ring hollow. Indeed, his assertion that Americans "are not a warlike people" and that "we always seek to live in peace" went a long way toward inoculating himself against Carter's "warmonger" label. In fact, Reagan would make peace a key element of the speech, invoking it constantly during his remarks.[17]

Three months later, Carter and Reagan would meet in Cleveland, Ohio, for their only debate of the presidential campaign. There Reagan revised the rhetorical questions he had asked in his acceptance speech: "Are you better off than you were four years ago? . . . Is America as respected throughout the world as it was?" If the people felt the answer to those questions was no, then Reagan asked them to join him in a "crusade" that would "take Government off the backs of the great people of this country, and turn you loose again to do those things that I know you can do so well, because you did them and made this country great."[18] Simple but powerful words, and ones that Americans wanted to hear. On Election Day, Carter was crushed. Not since Reagan's hero FDR would a challenger score such an impressive performance against an incumbent president, as Reagan along with Republicans in the House and Senate won a landslide victory and an electoral mandate to remake America.

## REAGAN'S LEGACY

The effect on the country was seismic. After more than fifty years in political exile, the conservative movement had finally reclaimed the mantle of presidential leadership. But the impact of Reagan's election would be felt long after Election Day. His victory signaled a fundamental shift in the nation's politics from activist government to a more restrained conservative model. In many respects, Reagan's win would be as consequential to the nation's long-term politics as Roosevelt's was in 1932. On foreign policy, a more muscular and aggressive approach to containing Communism would take root, characterized by the defense buildup of the early 1980s and President Reagan's rhetorical attacks on the Soviet Union. Moreover, Reagan's final words of his acceptance speech, in which he asked the convention crowd to join together in a moment of silent prayer, signaled the shifting power base of the party toward more socially conservative and religious voters.

Although the reality of Reagan's presidency would not always match the conservative rhetoric (government grew, taxes were frequently raised during the Reagan years, and this lifelong anti-Communist would sign one of the more far-reaching arms reductions treaties with the Soviet Union), the attitude of the country toward their government had been transformed. No longer would the American people look to the nation's political leaders for big-government initiatives to correct the nation's ills. When attempted, as with Bill Clinton's 1993 health care initiative, they would fail spectacularly. The pendulum in American politics had shifted to the right, and for the next three decades, every political campaign would be fought on GOP turf.

## *Ronald Reagan Accepts the Republican Nomination for President, Detroit, July 17, 1980*

Mr. Chairman, Mr. Vice President to be, this convention, my fellow citizens of this great nation:

With a deep awareness of the responsibility conferred by your trust, I accept your nomination for the presidency of the United States . . .

This convention has shown to all America a party united, with positive programs for solving the nation's problems; a party ready to build a new consensus with all those across the land who share a community of values embodied in these words: family, work, neighborhood, peace and freedom.

I know we have had a quarrel or two, but only as to the method of attaining a goal. There was no argument about the goal. As president, I will establish a liaison with the 50 governors to encourage them to eliminate, where it exists, discrimination against women. I will monitor federal laws to insure their implementation and to add statutes if they are needed.

More than anything else, I want my candidacy to unify our country, to renew the American spirit and sense of purpose. I want to carry our message to every American, regardless of party affiliation, who is a member of this community of shared values.

Never before in our history have Americans been called upon to face three grave threats to our very existence, any one of which could destroy us. We face a disintegrating economy, a weakened defense and an energy policy based on the sharing of scarcity.

The major issue of this campaign is the direct political, personal and moral responsibility of Democratic Party leadership—in the White House and in Congress—for this unprecedented calamity which has befallen us. They tell us they have done the most that humanly could be done. They say that the United States has had its day in the sun; that our nation has passed its zenith. They expect you to tell your children that the American people no longer have the will to cope with their problems; that the future will be one of sacrifice and few opportunities.

My fellow citizens, I utterly reject that view. The American people, the most generous on earth, who created the highest standard of living, are not going to accept the notion that we can only make a better world for others by moving backwards ourselves. Those who believe we can have no business leading the nation.

I will not stand by and watch this great country destroy itself under mediocre leadership that drifts from one crisis to the next, eroding our national will and purpose. We have come together here because the American people deserve better from those to whom they entrust our nation's highest offices, and we stand united in our resolve to do something about it.

We need rebirth of the American tradition of leadership at every level of government and in private life as well. The United States of America is unique in world history because it has a genius for leaders—many leaders—on many levels. But, back in 1976, Mr. Carter said, "Trust me." And a lot of people did. Now, many of those people are out of work. Many have seen their savings eaten away by inflation. Many others on fixed incomes, especially the elderly, have watched helplessly as the cruel tax of inflation wasted away their purchasing power. And, today, a great many who trusted Mr. Carter wonder if we can survive the Carter policies of national defense.

"Trust me" government asks that we concentrate our hopes and dreams on one man; that we trust him to do what's best for us. My view of government places trust not in one person or one party, but in those values that transcend persons and parties. The trust is where it belongs—in the people. The responsibility to live up to that trust is where it belongs, in their elected leaders. That kind of relationship, between the people and their elected leaders, is a special kind of compact.

Three hundred and sixty years ago, in 1620, a group of families dared to cross a mighty ocean to build a future for themselves in a new world. When they arrived at Plymouth, Massachusetts, they formed what they called a "compact"; an agreement among themselves to build a community and abide by its laws.

The single act—the voluntary binding together of free people to live under the law—set the pattern for what was to come.

A century and a half later, the descendants of those people pledged their lives, their fortunes and their sacred honor to found this nation. Some forfeited their fortunes and their lives; none sacrificed honor.

Four score and seven years later, Abraham Lincoln called upon the people of all America to renew their dedication and their commitment to a government of, for and by the people.

Isn't it once again time to renew our compact of freedom; to pledge to each other all that is best in our lives; all that gives meaning to them—for the sake of this, our beloved and blessed land?

Together, let us make this a new beginning. Let us make a commitment to care for the needy; to teach our children the values and the virtues handed down to us by our families; to have the courage to defend those values and the willingness to sacrifice for them.

Let us pledge to restore, in our time, the American spirit of voluntary service, of cooperation, of private and community initiative; a spirit that flows like a deep and mighty river through the history of our nation.

As your nominee, I pledge to restore to the federal government the capacity to do the people's work without dominating their lives. I pledge to you a government that will not only work well, but wisely; its ability to act tempered by prudence and its willingness to do good balanced by the knowledge that government is never more dangerous than when our desire to have it help us blinds us to its great power to harm us.

The first Republican president once said, "While the people retain their virtue and their vigilance, no administration by any extreme of wickedness or folly can seriously injure the government in the short space of four years."

If Mr. Lincoln could see what's happened in these last three-and-a-half years, he might hedge a little on that statement. But, with the virtues that our legacy as a free people and with the vigilance that sustains liberty, we still have time to use our renewed compact to overcome the injuries that have been done to America these past three-and-a-half years.

First, we must overcome something the present administration has cooked up: a new and altogether indigestible economic stew, one part inflation, one part high unemployment, one part recession, one part runaway taxes, one part deficit spending and seasoned by an energy crisis. It's an economic stew that has turned the national stomach.

Ours are not problems of abstract economic theory. Those are problems of flesh and blood; problems that cause pain and destroy the moral fiber of real people who should not suffer the further indignity of being told by the government that it is all somehow their fault . . .

The head of a government which has utterly refused to live within its means . . . dares to point the finger of blame at business and labor, both of which have been engaged in a losing struggle just trying to stay even.

High taxes, we are told, are somehow good for us, as if, when government spends our money it isn't inflationary, but when we spend it, it is.

Those who preside over the worst energy shortage in our history tell us to use less, so that we will run out of oil, gasoline, and natural gas a little more slowly. Conservation is desirable, of course, for we must not waste energy. But conservation is not the sole answer to our energy needs.

. . . Large amounts of oil and natural gas lay beneath our land and off our shores, untouched because the present administration seems to believe the American people would rather see more regulation, taxes and controls than more energy.

. . . Make no mistake. We will not permit the safety of our people or our environment heritage to be jeopardized, but we are going to reaffirm that the economic prosperity of our people is a fundamental part of our environment.

Our problems are both acute and chronic, yet all we hear from those in positions of leadership are the same tired proposals for more government tinkering, more meddling and more control— all of which led us to this state in the first place.

Can anyone look at the record of this administration and say, "Well done"? Can anyone compare the state of our economy when the Carter Administration took office with where we are today and say, "Keep up the good work"? Can anyone look at our reduced standing in the world today and say, "Let's have four more years of this"?

I believe the American people are going to answer these questions the first week of November and their answer will be, "No— we've had enough." And, then it will be up to us—beginning next January 20th—to offer an administration and congressional leadership of competence and more than a little courage.

We must have the clarity of vision to see the difference between what is essential and what is merely desirable, and then the courage to bring our government back under control and make it acceptable to the people.

It is essential that we maintain both the forward momentum of economic growth and the strength of the safety net beneath those in society who need help. We also believe it is essential that the integrity of all aspects of Social Security are preserved.

Beyond these essentials, I believe it is clear our federal government is overgrown and overweight. Indeed, it is time for our government to go on a diet. Therefore, my first act as chief executive will be to impose an immediate and thorough freeze on federal hiring. Then, we are going to enlist the very best minds from business, labor and whatever quarter to conduct a detailed review of every department, bureau and agency that lives by federal appropriations. We are also going to enlist the help and ideas of many dedicated and hard working government employees at all levels who want a more efficient government as much as the rest of us do. I know that many are demoralized by the confusion and waste they confront in their work as a result of failed and failing policies.

Our instructions to the groups we enlist will be simple and direct. We will remind them that government programs exist at the sufferance of the American taxpayer and are paid for with money earned by working men and women. Any program that represents a waste of their money—a theft from their pocketbooks—must have that waste eliminated or the program must go—by executive order where possible; by congressional action where necessary. Everything that can be run more effectively by state and local government we shall turn over to state and local government, along with the funding sources to pay for it. We are going to put an end to the money merry-go-round where our money becomes Washington's money, to be spent by the states and cities exactly the way the federal bureaucrats tell them to.

. . . We are going to put an end to the notion that the American taxpayer exists to fund the federal government. The federal government exists to serve the American people. On January 20th, we are going to re-establish that truth.

Also on that date we are going to initiate action to get substantial relief for our taxpaying citizens and action to put people back to work. None of this will be based on any new form of monetary tinkering or fiscal sleight-of-hand. We will simply apply to government the common sense we all use in our daily lives.

Work and family are at the center of our lives; the foundation of our dignity as a free people. When we deprive people of what they have earned, or take away their jobs, we destroy their dignity and undermine their families. We cannot support our families unless there are jobs; and we cannot have jobs unless people have both money to invest and the faith to invest it.

There are concepts that stem from an economic system that for more than 200 years has helped us master a continent, create a previously undreamed of prosperity for our people and has fed millions of others around the globe. That system will continue to serve us in the future if our government will stop ignoring the basic values on which it was built and stop betraying the trust and good will of the American workers who keep it going.

The American people are carrying the heaviest peacetime tax burden in our nation's history—and it will grow even heavier, under present law, next January. We are taxing ourselves into economic exhaustion and stagnation, crushing our ability and incentive to save, invest and produce.

This must stop. We must halt this fiscal self-destruction and restore sanity to our economic system.

I have long advocated a 30 percent reduction in income tax rates over a period of three years. This phased tax reduction would begin with a 10 percent "down payment" tax cut in 1981, which the Republican in Congress and I have already proposed.

A phased reduction of tax rates would go a long way toward easing the heavy burden on the American people. But, we should not stop here.

Within the context of economic conditions and appropriate budget priorities during each fiscal year of my presidency, I would strive to go further. This would include improvement in business depreciation taxes so we can stimulate investment in order to get plants and equipment replaced, put more Americans back to work and put our nation back on the road to being competitive in world commerce. We will also work to reduce the cost of government as a percentage of our gross national product.

The first task of national leadership is to set honest and realistic priorities in our policies and our budget and I pledge that my administration will do that.

When I talk of tax cuts, I am reminded that every major tax cut in this century has strengthened the economy, generated renewed productivity and ended up yielding new revenues for the government by creating new investment, new jobs and more commerce among our people.

The present administration has been forced by us Republicans to play follow-the-leader with regard to a tax cut. But, in this election year we must take with the proverbial "grain of salt" any tax cut proposed by those who have given us the greatest tax increase in our history. When those in leadership give us tax increases and tell us we must also do with less, have they thought about those who have always had less—especially the minorities? This is like telling them that just as they step on the first rung of the ladder of opportunity, the ladder is being pulled out from under them. That may be the Democratic leadership's message to the minorities, but it won't be ours. Our message will be: we have to move ahead, but we're not going to leave anyone behind. Thanks to the economic policies of the Democratic Party, millions of Americans find themselves out of work. Millions more have never even had a fair chance to learn new skills, hold a decent job, or secure for themselves and their families a share in the prosperity of this nation.

It is time to put America back to work; to make our cities and towns resound with the confident voices of men and women of all races, nationalities and faiths bringing home to their families a decent paycheck they can cash for honest money.

For those without skills, we'll find a way to help them get skills.

For those without job opportunities, we'll stimulate new opportunities, particularly in the inner cities where they live.

For those who have abandoned hope, we'll restore hope and we'll welcome them into a great national crusade to make America great again!

When we move from domestic affairs and cast our eyes abroad, we see an equally sorry chapter on the record of the present administration.

A Soviet combat brigade trains in Cuba, just 90 miles from our shores.

A Soviet army of invasion occupies Afghanistan, further threatening our vital interests in the Middle East.

America's defense strength is at its lowest ebb in a generation, while the Soviet Union is vastly outspending us in both strategic and conventional arms.

Our European allies, looking nervously at the growing menace from the East, turn to us for leadership and fail to find it.

And, incredibly more than 50 of our fellow Americans have been held captive for over eight months by a dictatorial foreign power that holds us up to ridicule before the world.

Adversaries large and small test our will and seek to confound our resolve, but we are given weakness when we need strength; vacillation when the times demand firmness.

The Carter Administration lives in the world of make-believe. Every day, drawing up a response to that day's problems, troubles, regardless of what happened yesterday and what will happen tomorrow.

The rest of us, however, live in the real world. It is here that disasters are overtaking our nation without any real response from Washington.

This is make-believe, self-deceit and—above all—transparent hypocrisy.

For example, Mr. Carter says he supports the volunteer army, but he lets military pay and benefits slip so low that many of our enlisted personnel are actually eligible for food stamps . . . I do not favor a peacetime draft or registration, but I do favor pay and benefit levels that will attract and keep highly motivated men and women in our volunteer forces and an active reserve trained and ready for an instant call in case of an emergency.

There may be a sailor at the helm of the ship of state, but the ship has no rudder . . . Who does not feel a growing sense of unease as our allies, facing repeated instances of an amateurish and confused administration, reluctantly conclude that America is unwilling or unable to fulfill its obligations as the leader of the free world?

Who does not feel rising alarm when the question in any discussion of foreign policy is no longer, "Should we do something?", but "Do we have the capacity to do anything?"

The administration which has brought us to this state is seeking your endorsement for four more years of weakness, indecision, mediocrity and incompetence. No American should vote until he or she has asked, is the United States stronger and more respected now than it was three-and-a-half years ago? Is the world today a safer place in which to live?

It is the responsibility of the president of the United States, in working for peace, to insure that the safety of our people cannot successfully be threatened by a hostile foreign power. As president, fulfilling that responsibility will be my number one priority.

We are not a warlike people. Quite the opposite. We always seek to live in peace. We resort to force infrequently and with great reluctance—and only after we have determined that it is absolutely necessary. We are awed—and rightly so—by the forces of destruction at loose in the world in this nuclear era. But neither can we be naive or foolish. Four times in my lifetime America has gone to war, bleeding the lives of its young men into the sands of beachheads, the fields of Europe and the jungles and rice paddies of Asia. We know only too well that war comes not when the forces of freedom are strong, but when they are weak. It is then that tyrants are tempted.

We simply cannot learn these lessons the hard way again without risking our destruction.

Of all the objectives we seek, first and foremost is the establishment of lasting world peace. We must always stand ready to negotiate in good faith, ready to pursue any reasonable avenue that holds forth the promise of lessening tensions and furthering the prospects of peace. But let our friends and those who may wish us ill take note: the United States has an obligation to its citizens and to the people of the world never to let those who would destroy freedom dictate the future course of human life on this planet. I would regard my election as proof that we have renewed our resolve to preserve world peace and freedom. This nation will once again be strong enough to do that.

This evening marks the last step—save one—of a campaign that has taken Nancy and me from one end of this great land to the other, over many months and thousands of miles. There are those who question the way we choose a president; who say that our process imposes difficult and exhausting burdens on those who seek the office. I have not found it so.

It is impossible to capture in words the splendor of this vast continent which God has granted as our portion of this creation. There are no words to express the extraordinary strength and character of this breed of people we call Americans.

Everywhere we have met thousands of Democrats, Independents, and Republicans from all economic conditions and walks of life bound together in that community of shared values of family, work, neighborhood, peace and freedom. They are concerned, yes, but they are not frightened. They are disturbed, but not dismayed. They are the kind of men and women Tom Paine had in mind when he wrote—during the darkest days of the

American Revolution—"We have it in our power to begin the world over again."

Nearly 150 years after Tom Paine wrote those words, an American president told the generation of the Great Depression that it had a "rendezvous with destiny." I believe that this generation of Americans today has a rendezvous with destiny.

Tonight, let us dedicate ourselves to renewing the American compact. I ask you not simply to "Trust me," but to trust your values—our values—and to hold me responsible for living up to them. I ask you to trust that American spirit which knows no ethnic, religious, social, political, regional, or economic boundaries; the spirit that burned with zeal in the hearts of millions of immigrants from every corner of the Earth who came here in search of freedom.

Some say that spirit no longer exists. But I have seen it—I have felt it—all across the land; in the big cities, the small towns and in rural America. The American spirit is still there, ready to blaze into life if you and I are willing to do what has to be done; the practical, down-to-earth things that will stimulate our economy, increase productivity and put America back to work. The time is now to resolve that the basis of a firm and principled foreign policy is one that takes the world as it is and seeks to change it by leadership and example; not by harangue, harassment or wishful thinking.

The time is now to say that while we shall seek new friendships and expand and improve others, we shall not do so by breaking our word or casting aside old friends and allies.

And, the time is now to redeem promises once made to the American people by another candidate, in another time and another place. He said, "For three long years I have been going up and down this country preaching that government—federal, state, and local—costs too much. I shall not stop that preaching. As an immediate program of action, we must abolish useless offices. We must eliminate unnecessary functions of government, . . . we must consolidate subdivisions of government and, like the private citizen, give up luxuries which we can no longer afford.

"I propose to you, my friends, and through you that government of all kinds, big and little be made solvent and that the example be set by the president of the United State and his Cabinet."

So said Franklin Delano Roosevelt in his acceptance speech to the Democratic National Convention in July 1932.

The time is now, my fellow Americans, to recapture our destiny, to take it into our own hands. But, to do this will take many of us, working together. I ask you tonight to volunteer your help in this cause so we can carry our message throughout the land.

Yes, isn't now the time that we, the people, carried out these unkept promises? Let us pledge to each other and to all America on this July day 48 years later, we intend to do just that.

I have thought of something that is not part of my speech and I'm worried over whether I should do it.

Can we doubt that only a Divine Providence placed this land, this island of freedom, here as a refuge for all those people in the world who yearn to breathe freely: Jews and Christians enduring persecution behind the Iron Curtain, the boat people of Southeast Asia, of Cuba and Haiti, the victims of drought and famine in Africa, the freedom fighters of Afghanistan and our own countrymen held in savage captivity.

I'll confess that I've been a little afraid to suggest what I'm going to suggest—I'm more afraid not to—that we begin our crusade joined together in a moment of silent prayer. God bless America.

## Chapter 17

# THE LIBERALS STRIKE BACK

Mario Cuomo, Jesse Jackson, and Walter Mondale
Lay Out a Liberal Political Agenda for
a Skeptical Electorate: 1984

IN THE SUMMER of 1984, the Democratic Party found itself in a true crisis, caught between the traditions of the past and the political realities of the 1980s. While the debacle of the Democrats' overwhelming defeat in 1980 had been temporarily offset by gains in the 1982 midterm elections, the philosophical tone and tenor of the nation had moved to the right. Ronald Reagan and his ideological cohorts had capitalized on the American people's growing mistrust of government to score great political success. No longer did most Americans view government as part of the solution, but in the words of Reagan's inaugural address, government had become "part of the problem."

It had been a long time coming, but by the dawn of the 1980s the needs and desires of the American people had dramatically changed. The urgencies of the New Deal had been replaced by concerns over crime, taxes, and above all holding on to the economic gains that so many Americans had achieved. Over the past thirty years, millions of Americans had entered the middle class, and the old class warfare rhetoric that Roosevelt and Truman had perfected in the 1930s and '40s was no longer resonating with the American people.

In many respects, the Democrats were a victim of their own success—the activist government and new economic and educational programs that characterized the New Deal had given millions the opportunity for a true middle-class existence. When FDR pledged to help the "forgotten man," he was talking about a healthy percentage of the American people. By 1984, the typical "forgotten man" had become a middle manager living in suburbia with two children, a mortgage to pay off, and a gnawing fear about how he or she was going to make ends meet. More and more families now had two wage earners. As the American people's financial and political concerns were changing, the Democrats were seemingly still wedded to the ideologies of the past, unwilling and perhaps unable to evolve.

For millions of Americans, the Democrats were becoming the party of big-government solutions, loyalty to liberal interest groups, and tax-and-spend economic policies. The party's failure to articulate an aspirational message of national greatness, which of course Reagan perfected, as well as the seeming elitism of the party's political philosophy had turned many Americans off. Quite simply, the concept of activist government as defined by Roosevelt's New Deal, Truman's Fair Deal, Kennedy's New Frontier, and Johnson's Great Society was, by the 1980s, no longer embraced by the electorate.[1]

The populism that had once driven the Democrats' success was now seen as reserved for the poor, not the middle class. Reforms in the party's structure had opened the party to new special interest groups, who were given ample voice and opportunity to express their views. The Democratic Party, which once a coalition of working-class Americans, had become to many an amalgamation of cause-oriented groups increasingly to the left of the American people.[2] Issues such as affirmative action, gay rights, welfare, busing, the nuclear freeze, human rights, and other liberal causes were becoming front and center in Democratic speeches, as opposed to the bread-and-butter, pocketbook issues that were of greatest concern to most Americans.

By 1984 the white ethnics (the so-called Reagan Democrats) and southern voters, who once had been the backbone of the New Deal coalition, were abandoning the party in droves. When given a choice between what they perceived as big and unresponsive government and the Republican philosophy of limited government, they were choosing the latter. As President Reagan would say when accepting his renomination for president, "The choices this year are not just between two different personalities or between two different political parties. They're between two different visions of the future."

No event would provide America with a better contrast between these two choices, while also reinforcing the reigning stereotypes of the Democratic Party, than the 1984 Democratic convention in San Francisco and the speeches examined in this chapter.

## A BRUISING PRIMARY

As Democrats gathered in the city by the bay, party delegates were limping toward the finish line of what had been a difficult and trying primary battle. The nominee, former vice president Walter Mondale, had been bruised, bloodied, and almost upended in his race for the nomination. The choice of New York congresswoman Geraldine Ferraro as his running mate, the first woman to appear on a presidential ticket, had given the party a momentary boost in spirits, but the challenges facing Democrats were not going to be solved so easily.

Mondale had taken the traditional front-runner route to the nomination, lining up key labor and special-interest support and raising far more money than his rivals. An old-style New Deal

Democrat, Mondale maintained strong appeal among the party activists who dominated Democratic Party politics. But for all of Mondale's political achievements, he lacked a real vision for the party or the country. In the words of pollster Pat Caddell, Mondale's campaign didn't inspire or energize Democrats; it simply "existed."[3] When Gary Hart and his centrist "New Ideas" platform emerged, Mondale had no strong reservoir of emotional support in the party to fall back on. Mondale's seemingly easy route to the nomination suddenly took an unexpected detour.

Hart was at the time a little-known Democratic senator from Colorado who'd barely registered on early public opinion polls. But the faltering campaigns of other, more centrist candidates, particularly Ohio senator and former astronaut John Glenn, as well as Hart's efforts to establish a foothold in the early primary state of New Hampshire gave his candidacy greater visibility. Moreover, his effort to chart a new course for the party and break away from traditional Democratic thinking struck a chord with not only moderate and independent voters but also younger Americans, for whom the New Deal was merely a chapter in a history book. His stunning victory in the New Hampshire primary thrust his candidacy to the forefront and positioned him as the logical alternative to Mondale's traditional liberalism.

But Hart's "New Ideas" were, for many, much more of a public relations device than a genuine effort to transform long-held Democratic positions. Even as Hart continued to win primaries, new questions were raised about his background, and it was revealed that significant numbers of his supporters didn't actually know what he believed in.[4] Hart was defining his campaign by opposition to liberal politics but was failing to present Democratic primary voters with a vision of the future. It was the same problem facing Mondale, but the latter's position as the front-runner gave him a bit more leeway. The need for Democrats to move decisively toward the center and craft a unique political narrative that would inspire voters once again would come in time . . . just not in 1984.

But Mondale's challenge wouldn't come only from the center. In November, longtime civil rights activist and minister Jesse Jackson entered the Democratic primary race. It was a historic moment for both the party and the country: here was the first serious African American contender for the White House. However, Jackson presented a genuine dilemma for Mondale and the Democrats. On one hand, he was the key to ensuring strong support from African American voters for the party. On the other hand, Jackson's presence in the primaries threatened to upset more conservative Democrats and Jewish voters, who viewed Jackson with enormous suspicion. When he was quoted using the epithet *Hymietown* (derived from a derogatory term for Jews) to describe New York City and refused to separate himself from the Nation of Islam leader Louis Farrakhan, the hostility from Jewish voters grew even stronger.

Yet long after the other candidates had left the race (and it was clear his hope for the nomination had passed) Jackson stayed on, fighting it out with Hart and Mondale. Jackson's candidacy instilled enormous pride in African American voters across the country. Among whites, however, Jackson's support was minimal at best. While this reflected in part out-and-out racism, it was also a question of Jackson's aggressive style, which alarmed many white voters and reminded them of the radical black movements of the 1960s and early '70s. (This is not to mention the fact that Jackson had never held elected office and was in many respects unqualified to be president. As former Washington, D.C., mayor Marion Barry famously said of Jackson, he "don't want to run nothing but his mouth.") In the end, Jackson had little hope of winning the nomination, but if his goal was to become the voice of black America, on this point he was clearly the victor. Jackson would end up making history in 1984, becoming the first black man to win a presidential primary in American history, as nationwide more than 20 percent of Democratic primary voters cast a ballot for him.

But for Mondale, it was a different story. His fund-raising and institutional advantage would turn out to be too much for Hart. However, the bruising primary had taken a significant (and in some respects fatal) toll on his ability to win a general election. Faced with Hart's challenge, Mondale had been forced to move to the left to energize his base supporters. Conversely, Jackson's entry into the race and his close association with the party threatened to alienate the same moderate white voters who had abandoned the party in 1968 and 1972. Neither Hart nor Mondale had been willing to attack Jackson on the campaign trail or during debates for fear of alienating African American voters. Yet, at the same time, the threat of a white backlash constantly hung over both campaigns.

To make matters worse, Mondale had won only eleven out of twenty-nine contested primaries. He had ensured his nomination victory by following arcane delegate rules to win the support of superdelegates to the Democratic convention. The onetime front-runner barely had the support of his own party, winning less than a majority of all primary votes cast. In short, Mondale had done little to change the party's image among white middle-class voters—the segment of the electorate that had been the backbone of the New Deal coalition and whose defection in 1980 had led to the Reagan landslide. The Democratic convention in San Francisco would only serve to make his challenge that much greater.

## Cuomo Rallies the Faithful

New York governor Mario Cuomo, a rising star in the party, had been asked to give the keynote speech at the convention. Cuomo was known as a spellbinding orator, but his rhetoric was decidedly left of center. This, however, was his first moment on a national stage, and in one of the most famous convention addresses in American history, Cuomo wowed Democrats and the nation with moving oratory that, following in the footsteps of Bryan, Wilson, and FDR, once again established the Democratic Party as the party of poor and working-class Americans.

At the outset of his speech, Cuomo harked back to the class warfare rhetoric that had long brought success for Democrats, "The difference between Democrats and Republicans has always been measured in courage and confidence," he reminded the audience. "The Republicans believe that the wagon train will not make it to the frontier unless some of the old, some of the young, some of the weak are left behind by the side of the trail. The strong they tell us will inherit the land."

But this survival-of-the-fittest ideology stood in stark contrast to the philosophy of Democrats. "We Democrats believe that we can make it all the way with the whole family intact. And we have more than once," argued Cuomo.

> Ever since Franklin Roosevelt lifted himself from his wheelchair to lift this nation from its knees. Wagon train after wagon train, to new frontiers of education, housing, peace; the whole family aboard; constantly reaching out to extend and enlarge that family; lifting them up into the wagon on the way; Blacks and Hispanics and people of every ethnic group, and Native Americans—all those struggling to build their families and claim some small share of America. For nearly 50 years we carried them all to new levels of comfort and security and dignity, even affluence; and remember this, some of us in this room today are here only because this nation had that kind of confidence. And it would be wrong to forget that.

Cuomo had a point—it would be wrong to forget the achievements of the past. But now was the time for looking forward as well. In this sense, Cuomo's speech was far more focused on protecting the gains that Americans had made under Democratic administrations as opposed to offering new ideas for meeting the challenges of the future.

Cuomo called on Democrats to guide the American people toward their way of thinking. "We must get the American public to look past the glitter, beyond the showmanship—to the reality, the hard substance of things. And . . . bring people to their senses," Cuomo passionately argued. He told the assembled delegates, "We must make the American people understand this deficit because they don't," and he bemoaned that the "disastrous quality" of the President's record was "not more fully understood by the American people." How did he explain this apparent disconnect? "I can only attribute [it] to the President's amiability and the failure by some to separate the salesman from the product," said Cuomo. Such words smacked of paternalism, a sense that Americans were not smart enough to see the "real" troubles in America.

At a time when much of the electorate was happy with the direction of the country (the so-called satisfaction index, which gauged the American people's satisfaction with the way things were going in the country, reached 50 percent—its highest point ever) and with the economy on the upswing, Cuomo was reflecting a vision of America that ran counter to what millions were seeing outside their own windows and in their neighborhoods.[5] The economic uncertainty to which Cuomo spoke resonated with some, but it didn't fully reflect the concerns of middle-class America.

When Cuomo attacked the president for his vision of America as "a shining city on a hill," he urged the president to get out and see the real suffering in America. He urged Reagan to remember that there were "more families in trouble" and "more and more people who need help but can't find it." He spoke of the nation's cities and the "elderly people who tremble in the basements of the houses there," the "people who sleep in the city streets, in the gutter," and the "ghettos where thousands of young people, without a job or an education, give their lives away to drug dealers every day." "There is despair, Mr. President, in the faces that you don't see, in the places that you don't visit in your shining city," said Cuomo.

Cuomo called on Reagan to visit more places such as "Appalachia where some people still live in sheds . . . Lackawanna where thousands of unemployed steel workers wonder why we subsidize foreign steel . . . a shelter in Chicago." Again, Cuomo was highlighting real problems and concerns, but were these places with which most Americans could identify? In his summation, Cuomo lays out his beliefs and those of the party;

> We believe, as Democrats, that a society as blessed as ours, the most affluent democracy in the world's history, one that can spend trillions on instruments of destruction, ought to be able to help the middle class in its struggle, ought to be able to find work for all who can do it, room at the table, shelter for the homeless, care for the elderly and infirm and hope for the destitute. And we proclaim as loudly as we can the utter insanity of nuclear proliferation and the need for a nuclear freeze, if only to affirm the simple truth that peace is better than war because life is better than death.

It was captivating rhetoric, firmly rooted in the party's great traditions. Moreover, it was a legitimate criticism of the president and of an uneven economic recovery that left millions of Americans behind. But it wasn't a recipe for political success. When it came to rallying the faithful, Cuomo had done his job. He had delivered a memorable and beautiful speech in the booming and insistent voice for which Cuomo was well known. Senator Barry Goldwater called it "one of the best speeches I've ever heard."

Even President Reagan praised the remarks.[6] To this day, Cuomo's keynote address is one that millions of Americans remember as one of the most poignant and memorable political speeches. It is a tribute to Cuomo's unique oratorical skills. But when it came to energizing moderate and conservative voters, and above all rallying popular support for Democrats, Cuomo's New Deal–style rhetoric did little for the party or Mondale (who was never even mentioned).

While the speech was an extraordinary personal success for Cuomo, the soaring class warfare rhetoric was a further reminder to America of the liberal orientation of the Democratic Party. While Ronald Reagan was providing the country with an equally soaring message about American greatness and renewal and sounding a clarion call of American individualism, Cuomo and the Democrats came across as negative, even whiny—no matter how right their political statements may have seemed to themselves.

## Finding "Common Ground"

As Jesse Jackson prepared to address the assembled delegates in San Francisco, he would deliver a political speech unlike any other ever heard at a Democratic convention. Jackson's appearance at the convention was a historic moment for the nation. Eight years earlier, African American congresswoman Barbara Jordan had delivered a rousing keynote address at the 1976 Democratic convention. But this was different. Jackson had earned 3.5 million votes in the Democratic primaries. He represented a true and rising force in American politics.

Jackson's performance in the primaries earned him a prime speaking slot at the convention—and he hardly disappointed. Rhetorical scholars Martha Solomon and Paul Stewart nicely summed up Jackson's unique oratorical approach: "Experiencing a Jackson speech is like a long automobile excursion—you know where it began and where it is supposed to end, but in between is fraught with detours, and surprises, as well as long familiar stretches."[7]

This circuitous approach is a good description of the type of speech Jackson delivered, which seemed more rooted in his past role as a preacher than in his present role as a political leader. It would be a fool's errand even to attempt to highlight all the memorable metaphors and analogies that dotted this speech. Suffice it to say that Jackson brought every rhetorical trick of the trade to the table. Yet for many what was so surprising about the speech was his initially chastened tone.

To his great credit, Jackson owned up to his own misstatements and hurtful words on the campaign trail (the more cynical might argue they came about seven months too late). "If in my low moments, in word, deed or attitude, through some error of temper, taste and tone, I have caused anyone discomfort, created pain, or revived someone's fears, that was not my truest self. If there were occasions when my grape turned into a raisin and my joy bell lost its resonance, please forgive me . . . I am not a perfect servant. I am a public servant. I'm doing my best against the odds. As I develop and serve, be patient. God is not finished with me yet." Here Jackson combines well-crafted metaphors with his familiar alliteration and places them in a veneer of humility and a plea for forgiveness.

Yet it was his image of the "Rainbow Coalition" and a call for social justice for the nation's most vulnerable citizens that came to define this address. Jackson said, "America is not like a blanket—one piece of unbroken cloth, the same color, the same texture, the same size. America is more like a quilt—many patches, many pieces, many colors, many sizes, all woven and held together by a common thread. The white, the Hispanic, the black, the Arab, the Jew, the woman, the Native American, the small farmer, the businessperson, the environmentalist, the peace activist, the young, the old, the lesbian, the gay and the disabled make up the American quilt." This image of the Democratic Party as a grand quilt bringing together disparate forces under one banner was an evocative image and one that spoke to the party's inclusive message. Yet at the same time, it once again reminded Americans of the identity politics that so often characterized Democratic politics in the post-1968 era.

Moreover, Jackson's call for greater government assistance for the downtrodden and a national mission "to feed the hungry, to clothe the naked, to house the homeless, to teach the illiterate, to provide jobs for the jobless and to choose the human race over the nuclear race" were straight out of the old Democratic playbook. In an era of small-government conservatism, he bemoaned cuts in government programs such as energy assistance to the poor, breakfast and lunch programs for children, and job training. At a time when the Cold War was heating up, he called for a foreign policy "characterized by mutual respect, not by gunboat diplomacy, big stick diplomacy and threats."

This is not to say that it is wrong to talk about social justice on the campaign trail. But these calls must be balanced. Many Americans empathized with the plight of those in need, but listening to these speeches, one could be forgiven for believing that those in need were the only Americans who mattered to Democrats.[8]

To be sure, the Republicans hardly ran what anyone would consider an issue-laden campaign—Reagan's "Morning in America" reelection campaign was far more about showmanship and flash than a substantive debate on the challenges facing America in the 1980s. But when you have an ideological advantage, you can get away with sizzle rather than steak—just ask Harry Truman. Reagan constantly reminded Americans how far the country had come, of the potential of America in the 1980s, and of his brimming confidence in the future.

At the GOP convention in Dallas that August, he would contrast the GOP message of "hope, confidence, and growth" with the Democratic message of "pessimism, fear, and limits." He would go on to say that Democrats were living "in the past, seeking to apply the old and failed policies to an era that has passed them by. Ours learns from the past and strives to change by boldly charting a new course for the future. Theirs lives by promises, the bigger, the better. We offer proven, workable answers."[9] It was a view shared by the American people.

## MONDALE TELLS THE TRUTH . . . AND SHOOTS HIMSELF IN THE FOOT

For all their eloquence, Jackson and Cuomo did little to arrest the Democrats' continuing decline—if anything, their messages likely reinforced it and placed the country in even greater lock-step with the conservative populism being preached by Ronald Reagan and the Republican Party. Yet it would be Walter Mondale who would make the greatest misstep of the 1984 Democratic convention.

It's not often that a major public figure commits political suicide in front of millions of people, but at the 1984 Democratic convention in San Francisco that's exactly what Walter Mondale did. The great irony of Mondale's self-immolation was that he had begun his acceptance speech by taking exactly the right approach to appeal to dubious independent and moderate voters:

> We know that America must have a strong defense, and a sober view of the Soviets. We know that government must be as well-managed as it is well-meaning. We know that a healthy, growing private economy is the key to the future. We know that Harry Truman spoke the truth when he said: "A President . . . has to be able to say yes and no, but mostly

no." Look at our platform. There are no defense cuts that weaken our security; no business taxes that weaken our economy; no laundry lists that raid our Treasury. We are wiser, stronger, and focused on the future. If Mr. Reagan wants to re-run the 1980 campaign: Fine. Let them fight over the past. We're fighting for the American future—and that's why we're going to win this campaign.[10]

These words were delivered with a clear and unambiguous intention—to confront head-on the most negative stereotypes that many millions had of the Democratic Party. Yet only moments later it was Walter Mondale who would remind the American people of the party's greatest liability.

If there was one overriding negative public perception that defined the Democratic Party in the 1980s, it was the toxic label of "tax-and-spend liberals." For years, Republicans had accused Democrats of taking the American people's hard-earned tax dollars and spending them on Great Society programs geared toward helping poor minorities. With the notable exception of the 1976 post-Watergate election, the strategy generally worked like a charm.

So when Walter Mondale strode to the stage to deliver his acceptance speech, the *last* thing he should have told the American people was that he intended to raise their taxes. But that's exactly what he did.

Whoever is inaugurated in January, the American people will have to pay Mr. Reagan's bills. The budget will be squeezed. Taxes will go up. And anyone who says they won't is not telling the truth to the American people. I mean business. By the end of my first term, I will reduce the Reagan budget deficit by two-thirds. Let's tell the truth . . . Mr. Reagan will raise taxes, and so will I. He won't tell you. I just did.[11]

Mondale believed that only through boldness and candor could he convince the American people to give his candidacy a fighting chance. Moreover, he genuinely believed that the nation's growing deficit needed to be addressed. To his credit, Mondale refused to duck what nearly everyone in Washington knew to be the truth—that taxes would have to be raised in order to correct the deficit begun by President Reagan's 1981 budget of tax cuts and higher defense spending. Two years later, Mondale's words would be proved prophetic as Reagan signed off on one of the largest tax increases in the nation's history.[12]

Mondale showed great political courage, but it didn't translate into political gold. Indeed, one man's political courage is another man's example of being hopelessly out of touch. These disastrous words only served to reinforce the image of the Democratic Party as a party of tax-and-spend liberals, strengthening conservative efforts to reduce the scope and influence of government in the process. As Jack Germond and Jules Witcover put it, "Fritz Mondale's determination to be the candidate of candor moved him to make a statement that in a flash conveyed to voters that he wasn't any different after all from the long line of New Deal Democrats from which he had so conspicuously descended. And in that flash of candor, his slim chances to upset Reagan very probably went down the drain."[13]

Mondale never had much of a chance of beating Ronald Reagan at the ballot box, but his honesty at the convention ended any hope for victory. The tax-and-spend label would become a millstone around the neck of his candidacy. It was a landslide defeat for the Democrats as Reagan piled up forty-nine states, creating a true political realignment in the country. If the win in 1980 was a result, in some measure, of the unpopularity of Jimmy Carter, the victory in 1984 was all Reagan's and even more so a victory for the conservative movement. Now the Republicans had not only the White House but also the overriding support of the American people.

A closer look inside the results provides even more context to the breadth of the Democratic Party's loss and its alienation from white, middle-class America. Mondale won majority support from only African Americans, Hispanics, and Jews as well as the unemployed, union members, voters with incomes below $12,500, and women who didn't have a high school education. This was a narrow political base, and it demonstrated the extent to which the Republicans had made significant inroads into those communities that once had strongly supported Democrats. For better or for worse, when it came to the role of government in their lives the American people were unambiguous: less was better. Stirring rhetoric, no matter how beautiful, no matter how moving, and no matter how memorable, wasn't about to change that.

## *Mario Cuomo Reminds Ronald Reagan of the Nation Beyond His "City on the Hill," San Francisco, July 16, 1984*

Please allow me to skip the stories and the poetry and the temptation to deal in nice but vague rhetoric. Let me instead use this valuable opportunity to deal immediately with the questions that should determine this election and that we all know are vital to the American people.

Ten days ago, President Reagan admitted that although some people in this country seemed to be doing well nowadays, others were unhappy, even worried, about themselves, their families and their futures. The President said that he didn't understand that fear. He said, "Why, this country is a shining city on a hill." And the President is right. In many ways we are "a shining city on a hill."

But the hard truth is that not everyone is sharing in this city's splendor and glory. A shining city is perhaps all the President sees from the portico of the White House and the veranda of his ranch, where everyone seems to be doing well. But there's another city, there's another part to the shining city, the part where some people can't pay their mortgages and most young people can't afford one, where students can't afford the education they need and middle-class parents watch the dreams they hold for their children evaporate.

In this part of the city there are more poor than ever, more families in trouble, more and more people who need help but can't find it. Even worse: There are elderly people who tremble in the basements of the houses there. And there are people who sleep in the city streets, in the gutter, where the glitter doesn't show. There are ghettos where thousands of young people, without a job or an education, give their lives away to drug dealers every day. There is despair, Mr. President, in the faces that you don't see, in the places that you don't visit in your shining city.

. . . Mr. President you ought to know that this nation is more a "Tale of Two Cities" than it is just a "Shining City on a Hill."

Maybe, maybe, Mr. President, if you visited some more places; maybe if you went to Appalachia where some people still live in sheds; maybe if you went to Lackawanna where thousands of unemployed steel workers wonder why we subsidize foreign steel. Maybe, Mr. President, if you stopped in at a shelter in Chicago and spoke to the homeless there; maybe, Mr. President, if you asked a woman who had been denied the help she needed to feed her children because you said you needed the money for a tax break for a *millionaire* or for a missile we couldn't afford to use; maybe, Mr. President, but I'm afraid not.

Because, the truth is, ladies and gentlemen, that this is how we were warned it would be. President Reagan told us from the very beginning that he believed in a kind of social Darwinism—survival of the fittest. "Government can't do everything," we were told. "So it should settle for taking care of the strong and hope that economic ambition and charity will do the rest. Make the rich richer, and what falls from the table will be enough for the middle class and those who are trying desperately to work their way into the middle class."

You know, the Republicans called it trickle-down when Hoover tried it. Now they call it supply-side, but it's the same shining city for those relative few who are lucky enough to live in its good neighborhoods. But for the people who are excluded, for the people who are locked out—all they can do is stare from a distance at that city's glimmering towers.

It's an old story. It's as old as our history. The difference between Democrats and Republicans has always been measured in courage and confidence. The Republicans believe that the wagon train will not make it to the frontier unless some of the old, some of the young, some of the weak are left behind by the side of the trail. The strong they tell us will inherit the land!

We Democrats believe in something else. We Democrats believe that we can make it all the way with the whole family intact. And we have more than once, ever since Franklin Roosevelt lifted himself from his wheelchair to lift this nation from its knees. Wagon train after wagon train, to new frontiers of education, housing, peace; the whole family aboard; constantly reaching out to extend and enlarge that family; lifting them up into the wagon on the way; Blacks and Hispanics and people of every ethnic group, and Native Americans—all those struggling to build their families and claim some small share of America. For nearly 50 years we carried them all to new levels of comfort and security and dignity, even affluence; and remember this, some of us in this room today are here only because this nation had that kind of confidence. And it would be wrong to forget that.

So, here we are at this convention to remind ourselves where we come from and to claim the future for ourselves and for our children. Today, our great Democratic Party, which has saved this nation from depression, from fascism, from racism, from corruption, is called upon to do it again—this time to save the nation from confusion and division, from the threat of eventual fiscal disaster, and most of all from the fear of a nuclear holocaust—but that's not going to be easy . . . In order to succeed, we must answer our opponent's polished and appealing rhetoric with a more telling reasonableness and rationality.

We must win this case on the merits. We must get the American public to look past the glitter, beyond the showmanship—to the reality, the hard substance of things. And we'll do it, not so much with speeches that sound good as with speeches that are good and sound; not so much with speeches that will bring people to their feet as with speeches that will bring people to their senses. We must make the American people hear our "Tale of

Two Cities." We must convince them that we don't have to settle for two cities, that we can have one city, indivisible, shining
for all of its people.

Now, we will have no chance to do that if what comes out of
this convention is a babble of arguing voices. If that's what's heard
throughout the campaign—dissident sounds from all sides—we
will have no chance to tell our message. To succeed we will have
to surrender some small parts of our individual interests, to build a
platform that we can all stand on, at once and comfortably.
Proudly singing out, we need a platform we can all agree to so
that we can sing out the truth for the nation to hear, in chorus, its
logic so clear and commanding that no slick Madison Avenue
commercial, no amount of geniality, no martial music will be able
to muffle the sound of the truth.

And we Democrats must unite. We Democrats must unite so
that the entire nation can unite, because surely the Republicans
won't bring this country together. Their policies divide the nation
into the lucky and the left-out, into the royalty and the rabble.
The Republicans are willing to treat that division as victory. They
would cut this nation in half, into those temporarily better off and
those worse off than before. And they would call that division recovery.

Now we should not be embarrassed or dismayed or chagrined
if the process of unifying is difficult, even wrenching at times. Remember that unlike any other party, we embrace men and
women of every color, every creed, every orientation, every economic class. In our family are gathered everyone from the abject
poor of Essex County in New York to the enlightened affluent of
the gold coasts at both ends of the nation. And in between is the
heart of our constituency: the middle class, the people not rich
enough to be worry-free but not poor enough to be on welfare;
the middle class—those people who work for a living because

they have to, not because some psychiatrist told them it was a convenient way to fill the interval between birth and eternity—white collar and blue collar, young professionals—men and women in small business desperate for the capital and contracts that they need to prove their worth.

We speak for the minorities who have not yet entered the mainstream. We speak for ethnics who want to add their culture to the magnificent mosaic that is America. We speak for women who are indignant that this nation refuses to etch into its governmental commandments the simple rule "thou shalt not sin against equality," a rule so simple—I was going to say, and I perhaps dare not but I will; its a commandment so simple it can be spelled in three letters—ERA!

We speak for young people demanding an education and a future. We speak for senior citizens who are terrorized by the idea that their only security, their Social Security, is being threatened. We speak for millions of reasoning people fighting to preserve our environment from greed and from stupidity. And we speak for reasonable people who are fighting to preserve our very existence from a macho intransigence that refuses to make intelligent attempts to discuss the possibility of nuclear holocaust with our enemy. They refuse because they believe we can pile missiles so high that they will pierce the clouds and the sight of them will frighten our enemies into submission.

Now we're proud of this diversity. As Democrats we're grateful for it, we don't have to manufacture it the way the Republicans will next month in Dallas, by propping up mannequin delegates on the convention floor. But we—while we're proud of this diversity—we pay a price for it. The different people that we represent have different points of view. And sometimes they compete and even debate, and even argue. That's what our primaries were all about. But now the primaries are over, and it is time when we pick our candidates and our platform here to lock arms and move into this campaign together.

If you need any more inspiration to put some small part of your own difference aside to create this consensus then all you need to do is to reflect on what the Republican policy of "divide and cajole" has done to this land since 1980. Now the President has asked the American people to judge him on whether or not he's fulfilled the promises he made four years ago. I believe as Democrats we ought to accept that challenge. And just for a moment let us consider what he has said and what he's done.

Inflation is down since 1980, but not because of the supply-side miracle promised to us by the President. Inflation was reduced the old-fashioned way, with a recession, the worst since 1932. We could have brought inflation down that way. How did he do it? 55,000 bankruptcies, two years of massive unemployment, 200,000 farmers and ranchers forced off the land, more homeless than at any time since the Great Depression in 1932 . . . more hungry, more poor—most of them women— and he paid one other thing, a nearly $200 billion deficit threatening our future.

Now we must make the American people understand this deficit because they don't. The President's deficit is a direct and dramatic repudiation of his promise in 1980 to balance the budget by 1983 . . . It is a mortgage on our children's future that can be paid only in pain and that could bring this nation to its knees.

Now don't take my word for it, I'm a Democrat. Ask the Republican investment bankers on Wall Street what they think the chances of this recovery being permanent are. You see, if they're not too embarrassed to tell you the truth, they'll say that they're appalled and frightened by the President's deficit. Ask them what they think of our economy, now that it's been driven by the distorted value of the dollar back to its colonial condition . . .

What chance would the Republican candidate have had in

1980 if he had told the American people that he intended to pay for his so-called economic recovery with bankruptcies, unemployment, more homeless, more hungry and the largest government debt known to humankind? If he had told the voters in 1980 that truth would American voters have signed the loan certificate for him on Election Day? Of course not! That was an election won under false pretenses. It was won with smoke and mirrors and illusions. And that's the kind of recovery we have now as well.

And what about foreign policy? They said that they would make us and the whole world safer. They say they have. By creating the largest defense budget in history—one that even they now admit is excessive—by escalating to a frenzy the nuclear arms race, by incendiary rhetoric, by refusing to discuss peace with our enemies, by the loss of 279 young Americans in Lebanon in pursuit of a plan and a policy that no one can find or describe.

. . . Of course Democrats are for a strong defense. Of course Democrats believe that there are times that we must stand and fight, and we have. Thousands of us have paid for freedom with our lives, but always, when this country has been at its best, our purposes were clear. Now they're not. Now our allies are as confused as our enemies. Now we have no real commitment to our friends or to our ideals, not to human rights, not to the *refuseniks*, not to Sakharov, not to Bishop Tutu and the others struggling for freedom in South Africa.

We have in the last few years spent more than we can afford. We have pounded our chests and made bold speeches, but we lost 279 young Americans in Lebanon and we live behind sandbags in Washington. How can anyone say that we are safer, stronger or better?

That is the Republican record. That its disastrous quality is not more fully understood by the American people I can only attribute to the President's amiability and the failure by some to separate the salesman from the product.

Now it's up to us. Now it's up to you and to me to make the case to America. And to remind Americans that if they are not happy with all that the President has done so far, they should consider how much worse it will be if he is left to his radical proclivities for another four years unrestrained.

. . . Where would four years more take us? How much larger will the deficit be? How much deeper the cuts in programs for the struggling middle class and the poor to limit that deficit? How high will the interest rates be? How much more acid rain killing our forests and fouling our lakes?

And, ladies and gentlemen, please think of this: What kind of Supreme Court will we have?

We must ask ourselves what kind of court and country will be fashioned by the man who believes in having government mandate people's religion and morality, the man who believes that trees pollute the environment, the man that believes that the laws against discrimination against people go too far, a man who threatens Social Security and Medicaid and help for the disabled. How high will we pile the missiles? How much deeper will the gulf be between us and our enemies? And, ladies and gentlemen, will four years more make meaner the spirit of the American people? This election will measure the record of the past four years. But more than that, it will answer the question of what kind of people we want to be.

We Democrats still have a dream. We still believe in this nation's future. And this is our answer to the question. This is our credo:

We believe in only the government we need, but we insist on all the government we need.

We believe in a government that is characterized by fairness and reasonableness, a reasonableness that goes beyond labels, that doesn't distort or promise to do things that we know we can't do.

We believe in a government strong enough to use words like

"love" and "compassion" and smart enough to convert our no-
blest aspirations into practical realities.

We believe in encouraging the talented, but we believe that
while survival of the fittest may be a good working description of
the process of evolution, a government of humans should elevate
itself to a higher order.

Our government should be able to rise to the level where it
can fill the gaps that are left by chance or by a wisdom we don't
fully understand. We would rather have laws written by the patron of this great city, the man called the "world's most sincere
Democrat," St. Francis of Assisi, than laws written by Darwin.

We believe, as Democrats, that a society as blessed as ours, the
most affluent democracy in the world's history, one that can
spend trillions on instruments of destruction, ought to be able to
help the middle class in its struggle, ought to be able to find work
for all who can do it, room at the table, shelter for the homeless,
care for the elderly and infirm and hope for the destitute. And we
proclaim as loudly as we can the utter insanity of nuclear prolifer-
ation and the need for a nuclear freeze, if only to affirm the simple truth that peace is better than war because life is better than
death.

We believe in firm but fair law and order. We believe proudly
in the union movement. We believe in privacy for people, open-
ness by government. We believe in civil rights and we believe in
human rights.

We believe in a single fundamental idea that describes better
than most textbooks and any speech that I could write what a
proper government should be: the idea of family, mutuality, the
sharing of benefits and burdens for the good of all; feeling one another's pain, sharing one another's blessings; reasonably, honestly,
fairly, without respect to race or sex or geography or political affiliation.

We believe we must be the family of America; recognizing that at the heart of the matter we are bound one to another; that the problems of a retired school teacher in Duluth are our problems, that the future of the child in Buffalo is our future, that the struggle of a disabled man in Boston to survive and live decently is our struggle, that the hunger of a woman in Little Rock is our hunger, that the failure anywhere to provide what reasonably we might, to avoid pain, is our failure.

For 50 years we Democrats created a better future for our children, using traditional Democratic principles as a fixed beacon, giving us direction and purpose, but constantly innovating, adapting to new realities: Roosevelt's alphabet programs; Truman's NATO and the GI Bill of Rights; Kennedy's intelligent tax incentives and the Alliance for Progress; Johnson's civil rights; Carter's human rights and the nearly miraculous Camp David Peace Accord.

Democrats did it, and Democrats can do it again. We can build a future that deals with our deficit. Remember this, that 50 years of progress under our principles never cost us what the last four years of stagnation have. And we can deal with the deficit intelligently, by shared sacrifice, with all parts of the nation's family contributing, building partnerships with the private sector, providing a sound defense without depriving ourselves of what we need to feed our children and care for our people. We can have a future that provides for all the young of the present by marrying common sense and compassion.

We know we can, because we did it for nearly 50 years before 1980. And we can do it again, if we do not forget that this entire nation has profited by these progressive principles, that they helped lift up generations to the middle class and higher, that they gave us a chance to work, to go to college, to raise a family, to own a house, to be secure in our old age, and, before that, to reach heights that our own parents would not have dared dream of.

That struggle to live with dignity is the real story of the shining city. And it's a story, ladies and gentlemen, that I didn't read in a book or learn in a classroom. I saw it and lived it, like many of you. I watched a small man with thick calluses on both his hands work 15 and 16 hours a day. I saw him once literally bleed from the bottoms of his feet—a man who came here uneducated, alone, unable to speak the language, who taught me all I needed to know about faith and hard work by the simple eloquence of his example. I learned about our kind of democracy from my father. And I learned about our obligation to each other from him and my mother. They asked only for a chance to work and to make the world better for their children, and they asked to be protected in those moments when they would not be able to protect themselves. This nation and this nation's government did that for them.

And that they were able to build a family and live in dignity and see one of their children go from behind their little grocery store in South Jamaica on the other side of the tracks where he was born, to occupy the highest seat in the greatest state in the greatest nation in the only world we know is an ineffably beautiful tribute to the democratic process.

And ladies and gentlemen, on January 20, 1985, it will happen again, only on a much, much grander scale. We will have a new President of the United States, a Democrat born not to the blood of kings but to the blood of pioneers and immigrants. And we will have America's first woman Vice President, the child of immigrants, and she will open with one magnificent stroke a whole new frontier for the United States.

Now it will happen if we make it happen; if you and I make it happen. And I ask you now, ladies and gentlemen, brothers and sisters—for the good of all of us, for the love of this great nation, for the family of America, for the love of God—please make this nation remember how futures are built.

## *Jesse Jackson Describes His Vision of the "Rainbow Coalition," San Francisco, July 17, 1984*

Tonight we come together bound by our faith in a mighty God, with genuine respect for our country, and inheriting the legacy of a great party—a Democratic Party—which is the best hope for redirecting our nation on a more humane, just and peaceful course.

This is not a perfect party. We are not a perfect people. Yet, we are called to a perfect mission: to feed the hungry, to clothe the naked, to house the homeless, to teach the illiterate, to provide jobs for the jobless, and to choose the human race over the nuclear race.

We are gathered here this week to nominate a candidate and write a platform which will expand, unify, direct and inspire our party and the nation to fulfill this mission.

My constituency is the damned, disinherited, disrespected and the despised.

They are restless and seek relief. They've voted in record numbers. They have invested the faith, hope, and trust that they have in us. The Democratic Party must send them a signal that we care. I pledge my best not to let them down.

There is the call of conscience: redemption, expansion, healing and unity. Leadership must heed the call of conscience, redemption, expansion, healing and unity, for they are the key to achieving our mission.

Time is neutral and does not change things. With courage and initiative leaders change things. No generation can choose the age or circumstances in which it is born, but through leadership it can choose to make the age in which it is born an age of enlightenment—an age of jobs, and peace, and justice.

Only leadership—that intangible combination of gifts, discipline, information, circumstance, courage, timing, will and divine inspiration—can lead us out of the crisis in which we find ourselves.

Leadership can mitigate the misery of our nation. Leadership can part the waters and lead our nation in the direction of the Promised Land. Leadership can lift the boats stuck at the bottom.

I have had the rare opportunity to watch seven men, and then two, pour out their souls, offer their service and heed the call of duty to direct the course of our nation.

There is a proper season for everything. There is a time to sow and a time to reap. There is a time to compete, and a time to cooperate.

I ask for your vote on the first ballot as a vote for a new direction for this party and this nation; a vote for conviction, a vote for conscience.

But I will be proud to support the nominee of this convention for the president of the United States of America.

I have watched the leadership of our party develop and grow. My respect for both Mr. Mondale and Mr. Hart is great.

I have watched them struggle with the cross-winds and cross-fires of being public servants, and I believe that they will both continue to try to serve us faithfully. I am elated by the knowledge that for the first time in our history a woman, Geraldine Ferraro, will be recommended to share our ticket.

Throughout this campaign, I have tried to offer leadership to the Democratic Party and the nation.

If in my high moments, I have done some good, offered some service, shed some light, healed some wounds, rekindled some hope or stirred someone from apathy and indifference, or in any way along the way helped somebody, then this campaign has not been in vain.

For friends who loved and cared for me, and for a God who spared me, and for a family who understood, I am eternally grateful.

If in my low moments, in word, deed or attitude, through some error of temper, taste or tone, I have caused anyone discomfort, created pain, or revived someone's fears, that was not my truest self.

If there were occasions when my grape turned into a raisin and my joy bell lost its resonance, please forgive me. Charge it to my head and not to my heart. My head is so limited in its finitude; my heart is boundless in its love for the human family. I am not a perfect servant. I am a public servant. I'm doing my best against the odds. As I develop and serve, be patient. God is not finished with me yet.

The campaign has taught me much: that leaders must be tough enough to fight, tender enough to cry, human enough to make mistakes, humble enough to admit them, strong enough to absorb the pain, and resilient enough to bounce back and keep on moving. For leaders, the pain is often intense. But you must smile through your tears and keep moving with the faith that there is a brighter side somewhere.

I went to see Hubert Humphrey three days before he died. He had just called Richard Nixon from his dying bed, and many people wondered why. And, I asked him.

He said, "Jesse, from this vantage point, with the sun setting in my life, all of the speeches, the political conventions, the crowds and the great fights are behind me now. At a time like this you are forced to deal with your irreducible essence, forced to grapple with that which is really important to you. And what I have concluded about life," Hubert Humphrey said, "when all is said and done, we must forgive each other, and redeem each other, and move on."

. . . Our flag is red, white and blue, but our nation is rainbow—red, yellow, brown, blacks and white—we're all precious in God's sight. America is not like a blanket—one piece of unbroken cloth, the same color, the same texture, the same size. America is more like a quilt—many patches, many pieces, many colors, many sizes, all woven and held together by a common thread.

The white, the Hispanic, the black, the Arab, the Jew, the

woman, the Native American, the small farmer, the businessperson, the environmentalist, the peace activist, the young, the old, the lesbian, the gay, and the disabled make up the American quilt.

Even in our fractured state, all of us count and fit somewhere. We have proven that we can survive without each other. But we have not proven that we can win or make progress without each other. We must come together.

From Fannie Lou Hamer in Atlantic City in 1964 to the Rainbow Coalition in San Francisco today; from the Atlantic to the Pacific, we have experienced pain but progress as we ended American apartheid laws; we got public accommodations; we secured voting rights; we obtained open housing; as young people got the right to vote; we lost Malcolm, Martin, Medgar, Bobby and John and Viola.

The team that got us here must be expanded, not abandoned. Twenty years ago, tears welled up in our eyes as the bodies of Schwerner, Goodman and Chaney were dredged from the depths of a river in Mississippi. Twenty years later, our communities, black and Jewish, are in anguish, anger and pain.

. . . We are co-partners in a long and rich religious history—the Judeo-Christian tradition. Many blacks and Jews have a shared passion for social justice at home and peace abroad. We must seek a revival of the spirit, inspired by a new vision and new possibilities . . . We are bound by Dr. Martin Luther King Jr. and Rabbi Abraham Heschel, crying out from their graves for us to reach common ground. We are bound by shared blood and shared sacrifices. We are much too intelligent; much too bound by our Judeo-Christian heritage; much too victimized by racism, sexism, militarism and anti-Semitism; much too threatened as historical scapegoats to go on divided one from another. We must turn from finger-pointing to clasped hands. We must share our burdens and our joys with each other once again. We must turn to each other and not on each other and choose higher ground.

Twenty years later, we cannot be satisfied by just restoring the old coalition. Old wine skins must make room for new wine. We must heal and expand. The Rainbow Coalition is making room for Arab-Americans . . . The Rainbow Coalition is making room for Hispanic-Americans . . . The Rainbow is making room for the Native Americans, the most exploited people of all, a people with the greatest moral claim amongst us . . . The Rainbow Coalition includes Asian-Americans, now being killed in our streets—scapegoats for the failures of corporate, industrial and economic policies. The Rainbow is making room for the young Americans. Twenty years ago, our young people were dying in a war for which they could not even vote. But 20 years later, Young America has the power to stop a war in Central America and the responsibility to vote in great numbers . . .

The Rainbow includes disabled veterans. The color scheme fits in the Rainbow. The disabled have their handicap revealed and their genius concealed; while the able-bodied have their genius revealed and their disability concealed. But ultimately we must judge people by their values and their contribution. Don't leave anybody out. I would rather have Roosevelt in a wheelchair than Reagan on a horse.

The Rainbow is making room for small farmers. They have suffered tremendously under the Reagan regime . . . The Rainbow includes lesbians and gays. No American citizen ought be denied equal protection under the law.

We must be unusually committed and caring as we expand our family to include new members. All of us must be tolerant and understanding as the fears and anxieties of the rejected and of the party leadership express themselves in many different ways. Too often what we call hate—as if it were deeply rooted in some philosophy or strategy—is simply ignorance, anxiety, paranoia, fear and insecurity. To be strong leaders, we must be long-suffering as we seek to right the wrongs of our party and our nation. We must expand our party, heal our party and unify our party. That is our mission in 1984.

. . . Jesus said that we should not be judged by the bark we wear but by the fruit that we bear. Jesus said that we must measure greatness by how we treat the least of these.

President Reagan says the nation is in recovery. Those 90,000 corporations that made a profit last year but paid no federal taxes are recovering. The 37,000 military contractors who have benefited from Reagan's more than doubling the military budget in peacetime, surely they are recovering. The big corporations and rich individuals who received the bulk of the three-year, multibillion tax cut from Mr. Reagan are recovering. But no such recovery is under way for the least of these. Rising tides don't lift all boats, particularly those stuck on the bottom.

For the boats stuck at the bottom there is a misery index. This administration has made life more miserable for the poor. Its attitude has been contemptuous. Its policies and programs have been cruel and unfair to working people. They must be held accountable in November for increasing infant mortality among the poor. In Detroit, one of the great cities of the Western world, babies are dying at the same rate as Honduras, the most underdeveloped nation in our hemisphere.

This administration must be held accountable for policies that contribute to the growing poverty in America. Under President Reagan, there are now 34 million people in poverty, 15 percent of our nation. Twenty-three million are white, 11 million black, Hispanic, Asian and others. Mostly women and children. By the end of this year, there will be 41 million people in poverty. We cannot stand idly by. We must fight for change, now.

Under this regime we look at Social Security. The 1981 budget cuts included nine permanent Social Security benefits cuts totaling $20 billion over five years.

Small businesses have suffered under Reagan tax cuts. Only 18 percent of total business tax cuts went to them—82 percent to big business.

Health care under Mr. Reagan has been sharply cut.

Education under Mr. Reagan has been sharply cut.

Under Mr. Reagan there are now 9.7 million female-head families. They represent 16 percent of all families, half of all of them are poor. Seventy percent of all poor children live in a house headed by a woman, where there is no man.

Under Mr. Reagan, the administration has cleaned up only 6 of 545 priority toxic waste dumps.

Farmers' real net income was only about half its level in 1979.

Many say that the race in November will be decided in the South. President Reagan is depending on the conservative South to return him to office. But the South, I tell you, is unnaturally conservative. The South is the poorest region in our nation and, therefore, has the least to conserve. In his appeal to the South, Mr. Reagan is trying to substitute flags and prayer cloths for food, and clothing, and education, health care and housing. But President Reagan who asks us to pray, and I believe in prayer—I've come this way by the power of prayer. But, we must watch false prophecy.

He cuts energy assistance to the poor, cuts breakfast programs from children, cuts lunch programs from children, cuts job training from children and then says, when at the table, "let us pray." Apparently he is not familiar with the structure of a prayer. You thank the Lord for the food that you are about to receive, not the food that just left.

I think that we should pray. But don't pray for the food that left, pray for the man that took the food to leave. We need a change. We need a change in November.

Under President Reagan, the misery index has risen for the poor, but the danger index has risen for everybody.

Under this administration we've lost the lives of our boys in Central America, in Honduras, in Grenada, in Lebanon.

A nuclear standoff in Europe. Under this administration, one-third of our children believe they will die in a nuclear war. The danger index is increasing in this world.

With all the talk about defense against Russia, the Russian submarines are closer and their missiles are more accurate. We live in a world tonight more miserable and a world more dangerous.

While Reaganomics and Reaganism is talked about often, so often we miss the real meaning. Reaganism is a spirit. Reaganomics represents the real economic facts of life.

In 1980, Mr. George Bush, a man with reasonable access to Mr. Reagan, did an analysis of Mr. Reagan's economic plan. Mr. Bush concluded Reagan's plan was "voodoo economics." He was right. Third-party candidate John Anderson said that the combination of military spending, tax cuts and a balanced budget by '84 could be accomplished with blue smoke and mirrors. They were both right.

Mr. Reagan talks about a dynamic recovery. There is some measure of recovery, three and a half years later. Unemployment has inched just below where it was when he took office in 1981. But there are still 8.1 million people officially unemployed, 11 million working only part-time jobs. Inflation has come down, but let's analyze for a moment who has paid the price for this superficial economic recovery.

Mr. Reagan curbed inflation by cutting consumer demand. He cut consumer demand with conscious and callous fiscal and monetary policy. He used the federal budget to deliberately induce unemployment and curb social spending. He then weighed and supported tight monetary policies of the Federal Reserve Board to deliberately drive up interest rates—again to curb consumer demand created through borrowing.

Unemployment reached 10.7 percent; we experienced skyrocketing interest rates; our dollar inflated abroad; there were record bank failures; record farm foreclosures; record business bankruptcies; record budget deficits, record trade deficits. Mr.

Reagan brought inflation down by destabilizing our economy and disrupting family life.

He promised in 1980 a balanced budget, but instead we now have a record $200 billion budget deficit. Under President Reagan, the cumulative budget deficit for his four years is more than the sum total of deficits from George Washington to Jimmy Carter combined. I tell you, we need a change.

How is he paying for these short-term jobs? Reagan's economic recovery is being financed by deficit spending—$200 billion a year. Military spending, a major cause of this deficit, is projected over the next five years to be nearly $2 trillion, and will cost about $40,000 for every taxpaying family.

. . . The U.S. used to be the largest exporter of capital, but under Mr. Reagan we will quite likely become the largest debtor nation. About two weeks ago, on July 4, we celebrated our Declaration of Independence. Yet every day, supply-side economics is making our nation more economically dependent and less economically free. Five to six percent of our gross national product is now being eaten up with President Reagan's budget deficit.

To depend on foreign military powers to protect our national security would be foolish, making us dependent and less secure. Yet Reaganomics has us increasingly dependent on foreign economic sources . . .

We have a challenge as Democrats: support a way out. Democracy guarantees opportunity, not success. Democracy guarantees the right to participate, not a license for either the majority or a minority to dominate. The victory for the Rainbow Coalition in the platform debates today was not whether we won or lost; but that we raised the right issues. We cannot afford to lose the vote; issues are negotiable. We cannot afford to avoid raising the right questions. Our self respect and our moral integrity were at stake. Our heads are perhaps bloodied but not bowed. Our backs are straight. We can go home and face our people. Our vision is clear. When we think, on this journey from slave-ship to championship, we've gone from the planks of the boardwalk in Atlantic City in 1964 to fighting to have the right planks in the platform in San Francisco in '84. There is a deep and abiding sense of joy in our soul, despite the tears in our eyes. For while there are missing planks, there is a solid foundation upon which to build. Our party can win. But we must provide hope that will inspire people to struggle and achieve; provide a plan to show the way out of our dilemma, and then lead the way.

. . . If we want a change in this nation, reinforce that Voting Rights Act—we'll get 12 to 20 black, Hispanic, female and progressive congresspersons from the South. We can save the cotton, but we've got to fight the boll weevil—we've got to make a judgment.

It's not enough to hope ERA will pass; how can we pass ERA? If blacks vote in great numbers, progressive whites win. It's the only way progressive whites win. If blacks vote in great numbers, Hispanics win. If blacks, Hispanics and progressive whites vote, women win. When women win, children win. When women and children win, workers win. We must all come up together.

. . . Our foreign policy must be characterized by mutual respect, not by gunboat diplomacy, big stick diplomacy and threats. Our nation at its best feeds the hungry. Our nation at its worse will mine the harbors of Nicaragua; at its worst, will try to overthrow that government; at its worst, will cut aid to American education and increase aid to El Salvador; at its worst our nation will have partnership with South Africa. That's a moral disgrace.

When we look at Africa, we cannot just focus on apartheid in southern Africa. We must fight for trade with Africa, and not just aid to Africa. We cannot stand idly by and say we will not relate to Nicaragua unless they have elections there and then embrace military regimes in Africa, overthrowing democratic governments in Nigeria and Liberia and Ghana. We must fight for democracy all around the world, and play the game by one set of rules.

Peace in this world. Our present formula for peace in the Middle East is inadequate; it will not work. There are 22 nations in the Middle East. Our nation must be able to talk and act and influence all of them . . .

There is a way out. Jobs. Put Americans back to work. When I was a child growing up in Greenville, S.C., the reverend used to preach every so often a sermon about Jesus. He said, if I be lifted up, I'll draw all men unto me. I didn't quite understand what he meant as a child growing up. But I understand a little better now. If you raise up truth, it's magnetic. It has a way of drawing people. With all this confusion in this convention—there is bright lights and parties and big fun—we must raise up the simple proposition: if we lift up a program to feed the hungry, they'll come running. If we lift up a program to study war no more, our youth will come running. If we lift up a program to put America back to work, an alternative to welfare and despair, they will come working. If we cut that military budget without cutting our defense, and use that money to rebuild bridges and put steelworkers back to work, and use that money, and provide jobs for our citizens, and use that money to build schools and train teachers and educate our children, and build hospitals and train doctors and train nurses, the whole nation will come running to us.

As I leave you now, vote in this convention and get ready to go back across this nation in a couple of days, in this campaign, I'll try to be faithful by my promise. I'll live in the old barrios, and ghettos and reservations, and housing projects. I have a message for our youth. I challenge them to put hope in their brains, and not dope in their veins. I told them like Jesus, I, too, was born in a slum, but just because you're born in a slum, does not mean the slum is born in you, and you can rise above it if your mind is made up. I told them in every slum, there are two sides. When I see a broken window, that's the slummy side. Train that youth to be a glazier, that's the sunny side. When I see a missing brick, that's the slummy side. Let that child in the union, and become a brickmason, and build, that's the sunny side. When I see a missing door, that's the slummy side. Train some youth to become a carpenter, that's the sunny side. When I see the vulgar words and hieroglyphics of destitution on the walls, that's the slummy side. Train some youth to be a painter, an artist—that's the sunny side. We need this place looking for the sunny side because there's a brighter side somewhere. I am more convinced than ever that we can win. We'll vault up the rough side of the mountain; we can win. I just want young America to do me one favor.

Exercise the right to dream. You must face reality—that which is. But then dream of the reality that ought to be, that must be. Live beyond the pain of reality with the dream of a bright tomorrow. Use hope and imagination as weapons of survival and progress. Use love to motivate you and obligate you to serve the human family.

Young America, dream. Choose the human race over the nuclear race. Bury the weapons and don't burn the people. Dream of a new value system. Teachers, who teach for life, and not just for a living, teach because they can't help it. Dream of lawyers more concerned with justice than a judgeship. Dream of doctors more concerned with public health than personal wealth. Dream [of] preachers and priests who will prophesy and not just profiteer. Preach and dream. Our time has come.

Our time has come. Suffering breeds character. Character breeds faith. And in the end, faith will not disappoint.

Our time has come. Our faith, hope and dreams will prevail. Our time has come. Weeping has endured for the night. And, now joy cometh in the morning.

Our time has come. No graves can hold our body down.

Our time has come. No lie can live forever.

Our time has come. We must leave racial battleground and come to economic common ground and moral higher ground. America, our time has come.

We've come from disgrace to Amazing Grace, our time has come.

Give me your tired, give me your poor, your huddled masses who yearn to breathe free and come November, there will be a change because our time has come.

Thank you and God bless you.

## Chapter 18

# MURPHY BROWN AND
# THE CULTURE WARS

## Dan Quayle and Pat Buchanan Bring Family Values
## to the Campaign Trail: 1992

THROUGHOUT MUCH OF the twentieth century, the debate in presidential campaigns about the responsibilities of the federal government revolved largely around economic, international, and later racial issues. In the 1990s, a new question took on increased prominence—cultural values and in particular religious faith. This was certainly not the first time Americans had debated contentious social matters. Nor was it the first time that religion began to play a major role in American politics. But what was once a sideshow became front and center in the 1990s and into the twenty-first century. While the role of cultural values had began to gather steam a decade before, it truly reached its nadir in the 1992 race for the White House and speeches by two conservative politicians—Vice President Dan Quayle and failed Republican candidate Pat Buchanan.

The presidential election of 1992 was one of the most memorable in recent history. There were charges of draft dodging and adultery; talk shows and town hall debates became the new venue for political discourse; and a populist billionaire from Texas scored one of the best showings ever for a third-party candidate. James Carville's famous campaign slogan, "It's the economy, stupid," reminds us of the crucial question in the race, but that didn't stop Republican candidates from trying to focus on an issue that was steadily moving to the forefront of the GOP's national campaign strategy—"family values," or cultural issues such as abortion, family structure, attitudes toward homosexuality, and religious concerns. Not only did these issues play well with the increasingly conservative Republican base, but they resonated with millions of Americans fearful of technological and social upheaval. In 1992, both Quayle and Buchanan would make every effort to bring family and cultural values to the forefront.

## Quayle "Makes Some News"

Dan Quayle has long been the butt of national jokes for his alleged lack of intellectual depth, privileged upbringing, and tendency toward verbal gaffes and miscues. During the 1988 vice presidential debate, Quayle bore the brunt of one of the harshest attacks in American political history when Democratic vice presidential nominee Lloyd Bentsen took umbrage with Quayle's invoking of John F. Kennedy in defending his lack of political experience. "Senator, I served with Jack Kennedy," Bentsen intoned. "I knew Jack Kennedy. Jack Kennedy was a friend of mine. Senator, you're no Jack Kennedy."[1] For many Americans, the broadside solidified Quayle's sophomoric image.

Yet for all of Quayle's seeming liabilities, he was quite popular among socially conservative voters, many of whom viewed the more moderate George H. W. Bush with suspicion. The conservative wing of the Republican Party saw Quayle as their most prominent advocate in the administration. Moreover, in the face of a struggling economy and the rise of the populist billionaire Ross Perot, it was imperative for the Bush-Quayle ticket to change the political equation and focus the election on the issues that played more to the GOP's strengths. Even a generation after 1968, the Republicans remained the party of social order and cultural values. Behind in the polls, Quayle found his work cut out for him. But national events would soon create a political opening.

In April 1992, Los Angeles erupted in a spasm of violence over not-guilty verdicts for four white police officers accused of beating black motorist Rodney King—an event captured on video and broadcast across the country. The riots led to billions of dollars in property losses as businesses were looted and burned to the ground, and fifty-three people were killed in the deadly violence.

Politically, the riots were viewed along strictly partisan lines—Democrats attacked the Bush and Reagan administrations for ignoring urban issues over the previous dozen years, while Republicans blamed liberal social programs, in particular welfare, for the social pathologies of America's inner cities. In May, Quayle traveled to California and San Francisco's Commonwealth Club to offer his perspective.

The speech represented Quayle's effort to explain why the riots happened and what could be done to prevent such violence from occurring in the future. While some, particularly on the left, had placed responsibility for the deadly spasm of violence on larger societal and economic issues, Quayle would have none of it, blaming the "rioters" and the "killers" and arguing that "there is simply no excuse for the mayhem that followed" the King verdict.

But Quayle would go much further then just blaming the perpetrators themselves. He argued that the "lawless social anarchy" seen during the LA riots was not due to diminished economic opportunity or endemic inner-city poverty but instead was a result of the "breakdown of the family structure, personal responsibility and social order in too many areas of our society." Quayle aimed his fire on a familiar conservative target, namely, "a welfare ethos that impedes individual efforts to move ahead in society and hampers their ability to take advantage of the opportunities America offers." Moreover, he asserted that these changes have created a permanent underclass, mired in a cycle of poverty, violence and above all, out-of-wedlock births.

While Quayle did say that "it would be overly simplistic to blame this social breakdown on the programs of the Great Society alone," he also didn't offer any larger economic and demographic explanations for the violence. In fact, these issues seemed to play no role in Quayle's thinking. Instead, he linked the tendency among some baby boomers in the 1960s to "declare war against traditional values" to the problems of America's inner cities in 1992, arguing that "inter-generational poverty that troubles us so much is *predominantly* a poverty of values."

Attacks on welfare and the "culture of dependency" were not new and had even been accepted by some Democrats. For example, one could imagine Quayle's argument that it was "time to talk again about the family, hard work, integrity and personal responsibility" coming out of the mouth of Bill Clinton. Quayle's focus on illegitimacy and his assertion that "two parents married to each other are better, in most cases, for children than one" was one that was likely embraced by most Americans. It would have been difficult for any politician to seriously question Quayle's notion that two-parent households were far preferable to those led by a single parent. Quayle bolstered his argument by offering statistics that indicated the number of black families headed by married couples had gone from 68 percent in 1967 to 48 percent in 1991 and that the illegitimacy rate among black families had risen from 28 percent in 1965 to 65 percent in 1989. In addition, Quayle argued that unemployment and homicide rates had significantly increased in the same period. While these numbers told a sobering tale, the cause-and-effect relationship between out-of-wedlock births and these social maladies was less clear.

A year later, in a widely publicized article in the *Atlantic Monthly* titled "Dan Quayle Was Right," Barbara Dafoe Whitehead made an even stronger case than Quayle about the dangers of illegitimacy, asserting that "according to a growing body of social-scientific evidence, children in families disrupted by divorce and out-of-wedlock birth do worse than children in intact families on several measures of well-being. Children in single-parent families are six times as likely to be poor. They are also likely to stay poor longer . . . Children in single-parent families are two to three times as likely as children in two-parent families to have emotional and behavioral problems. They are also more likely to drop out of high school, to get pregnant as teenagers, to abuse drugs, and to be in trouble with the law."[2] In attacking the epidemic of fatherlessness, especially in America's inner cities, Quayle certainly had a legitimate point.

Indeed, if the vice president had stopped there, the Commonwealth Club speech might have been the political equivalent of the proverbial tree falling in the forest. Quayle had been giving such "values speeches" for several months, with few members of the national press paying much attention.[3] What raised the profile of the speech and helped ensure that family values would be debated on the campaign trail in 1992 was the straw man that Quayle used at the end of his remarks: a fictional TV character named Murphy Brown.

Played by the actress Candice Bergen, the character on CBS's hit show by the same name had recently had a child out of wedlock—a decision derided by Quayle. "It doesn't help matters," said Quayle, "when primetime TV has Murphy Brown, a character who supposedly epitomizes today's intelligent, highly paid professional woman, mocking the importance of fathers by

bearing a child alone and calling it just another lifestyle choice."
Quayle had never actually seen the show, and it wasn't immediately clear that anyone on his staff had seen it either—or fully understood its impact on American pop culture. While Quayle's staff knew that the inclusion of Murphy Brown would most certainly "make some news," they severely underestimated the firestorm that was about to come.[4]

For days, the Murphy Brown story became the nation's dominant news item, featured prominently on the nightly news, in editorial pages around the country, and of course on the nation's newest political medium, talk radio. In New York, the *Daily News* screamed out "Quayle to Murphy Brown: You Tramp!" and David Letterman ran a Top Ten list titled "Dan Quayle's Top 10 Other Complaints About TV."[5]

The problem for Quayle was the context of his comment. The attack on Brown and in particular the notion that she was "mocking the importance of fathers" was, for lack of a better word, absurd. (In fact, later Bergen would say she agreed with much of the speech's content, particularly the notion that fathers were crucially important to child rearing.)[6] It was one thing to criticize the show for glamorizing a so-called poor lifestyle choice, but to link the violence in Los Angeles and the generation-long epidemic of out-of-wedlock births in poor communities to a television program struck many as inappropriate and inaccurate. Moreover, pro-choice advocates, including *Murphy Brown*'s executive producer, pointed to the very real inconsistency of a pro-life supporter such as Quayle criticizing a woman for having a baby. Quayle was attacked anew, not only by Hollywood but increasingly by newspaper columnists around the country.

There were serious policy elements to the Murphy Brown speech, and Quayle's argument was certainly reflective of the larger conservative perspective on the problems of the underclass and the policy solutions for inner-city poverty and illegitimacy.

Yet, perversely, any larger aspirations Quayle might have had for the speech were a victim of past Republican political success. For years the GOP had attacked welfare recipients and had done so in coded political language that was intended not to lift people up but to garner votes on Election Day. Quayle's effort to shift the discussion to a substantive debate about welfare reform and father-lessness would be hamstrung by the inclination of many to view the speech through the context of more than twenty years of GOP attacks on the welfare system.

In addition, the speech was based far more on a "diagnosis" of the problem of inner-city poverty and on casting blame rather than outlining substantive policy cures. Quayle's gratuitous attacks not only on the Murphy Brown character but also on Hollywood further diminished any chance of a serious political discussion. In-deed, Quayle was channeling his inner George Wallace when he argued that the political arena was an appropriate area for debates about moral values, "even though our cultural leaders in Holly-wood, network TV and the national newspapers routinely jeer" at such a discussion. Quayle's attacks on Hollywood and his invok-ing of the nation's moral and cultural failings would continue through the fall campaign—as did the GOP's focus on family values.

A few weeks later Quayle again attacked America's "cultural elites," who he claimed were mocking America's traditional val-ues. He bragged that he wore the scorn of the mainstream media like a "badge of honor."[7] At the conservative Manhattan Institute, Quayle would go even further, claiming of the "cultural elite," "They are laughing at America itself, at the families that have al-ways done the real work of building our great nation. They are mocking the source of our nation's greatness, the source of our goodness and our hope for the future."[8]

From Quayle's perspective, the speech was an enormous suc-cess. The country was beginning a national discussion on an issue that was sure to mobilize and energize conservative GOP voters. Moreover, the discussion of family values would help remind Americans of Bill Clinton's own deficiencies in that area. In the end, the Murphy Brown speech did more to position the 1992 campaign on positive terrain for Republicans than it did to change the terms of the national debate on poverty issues. Indeed, Quayle's conclusion to the speech, a rather tepid call to "let the national debate roar on," could hardly be considered a unifying message for the nation.

## A "CULTURAL WAR" IN AMERICA

When it came to division, however, Quayle would have to take a backseat to Pat Buchanan, who took the message of America's faltering moral values in a much more partisan and mean-spirited direction. Buchanan had launched an insurgent campaign from the right against George Bush, scoring an improbable 38 percent of the vote in the New Hampshire Republican primary. Buchanan went on to garner approximately three million votes in the GOP primaries, an impressive showing against an incumbent president. Buchanan's success entitled him to a key speaking spot at the party's national convention and at the opening of the quadrennial gathering in Houston, he hardly disappointed his supporters.

Buchanan was a speechwriter by trade, having written for both Presidents Nixon and Reagan, and his background as a presidential scribe was reflected in his punchy and direct rhetoric. He threw out some choice one-liners, mocking Bill Clinton's foreign policy experience as consisting of a "breakfast once at the International House of Pancakes." But this was not a speech that would be remembered for its humor. Instead it was Buchanan's unabashed attacks on the "homosexual rights movement," "unrestricted abortion on demand," and the "radical feminism" of Hillary Clinton that would be remembered by most Americans.

Decrying the "raw sewage of pornography" and "environmental extremists who put birds and rats and insects ahead of families, workers and jobs," Buchanan laid out, in no uncertain terms, what he believed were the stakes in the 1992 election. "My friends, this election . . . is about who we are. It is about what we believe and what we stand for as Americans. There is a religious war going on in this country for the soul of America. It is a cultural war as critical to the kind of nation we shall be as the Cold War itself . . . And in that struggle for the soul of America, Clinton and Clinton are on the other side and George Bush is on our side."

This was a type of political attack that had rarely before appeared in twentieth-century political orutory. It's certainly one thing to attack an opponent's policy positions, to argue that he or she was wrong on the major issues of the day, but Buchanan was raising the bar to unprecedented heights. He was basically calling the GOP's Democratic opponents personally immoral. Rarely before had a major politician posed religious and cultural divisions in such absolute and highly divisive terms. If Bill and Hillary Clinton were on the wrong side of a religious and cultural war, what was the appropriate response? Buchanan was deriding the two as morally incapable of leading the nation. Even Goldwater's harsh 1964 rhetoric would seem tame in comparison to Buchanan's words.

Buchanan wasn't alone in the stridency of his rhetorical attacks. Televangelist Pat Robertson called the Democratic Party an "insidious plague" on the nation and said, "When Bill and Hillary Clinton talk about family values, they are not talking about either families or values. They are talking about a radical plan to destroy the traditional family and transfer its functions to the federal government." This was an unbelievable attack—one hardly based on any substantive reading of the couple's political and policy positions.[9] But Robertson's vitriolic tone was par for the course.

According to Jack Germond and Jules Witcover, who had covered numerous presidential campaigns, the "moral element," as expressed by the various GOP speakers, "was something new at this level of American politics . . . The delegates of the religious right were a different breed of activists who believed those who disagreed with them were not just wrong, but evil."[10] Even Quayle thought that Buchanan had gone too far.[11]

To be sure, many Americans were concerned about the nation's moral climate, but a cultural war was too much. As *Newsweek*'s summary of the 1992 campaign described the proceedings, "For four nights in Houston, it was as if the melancholy state of the union counted for little against the scarlet sins of liberals, lesbians, gays, Democrats, feminists, Congress, Greens, trial lawyers, single women who had babies, all women who aborted them—and, at the head of their advancing columns, Bill and Hillary Clinton."[12] There is an old standby in American politics that softer issues play better in years when the economy is strong. Certainly that was the case in 1988, when George Bush ran on a platform of crime fighting and patriotic, even cultural matters to defeat his opponent, Michael Dukakis. But in 1992, Americans were concerned about the economy. They were worried about their jobs and their health care. The focus by Buchanan and the GOP on questions of character and cultural values may have played well with some conservative voters, but most Americans were concerned about their pocketbooks, and the Republicans were offering little in that area.

However, while Buchanan and Quayle's focus on family values would fall short in 1992, the cultural war of which Buchanan spoke would end up taking on a life of its own. Over the next dozen years, as the country was roiled by presidential sex scandals and debates over gay marriage, the cultural and social attitudes of the nation would move front and center in American politics. By 2004, 22 percent of Americans would report in presidential exit polls that moral values were the single most important issue in determining how they cast their ballot—higher than any other concern.[13]

The social conservative movement had been successful in making the argument that the morality of America and its cultural values were issues of serious public policy debate. For millions of Americans, these questions were quickly becoming a crucial factor in how they viewed their government and its elected leaders.

## *Vice President Dan Quayle Takes on Murphy Brown,*
### *San Francisco, May 19, 1992*

Ladies and gentlemen, it's great to be back with you and, as you may know, I've just returned from a weeklong trip to Japan . . . Though we have had our differences, especially in the area of trade, our two countries, with 40 percent of the world's GNP, are committed to a global partnership on behalf of peace and economic growth. But in the midst of all these discussions of international affairs, obviously I was asked many times in Japan about the recent events in Los Angeles.

From the perspective of many Japanese, the ethnic diversity of our culture is a weakness compared to their homogeneous society. I beg to differ with my host. I explained that our diversity is our strength and I explained that the immigrants who come to our shores have made and continue to make vast contributions to our culture and to our economy. It is wrong to imply that the Los Angeles riots were an inevitable outcome of our diversified society. But the question that I tried to answer in Japan is one that needs answering here. What happened? Why? And most importantly, how can we prevent it in the future?

One response has been predictable. Instead of denouncing wrongdoing, some have shown tolerance for rioters. Some have enjoyed saying "I told you so." And some have simply made excuses for what happened. All of this has been accompanied by pleas for more money. I'll readily accept that we need to understand what happened, but I reject the idea that we should tolerate or excuse it.

When I have been asked during these last weeks who caused the riots and the killings in L.A., my answer has been direct and simple. Who is to blame for the riots? The rioters are to blame. Who is to blame for the killings? The killers are to blame. Yes, I can understand how people were shocked and outraged by the verdict in the Rodney King trial. But, my friends, there is simply no excuse for the mayhem that followed. To apologize or in any way to excuse what happened is wrong. It is a betrayal of all those people equally outraged and equally disadvantaged who did not loot, who did not riot, and who were, in many cases, victims of the rioting. No matter how much you may disagree with the verdict, the riots were wrong. If we as a society don't condemn what is wrong, how can we teach our children what is right? But after condemning the riots, we do need to try to understand the underlying situation.

In a nutshell, I believe the lawless social anarchy that we saw is directly related to the breakdown of the family structure, personal responsibility and social order in too many areas of our society. For the poor, the situation is compounded by a welfare ethos that impedes individual efforts to move ahead in society and hampers their ability to take advantage of the opportunities America offers. If we don't succeed in addressing these fundamental problems and in restoring basic values, any attempt to fix what's broken, will fail. One reason I believe we won't fail is that we have come so far in the last 25 years. There's no question that this country has had a terrible problem with race and racism. The evil of slavery has left a long and ugly legacy.

But we have faced racism squarely and we have made progress in the past quarter of a century. With landmark civil rights bills of the 1960s, we moved legal barriers to allow full participation by blacks in the economic, social and political life of the nation. By any measure, the America of 1992 is more egalitarian, more integrated and offers more opportunities to black Americans and all other minority members than the America of 1964. There is more to be done, but I think that all of us can be proud of our progress. And let's be specific about one aspect of this progress. The country now has a black middle class that barely existed a quarter-century ago. Since 1967, the median income of black two-parent families has risen by 60 percent in real terms. The number of black college graduates has skyrocketed. Black men and women have achieved real political power. Black mayors head 48 of our largest cities, including Los Angeles. These are real achievements, but as we all know, there's another side to that bright landscape.

During this period of progress, we have also developed a culture of poverty. Some call it the underclass that is far more violent and harder to escape than it was a generation ago. The poor you always have with you, scripture tells us, and in America we have always had poor people. But in this dynamic, prosperous nation, poverty has traditionally been a stage through which people pass on their way to joining the great middle class. And if one generation didn't get very far up the ladder, their ambitious, better-educated children would. But the underclass seems to be a new phenomenon. It is a group whose members are dependent on welfare for very long stretches and whose young men are often drawn into lives of crime. There is far too little upward mobility, because the underclass is disconnected from the rules of American society. And these problems have, unfortunately, been particularly acute for black Americans.

Let me share with you a few statistics on the difference between black poverty in the 1960s and now. In 1967, 68 percent of black families were headed by married couples. In 1991, only 48 percent of black families were headed by both a husband and a wife. In 1965, the illegitimacy rate among black families was 28 percent. In 1989, 65 percent, two-thirds of all black children were born with never-married mothers. In 1951, 9 percent of black youths between 16 and 19 were unemployed. In 1965, it was 23 percent. In 1980, it was 35 percent. By 1989, the number had declined slightly, but it was still 32 percent. The leading cause of death of young black males today is homicide.

It would be overly simplistic to blame this social breakdown on the programs of the Great Society alone. It would be absolutely wrong to blame it on the growth and success most Americans enjoyed during the 1980s. Rather, we are in large measure reaping the consequences of the decades of changes in social mores.

I was born in 1947, so I'm considered one of those baby boomers that we keep reading about. But let's look at one unfortunate legacy of the so-called boomer generation. When we were young, it was fashionable to declare war against traditional values. Indulgence and self-gratification seemed to have no consequences. Many of our generation glamorized casual sex and drug use, evaded responsibility and trashed authority. Today, the boomers are middle-aged and middle class. The responsibility of having families has helped many recover traditional values. And, of course, the great majority of those in the middle class survived the turbulent legacy of the '60s and '70s. But many of the poor, with less to fall back on, did not. The inter-generational poverty that troubles us so much today is predominantly a poverty of values.

Our inner cities are filled with children having children, with people who have not been able to take advantage of educational opportunities, with people who are dependent on drugs or the narcotic of welfare. To be sure, many people in the ghetto struggle very hard against these tides and sometimes win. But too many people feel they have no hope and nothing to lose. This poverty is, again, fundamentally a poverty of values. Unless we change the basic rules of society in our inner cities, we cannot expect anything else to change. We will simply get more of what we saw three weeks ago. New thinking, new ideas, new strategies are needed. For the government, transforming underclass culture means that our policies and our programs must create a different incentive system. Our policy must be premised on and must reinforce values such as family, hard work, integrity, personal responsibility. I think we can all agree the government's first obligation is to maintain order. We are a nation of laws, not looting. It has become clear that the riots were fueled by the vicious gangs that terrorize the inner cities. We are committed to breaking those gangs and restoring law and order.

As James Q. Wilson has written, programs of economic restructuring will not work so long as gangs control the streets. Some people say law and order are code words. Well, they are code words, code words for safety, getting control of the streets and freedom from fear. And let's not forget that in 1990, 84 percent of the crimes committed by blacks were committed against blacks. We are for law and order. If a single mother raising her children in the ghetto has to worry about drive-by shootings, drug deals or whether her children will join gangs and die violently, the difficult task becomes next to impossible. We're for law and order because we can't expect children to learn in dangerous schools. We're for law and order because if property isn't protected, who will build the businesses, who will make the investment? . . .

Safety is absolutely necessary, but it's not sufficient. Our urban strategy is to empower the poor by giving them control over their lives. To do that, our urban agenda includes fully funding the Home Ownership and Opportunity for People Everywhere program. HOPE, as we call it, will help public housing residents become homeowners. Subsidized housing all too often merely made rich investors richer. Home ownership will give the poor a stake in their neighborhood and a chance to build equity. Creating enterprise zones by slashing taxes in targeted areas, including a zero capital gains tax to spur entrepreneurship, economic development and job creation in the inner cities.

Instituting our education strategy, America 2000, to raise academic standards and to give the poor the same choices about how and where to educate their children that the rich people have. Promoting welfare reform to remove the penalties for marriage, create incentives for saving and give communities greater control over how the programs are administered. These programs are empowerment programs. They are based on the same principles as the Job Training

Partnership Act, which aimed to help disadvantaged young people and dislocated workers to develop their skills, to give them an opportunity to get ahead in life.

Empowering the poor will strengthen families, and right now the failure of our families is hurting America deeply. When family fails, society fails. The anarchy and lack of structure in our inner cities are a testament to how quickly civilization falls apart when the family foundation crashes. Children need love and discipline; they need mothers and fathers. A welfare check is not a husband, the state is not a father. It is from parents that children learn how to behave in society. It is from parents, above all, that children come to understand values and themselves as men and women, mothers and fathers. And for those who are concerned about children growing up in poverty, we should know this—marriage is probably the best anti-poverty program of all.

Among families headed by married couples today, there is a poverty rate of 5.7 percent. But 33.4 percent of the families headed by a single mother are in poverty. Nature abhors a vacuum. Where there are no mature, responsible men around to teach boys how to be good men, gangs serve in their place. In fact, gangs have become a surrogate family for much of a generation of inner-city boys. I recently visited with some former gang members in Albuquerque, New Mexico. In a private meeting, they told me why they had joined gangs. These teenage boys said that gangs gave them a sense of security. They made them feel wanted and useful. They got support from their friends and they said, "It was like having family." Like family? Unfortunately, that says it all.

The system perpetuates itself as these young men father children whom they have no intention of caring for, by women whose welfare checks support them. Teenage girls mired in the same hopelessness lack sufficient motive to say no to this trap. Answers to our problems won't be easy, my friends. We can start by dismantling a welfare system that encourages dependency and subsidizes broken families. We can attach conditions such as school attendance or work to welfare. We can limit the time a recipient gets benefits. We can stop penalizing marriage for welfare mothers. We can enforce child-support payments. Ultimately, however, marriage is a moral issue that requires cultural consensus and the use of social sanctions.

Bearing babies irresponsibly is simply wrong. Failing to support children one has fathered is wrong and we must be unequivocal about this. It doesn't help matters when primetime TV has Murphy Brown, a character who supposedly epitomizes today's intelligent, highly paid professional woman, mocking the importance of fathers by bearing a child alone and calling it just another lifestyle choice. I know it's not fashionable to talk about moral values, but we need to do it! Even though our cultural leaders in Hollywood, network TV and the national newspapers routinely jeer at them, I think most of us in this room know that some things are good and other things are wrong. And now, it's time to make the discussion public. It's time to talk again about the family, hard work, integrity and personal responsibility. We cannot be embarrassed out of our belief that two parents married to each other are better, in most cases, for children than one. That honest work is better than handouts or crime. That we are our brother's keepers. That is worth making an effort, even when the rewards aren't immediate.

So, I think the time has come to renew our public commitment to our Judeo-Christian values in our churches and synagogues, our civic organizations and our schools. We are, as our children recite each morning, one nation under God. That's a useful framework for acknowledging a duty and an authority higher than our own pleasures and personal ambition. If we live more thoroughly by these values, we would live in a better society. For the poor, renewing these values will give the people the strength to help themselves by acquiring the tools to achieve self-sufficiency, a good education, job training, and property. Then they will move from permanent dependence to dignified independence.

. . . I believe that the Bush administration's empowerment agenda will help the poor gain that power by creating opportunity and letting people make the choices that free citizens must make.

Though our hearts have been pained by the events in Los Angeles, we should take this tragedy as an opportunity for self-examination and progress. So let the national debate roar on. I, for one, will join it. The President will lead it, the American people will participate in it, and as a result, we will become an even stronger nation. Thank you very much and God bless you.

## *Pat Buchanan Declares the Existence of a "Cultural War" in America, Houston, August 17, 1992*

Listen my friends, we may have taken the long way home, but we finally got here.

. . . Like many of you last month, I watched that giant masquerade ball up at Madison Square Garden—where 20,000 radicals and liberals came dressed up as moderates and centrists—in the greatest single exhibition of cross-dressing in American political history.

One by one, the prophets of doom appeared at the podium. The Reagan decade, they moaned, was a terrible time in America; and they said the only way to prevent even worse times is to entrust our nation's fate and future to the party that gave us McGovern, Mondale, Carter and Michael Dukakis.

. . . The American people are not going to go back to the discredited liberalism of the 1960s and the failed liberalism of the 1970s—no matter how slick the package in 1992.

No, the malcontents of Madison Square Garden notwithstanding, the 1980s were not terrible years in America. They were great years. You know it. And I know it. And everyone knows it except for the carping critics who sat on the sidelines of history, jeering at one of the great statesmen of modern time, Ronald Reagan.

Remember the time of Jimmy Carter's days of malaise? Ronald Reagan crafted the greatest peacetime recovery in U.S. history— 3 million new businesses created, and 20 million new jobs.

Under the Reagan Doctrine, one by one, it was the communist dominos that began to fall. First, Grenada was liberated by U.S. airborne troops and the U.S. Marine Corps.

Then, the mighty Red Army was driven out of Afghanistan with American weapons. In Nicaragua, that squalid Marxist regime was forced to hold free elections—by Ronald Reagan's contra army—and the communists were thrown out of power.

Fellow Americans, we ought to remember, it was under our

party that the Berlin Wall came down, and Europe was reunited. It was under our party that the Soviet Empire collapsed, and the captive nations broke free.

You know, it is said that every president will be remembered in history with but a single sentence. George Washington was the father of our country. Abraham Lincoln preserved the Union. And Ronald Reagan won the Cold War. And it is just about time that my old colleagues, the columnists and commentators, looking down on us tonight from their sky boxes and anchor booths, gave Ronald Reagan the full credit he deserves—for leading America to victory in the Cold War.

Most of all, my friends, Ronald Reagan made us proud to be Americans again. We never felt better about our country; and we never stood taller in the eyes of the world than when the Gipper was at the helm.

But we are here tonight, my friends, not only to celebrate, but to nominate. And an American president has many, many roles.

He is our first diplomat, the architect of American foreign policy. And which of these two men is more qualified for that role? George Bush has been U.N. ambassador, director of the CIA, envoy to China. As vice president, George Bush co-authored and co-signed the policies that won the Cold War. As president, George Bush presided over the liberation of Eastern Europe and the termination of the Warsaw Pact.

And what about Mr. Clinton? Well, Bill Clinton couldn't find 150 words to discuss foreign policy in an acceptance speech that lasted almost an hour . . . Bill Clinton's foreign policy experience is pretty much confined to having had breakfast once at the International House of Pancakes.

. . . Under President George Bush, more human beings escaped from the prison house of tyranny to freedom than in any other four-year period in history.

And for any man to call this the record of failure is the cheap

political rhetoric of politicians who only know how to build themselves up by tearing America down, and we don't want that kind
of leadership in the United States.

The presidency, my friends, is also an office that Theodore
Roosevelt called America's bully pulpit. Harry Truman said it was
preeminently a place of moral leadership. George Bush is a defender of right-to-life, and a champion of the Judeo-Christian values and beliefs upon which this America was founded.

Mr. Clinton, however, has a different agenda.

At its top is unrestricted, unrestricted abortion on demand.
When the Irish-Catholic governor of Pennsylvania, Robert Casey,
asked to say a few words on behalf of the 25 million unborn children destroyed since *Roe v. Wade*, Bob Casey was told there was no
room for him at the podium at Bill Clinton's convention and no
room at the inn.

Yet a militant leader of the homosexual rights movement could
rise at that convention and say: "Bill Clinton and Al Gore represent the most pro-lesbian and pro-gay ticket in history." And so
they do.

Bill Clinton says he supports school choice—but only for state-
run schools. Parents who send their children to Christian schools,
or private schools or Jewish schools or Catholic schools need not
apply.

Elect me, and you get two for the price of one, Mr. Clinton
says of his lawyer-spouse. And what does Hillary believe? Well,
Hillary believes that 12-year-olds should have the right to sue their
parents. And Hillary has compared marriage and the family as institutions to slavery and life on an Indian reservation.

Well, speak for yourself, Hillary.

Friends, my friends, this is radical feminism. The agenda that
Clinton and Clinton would impose on America—abortion on
demand, a litmus test for the Supreme Court, homosexual rights,
discrimination against religious schools, women in combat units—

that's change, all right. That's not the kind of change America needs. It's not the kind of change America wants. And it is not the kind of change we can abide in a nation that we still call God's country.

A president of the United States is also America's commander-in-chief. He's the man we authorize to send fathers and sons and brothers and friends into battle.

George Bush was 17 years old when they bombed Pearl Harbor. He left his high school graduation, he walked down to the recruiting office, and signed up to become the youngest fighter pilot in the Pacific war. And Bill Clinton?

. . . I'll tell you where he was. When Bill Clinton's time came in Vietnam, he sat up in a dormitory in Oxford, England, and figured out how to dodge the draft.

Let me ask the question of this convention. Which of these two men has won the moral authority to send young Americans into battle? I suggest, respectfully, it is the American patriot and war hero, Navy Lieutenant J.G. George Herbert Walker Bush.

My fellow Americans, this campaign is about philosophy, and it is about character; and George Bush wins on both counts. And it is time all of us came home and stood beside him.

As his running mate, Mr. Clinton chose Albert Gore. But just how moderate is Prince Albert? Well, according to the Taxpayers Union, Al Gore beat out Teddy Kennedy, two straight years, for the title of biggest spender in the U.S. Senate, and Teddy Kennedy isn't moderate about anything. I'm not kidding about Teddy. How many other 60-year-olds do you know who still go to Florida for spring break?

You know, at that great big costume party they held up in New York, Mr. Gore made a startling declaration. Henceforth, Albert Gore said, the central organizing principle of governments everywhere must be the environment. Wrong, Albert!

The central organizing principle of this republic is freedom.

And from the ancient forests of Oregon and Washington, to the Inland Empire of California, America's great middle class has got to start standing up to these environmental extremists who put birds and rats and insects ahead of families, workers and jobs.

One year ago, my friends, I could not have dreamt that I would be here tonight. I was just one of many panelists on what President Bush calls "those crazy Sunday talk shows."

But I disagreed with the president; and so we challenged the president in the Republican primaries and we fought as best we could. From February to June, President Bush won 33 primaries. I can't recall exactly how many we won. I'll get you the figure tomorrow.

But tonight I want to speak from the heart, to the 3 million Americans who voted for Pat Buchanan for president. I will never forget you, nor the great honor you have done me. But I do believe, I do believe deep in my heart, that the right place for us to be now—in this presidential campaign—is right beside George Bush.

This party is my home. This party is our home, and we've got to come home to it. And don't let anyone tell you any different.

Yes, we disagreed with President Bush, but we stand with him for the freedom of choice religious schools. And we stand with him against the amoral idea that gay and lesbian couples should have the same standing in law as married men and women. We stand with President Bush for right-to-life, and for voluntary prayer in the public schools.

And we stand against putting our wives and daughters and sisters into combat units of the United States Army. And we stand, my friends, we also stand with President Bush in favor of the right of small towns and communities to control the raw sewage of pornography that so terribly pollutes our popular culture.

We stand with President Bush in favor of federal judges who interpret the law as written, and against would-be Supreme Court justices like Mario Cuomo who think they have a mandate to re-write the Constitution.

My friends, this election is about more than who gets what. It is about who we are. It is about what we believe and what we stand for as Americans. There is a religious war going on in this country for the soul of America. It is a cultural war as critical to the kind of nation we shall be as the Cold War itself, for this war is for the soul of America. And in that struggle for the soul of America, Clinton and Clinton are on the other side, and George Bush is on our side.

And so, to the Buchanan brigades out there, we have to come home, and stand beside George Bush.

In those six months campaigning from Concord, New Hampshire to California, I came to know our country better than I had known it ever before in my life, and I gathered up memories that are going to be with me the rest of my days.

There was that day-long ride through the great state of Georgia in a bus Vice President Bush himself had used in 1988 called Asphalt One. The ride ended in a 9:00 P.M. speech in a tiny town in southern Georgia called Fitzgerald.

There were those workers at the James River Paper Mill, in northern New Hampshire in a town called Groveton—tough, hardy men. None of them would say a word to me as I came down the line, shaking their hands one by one. They were under threat of losing their jobs at Christmas. As I moved down the line, one tough fellow about my age just looked up and said to me, "Save our jobs."

Then there was the legal secretary that I met at the Manchester airport Christmas Day who came running up to me and said, "Mr. Buchanan, I'm going to vote for you." And then she broke down weeping and she said, "I've lost my job, I don't have any money, and they're going to take away my little girl. What am I going to do?"

My friends, these people are our people. They don't read Adam Smith or Edmund Burke, but they came from the same schoolyards and the same playgrounds and towns as we came from. They share our beliefs and convictions, our hopes and our dreams. These are the conservatives of the heart. They are our people. And we need to reconnect with them. We need to let them know we know how bad they're hurting. They don't expect miracles of us, but they need to know we care.

There were the people, of Hayfork, a tiny town up in California's Trinity Alps, a town that is now under a sentence of death because a federal judge has set aside 9 million acres for the habitat of the spotted owl—forgetting about the habitat of the men and women who live and work in Hayfork.

And there were the brave people of Koreatown who took the worst of those L.A. riots, but still live the family values we treasure, and who still believe deeply in the American dream.

Friends, in those wonderful 25 weeks of our campaign, the saddest days were the days of that riot in L.A., the worst riot in American history. But out of that awful tragedy can come a message of hope. Hours after that awful tragedy can come a message of hope.

Hours after that riot ended I went down to the Army compound in south Los Angeles where I met the troopers of the 18th Cavalry who had come to save the city of Los Angeles. An officer of the 18th Cav said, "Mr. Buchanan, I want you to talk to a couple of our troopers." And I went over and I met these young fellas. They couldn't have been 20 years old, and they recounted their story.

They had come into Los Angeles late in the evening of the second day, when the rioting was still going on, and two of them walked up a dark street, where the mob had burned and looted every building on the block but one, a convalescent home for the aged. And the mob was headed in to ransack and loot the apartments of the terrified old men and women inside. The troopers came up the street, M-16s at the ready, and the mob threatened and cursed, but the mob retreated because it had met the one thing that could stop it: force, rooted in justice, and backed by moral courage.

Greater love than this hath no man than that he lay down his life for his friend. Here were 19-year-old boys ready to lay down their lives to stop a mob from molesting old people they did not even know. And as those boys took back the streets of Los Angeles, block by block, my friends, we must take back our cities, and take back our culture, and take back our country.

God bless you, and God bless America.

## Chapter 19

# "I STILL BELIEVE IN A PLACE CALLED HOPE"

Bill Clinton Takes on His Own Party and
Reclaims the Political Center for Democrats:
1992–1996

I MAGE MAKING HAS always been a fundamental part of the speechwriting process, particularly on the campaign trail. From Bryan's embodiment of the common man and FDR's invocation of active and engaged government to Kennedy's generational call to arms and Harding's return to normalcy, speechmaking has always gone hand in hand with the core public relations aspect of American presidential campaigns. Unlike in a parliamentary system, Americans vote as much for the man or woman as they do for the party. Thus creating the right public persona is a crucial element of the campaign process.

Few modern American politicians have been as effective at marrying speechmaking with image making as the nation's forty-second president, William Jefferson Clinton. In 1991, when he began his race for the Democratic nomination for president, the party had an almost fatal image with the American electorate—the party of "tax and spend," and the "coddling" of criminals and welfare recipients. In both his runs for the White

House, Clinton would spend much of his time eradicating those images and transforming the Democratic Party from a left-leaning, special-interest-focused party into one that was seen as embodying opportunity, individual responsibility, and defending the middle class. In a mere four years, Clinton recast the Democratic Party, but also created a new model for the role of government in American society—an updated New Deal that reflected America's desire for a more restrained federal government.

In the fall of 1991 few Americans would have expected that a relatively unknown governor from Arkansas would be the person to remake the Democratic Party and return Democrats to the halls of power after twelve years in exile. In fact, in the fall of 1991 not many people expected the 1992 race for the White House to be anything more than an overwhelming victory for the highly popular incumbent, George H. W. Bush.

Many of the Democrats' bigger names were begging off a national campaign, convinced that Bush, the hero of the Gulf War, could not be defeated. But then, Bill Clinton was not an ordinary Democrat. The former chairman of the centrist Democratic Leadership Committee, Clinton had consistently shown a willingness to challenge liberal orthodoxies and seek centrist solutions to public policy challenges.

During the early Democratic primaries Clinton had weathered a withering spate of attacks based largely on personal issues, namely, his alleged womanizing and his efforts to avoid military service during the Vietnam War. Against more formidable primary opposition, it is doubtful Clinton would have survived this double dose of bad press. But Clinton was blessed in 1992 to face one of the weakest crops of presidential candidates in recent Democratic politics. In 1988, eight prominent Democrats sought the party's nomination. In 1992, Clinton's biggest rivals were a former senator, Paul Tsongas, who had minimal name recognition and a dour public persona, and a former governor of California,

Jerry Brown, who had long ago been nicknamed "Governor Moonbeam."

A weak primary field was not Clinton's only blessing. President Bush, who had once seemed so invincible, was in the midst of a startling and largely unexpected fall from political grace. At the end of the Gulf War in March 1991, Bush had a stratospheric 91 percent approval rating, but a weakening economy combined with growing unemployment sent his poll numbers decidedly back to earth. Just a year later he was an incumbent at serious risk of losing reelection.

Yet Clinton was initially unable to capitalize on Bush's weakening position. Not only did he come out of the primary season badly hurt by the personal attacks against him, but the rising political movement around Texas billionaire Ross Perot threatened to eclipse his candidacy. In the late spring of 1992, Clinton was running third in public opinion polls, scoring just over a quarter of the popular vote.

Clinton's centrist message wasn't getting across—Perot was increasingly seen as the real agent of change in the presidential race. Clinton needed to shake up the campaign, and a speaking engagement at the Reverend Jesse Jackson's Rainbow Coalition gave him just that opportunity.

## The "Sister Souljah Moment"

Jesse Jackson and Bill Clinton were not political allies and they weren't good friends. In fact, in May 1991, Clinton had deliberately excluded him from a meeting of moderate Democrats in Cleveland, Ohio. Clinton's reluctance to be too closely identified with Jackson was not terribly surprising. Throughout his nascent political career, Jackson had been both a boon to Democrats, rallying liberals and minority voters, but also a thorn, reminding voters of the party's strong link with identity politics and in particular

African American voters. The perception of the party as beholden to leaders such as Jackson had been used to great and dastardly political effect by a series of Republican politicians, from Nixon's law-and-order campaign of 1968 to Ronald Reagan's 1980 attack on "welfare queens" and the infamous Willie Horton ad in the 1988 race for the White House.

Moreover, in April 1992, Los Angeles had erupted in fearsome violence after four police officers accused of beating up a black motorist, Rodney King, were acquitted. The Bush White House had fallen back on old and often successful habits, invoking the Great Society programs of the 1960s as a cause of the violence. Racial politics had split up the New Deal Coalition and driven countless white Democratic and independent voters into the arms of the GOP. The same could happen again in 1992 without a full-throated response by Democrats. A relatively unknown militant rapper named Sister Souljah (née Lisa Williamson) would give Clinton the chance he needed.

In many respects, no event did more to recast the Democratic Party and present Bill Clinton as a "New Democrat" than his address to the Rainbow Coalition in June 1992. It was a speech that was not broadcast on television, and few Americans heard or read the complete speech. Yet it was perhaps the most important campaign speech of Clinton's two runs for national office and one of the more influential political statements of the past twenty years.

In a recitement of his key campaign themes, with a particular focus on his urban and economic empowerment agenda, Clinton took on the Rainbow Coalition—and in particular Jackson, who was sitting only a few feet away—for hosting the rapper at their conference.

Clinton recounted Souljah's controversial and hate-filled statements, noting that she had told the *Washington Post*, "If black people kill black people every day, why not have a week and kill

white people. So you're a gang member and normally kill somebody. Why not kill a white person."[1]

While defending the rapper's right to speak her mind, Clinton
said that her comments "were filled with the kind of hatred that
you do not honor today and tonight."[2] To be sure, the effectiveness of Clinton's attack was heightened by the utterly indefensible
nature of Souljah's comments.

But then Clinton took a harder shot at the assembled group,
noting that "if you took the words white and black and reversed
them, you might think David Duke was giving that speech."[3]
Duke was a former Grand Wizard of the KKK who had run for
governor of Louisiana in 1991. The linking of a group helmed by
Jackson with an odious figure such as Duke was exactly the kind
of comment guaranteed to raise temperatures in the room—and
garner headlines the next day.

Yet, ever the conciliator, Clinton spoke of his own mistakes in
playing golf in a country club that excluded African Americans. "I
was criticized for doing it . . . I was rightly criticized for doing it.
I made a mistake. And I said I would never do that again. And I
think all of us have got to be sensitive to that. We can't get anywhere in this country, pointing the finger at one another across
racial lines. If we do that, we're dead and they will beat us."[4]

By addressing his own mistakes and calling for racial reconciliation, Clinton could persuasively argue that he was being
even-handed in his discussion of Souljah's words. As an emerging
national figure, Clinton had made a point of reaching out to a
new generation of black elected officials in an effort to minimize the influence of traditional civil rights leaders such as Jackson. As governor of Arkansas, he enjoyed enormous popularity
among local black voters, who were the bedrock of his political
support.[5] As a result, charges of political opportunism against
Clinton were harder to make stick (even if they may have
seemed germane).

Clinton's attack on Souljah also played into the key themes of his campaign. First, like Adlai Stevenson forty years earlier, he was willing to speak unpleasant truths to entrenched groups, a political tactic called counterscheduling. Clinton had used this approach in a speech in Macomb County, Michigan, the home of so-called Reagan Democrats who had deserted the party because of its social policies. There he pledged a reinvigorated Democratic Party, while also calling on the largely white crowd to "stop voting along the racial divide." Clinton argued that the nation's problems were not "racial in nature," but a question of "economics" and "values."[6] He took a similar message to Wall Street, where he was booed for calling the 1980s a "decade of greed" and criticizing capital gains tax cuts.[7] Those speeches helped Clinton cultivate the notion that he was a different kind of Democrat—and unlike the perpetually dour Stevenson, he wasn't facing the most popular man in America on Election Day.

Second, the Souljah speech was part of what historian Jeremy Mayer describes as the "deracialized economic rhetoric" that had come to define Clinton's campaign.[8] The governor's message was one of unity, of the need for Americans to come together and ensure widespread economic opportunity; as Clinton liked to say, "We don't have an American to waste." By excoriating Sister Souljah while also calling for racial reconciliation and a cooling-off of racial tempers, he was able to play up his image as a unifying figure.

The reaction to the speech was predictable and even more beneficial to Clinton's campaign. Jackson attacked Clinton, asserting that the candidate had a "character flaw." He even went so far as to defend the rapper and claimed that she had been misunderstood. Clinton couldn't have asked for much more. He was able to separate himself from the controversial Jackson while also taking the high road by arguing that he had done nothing more than point out racial intolerance. At a news conference several days later he once again put the onus on Jackson, noting, "I criticized divisive language by Sister Souljah. If Jesse Jackson wants to align himself with that now and claim that's the way he felt, then that's his business."[9] When Jackson said after the speech that many people were "aggrieved" by Clinton's comment, he would have been hard pressed to find many white voters (or, for that matter, many black voters) who felt the same way.[10]

For a generation, the Democratic Party was perceived as the captive of special-interest groups, none more powerful than African Americans. For millions of Americans, economic liberalism and government activism had become inextricably linked to racial liberalism and identity politics. With just a few words, Clinton tore that perception to shreds, demonstrating that he was a politician willing to speak candidly to even the most entrenched party constituencies, but also that he was striving to make government responsive to all Americans. By taking race off the table, Clinton was now able to sound traditional populist themes and recast Democrats as, once again, the "party of the people." (Clinton's actions would even coin a new political phrase—a "Sister Souljah moment.") Nine months later, many voters would cite the Sister Souljah speech as a reason for helping make Clinton the first Democrat to win a national election in sixteen years. A white Philadelphia electrician may have best summed up the impact Clinton's words had on some blue collar voters: "The day he told off that fucking Jackson is the day he got my vote."[11]

## DEFENDER OF THE MIDDLE CLASS

But Clinton's change in rhetoric and governing philosophy was about more than distancing himself from liberal interest groups. Clinton's ultimate success was in convincing a wide swath of Americans that the party was willing to change its ideological tone and focus greater attention on the pocketbook issues that directly affected the middle class.

This new approach to the role of government in the lives of the American people is summed up presciently in the opening paragraph of Clinton's acceptance speech to the Democratic National Convention in 1992: "In the name of all the people who do the work, pay the taxes, raise the kids and play by the rules, in the name of the hard-working Americans who make up our forgotten middle class, I accept your nomination for President of the United States. I am a product of that middle class. And when I am President you will be forgotten no more."

To some, this may seem like boilerplate, but after decades of Democratic dalliances with liberal policies and warmed-over New Deal–style rhetoric, these words represented a true philosophical shift for Democrats. It was in a very real sense a new New Deal, focused on addressing the reality of 1990s middle-class, post-industrial, suburban America. The party platform contained language that would have been unimaginable only a few years earlier: "governments don't raise children, people do"; a rejection of "the big government theory that says we can hamstring business and tax and spend our way to prosperity"; and most critically a call for government to "once again make responsibility an instrument of national purpose."[12] The party was making a concerted effort to reach out to middle-class voters—the same once loyal Democrats who voted in droves for Ronald Reagan and George Bush—with an ideological approach that matched the American people's aspirations.

Clinton went a step further in breaking with the past by emphasizing centrist policies such as "ending welfare as we know it," putting "100,000 new police officers on the streets of American cities," and calling for a middle-class tax cut.

Here we see the birth pangs of the so-called triangulation theory that would later come to define Clinton's second run for the White House—in short, a concerted effort to stake out centrist ground between right and left, where most Americans truly

defined themselves politically. Clinton was unabashed in his call
for a "third way" in American politics:

> Now, I don't have all the answers. But I do know the old
> ways don't work. Trickle down economics has sure failed.
> And big bureaucracies, both private and public, they've failed,
> too. That's why we need a new approach to government—
> a government that offers more empowerment and less
> entitlement . . . a government that is leaner, not meaner.
> A government that expands opportunity, not bureaucracy—
> a government that understands that jobs must come from
> growth in a vibrant and vital system of free enterprise.

Even this tacit acknowledgment of the power of the private
sector in creating jobs and spurring the economy was unusual language from a Democrat seeking the White House.

This effort to reach out to the middle class was a logical progression from Clinton's Sister Souljah speech. For years, economic liberalism had been associated with government activism
and programs for poor and minority Americans. When Clinton
separated himself from Jackson, he was saying to the middle class,
"I'm going to make government work for you." In his acceptance
speech at the Democratic convention he made the connection
even more explicit.

In homage to past Democratic glory, Clinton invoked the idea
of a "New Covenant," not only aping JFK's New Frontier from
the 1960 campaign for the White House but also adding a religious element to his political message:

> I call this approach a New Covenant—a solemn agreement
> between the people and their government—based not simply
> on what each of us can take but what all of us must give to

our nation. We offer our people a new choice based on old values. We offer opportunity. We demand responsibility. We will build an American community again. The choice we offer is not conservative or liberal. In many ways, it is not even Republican or Democratic. It's different. It is new. And it will work. It will work because it is rooted in the vision and the values of the American people.

Though rhetorically it may have reminded listeners of Kennedy's 1960 call to arms, the context was quite different. JFK was asking for Americans to sacrifice in pursuit of great and noble national goals. Clinton's crusade was far more limited and inward-looking—this was about what the country could do for the American people, as opposed to the other way around. Nonetheless, Clinton's restrained rhetoric was symptomatic of the times and more reflective of an electorate that had become suspicious of grandiose government solutions and was more inclined to see government as a benign but limited force rather an engine of social change.

To be sure, "it was the economy, stupid" helped, but it was also this new Democratic approach, spearheaded by Clinton, that returned Democrats to the White House after a twelve-year hiatus.

Finally, Clinton left the nation with a hopeful, affirmative message for the future. Imploring Americans to move beyond the narrow politics of the past that had been used by countless Republican politicians to define the party, Clinton called on the electorate to come together:

Tonight every one of you knows deep in your heart that we are too divided. It is time to heal America. And so we must say to every American: look beyond the stereotypes that blind us. We need each other. All of us, we need each other. We don't have a person to waste. And yet, for too long, politicians have told the most of us that are doing all right that what's really wrong with America is the rest of us. Them. Them the minorities. Them the liberals. Them the poor. Them the homeless. Them the people with disabilities. Them the gays. We've gotten to where we've nearly them'd ourselves to death. Them, and them, and them. But this is America. There is no them; there is only us. One nation, under God, indivisible, with liberty, and justice, for all.

This color-blind approach to identity politics was picture-perfect Clinton. It allowed him to call for racial and cultural reconciliation, all the while not endorsing any specific steps for such reconciliation to occur. It was almost post-racial in its approach.[13] By invoking the Pledge of Allegiance, Clinton was able to repudiate his predecessor as party nominee, Michael Dukakis, who had famously vetoed a bill in Massachusetts calling on teachers to recite the Pledge—a fact that his opponent, George Bush, reminded the electorate of often.

At the end, Clinton echoed Kennedy again and cast his election in tough, but hopeful terms, noting that Americans have always believed in two things: "that tomorrow can be better than today, and second, that each of us has a personal, moral responsibility to make it so." This was as close as Clinton would come to calling for genuine sacrifice from the American people. Finally, in a brilliant turn of phrase, he echoed his hometown of Hope, Arkansas, by sounding an uplifting tone for the future: "I still believe in a place called Hope." This was the sort of visionary ideal that Clinton's centrist predecessor, Gary Hart, had lacked in 1984. Clinton was bringing together a renunciation of Mondale-style interest-group politics with a narrative of national greatness, à la Ronald Reagan. It resounded with the American people and seemed to demonstrate that Clinton was truly a new type of Democrat.

In indomitable Clinton style, he spoke for an extraordinary

fifty-four minutes. Television cameras even captured some younger participants in the hall visibly yawning. No one would ever accuse Bill Clinton of brevity in his speechmaking. Moreover, the Arkansas governor employed a unique, confessional style that others had used before, but never as successfully. His address was couched in personal terms that would have seemed unimaginable to JFK or FDR. In an effort to improve his personal image with the electorate, Clinton told the audience of his love for his mother, the fact he never knew his father, even the joy he felt at holding his daughter. This was something new, what some would call the Oprah-ization of American politics, where no question and no emotion were seemingly off-limits for public discussion. Clinton's "I feel your pain" approach to campaigning would place new demands on presidential candidates to do more than discuss policy options on the campaign trail, laying themselves out to audiences like an open book.

## TRIANGULATION

Though Clinton was able to wrestle down many of the negative stereotypes that haunted Democrats in 1992, the results of the disastrous 1994 midterm election showed that Americans remained unconvinced. Clinton and the Democrats had yet to cast off their liberal image. In the wake of losing control of the House and Senate, and reduced at one point to pathetically declaring his relevance in the political process, Clinton spent much of 1995 seemingly playing second fiddle to the new Speaker of the House, Newt Gingrich, and the GOP's "Contract with America." But through a carefully calibrated strategy that extolled Clinton's centrist virtues and a willingness to embrace policies traditionally identified with Republicans, the president once again remade his political image—and that of his party.

Republicans had been pushing hard for a balanced budget, and

Democrats in Congress as well as a strong liberal faction in the White House resisted the move. But Clinton understood that a mere two and a half years after Ross Perot's impressive showing in the 1992 election, the issue of deficit reduction and balancing the budget captured the public imagination. Perot had won 19 percent of the vote in '92, running almost exclusively against profligate deficit spending in Washington, or what he called the "crazy aunt in the basement." In May 1994, Clinton gave a nationally televised address announcing his support for a balanced budget in seven years. Liberal Democrats howled in disgust, but Clinton's move allowed him to negotiate with Republicans on far better terms. Instead of appearing to be a laggard on deficit reduction, he was now committed to fiscal responsibility, while serving as the sole bulwark against Republican cuts in Medicare, Medicaid, education, and environmental spending—all programs where he enjoyed wide public support.

As the budget battle gathered steam in the fall of 1995 and the government was shut down for several weeks, public opinion again moved in Clinton's favor. No longer was he seen as the traditional Democrat who'd raised taxes and advocated a big-government health care plan in 1993. Now he was the moderate, fiscally responsible Democrat—the image that had defined his initial run for office—who stood up to the heartless and conservative GOP.

But Clinton was not done. He had transformed his image. He had become the defender of programs that most Americans believed were the fundamental and essential responsibility of government. However, there was one more step to be taken—creating a new model for how Americans viewed the role of government in their lives.

In his 1996 State of the Union address, Clinton took his first tentative step toward achieving that goal. He began by asking the American people three questions that to a large degree form the backdrop for this book—timeless issues about the American people's vision of their nation. "First, how do we make the American dream of opportunity for all a reality for all Americans who are willing to work for it? Second, how do we preserve our old and enduring values as we move into the future? And third, how do we meet these challenges together, as one America?"[14]

In 1928, Herbert Hoover argued that the private sector provided the answers to these questions. In the 1930s, FDR asserted that the federal government had a fundamental responsibility for ensuring economic opportunity. In the 1960s, Lyndon Johnson took FDR's New Deal a step further by declaring a War on Poverty, creating the infrastructure of the modern welfare state, and tackling the challenge of equal rights for all Americans. In the 1980s, Ronald Reagan declared that government was not a solution but a problem that needed to be solved. In short, over a century of American history the pendulum had swung toward both more and less government. As was his way, Clinton tried to stop the back and forth by keeping the pendulum firmly lodged in the center.

He declared, "We know big government does not have all the answers. We know there's not a program for every problem." And then in words that would come to define his presidency and set the terms for the election to come, Clinton declared, "The era of big government is over."[15]

But Clinton wasn't about to leave it at that. He went on to forcefully argue, "We cannot go back to the time when our citizens were left to fend for themselves. Instead, we must go forward as one America, one nation working together to meet the challenges we face together. Self-reliance and teamwork are not opposing virtues. We must have both."[16]

Then came his vision for the future:

I believe our new, smaller government must work in an old-fashioned American way—together with all of our citizens, through state and local governments, in the workplace, in religious, charitable and civic associations. Our goal must be to enable all our people to make the most of their own lives with stronger families, more educational opportunity, economic security, safer streets, a cleaner environment, in a safer world. To improve the state of our union, we must all ask more of ourselves; we must expect more of each other, and we must face our challenges together.[17]

While the election may have been ten months away, the political debate was being waged on Clinton's terms—no longer big government versus smaller government, but limited government versus no government. That was a debate Democrats could win, and it was one in which they were on the same side as the American people. For all intents and purposes, when Bill Clinton declared in the well of the U.S. House of Representatives that the era of big government was over, so too was the race for the White House in 1996.

While each of these speeches demonstrates Clinton's legendary image-making skills, they were also bolstered by concrete policy choices. Clinton *was* a New Democrat. This was not FDR's Hundred Days or Johnson's Great Society.

Clinton's philosophy represented, for lack of a better phrase, more digestible government. Americans didn't truly hate government, but they were suspicious of those who pledged to use the levers of the state for grandiose goals. Most Americans were taxpayers. They owned homes, stocks, and automobiles. They were concerned about what their children were seeing on television, about tobacco companies marketing their products to kids, and about whether the doors of college education would be open to their sons and daughters. They were concerned about pensions, health care, and family and medical leave. They wanted a government that stressed individual responsibility but also provided opportunity to those who were willing to better themselves. And they wanted Washington to live within its means. These were the ideas reflected not only in Clinton's State of the Union address but also in countless speeches given during the 1996 campaign for the White House.

There are some who have criticized Clinton for not implementing any big initiatives as president and for failing miserably when he tried, as with health care. But if a president's job in a representative democracy is to reflect the desires of the voters, few have done it better than Bill Clinton—and few have reflected it more effectively on the campaign trail.

## Bill Clinton Tells the Democratic Party, "I Still Believe in a Place Called Hope," New York, July 16, 1992

Tonight I want to talk with you about my hope for the future, my faith in the American people, and my vision of the kind of country we can build, together . . .

One sentence in the platform we built says it all: "The most important family policy, urban policy, labor policy, minority policy and foreign policy America can have is an expanding, entrepreneurial economy of high-wage, high-skill jobs."

And so, in the name of all the people who do the work, pay the taxes, raise the kids and play by the rules, in the name of the hard-working Americans who make up our forgotten middle class, I accept your nomination for President of the United States.

I am a product of that middle class. And when I am President you will be forgotten no more.

We meet at a special moment in history, you and I. The Cold War is over; Soviet Communism has collapsed; and our values—freedom, democracy, individual rights and free enterprise—they have triumphed all around the world. And yet just as we have won the Cold War abroad, we are losing the battles for economic opportunity and social justice here at home. Now that we have changed the world, it's time to change America.

I have news for the forces of greed and the defenders of the status quo: your time has come—and gone. It's time for a change in America.

Tonight ten million of our fellow Americans are out of work. Tens of millions more work harder for lower pay. The incumbent President says unemployment always goes up a little before a recovery begins. But unemployment only has to go up by one more person before a real recovery can begin. And, Mr. President, you are that man.

This election is about putting power back in your hands and

putting government back on your side. It's about putting people first.

You know, I've said that all across the country, and someone always comes back at me, as a young man did just this week at the Henry Street Settlement on the Lower East Side of Manhattan. He said, "That sounds good, Bill. But you're a politician. Why should I trust you?"

Tonight, as plainly as I can, I want to tell you who I am, what I believe, and where I want to lead America.

I never met my father. He was killed in a car wreck on a rainy road three months before I was born, driving home from Chicago to Arkansas to see my mother.

After that, my mother had to support us. So we lived with my grandparents while she went back to Louisiana to study nursing.

I can still see her clearly tonight through the eyes of a three-year-old: kneeling at the railroad station and weeping as she put me back on the train to Arkansas with my grandmother. She endured her pain because she knew her sacrifice was the only way she could support me and give me a better life.

My mother taught me. She taught me about family and hard work and sacrifice. She held steady through tragedy after tragedy. And she held our family, my brother and I, together through tough times. As a child, I watched her go off to work each day at a time when it wasn't always easy to be a working mother.

As an adult, I've watched her fight off breast cancer. And again she has taught me a lesson in courage. And always, always she taught me to fight.

That's why I'll fight to create high-paying jobs so that parents can afford to raise their children today. That's why I'm so committed to making sure every American gets the health care that saved my mother's life, and that women's health care gets the same attention as men's. That's why I'll fight to make sure women in this country receive respect and dignity—whether they work in the home, out of the home, or both. You want to know where I get my fighting spirit? It all started with my mother.

Thank you, Mother. I love you.

When I think about opportunity for all Americans, I think about my grandfather.

He ran a country store in our little town of Hope. There were no food stamps back then, so when his customers—whether they were white or black, who worked hard and did the best they could, came in with no money—well, he gave them food anyway—just made a note of it. So did I. Before I was big enough to see over the counter, I learned from him to look up to people other folks looked down on.

My grandfather just had a grade-school education. But in that country store he taught me more about equality in the eyes of the Lord than all my professors at Georgetown; more about the intrinsic worth of every individual than all the philosophers at Oxford; and he taught me more about the need for equal justice than all the jurists at Yale Law School.

If you want to know where I come by the passionate commitment I have to bringing people together without regard to race, it all started with my grandfather.

I learned a lot from another person, too. A person who for more than 20 years has worked hard to help our children—paying the price of time to make sure our schools don't fail them. Someone who traveled our state for a year, studying, learning, listening, going to PTA meetings, school board meetings, town hall meetings, putting together a package of school reforms recognized around the nation, and doing it all while building a distinguished legal career and being a wonderful loving mother.

That person is my wife.

Hillary taught me. She taught me that all children can learn, and that each of us has a duty to help them do it. So if you want to know why I care so much about our children and our future; it all started with Hillary. I love you.

Frankly, I'm fed up with politicians in Washington lecturing the rest of us about "family values." Our families have values. But our government doesn't.

I want an America where "family values" live in our actions, not just in our speeches—an America that includes every family, every traditional family and every extended family, every two-parent family, every single-parent family, and every foster family—every family.

I do want to say something to the fathers in this country who have chosen to abandon their children by neglecting to pay their child support: take responsibility for your children or we will force you to do so. Because governments don't raise children; parents do. And you should.

And I want to say something to every child in America to-night who is out there trying to grow up without a father or a mother: I know how you feel. You're special, too. You matter to America.

And don't ever let anybody tell you you can't become what-ever you want to be. And if other politicians make you feel like you're not a part of their family, come on and be part of ours.

The thing that makes me angriest about what's gone wrong in the last 12 years is that our government has lost touch with our values, while our politicians continue to shout about them. I'm tired of it.

I was raised to believe its that the American Dream was built on rewarding hard work. But we have seen the folks in Washington turn the American ethic on its head. For too long, those who play by the rules and keep the faith have gotten the shaft, and those who cut corners and cut deals have been rewarded. People are working harder than ever, spending less time with their children, working nights and weekends at their jobs instead of going to PTA and Little League or Scouts, and their incomes are still going down. Their taxes are going up, and the costs of health care, housing and education are going through the roof. Meanwhile, more and more of our best people are falling into poverty—even when they work forty hours a week.

Our people are pleading for change, but government is in the way. It has been hijacked by privileged, private interests. It has forgotten who really pays the bills around here—it's taking more of your money and giving you less in return.

We have got to go beyond the brain-dead politics in Washington, and give our people the kind of government they deserve: a government that works for them.

A President ought to be a powerful force for progress. But right now I know how President Lincoln felt when General McClellan wouldn't attack in the Civil War. He asked him, "If you're not going to use your army, may I borrow it?"

And so I say, George Bush, if you won't use your power to help America, step aside. I will.

Our country is falling behind. The President is caught in the grip of a failed economic theory. We have gone from first to thirteenth in the world in wages since Reagan and Bush have been in office. Four years ago, candidate Bush said America is a special place, not just "another pleasant country on the U.N roll call, between Albania and Zimbabwe." Now, under President Bush, America has an unpleasant economy stuck somewhere between Germany and Sri Lanka. And for most Americans, Mr. President, life's a lot less kind and a lot less gentle than it was before your Administration took office.

Our country has fallen so far, so fast that just a few months ago the Japanese Prime Minister actually said he felt "sympathy" for the United States. Sympathy. When I am your President, the rest of the world will not look down on us with pity, but up to us with respect again.

What is George Bush doing about our economic problems? Now, four years ago he promised us fifteen million new jobs by this time. And he's over fourteen million short. Al Gore and I can do better.

He has raised taxes on the people driving pick-up trucks, and lowered taxes on people riding in limousines. We can do better.

He promised to balance the budget, but he hasn't even tried. In fact, the budgets he has submitted have nearly doubled the debt. Even worse, he wasted billions and reduced our investment in education and jobs. We can do better.

So if you are sick and tired of a government that doesn't work to create jobs; if you're sick and tired of a tax system that's stacked against you; if you're sick and tired of exploding debt and reduced investments in our future—or if, like the great civil rights pioneer Fannie Lou Hamer, you're just plain old sick and tired of being sick and tired—then join us, work with us, win with us. And we can make our country the country it was meant to be.

Now, George Bush talks a good game. But he has no game plan to rebuild America from the cities to the suburbs to the countryside so that we can compete and win again in the global economy. I do.

He won't take on the big insurance companies and the bureaucracies to control health costs and give us affordable health care for all Americans. But I will.

He won't even implement the recommendations of his own Commission on AIDS. But I will.

He won't streamline the federal government, and change the way it works; cut a hundred thousand bureaucrats, and put a hundred thousand new police officers on the streets of American cities. But I will.

He has never balanced a government budget. But I have, eleven times.

He won't break the stranglehold the special interests have on our elections and the lobbyists have on our government. But I will.

He won't give mothers and fathers the simple chance to take some time off from work when a baby is born or a parent is sick. But I will.

We're losing our family farms at a rapid rate, and he has no commitment to keep family farms in the family. But I do.

He's talked a lot about drugs, but he hasn't helped people on the front line to wage that war on drugs and crime. But I will.

He won't take the lead in protecting the environment and creating new jobs in environmental technology. But I will.

You know what else? He doesn't have Al Gore and I do . . .

And George Bush won't guarantee a woman's right to choose. I will. Listen, hear me now: I am not pro-abortion. I am pro-choice strongly. I believe this difficult and painful decision should be left to the women of America. I hope the right to privacy can be protected, and we will never again have to discuss this issue on political platforms. But I am old enough to remember what it was like before *Roe v. Wade*. And I do not want to return to the time when we made criminals of women and their doctors.

Jobs. Education. Health care. These are not just commitments from my lips. They are the work of my life.

Our priorities must be clear: we will put our people first again. But priorities without a clear plan of action are just empty words. To turn our rhetoric into reality we've got to change the way government does business—fundamentally. Until we do, we'll continue to pour billions of dollars down the drain.

The Republicans have campaigned against big government for a generation. But have you noticed? They've run this big government for a generation. And they haven't changed a thing. They

don't want to fix government. They still want to campaign against it, and that's all.

But, my fellow Democrats, it's time for us to realize that we've got some changing to do too. There is not a program in government for every problem. And if we want to use government to help people, we've got to make it work again.

Because we are committed in this convention and in this platform to making these changes, we are, as Democrats, in the words that Ross Perot himself spoke today, a revitalized Democratic party. I am well aware that all those millions of people who rallied to Ross Perot's cause wanted to be in an army of patriots for change. Tonight I say to them: join us and together we will revitalize America.

Now, I don't have all the answers. But I do know the old ways don't work. Trickle down economics has sure failed. And big bureaucracies, both private and public, they've failed, too.

That's why we need a new approach to government—a government that offers more empowerment and less entitlement, more choices for young people in the schools they attend, in the public schools they attend, and more choices for the elderly and for people with disabilities and the long-term care they receive—a government that is leaner, not meaner. A government that expands opportunity, not bureaucracy—a government that understands that jobs must come from growth in a vibrant and vital system of free enterprise. I call this approach a New Covenant—a solemn agreement between the people and their government—based not simply on what each of us can take but on what all of us must give to our nation.

We offer our people a new choice based on old values. We offer opportunity. We demand responsibility. We will build an American community again. The choice we offer is not conservative or liberal. In many ways it's not even Republican or Democratic. It's different. It's new. And it will work.

It will work because it is rooted in the vision and the values of the American people. Of all the things George Bush has ever said that I disagree with, perhaps the thing that bothers me most is how he derides and degrades the American tradition of seeing—and seeking—a better future. He mocks it as "the vision thing."

But remember just what the Scripture says: "Where there is no vision the people perish."

I hope nobody in this great hall tonight or in our beloved country has to go through tomorrow without a vision. I hope no one ever tries to raise a child without a vision. I hope nobody ever starts a business or plants a crop in the ground without a vision—for where there is no vision the people perish.

One of the reasons we have so many children in so much trouble in so many places in this nation is because they have seen so little opportunity, so little responsibility, and so little loving, caring community that they literally cannot imagine the life we are calling them to lead. And so I say again, where there is no vision America will perish.

What is the vision of our New Covenant?

An America with millions of new jobs in dozens of new industries moving confidently toward the 21st Century. An America that says to entrepreneurs and business people: We will give you more incentives and more opportunity than ever before to develop the skills of your workers and create American jobs and American wealth in the new global economy. But you must do your part; you must be responsible. American companies must act like American companies again—exporting products, not jobs. That's what this New Covenant is all about.

An America in which the doors of college are thrown open once again to the sons and daughters of stenographers and steelworkers. We'll say: Everybody can borrow the money to go to college. But you must do your part. You must pay it back—from your paychecks, or better yet, by going back home and serving

your communities. Just think of it. Think of it; millions of energetic young men and women, serving their country by policing the streets, or teaching the children or caring for the sick, or working with the elderly or people with disabilities, or helping young people to stay off drugs and out of gangs, giving us all a sense of new hope and limitless possibilities. That's what this New Covenant is all about.

An America in which health care is a right, not a privilege. In which we say to all of our people: Your government has the courage—finally—to take on the health care profiteers and make health care affordable for every family. But you must do your part: preventive care, prenatal care, childhood immunization; saving lives, saving money, saving families from heartbreak. That's what the New Covenant is all about.

An America in which middle class incomes—not middle class taxes—are going up. An America, yes, in which the wealthiest few—those making over $200,000 a year—are asked to pay their fair share. An America in which the rich are not soaked—but the middle class is not drowned either. Responsibility starts at the top; that's what the New Covenant is all about.

An America where we end welfare as we know it. We will say to those on welfare: you will have and you deserve the opportunity through training and education, through child care and medical coverage, to liberate yourself. But then, when you can, you must work, because welfare should be a second chance, not a way of life. That's what the New Covenant is all about.

An America with the world's strongest defense; ready and willing to use force, when necessary. An America at the forefront of the global effort to preserve and protect our common environment—and promoting global growth. An America that will not coddle tyrants, from Baghdad to Beijing. An America that champions the cause of freedom and democracy, from Eastern Europe to Southern Africa, and in our own hemisphere in Haiti and Cuba.

The end of the Cold War permits us to reduce defense spending while still maintaining the strongest defense in the world. But we must plow back every dollar of defense cuts into building American jobs right here at home. I know well that the world needs a strong America, but we have learned that strength begins at home.

But the New Covenant is about more than opportunities and responsibilities for you and your families. It's also about our common community. Tonight every one of you knows deep in your heart that we are too divided.

It is time to heal America. And so we must say to every American: look beyond the stereotypes that blind us. We need each other.

All of us, we need each other. We don't have a person to waste.

And yet, for too long, politicians have told the most of us that are doing all right that what's really wrong with America is the rest of us. Them. Them the minorities. Them the liberals. Them the poor. Them the homeless. Them the people with disabilities. Them the gays. We've gotten to where we've nearly them'd ourselves to death. Them, and them, and them. But this is America. There is no them; there is only us. One nation, under God, indivisible, with liberty, and justice, for all.

That is our Pledge of Allegiance, and that's what the New Covenant is all about.

How do I know we can come together to make change happen? Because I have seen it in my own state. In Arkansas we're working together and we're making progress. No, there is no Arkansas miracle. But there are a lot of miraculous people. And because of them, our schools are better, our wages are higher, our factories are busier, our water is cleaner, and our budget is balanced. We're moving ahead.

I wish I could say the same thing about America under the

incumbent President. He took the richest country in the world and brought it down. We took one of the poorest states in America and lifted it up.

And so I say to those who would criticize Arkansas: come on down. Especially if you're from Washington—come to Arkansas. You'll see us struggling against some problems we haven't solved yet. But you'll also see a lot of great people doing amazing things. And you might even learn a thing or two.

In the end, the New Covenant simply asks us all to be Americans again—old-fashioned Americans for a new time. Opportunity. Responsibility. Community. When we pull together, America will pull ahead. Throughout the whole history of this country, we have seen time and again that when we are united, we are unstoppable.

We can seize this moment, we can make it exciting and energizing and heroic to be an American again. We can renew our faith in ourselves and each other, and restore our sense of unity and community. Scripture says, our eyes have not yet seen, nor our ears heard, nor our minds imagined what we can build.

But I cannot do it alone. No President can. We must do it together. It won't be easy and it won't be quick. We didn't get into this mess overnight, and we won't get out of it overnight. But we can do it—with our commitment and our creativity and our diversity and our strength. I want every person in this hall and every citizen in this land to reach out and join us in a great new adventure to chart a bold new future.

As a teenager I heard John Kennedy's summons to citizenship. And then, as a student at Georgetown, I heard that call clarified by a professor I had, named Carroll Quigley, who said America was the greatest country in the history of the world because our people have always believed in two great ideas: first, that tomorrow can be better than today, and second, that each of us has a personal, moral responsibility to make it so.

That future entered my life the night our daughter Chelsea was born. As I stood in that delivery room, I was overcome with the thought that God had given me a blessing my own father never knew: the chance to hold my child in my arms.

Somewhere at this very moment, another child is born in America. Let it be our cause to give that child a happy home, a healthy family, a hopeful future. Let it be our cause to see that child reach the fullest of her God-given abilities. Let it be our cause that she grow up strong and secure, braced by her challenges, but never, never struggling alone; with family and friends and a faith that in America, no one is left out; no one is left behind.

Let it be our cause that when she is able, she gives something back to her children, her community, and her country. And let it be our cause to give her a country that's coming together, and moving ahead—a country of boundless hopes and endless dreams; a country that once again lifts up its people, and inspires the world.

Let that be our cause and our commitment and our New Covenant.

I end tonight where it all began for me: I still believe in a place called Hope.

# EPILOGUE

O F COURSE, GREAT oratory and image making on the campaign trail did not end with Bill Clinton and his effort to remake the Democratic Party. In 2000, George W. Bush would perform his own bit of political triangulation, smoothing the rough edges of the Republican Party's image by declaring himself a "compassionate conservative" and announcing in the kickoff to his campaign for president, "I am running because my party must match a conservative mind with a compassionate heart."[1] On the campaign trail, Bush would match this theme with a pledge to "restore honor and dignity" to the White House—a resonant trope considering the seediness and squalor of the Lewinsky scandal and President Clinton's impeachment.

The Democratic standard-bearer, Al Gore, would fall back on past Democratic terrain—in fact, very far back in the past—as he returned to the populist rhetoric of Truman and Roosevelt and declared he was fighting for the "people vs. the powerful." But this wasn't 1948 and populist rhetoric doesn't get you too far when the country is enjoying peace and prosperity, as it was in 2000.

In 2004, the specter of September 11 hung over the race from day one—a specter that President George W. Bush used to his clear political advantage. In his acceptance speech at the 2004 GOP national convention in New York City, Bush bookended his address with the events of September 11. At the beginning he said, "In the heart of this great city, we saw tragedy arrive on a quiet morning. We saw the bravery of rescuers grow with danger. We learned of passengers on a doomed plane who died with a courage that frightened their killers" and at the dramatic conclusion he sounded a note of rebirth: "Here buildings fell, here a nation rose." Bush evoked both the trauma and the heroism associated with the worst terrorist attack in American history and wrapped himself in its political mantle.[2]

With concerns raised about Democratic nominee Senator John Kerry's commitment to fighting terrorism as well as the quadrennial focus on Democratic "weakness" in regard to national security, Bush capitalized on the moment, focusing his speeches on traditional GOP themes such as military strength, national greatness, and advancing freedom around the globe, all the while projecting an image of resoluteness at a time of war in Iraq and national fear of another terrorist strike. Bush let others deliver the more stinging attacks. Few were harsher than Democratic senator Zell Miller of Georgia, who gave the keynote speech at the GOP convention. There he claimed Kerry would allow Paris to "decide when America needs defending," would arm the U.S. military with "spitballs," and had been "more wrong, more weak, and more wobbly than any other national figure."[3]

The Democrats did not lack for memorable rhetorical moments, but not necessarily for the right reasons. During the Democratic primaries, the most commented-upon speech was actually a "scream" from former Vermont governor Howard Dean, which pretty much put a fork in his presidential ambitions. At the Democratic convention in Boston, freshman Illinois senator Barack Obama would deliver one of the most stirring keynote speeches in American convention history. Sounding Clintonian themes, Obama's overarching message was one of much-needed national unity. Decrying the so-called red-state, blue-state divide in modern American politics, Obama declared, "There's not a liberal

America and a conservative America; there's the United States of America . . . We worship an awesome God in the blue states, and we don't like federal agents poking around our libraries in the red states. We coach Little League in the blue states and, yes, we've got some gay friends in the red states. There are patriots who opposed the war in Iraq, and there are patriots who supported the war in Iraq. We are one people, all of us pledging allegiance to the stars and stripes, all of us defending the United States of America."[4]

But these words, which sparked Obama's own campaign for the White House in 2008, could not overcome the nation's growing political and social divisions. If anything, the red-state, blue-state divide that Obama spoke of seemed even *more* pronounced after the 2004 election than it did before. When it came to John Kerry, oratory was not necessarily his strong point. Indeed, his best speech was perhaps one he could be criticized for having waited too long to deliver, a September 12, 2004, address at New York University that offered a rousing critique of the U.S. war effort in Iraq and the flawed political and military thinking that got America mired in Iraq in the first place. Delivered weeks or months earlier, it might have changed the very texture of the presidential campaign. Throughout the race, Kerry seemed incapable of finding just the right words to convince the American people that the time had come to switch horses in midstream. Comparing Bush's lyrical, concise, at times evangelical rhetoric to the often jumbled, disjointed, and sometime confusing oratory of Senator Kerry offers compelling evidence as to why President Bush narrowly won reelection.

As the country prepares once again to venture to the election booth in November 2008, the elongated primary season has featured a fascinating diversity of campaign speechmaking.

On the Democratic side, the overriding message was one of change. The sticking point, however, as it often is in American politics, was about the nature of that change. Barack Obama revised his 2004 speech at the Democratic convention with a message of political unity and national sacrifice that echoed the New Frontier rhetoric of John F. Kennedy in 1960. Indeed, Obama's soaring rhetoric became the touchstone of his campaign, sparking a populist movement that brought millions of new voters to the polls. If ever a presidential candidate demonstrated the power of oration on the campaign trail, it was Barack Obama. His main opponent, the somewhat rhetorically challenged Senator Hillary Clinton, was apt to quote Mario Cuomo's admonition "You campaign in poetry, you govern in prose" to make the argument that fancy words on the campaign trail will not bring real political change if you lack the experience to govern. From the left, former vice presidential nominee John Edwards harkened back to the language of Harry Truman with harsh us-versus-them attacks on "corporate greed," and a populist call to arms.

Among the Republican candidates, the rhetorical challenges were far greater as all of the candidates seemed plagued by the burden of President Bush's uncertain legacy. A message of "stay the course" would not do, but with the notable exception of Arkansas governor Mike Huckabee none of the candidates seemed inclined to deviate too drastically from the now increasingly standard GOP message of attacks on big government and fears of Islamic terrorism. This was particularly true of Arizona senator John McCain, who regularly railed against pork barrel spending in Washington and warned of "surrender" to Islamic terrorists in Iraq. All the Republicans seemed to lack what former President George H. W. Bush once derisively referred to as "the vision thing."

The most notable Republican speech of the 2008 primary race came from former Massachusetts governor Mitt Romney, who traveled to Texas to offer a defense of his Mormon faith. Unlike John F. Kennedy in 1960, Romney's remarks hardly qualified as a plea for religious tolerance and freedom. Instead the address was a rather obvious attempt to curry favor with those in American society who look most askance at the idea of separation of church and state. Romney's argument that "freedom requires religion just as religion requires freedom" and "freedom and religion endure together or perish alone" seemed to purposely exclude America's thirty million nonbelievers. For this speech, at least, Mitt Romney was no Jack Kennedy.

With the rhetorical divisions between Democrats and Republicans lining up in this manner, it seems like the Democrats' election to lose, but of course stranger things have happened—just ask Thomas Dewey. Indeed, the lack of a clear frontrunner on the Democratic side means there is a strong possibility that we will see the first brokered national convention in more than five decades. While political junkies are understandably excited at the possibility, John McCain will likely be the most direct beneficiary of continued indecision among Democrats. However, no matter who ends up the victor, it seems fairly clear that we are in store for one of the most exciting national elections in recent memory. I suppose we'll just have to stay tuned to the comings and goings on the campaign trail.

# ACKNOWLEDGMENTS

There are so many individuals, both professional and personal acquaintances, who helped me to complete this book. I am indebted to all of them, but two individuals stand out in particular and are deserving of my greatest appreciation. Will Lippincott is my agent, but in the course of putting together the proposal for this book and the writing process itself, he became my friend. He was there for me in the most difficult parts of the journey, he provided me with both professional and personal support, he believed in this project, and he worked with me closely to make this book as good as I believe it is. Without him, it never would have been published, and I am forever in his debt.

At the same time, this book would never have been written without the help of my research assistant, Diana Benton, who did a masterly job of helping me assemble my research materials. No task was too difficult or too arcane for her to accomplish. No article was too obscure for her to track down. Her commitment to the project as well as her editorial judgment raised many of these chapters to a far higher level and quite simply made this a better book. She is an extraordinarily talented person and I am quite confident that I will someday be telling people that I knew her when.

Although he was not as involved with the writing or researching of this book, my good friend John Buntin merits special acknowledgment. John took time from writing his book to provide me with a detailed analysis of many of the early chapters of this book. I am grateful not only for the time he took to read and offer these comments but even more so for being my close friend. I am privileged and humbled to have a friend like him. In addition, Lamar Robertson took the time to read several chapters from the book. But, in all honesty, his greatest gift was providing me with a much-needed outlet to help get me through the difficult roller-coaster experience of book writing. I probably spoke to Lamar more than any other person while I was writing this book, and I would say 99 percent of our conversations dwelled not one second on speechwriting. I wouldn't have had it any other way. I hope in 2008 we can celebrate a first-place victory.

I am also exceptionally thankful to the folks at Robinson, Lerer and Montgomery. They provided me with the much-needed flexibility to complete this book, and I am appreciative of their generosity, in particular to Pat Gallagher and Jim Badenhausen for their patience with what was often a difficult process. My special thanks to Jim for taking the time to read the chapter on Ronald Reagan. As one of the few Republicans that I spent time with on a regular basis, Jim's insights were extremely helpful.

As I worked on this book many of my friends and colleagues took time out of their busy schedules to read individual chapters and provide me with their thoughts. Jeremy Rosner, who probably more than any person is responsible for me being a speechwriter and hence is indirectly responsible for this book being written, graciously read the chapters on the 1984 campaign and on Bill Clinton. His insights significantly strengthened the final products. I am honored to count Jeremy not only as a mentor but also as a good friend.

Additionally, Matt Dallek, who knows far more about Ronald Reagan and the conservative political movement than I could reasonably hope to, gave me some of the most unvarnished thoughts on the chapters he read, and I am appreciative of not only his honesty but also the strength of his comments. Jeremy Mayer offered detailed thoughts on one of the more difficult chapters in the book. His book *Running on Race* is great, and frankly, when he offered positive words it was one of the best reinforcements I received.

Working on a project with Doug Schoen first got me thinking about this book, so I am particularly thankful to him not only for that but also for the many opportunities that he has given me over the years and the trust that he has repeatedly placed in me. He also took the time to scrutinize a chapter from the book, and I am appreciative of his incredibly positive comments. In addition, I also want to thank Dan Gerstein and of course my good friend Amy Gross, who though not a fan of politics offered me great comments and thoughts on the chapters she read.

Amy and the rest of the members of the LOST crew have become some of my closest friends, and I am grateful for the friendship and support they offered me while I was writing. In addition, I must say a word of thanks to Elmira, who bucked up my spirits during the most difficult part of this experience.

Theodore Sorensen, Robert Dallek, Dr. Martin Medhurst, Ethan Riegelhaupt, Lisa Schiffrin, and Don Nathan all took the time to speak with me, and I am grateful for their assistance. My students at Columbia were a never-ending source of good ideas and insightful commentary. Two, however, deserve particular praise: Dan Doktori and especially Reah Johnson. Both took time out of their busy schedules to conduct research. In particular, the chapter on Ronald Reagan never would have been written without Reah's assistance.

I must also say a word of thanks to my intrepid editor, Kathy Belden at Walker & Company. From day one she believed in this book and my vision for it, and she supported my efforts unstintingly. Her comments were always timely and on message and undoubtedly strengthened the final product you hold in your hands. In addition, George Gibson at Walker & Company saw this book's potential from the beginning and placed enormous faith in my judgment and my vision for it. He encouraged me to broaden its scope and make it into the comprehensive volume that it is.

Molly Lindley did such a great job helping me obtain permissions from occasionally recalcitrant sources—and, what's more, put up with my often late-night "Where do we stand?" e-mails. Thanks also go to my copy editor, Sue Warga, and Mike O'Connor of Walker & Company for putting up with my thin knowledge of grammar and atrocious handwriting!

In addition, I must also acknowledge the contribution of Alice Mayhew and Roger Labrie. Their comments on my initial outline helped to strengthen the eventual final product.

I probably spend more time in coffee shops than any normal person should, and the writing of this book only intensified my caffeine intake. To the folks at Doma, McNally Robinson, Grounded, S'Nice, Tillie's, and Smooch (both in the hood) . . . you don't know me, but I couldn't have written this book without you.

Finally, I owe my greatest thank-you to my family. From an early age they instilled in me a love and veneration for history. They always encouraged my academic pursuits, gave of themselves so that I could realize my dreams, and have been supportive of my efforts. Unlike other Jewish households, in my family the words "my son, the author" have far greater resonance then "my son, the doctor." My only regret is that my grandfather was not alive to see the publication of this book—but then I know somewhere he is smiling.

# NOTES

## Introduction

1. Theodore Sorensen, *Kennedy* (New York: Harper and Row, 1965), 177.
2. Alexis de Tocqueville, *Democracy in America* (New York: Vintage Books, 1945), 140–41.
3. Theodore H. White, *America in Search of Itself: The Making of the President, 1956–1980* (New York: Warner Books, 1982), 7.
4. Douglas L. Wilson, *Lincoln's Sword: The Presidency and the Power of Words* (New York: Vintage Books, 2006), 44.
5. Ralph Waldo Emerson, *Essays and Lectures* (New York: Library of America, 1983) 174.

## Chapter 1: THE GREAT COMMONER

1. Michael Kazin, *A Godly Hero: The Life of William Jennings Bryan* (New York: Alfred A. Knopf, 2006), xv.
2. Louis William Koenig, *Bryan: A Political Biography of William Jennings Bryan* (New York: G. P. Putnam's Sons, 1971), 24.
3. As quoted in Ronald Steel, "All You Need Is Love," *New York Review of Books*, June 22, 2006.
4. Richard Hofstadter, *The American Political Tradition and the Men Who Made It* (New York: Vintage Books, 1989), 242.
5. Eric Goldman, *Rendezvous with Destiny: A History of Modern American Reform* (Chicago: Ivan R. Dee, 2001), 55.

6. Hofstadter, *The American Political Tradition*, 245.
7. Kazin, *A Godly Hero*, 46.
8. Koenig, *Bryan*, 191–92.
9. William Harpine, "Bryan's 'A Cross of Gold': The Rhetoric of Polarization at the 1896 Democratic Convention," *Quarterly Journal of Speech* 87, 3 (2001): 297.
10. Koenig, *Bryan*, 195.
11. Kazin, *A Godly Hero*, xviii.
12. Paul W. Glad, *McKinley, Bryan and the People* (Philadelphia: J. B. Lippincott, 1964), 136–37.
13. Koenig, *Bryan*, 198.
14. "Democracy Is Ruptured," *Los Angeles Times*, July 7, 1896.
15. Ibid.
16. Koenig, *Bryan*, 198; Glad, *McKinley, Bryan and the People*, 139.
17. Kazin, *A Godly Hero*, 63.
18. Hofstadter, *The American Political Tradition*, 241.
19. As quoted in "A Famous Scene: A Famous Speech," *Atlanta Constitution*, July 12, 1896, 17.
20. As quoted in "Opinions of the Press on Bryan," *Chicago Daily Tribune*, July 11, 1896, 3.
21. Hofstadter, *The American Political Tradition*, 256.

*Chapter 2:* THE NEW NATIONALISM VERSUS THE NEW FREEDOM

1. Arthur Schlesinger Jr., *The Crisis of the Old Order: 1919–1933, The Age of Roosevelt* (Boston: Houghton Mifflin, 1957), 33.
2. Patricia O'Toole, *When Trumpets Call: Theodore Roosevelt After the White House* (New York: Simon and Schuster, 2005), 207.
3. Brett Flehinger, *The 1912 Election and the Power of Progressivism* (Boston: Bedford/St. Martin's, 2003), 36.
4. Schlesinger, *Crisis of the Old Order*, 18.
5. Eric Goldman, *Rendezvous with Destiny: A History of Modern American Reform* (Chicago: Ivan R. Dee, 2001), 208.
6. O'Toole, *When Trumpets Call*, 104–5.

7. James Chace, *1912: Wilson, Roosevelt, Taft and Debs—The Election That Changed the Country* (New York: Simon and Schuster, 2004), 57.

8. Theodore Roosevelt, *The New Nationalism*, with an introduction and notes by William Leuchtenburg (Englewood Cliffs, NJ: Prentice-Hall, 1961), 9.

9. Chace, *1912*, 57.

10. Goldman, *Rendezvous with Destiny*, 194.

11. Roosevelt, *The New Nationalism*, 8.

12. Chace, *1912*, 8.

13. Woodrow Wilson, *The New Freedom*, with an introduction and notes by William Leuchtenburg (Englewood Cliffs, NJ: Prentice-Hall, 1961), 5.

14. Woodrow Wilson, *Woodrow Wilson: Essential Political Writings*, ed. Ronald Pestritto (Lanham, MD: Lexington Books, 2005), 21.

15. Goldman, *Rendezvous with Destiny*, 213.

16. Wilson, *The New Freedom*, 2.

17. Richard Hofstadter, *The Age of Reform* (New York: Vintage Books, 1955), 249.

18. Goldman, *Rendezvous with Destiny*, 204.

19. Hofstadter, *The Age of Reform*, 249.

20. "Cheering Crowd Storms Wilson," *New York Times*, October 20, 1912, 1.

21. Richard Hofstadter, *The American Political Tradition and the Men Who Made It* (New York: Vintage Books, 1989), 331.

22. Chace, *1912*, 283.

23. Ibid., 220.

24. Ibid., 220–21.

## Chapter 3: A "RETURN TO NORMALCY"

1. Eugene H. Roseboom, *A History of Presidential Elections* (New York: Macmillan, 1964), 392.

2. Wesley Bagby, *The Road to Normalcy: The Presidential Campaign and Election of 1920* (Baltimore: John Hopkins University Press, 1968), 157.

3. John F. Wilson, "Harding's Rhetoric of Normalcy, 1920–1923," *Quarterly Journal of Speech* 48 (1962): 406–11.

4. Ibid., 408.

5. John Dean, *Warren G. Harding* (New York: Times Books, 2004), 73.

6. Ibid.

7. Robert G. Torricelli and Andrew Carroll, eds., *In Our Own Words: Extraordinary Speeches of the American Century* (New York: Pocket Books, 1999), 70.

8. Dean, *Warren G. Harding*, 72–73.

9. As discussed in Michael McGerr, *A Fierce Discontent: The Rise and Fall of the Progressive Movement in America, 1870–1920* (New York: Free Press, 2003).

10. Paul F. Boller, *Presidential Campaigns* (New York: Oxford University Press, 2004), 213.

11. Dean, *Warren G. Harding*, 67.

12. Bagby, *The Road to Normalcy*, 99.

13. Dean, *Warren G. Harding*, 67.

14. Rupert Hughes, "In Praise of Harding's Style," *New York Times*, October 24, 1920.

15. Dean, *Warren G. Harding*, 72.

16. Ibid.

17. Robert J. Brake, "The Porch and the Stump: Campaign Strategies in the 1920 Presidential Election," *Quarterly Journal of Speech* 55 (1969): 256.

18. Arthur M. Schlesinger Jr., *The Crisis of the Old Order: 1919–1933, The Age of Roosevelt* (Boston: Houghton Mifflin, 1957), 45.

*Chapter 4:* "RUGGED INDIVIDUALISM" VERSUS "BOLD, PERSISTENT EXPERIMENTATION"

1. Michael McGerr, *A Fierce Discontent: The Rise and Fall of the Progressive Movement in America, 1870–1920* (New York: Free Press, 2003), 8.

2. Ibid.

3. Ibid., 311–12.

4. Arthur M. Schlesinger Jr., *The Crisis of the Old Order: 1919–1933, The Age of Roosevelt* (Boston: Houghton Mifflin, 1957), 57.

5. Herbert Hoover, *American Individualism* (Garden City, NY: Doubleday, Page & Co., 1923).

6. Richard Hofstadter, *The American Political Tradition and the Men Who Made It* (New York: Vintage Books, 1989), 372.

7. Ibid., 394.

8. Ibid., 398.

9. Paul Steven Hudson, "A Call for 'Bold Persistent Experimentation': FDR's Oglethorpe University Commencement Address, 1932," *Georgia Historical Quarterly* 77, 2 (1994).

10. Steve Neal, *Happy Days Are Here Again: The 1932 Democratic Convention, the Emergence of FDR—and How America Was Changed Forever* (New York: William Morrow, 2004), 297.

11. Ibid.

12. Ibid., 301.

13. Ibid., 307.

14. Raymond Moley, *After Seven Years* (New York: Harper and Brothers, 1939), 28.

15. Ibid., 29.

16. Jonathan Alter, *The Defining Moment: FDR's Hundred Days and Triumph of Hope.* (New York: Simon and Schuster, 2006), 117–18.

17. Ibid., 118.

18. Eric Goldman, *Rendezvous with Destiny: A History of Modern American Reform* (Chicago: Ivan R. Dee, 2001), 323.

19. Alter, *The Defining Moment*, 132.

20. Conrad Black, *Franklin Delano Roosevelt: Champion of Freedom* (New York: Public Affairs, 2003), 245.

21. Davis Houck, "FDR's Commonwealth Club Address: Redefining Individualism, Adjudicating Greatness," *Rhetoric and Public Affairs* 7, 3 (2004): 265.

22. Ibid., 262.

23. Ibid., 272–273.

24. Alter, *The Defining Moment*, 129.

25. Houck, "FDR's Commonwealth Club Address," 273.

26. Hofstadter, *The American Political Tradition*, 411.
27. Goldman, *Rendezvous with Destiny*, 324.

## Chapter 5: "RENDEZVOUS WITH DESTINY"

1. Conrad Black, *Franklin Delano Roosevelt: Champion of Freedom* (New York: Public Affairs, 2003), 381–82.
2. Arthur M. Schlesinger Jr., *The Age of Roosevelt: The Politics of Upheaval* (Boston: Houghton Mifflin, 2003), 582.
3. Black, *Franklin Delano Roosevelt*, 384.
4. Schlesinger, *Age of Roosevelt*, 583.
5. Ibid.
6. Ibid., 584.
7. Harold Ickes, *The Secret Diary of Harold Ickes: The First 1000 Days* (New York: Simon and Schuster, 1953), 626.
8. Michael Waldman, comp., *My Fellow Americans: The Most Important Speeches of America's Presidents, from George Washington to George W. Bush* (Naperville, IL: Sourcebooks, 2003), 102.
9. Ibid.
10. John T. Woolley and Gerhard Peters, *The American Presidency Project* [online]. Santa Barbara: University of California (hosted), Gerhard Peters (database). Available at http://www.presidency.ucsb.edu/ws/?pid=15095.
11. As discussed in Black, *Franklin Delano Roosevelt*.
12. Isaiah Berlin, "The Natural," in Robert Vare, ed., *The American Idea: The Best of* Atlantic Monthly (New York: Doubleday, 2007), 236.
13. Schlesinger, *Age of Roosevelt*, 585.
14. Arthur M. Schlesinger Jr., *The Crisis of the Old Order: 1919–1933, The Age of Roosevelt* (Boston: Houghton Mifflin, 1957), 7.
15. Black, *Franklin Delano Roosevelt*, 390.
16. Schlesinger, *Age of Roosevelt*, 585.
17. Waldman, *My Fellow Americans*, 103.
18. Laura Crowell, "Franklin Roosevelt's Audience Persuasion in the 1936 Campaign," *Speech Monographs* 17 (1950): 60–61.

19. Ted Widmer, ed., *American Speeches: Political Oratory from Abraham Lincoln to Bill Clinton* (New York: Penguin, 2006), 424–25.

## *Chapter 6:* THE BIRTH OF A POLITICAL STEREOTYPE

1. Charles Peters, *Five Days in Philadelphia* (New York: Public Affairs, 2005), 51.
2. "With All My Heart . . ." *Time*, October 16, 1944.
3. Peters, *Five Days in Philadelphia*, 30.
4. Wendell Willkie, "I Accept the Nomination," *Vital Speeches of the Day*, September 1, 1940, 676.
5. Conrad Black, *Franklin Delano Roosevelt: Champion of Freedom* (New York: Public Affairs, 2003), 592.
6. Wayne S. Cole, *Roosevelt and the Isolationists, 1932–45* (Lincoln: University of Nebraska Press, 1983), 397.
7. Paul F. Boller, *Presidential Campaigns* (New York: Oxford University Press, 2004), 257.
8. Black, *Franklin Delano Roosevelt*, 592.
9. Boller, *Presidential Campaigns*, 258.
10. Cole, *Roosevelt and the Isolationists*, 398, 400.
11. Boller, *Presidential Campaigns*, 262.
12. Marquis Childs, "Washington Calling," *Washington Post*, September 23, 1944, 5.
13. Doris Kearns Goodwin, *No Ordinary Time: Franklin and Eleanor Roosevelt: The Home Front in World War II* (New York: Simon and Schuster, 1994), 547.
14. "The Old Magic," *Time*, October 2, 1944.
15. Marquis Childs, "Roosevelt's Speech," *Washington Post*, September 26, 1944, 6.
16. Halford Ryan Ross, *Franklin D. Roosevelt's Rhetorical Presidency* (New York: Greenwood Press, 1988).
17. Warren Moscow, "Roosevelt Record 'Desperately Bad,' Dewey Declares," *New York Times*, September 26, 1944, 1.

18. Zachary Karabell, *The Last Campaign: How Harry Truman Won the 1948 Election* (New York: Vintage Books, 2001), 151.

19. Ibid., 156.

20. David Valley, "Significant Characteristics of Democratic Presidential Nomination Acceptance Speeches," *Central States Speech Journal* 25 (1978): 58.

21. Karabell, *The Last Campaign*, 209.

22. Harry S Truman, *Miracle of '48: Harry Truman's Major Campaign Speeches and Selected Whistle-Stops*, ed. Steve Neal (Carbondale, IL: Southern Illinois University Press, 2003), 64.

23. Ibid., 74, 80, 92.

24. David McCullough, *Truman* (New York: Simon and Schuster, 1992), 661.

25. William Safire, *Lend Me Your Ears: Great Speeches in History* (New York: Norton, 1992), 803.

26. Jules Witcover, *Party of the People: A History of the Democrats* (New York: Random House, 2003), 435.

27. Cole S. Brembeck, "Harry Truman at the Whistle Stops," *Quarterly Journal of Speech* 28 (1952): 42.

28. Truman, *Miracle of '48*, 63.

29. Karabell, *The Last Campaign*, 262.

30. Lewis Gould, *Grand Old Party: A History of the Republicans* (New York: Random House, 2003), 320.

31. David Fromkin, *In the Time of the Americans: FDR, Truman, Eisenhower, Marshall, MacArthur—The Generation That Changed America's Role in the World* (New York: Vintage Books, 1996), 650.

32. Gould, *Grand Old Party*, 321.

33. William E. Leuchtenburg, *In the Shadow of FDR: From Harry Truman to Ronald Reagan* (Ithaca, NY: Cornell University Press, 1983), 33–34.

Chapter 7: "THE BRIGHT SUNSHINE OF HUMAN RIGHTS"

1. Conrad Black, *Franklin Delano Roosevelt: Champion of Freedom* (New York: Public Affairs, 2003), 1003.

2. David McCullough, *Truman* (New York: Simon and Schuster, 1992), 639.

3. Carl Solberg, *Hubert Humphrey: A Biography* (St. Paul, MN: Borealis Books, 2003), 14.

4. Peter Beinart, *The Good Fight: Why Liberals—and Only Liberals—Can Win the War on Terror and Make America Great Again* (New York: HarperCollins, 2006), 11.

5. L. Patrick Devlin, "Hubert Humphrey's 1948 Civil Rights Speech," *Communication Quarterly* 16 (1968): 44.

6. Dan Cohen, *Undefeated: The Life of Hubert H. Humphrey* (Minneapolis, MN: Lerner, 1978), 142.

7. Ibid., 143.

8. Devlin, "Hubert Humphrey's 1948 Civil Rights Speech," 44.

9. Solberg, *Hubert Humphrey*, 18.

10. Devlin, "Hubert Humphrey's 1948 Civil Rights Speech," 45.

11. Kari Frederickson, *The Dixiecrat Revolt and the End of the Solid South, 1932–1968* (Chapel Hill: University of North Carolina Press, 2001), 130–31.

12. Ibid., 140.

13. Devlin, "Hubert Humphrey's 1948 Civil Rights Speech," 46.

## Chapter 8: "LET'S TALK SENSE TO THE AMERICAN PEOPLE"

1. John Barlow Martin, *Adlai Stevenson of Illinois* (Garden City, NY: Doubleday, 1979), 641.

2. Adlai Stevenson, *Major Campaign Speeches of Adlai Stevenson* (New York: Random House, 1953), xxv.

3. Martin, *Adlai Stevenson*, 584.

4. Stevenson, *Major Campaign Speeches*, 4.

5. Ibid., 5.

6. Ibid., 6.

7. Martin, *Adlai Stevenson*, 637.

8. Porter McKeever, *Adlai Stevenson: His Life and Legacy* (New York: Quill, 1991), 196.

9. Stevenson, *Major Campaign Speeches*, 7, 9.

10. Ibid., 10.

11. Arthur M. Schlesinger Jr., *Journals: 1952–2000*, edited by Andrew Schlesinger and Stephen Schlesinger (New York: Penguin, 2007), 10.

12. Martin, *Adlai Stevenson*, 631.

13. Ibid., 635.

14. David Halberstam, *The Fifties* (New York: Villard, 1993), 220; Schlesinger, *Journals*, 12.

15. McKeever, *Adlai Stevenson*, 214.

16. Ibid.

17. Ibid.

18. "Stevenson on Freedom," *Washington Post*, August 28, 1952.

19. McKeever, *Adlai Stevenson*, 217.

20. Ibid., 234–36.

21. Ibid., 263

22. Ibid., 263–64.

23. Schlesinger, *Journals*, 79.

## *Chapter 9:* THE CHECKERS SPEECH

1. Kathleen Hall Jamieson, *Eloquence in an Electronic Age: The Transformation of Political Speechmaking* (New York: Oxford University Press, 1990), 63.

2. Garry Wills, *Nixon Agonistes: The Crisis of the Self-Made Man* (Boston: Houghton Mifflin, 1970), 95.

3. Ibid., 99.

4. Ibid., 98.

5. Roger Morris, *Richard Milhous Nixon: The Making of an American Politician* (New York: Henry Holt, 1990), 781.

6. Ibid., 781.

7. Ibid., 808.

8. Richard Nixon, *Six Crises* (New York: Doubleday, 1968), 105.

9. Morris, *Richard Milhous Nixon*, 807.

10. Ibid., 827.

11. Nixon, *Six Crises*, 117.

12. Ibid., 114.

13. Martha Cooper, "Ethos, a Cloth Coat and a Cocker Spaniel," in Lloyd E. Rohler and Roger Cook, eds., *Great Speeches for Criticism and Analysis* (Greenwood, IN: Alistair, 1988), 128.

14. Nixon, *Six Crises*, 120

15. Ibid.

16. David Halberstam, *The Fifties* (New York: Villard, 1993), 240.

17. Wills, *Nixon Agonistes*, 104.

18. Morris, *Richard Milhous Nixon*, 833.

19. David Greenberg, *Nixon's Shadow: The History of an Image* (New York: W. W. Norton, 2003), 32.

20. Eric Goldman, *The Crucial Decade* (New York: Alfred E. Knopf, 1956), 231.

21. Morris, *Richard Milhous Nixon*, 835.

22. Wills, *Nixon Agonistes*, 110.

23. Rohler and Cook, eds., *Great Speeches for Criticism and Analysis*, 132.

24. Ibid., 133.

25. "How Nation's Editors React to Nixon Speech," *Chicago Daily Tribune*, September 25, 1952, 4.

26. "Press of Nation Reacted to Nixon Talk," *Los Angeles Times*, September 25, 1952, 2.

27. Bill Henry, "By the Way . . . with Bill Henry," *Los Angeles Times*, September 25, 1952.

28. "How Nation's Editors React to Nixon Speech."

29. Ronald Steel, *Walter Lippmann and the American Century* (Boston: Little, Brown, 1980), 483.

30. Greenberg, *Nixon's Shadow*, 32.

31. Morris, *Richard Milhous Nixon*, 847.

32. Wills, *Nixon Agonistes*, 93.

## Chapter 10: "I Shall Go to Korea"

1. David Halberstam, *The Fifties* (New York: Villard, 1993), 209.

2. Martin Medhurst, *Dwight D. Eisenhower, Strategic Communicator* (Westport, CT: Greenwood, 1993), 29.

3. William Pickett, *Eisenhower Decides to Run: Presidential Politics and Cold War Strategy* (Chicago: Ivan R. Dee, 2000), 213.

4. Halberstam, *The Fifties*, 210.

5. Jeff Broadwater, *Eisenhower and the Anti-Communist Crusade* (Chapel Hill: University of North Carolina Press, 1992), 48

6. Ibid.

7. Stephen Hess, "Foreign Policy and Presidential Campaigns," *Foreign Policy* 8 (1972): 5.

8. Emmet John Hughes, *The Ordeal of Power: Memoir of the Eisenhower Years* (New York: Atheneum, 1963), 33.

9. As quoted in Garry Wills, *Nixon Agonistes: The Crisis of the Self-Made Man* (Boston: Houghton Mifflin, 1970), 122.

10. Hughes, *Ordeal of Power*, 34.

11. Author interview with Dr. Martin Medhurst.

12. Eric Goldman, *The Crucial Decade* (New York: Alfred E. Knopf, 1956), 232–33.

13. Ed Wyszynski, "'I Shall Go to Korea'—Ike's October Surprise." Available at www.thepoliticalbandwagon.com/articles/2002October.html.

14. Martin Medhurst, "Text and Context in the 1952 Presidential Campaign: Eisenhower's 'I Shall Go to Korea' Speech," *Presidential Studies Quarterly* 30, 3 (2000): 464.

## *Chapter 11:* THE NEW FRONTIER

1. Robert Dallek, *An Unfinished Life: John F. Kennedy, 1917–1963* (Boston: Little, Brown, 2003), 274.

2. Richard Slotkin, *Gunfighter Nation: The Myth of the Frontier in Twentieth Century America* (New York: Atheneum, 1992), 1–4.

3. Author interview with Theodore Sorensen.

4. "Kennedy's Frontier," *Washington Post*, July 16, 1960.

5. Theodore Sorensen, *Kennedy* (New York: Harper and Row, 1965), 178–79.

6. Barbara Leaming, *Jack Kennedy: The Education of a Statesman* (New York: W. W. Norton, 2006), 251.

7. Ibid., 237.

8. Peter Beinart, *The Good Fight: Why Liberals—and Only Liberals—Can Win the War on Terror and Make America Great Again* (New York: HarperCollins, 2006), 26.

9. Thurston Clarke, *Ask Not: The Inauguration of John F. Kennedy and the Speech That Changed America* (New York: Henry Holt, 2005), 79.

10. Leaming, *Jack Kennedy*, 230–32.

11. Dallek, *An Unfinished Life*, 289–90.

## Chapter 12: GETTING RELIGION ON THE CAMPAIGN TRAIL

1. David Henry, "Senator John F. Kennedy Encounters the Religious Question: 'I Am Not the Catholic Candidate for President,'" in Ross Ryan Halford, ed., *Oratorical Encounters: Selected Studies and Sources of Twentieth-Century Political Accusations and Apologies* (New York: Greenwood Press, 1988).

2. Theodore Sorensen, *Kennedy* (New York: Harper and Row, 1965), 142.

3. Robert Dallek, *An Unfinished Life: John F. Kennedy, 1917–1963* (Boston: Little, Brown, 2003), 282.

4. Sorensen, *Kennedy*, 188

5. Ibid.

6. Ibid.

7. Author interview with Theodore Sorensen.

8. Theodore White, *The Making of the President: 1960* (New York: Atheneum, 1988), 260.

9. Sorensen, *Kennedy*, 189.

10. Dallek, *An Unfinished Life*, 283.

11. Sorensen, *Kennedy*, 19.

12. Thomas J. Carty, *A Catholic in the White House? Religion, Politics, and John F. Kennedy's Presidential Campaign* (New York: Palgrave Macmillan, 2004), 4.

13. Sorensen, *Kennedy*, 192.

14. Ibid., 193.

15. "The Religious Issue," *New York Times*, September 14, 1960.

16. "Enough Said," *Washington Post*, September 14, 1960.

17. Harold Barrett, "John F. Kennedy Before the Greater Houston Ministerial Association," *Central States Speech Journal* 15, 4 (1964): 265.

18. Author interview with Robert Dallek.

19. Ibid.

20. White, *The Making of the President*, 262.

## Chapter 13: THE CONSERVATIVE MOMENT

1. Taylor Branch, "The Year the GOP Went South," *Washington Monthly*, March 11, 1998.

2. Barry Goldwater with Jack Casserly, *Goldwater* (New York: Doubleday, 1988), 183.

3. Rick Perlstein, *Before the Storm: Barry Goldwater and Unmaking of the American Consensus* (New York: Hill and Wang, 2001), 389.

4. Robert Dallek, *Flawed Giant: Lyndon Johnson and His Times, 1961–1973* (New York: Oxford University Press, 1998), 167.

5. Perlstein, *Before the Storm*, 439.

6. Dallek, *Flawed Giant*, 167.

7. John C. Hammerback, "Goldwater's Rhetoric of Rugged Individualism," *Quarterly Journal of Speech* 58 (1972): 179.

8. Louis Harris, "Communications Top Goldwater Problems," *Los Angeles Times*, July 13, 1964, 2.

9. Robert Alan Goldberg, *Barry Goldwater* (New Haven, CT: Yale University Press, 1995), 205.

10. Goldwater, *Goldwater*, 186.

11. "Peddler's Grandson," *Time*, July 24, 1964.

12. Goldwater, *Goldwater*, 185.

13. Perlstein, *Before the Storm*, 391.

14. Ibid., 392.

15. Goldwater, *Goldwater*, 186.

16. Goldberg, *Barry Goldwater*, 206.

17. Ibid.

18. Harold Faber, ed., *The Road to the White House* (New York: McGraw-Hill, 1965), 71.

19. Goldberg, *Barry Goldwater*, 207.

20. Perlstein, *Before the Storm*, 392.

21. Ibid.

22. Kurt W. Ritter, "American Political Rhetoric and the Jeremiad Tradition: Presidential Nomination Acceptance Addresses, 1960–1976," *Central States Speech Journal* 31 (1980): 170.

23. "President Lyndon Johnson, Remarks at the University of Michigan, May 22, 1964," *Public Papers of the Presidents of the United States: Lyndon B. Johnson, 1963–1964*, vol. 1, entry 357, 704–7 (Washington, D.C.: Government Printing Office, 1965).

24. Ibid.

25. Ibid.

26. Dallek, *Flawed Giant*, 168–69.

27. Faber, ed., *The Road to the White House*, 257.

28. Ibid., 259.

29. Robert Mason, *Richard Nixon and the Quest for a New Majority* (Chapel Hill: University of North Carolina Press, 2003), 10.

30. Thomas Byrne Edsall and Mary D. Edsall, *Chain Reaction: The Impact of Race, Rights, and Taxes on American Politics* (New York: W. W. Norton, 1991), 39.

31. Faber, ed., *The Road to the White House*, 68.

32. Jeremy Mayer, *Running on Race: Racial Politics in Presidential Campaigns, 1960–2000* (New York: Random House, 2002), 61.

*Chapter 14:* THE "FORGOTTEN AMERICANS"
AND THE POLITICS OF FEAR

1. Lewis Chester, Godfrey Hodgson, and Bruce Page, *An American Melodrama: The Presidential Campaign of 1968* (New York: Viking, 1969), 276.

2. Dan Carter, *From George Wallace to Newt Gingrich: Race in the Conservative Counterrevolution, 1963–1994* (Baton Rouge: Louisiana State University Press, 1996), 41.

3. Chester, Hodgson, and Page, *An American Melodrama*, 279.

4. Jeremy Mayer, *Running on Race: Racial Politics in Presidential Campaigns, 1960–2000* (New York: Random House, 2002), 67.

5. Marshall Frady, *Wallace: The Classic Portrait of Alabama Governor George Wallace* (New York: Random House, 1996), 9.

6. Dan T. Carter, *The Politics of Rage: George Wallace, the Origins of the New Conservatism, and the Transformation of American Politics* (New York: Simon and Schuster, 1995), 208.

7. Ibid., 211.

8. Ibid., 215.

9. Carter, *From George Wallace to Newt Gingrich*.

10. Jody Carlson, *George C. Wallace and the Politics of Powerlessness* (New Brunswick, NJ: Transaction, 1981).

11. Carter, *From George Wallace to Newt Gingrich*, 17.

12. Thomas Byrne Edsall and Mary D. Edsall, *Chain Reaction: The Impact of Race, Rights, and Taxes on American Politics* (New York: W. W. Norton, 1991), 71–72.

13. Frady, *Wallace*, 16–17.

14. Carter, *From George Wallace to Newt Gingrich*, 15.

15. Lloyd Rohler, *George Wallace: Conservative Populist* (Westport, CT: Praeger, 2004), 38.

16. Chester, Hodgson, and Page, *An American Melodrama*, 279.

17. Richard Hofstadter, "The Paranoid Style in American Politics," *Harper's*, November 1964, 77–86.

18. Stephen Lesher, *George Wallace: American Populist* (Reading, MA: Addison Wesley, 1994), 280.

19. Edsall and Edsall, *Chain Reaction*, 78.

20. Carter, *From George Wallace to Newt Gingrich*, 23.

21. Chester, Hodgson, and Page, *An American Melodrama*, 283.

22. Ibid., 497.

23. Ibid.

24. Mayer, *Running on Race*, 88.

25. David Greenberg, *Nixon's Shadow: The History of an Image* (New York: W. W. Norton, 2003), 17–20, 32–35.

26. Garry Wills, *Nixon Agonistes: The Crisis of the Self-Made Man* (Boston: Houghton Mifflin, 1970), 312.

27. Charles Kaiser, *1968 in America: Music, Politics, Chaos, Counterculture, and the Shaping of a Generation* (New York: Grove, 1988), 227.

28. Ibid.

## *Chapter 15:* America "Come Home"

1. Dominic Sandbrook, *Eugene McCarthy: The Rise and Fall of Post-War American Liberalism* (New York: Alfred A. Knopf, 2004), 184.

2. Charles Kaiser, *1968 in America: Music, Politics, Chaos, Counterculture, and the Shaping of a Generation* (New York: Grove, 1988), 246.

3. Ibid., 249.

4. Carl Solberg, *Hubert Humphrey: A Biography* (St. Paul, MN: Borealis Books, 2003), 381.

5. Ibid., 382–83.

6. Ibid., 382–84.

7. Kaiser, *1968 in America*, 249.

8. Theodore White, *The Making of the President: 1968* (New York: Simon and Schuster, 1970), 440.

9. R. W. Apple Jr., "Humphrey Vows Halt in Bombing if Hanoi Reacts," *New York Times*, October 1, 1968.

10. Sandbrook, *Eugene McCarthy*, 151; Kaiser, *1968 in America*, 177.

11. Sandbrook, *Eugene McCarthy*, 196.

12. Peter Beinart, *The Good Fight: Why Liberals—and Only Liberals—Can Win the War on Terror and Make America Great Again* (New York: HarperCollins, 2006), 52.

13. Theodore H. White, *The Making of the President: 1972* (New York: Atheneum, 1973), 236.

14. Kurt Ritter, "American Political Rhetoric and the Jeremiad Tradition: Presidential Nomination Acceptance Speeches, 1960–1976," *Central States Speech Journal* 31, 3 (1980): 155.

15. Arthur M. Schlesinger Jr., *Journals 1952–2000*, edited by Andrew Schlesinger and Stephen Schlesinger (New York: Penguin, 2007), 355.

16. Dan Carter, *From George Wallace to Newt Gingrich: Race in the Conservative Counterrevolution, 1963–1994* (Baton Rouge: Louisiana State University Press, 1996), 54.

17. Christopher Cooper and Greg Hitt, "Democrats Are in an Odd Position on Iraq," *Wall Street Journal*, April 7, 2004.

## *Chapter 16:* THE TRIUMPH OF CONSERVATISM

1. Author conversation with Don Nathan. Also, Jason Gray Zengerle, "Old Party, New Energy" *American Prospect*, November 30, 2002.

2. Theodore H. White, *America in Search of Itself* (New York: Warner, 1983), 265.

3. "Primary Sources: The 'Crisis of Confidence' Speech," *American Experience*. Available at http://www.pbs.org/wgbh/amex/carter/filmmore/ps_crisis.html.

4. NBC News/Associated Press Poll, September 13, 1979.

5. Steven F. Hayward, *The Age of Reagan, 1964–1980: The Fall of the Old Liberal Order* (Roseville, CA: Forum/Prima, 2001), 579.

6. Henry Z. Scheele, "Ronald Reagan's Acceptance Address: A Focus on American Values," *Western Journal of Speech Communication* 48 (1984): 51.

7. Richard Harwood, ed., *Pursuit of the Presidency: 1980* (New York: Berkley, 1980), 167.

8. Lewis Chester, Godfrey Hodgson, and Bruce Page, *An American Melodrama: The Presidential Campaign of 1968* (New York: Viking, 1969), 190.

9. Scheele, "Ronald Reagan's Acceptance Address," 52.

10. Harwood, ed., *Pursuit of the Presidency*, 254.

11. Jeff Greenfield, *The Real Campaign: How the Media Missed the Story of the 1980 Campaign* (New York: Summit, 1982), 159.

12. Ibid., 171–72.

13. Elizabeth Drew, *Portrait of an Election* (New York: Simon and Schuster, 1981), 193.

14. Matt Bai, "Innovation and Inertia," *TPM Book Club*, September 26, 2007. Available at http://www.tpmcafe.com/blog/bookclub/2007/sep/26/on_innovation_and_inertia.

15. William E. Leuchtenburg, *In the Shadow of FDR: From Harry Truman to Ronald Reagan* (Ithaca, NY: Cornell University Press, 1983), 225.

16. Greenfield, *The Real Campaign*, 173.

17. Scheele, "Ronald Reagan's Acceptance Address," 56.

18. Carter-Reagan Presidential Debate, October 28, 1980, debate transcript. Available at http://www.debates.org/pages/trans80b.html.

## Chapter 17: THE LIBERALS STRIKE BACK

1. Jack Germond and Jules Witcover, *Wake Us When It's Over: Presidential Politics of 1984* (New York: Macmillan, 1985), 14.

2. Ibid., 27.

3. Peter Goldman and Tony Fuller with Thomas M. DeFrank, *The Quest for the Presidency, 1984* (New York: Bantam, 1985), 141.

4. Germond and Witcover, *Wake Us When It's Over*, 190–94.

5. Goldman and Fuller, *The Quest for the Presidency*, 23.

6. David Henry, "The Rhetorical Dynamic of Mario Cuomo's 1984 Keynote Address: Situation, Speaker, Metaphor," *Southern Speech Communication Journal* 53 (1988): 105.

7. Martha A. Solomon and Paul B. Stewart, "Beyond the Rainbow," in Lloyd Rohler and Roger Cook, eds., *Great Speeches for Criticism and Analysis* (Greenwood, IN: Alistair, 1988), 73.

8. Paul Erickson, *Reagan Speaks: The Making of an American Myth* (New York: New York University Press, 1985), 98–100, 111–12.

9. John T. Woolley and Gerhard Peters, *The American Presidency Project* [online]. Santa Barbara: University of California (hosted), Gerhard Peters (database). Available at http://www.presidency.ucsb.edu/ws/?pid=40290.

10. Mondale's Acceptance Speech, July 19, 1984. Available at http://

www.cnn.com/ALLPOLITICS/1996/conventions/chicago/facts/famous.speeches/mondale.84.shtml.

11. Ibid.

12. Author interview with Jeremy Rosner.

13. Germond and Witcover, *Wake Us When It's Over*, 408.

## Chapter 18: MURPHY BROWN AND THE CULTURE WARS

1. Commission on Presidential Debates, debate transcript, October 5, 1988. Available at http://www.debates.org/pages/trans88c.html.

2. Barbara Dafoe Whitehead, "Dan Quayle Was Right," *Atlantic Monthly*, April 1993.

3. "Rocky Road to Houston," *Newsweek*, Special Election Issue, November/December 1992, 66.

4. Ibid.

5. Bill Carter, "CBS Is Silent, but Then There's Next Season," *New York Times*, May 21, 1992; James Gerstenzang and David Lauter, "Quayle's Morality Debate: Day 2 Politics: Critique of TV Show Puts White House into Center of Controversy," *Los Angeles Times*, May 21, 1992.

6. Associated Press, "Bergen: Quayle Was Right About Murphy," July 11, 2002.

7. Jack Germond and Jules Witcover, *Mad as Hell: Revolt at the Ballot Box, 1992* (New York: Warner Books, 1993), 413.

8. Craig Smith, "Dan Quayle on Family Values: Epideictic Appeals in Political Campaigns." Available at http://www.csulb.edu/~crsmith/quale.html.

9. http://www.patrobertson.com/Speeches/1992GOPConvention.asp.

10. Germond and Witcover, *Mad as Hell*, 413.

11. "Rocky Road to Houston," 69.

12. Ibid., 68.

13. http://www.cnn.com/ELECTION/2004/pages/results/states/US/P/oo/epolls.o.html.

## Chapter 19: "I Still Believe in a Place Called Hope"

1. Bill Clinton, "Remarks to the Rainbow Coalition National Convention," Washington, D.C., 13 June 1992. Available at http://www.ibiblio .org/pub/academic/political-science/speeches/clinton.dir/c23.txt.
2. Ibid.
3. Ibid.
4. Ibid.
5. Jeremy Mayer, *Running on Race: Racial Politics in Presidential Campaigns, 1960–2000* (New York: Random House, 2002), 239.
6. Bill Clinton, *My Life* (New York: Alfred A. Knopf, 2004), 395.
7. Ibid., 406.
8. Mayer, *Running on Race*, 241.
9. Gwen Ifill, "Clinton Won't Back Down in Tiff with Jackson over a Rap Singer," *New York Times*, June 20, 1992.
10. Gwen Ifill, "Clinton at Jackson Meeting: Warmth and Some Friction," *New York Times*, June 20, 1992.
11. As recounted in Dan Carter, *From George Wallace to Newt Gingrich: Race in the Conservative Counterrevolution, 1963–1994* (Baton Rouge: Louisiana State University Press, 1996), 100.
12. 1992 Democratic Party Platform, "A New Covenant with the American People," June 1992.
13. As discussed in Jeremy Mayer, *Running on Race*.
14. "Prepared Text for the President's State of the Union Message," *The New York Times*, January 24, 1996
15. Ibid.
16. Ibid.
17. Ibid.

## Epilogue

1. "Bush sounds 'Compassionate Conservative' Theme in Iowa," Associated Press, June 12, 1999. Available at http://www.cnn.com/ ALLPOLITICS/stories/1999/06/12/bush.campaign/.

2. President's Remarks at the 2004 Republican National Convention, September 2, 2004. Available at http://www.whitehouse.gov/news/releases/2004/09/20040902-2.html.

3. "Text of Zell Miller's RNC Speech," CBSNews, September 1, 2004. Available at http://www.cbsnews.com/stories/2004/09/01/politics/main640299.shtml.

4. "Transcript: Illinois Senate Candidate Barack Obama," July 27, 2004. Available at http://www.washingtonpost.com/wp-dyn/articles/A19751-2004Jul27.html.

# BIBLIOGRAPHIC ESSAY

One of the greatest challenges in putting together this book was the sheer breadth of historical material to consider. I was writing not just about one election or one period in history but about the political history of the entire twentieth century. My challenge was to understand not only the speeches I've included in this collection but also the historical context in which they were delivered.

I am forever in debt to my research assistant, Diana Benton, for the prodigious primary research she conducted. In almost every chapter in this book her work helped me to add some of the color and feel that, I believe, makes them that much more interesting a read. Nonetheless, due to a somewhat compressed time frame, I relied very heavily on secondary research for most of the historical background for this book. The historical spadework was done by far more accomplished historians than myself, and I am indebted to all of them, as we all should be, for their ability not only to bring history alive but also to help all of us better understand the world in which we live.

While many authors influenced my thinking on the essays in this book, several stand out, and their impact on me was truly vast. First and foremost is Richard Hofstadter and two of his most brilliant books, *American Political Thought* and *Age of Reform*. Both were essential in helping me understand not only the populist and progressive movement, but also the personalities of Bryan, Roosevelt, Wilson, Hoover, and FDR. Quite simply, I could not have written this book if not for those two books. In addition, Eric Goldman's wonderful history *Rendezvous with Destiny* was an essential primer for understanding the history of the reform impulse in twentieth-century America.

Arthur Schlesinger's historical trilogy of *The Crisis of the Old Order*, *The Coming of the New Deal*, and *The Politics of Upheaval* was invaluable not only in explaining the history around the birth of the New Deal but also describing in vivid detail the political brilliance of Franklin D. Roosevelt. In more contemporary times, without Theodore White's *Making of the President: 1960, 1964, 1968*, and *1972* I would have been lost. Not only is White a wonderful writer, but unlike many campaign writers, he was able to place his observations and conclusions into a larger political context. His exhaustive histories of these four elections as well as his analysis of the 1980 race in *America in Search of Itself: 1956–1980* were essential to my research. Finally, the campaign histories put together by Jack Germond and Jules Witcover from 1980 to 1992 provided much-needed color and political insights on each of those races.

While below I specifically reference the materials that informed each essay, several books were helpful across a number of chapters. These include Michael McGerr's *A Fierce Discontent: The Rise and Fall of the Progressive Movement in America, 1870–1920*, which describes well the conservative impulse of the progressive movement and its eventual failure; David Halberstam's *The Fifties*, which is a great piece of reportage and was indispensable for the three chapters in this book about the 1952 election; Lloyd Rohler and Roger Cook's *Great Speeches for Criticism and Analysis*, fourth edition, particularly its analyses of the Checkers, Houston Ministerial Association, and Jesse Jackson "Common Ground" speeches; David Fromkin's *In the Time of the Americans: FDR, Truman, Eisenhower, Marshall, MacArthur—The Generation That Changed America's Role in the World*, for its examination of the creation of the postwar internationalist consensus in American politics; Jeremy Mayer's *Running on Race*, which authoritatively examines the evolution of race as a crucial issue in American politics; and Thomas Edsall's *Chain Reaction*, which may be the single most underrated book about race and politics in America. In addition, I relied heavily on Paul Boller's *Presidential Campaigns: From George Washington to George W. Bush*; Kurt Ritter's article

"American Political Rhetoric and the Jeremiad Tradition: Presidential Nomination Acceptance Speeches, 1960–1976" in the *Central States Speech Journal* 31 (Fall 1980), Martin Medhurst's *Beyond the Rhetorical Presidency*; Jules Witcover's *Party of the People: A History of the Democrats*; Lewis Gould's *Grand Old Party: A History of the Republicans*; Library of America's *American Speeches: Political Oratory from Abraham Lincoln to Bill Clinton*, edited by Ted Widmer; Arthur Schlesinger's *Journals 1952–2000*; Max Lerner's *America as a Civilization: Life and Thought in the United States*; Matt Bai's *The Argument*; and, of course, Tocqueville's *Democracy in America*.

## Chapter 1: BRYAN

The aforementioned *American Political Thought* by Hofstadter was instrumental in the writing of this chapter. Michael Kazin's biography, *A Godly Hero*, provided essential insight into the psychology of Bryan and the extraordinary impact he had on ordinary Americans. Moreover, Kazin really brought home the revolutionary nature of "Cross of Gold," which I describe in some detail in chapter 1. Louis William Koenig's biography of Bryan was exhaustive and provided an important window into Bryan's upbringing and the extent to which it influenced his political philosophy. In addition, his book and Paul Glad's *McKinley, Bryan and the People* gave wonderful color and feel for the mood on the convention floor when the "Cross of Gold" was delivered. I never tired of reading these descriptions, and every volume I read about the speech brought home the incredible, almost cataclysmic response to Bryan's remarks. This last point was reinforced by the examination of press coverage of the speech.

While I read dozens of histories of the 1896 election, the most helpful sources included Michael McGerr's *A Fierce Discontent*, Michael Kazin's *The Populist Persuasion: An American History*, Lawrence Goodwyn's *The Populist Moment: A Short History of the Agrarian Revolt in America*, and of course Richard Hofstadter's *Age of Reform*, all of which provided background on the populist and progressive movements.

## *Chapter 2:* WILSON, THEODORE ROOSEVELT, AND TAFT

The election of 1912 is, with three possible exceptions, the most interesting and important election in American history. The only others worthy of consideration are 1860, 1932, and 1968. But from the perspective of this book, 1912 is likely the most important because of the philosophical divide it enshrined between the two parties and the extent to which it ensured the Republican Party would be a conservative political party. Due to its obvious importance, I probably read more about this election and its key protagonists than any other.

The obvious place to begin with the 1912 election is James Chace's wonderful campaign chronicle, *1912*, which is one of my favorite campaign histories. My one complaint with Chace's book is that he clearly favors Roosevelt and Debs over Woodrow Wilson. In some respects, it's hard to blame Chace; Wilson was a horribly flawed president whose racist views are a black mark on his historical record. However, conducting my research on this election and in particular reading his volume of campaign speeches, *Crossroads of Freedom*, really increased my appreciation for Wilson. He may have been stubborn and a lousy foreign policy president, but Wilson was a heck of a speechwriter and a pretty smart politician. I'll admit I spent countless hours debating exactly which speech of his to include in this collection. Any number of addresses would have more than fit the bill. As a result, if there is any complaint to be made about my research of this chapter it is that I focused too much on Wilson and not enough on Roosevelt.

I read more than a dozen histories of the 1912 race and biographies of Roosevelt and Wilson, and while they all played a small but important role, a few stood out. In particular, William Leuchtenburg's opening essays to the slim anthologies *The New Freedom* and *The New Nationalism* are fascinating and helped, on a fundamental level, explain the political and economic dynamics underlying the philosophies of Roosevelt and Wilson. Credit is also due to Brett Flehinger's *The 1912 Election and the Power of Progressivism*.

Hofstadter, Goldman, and Schlesinger were, as always, invaluable. Patricia O'Toole's *When Trumpets Call* provided great insight into Roosevelt's thinking in seeking to upend Taft in the Republican primary. Ronald Pestritto's *Woodrow Wilson: Essential Political Writings* gave resonance to Wilson's appreciation and understanding for the power of political rhetoric.

## Chapter 3: WARREN HARDING

It's possible to count the good biographies of Warren Harding on the fingers of one hand. He was a much-maligned president and not many historians have made a significant effort to rehabilitate him. The most comprehensive biography of Harding is Francis Russell's *The Shadow of Blooming Grove: Warren G. Harding in His Times*, which has by far the most voluminous collection of material one could ever hope to read about Warren Harding. In more contemporary times, rehabilitation credit must be given to former White House counsel and Watergate protagonist John Dean, who in his thin biography of Harding does a nice job of presenting him in a more positive light than he has historically been seen. Also useful for this chapter were Wesley Bagby's *The Road to Normalcy: The Presidential Campaign and Election of 1920* and the more recent *1920: The Year of the Six Presidents* by David Pietrusza.

This was one chapter where I relied rather heavily on the analysis of several scholarly journal articles. These included John F. Wilson's "Harding's Rhetoric of Normalcy, 1920–1923," from the *Quarterly Journal of Speech* 48 (1962): 406–11; Robert J. Brake's "The Porch and the Stump: Campaign Strategies in the 1920 Presidential Election," from the *Quarterly Journal of Speech* 55 (1969): 256–67; and my favorite, Rupert Hughes's October 24, 1920, essay in the *New York Times*, "In Praise of Harding's Style." In addition to these sources, this chapter was greatly assisted by Paul Boller's campaign history and Michael McGerr's history of progressivism.

## Chapters 4–6: FRANKLIN ROOSEVELT, HOOVER, AND TRUMAN

Like any good Democrat, I've always been a fan of Franklin D. Roosevelt, but researching this book really brought home to me his incredible talent and skill as a politician. He had an almost preternatural ability to sense popular opinion and find just the words to reflect the emotions and feelings of the American people. I'm constantly in awe of Roosevelt and grateful that we as Americans were so lucky to have such a man in the White House during twelve of the most important years in our nation's history. I consulted countless books for the completion of these chapters, but several stand out and merit recognition.

Besides the usual suspects of Goldman, Hofstadter, and Schlesinger, Conrad Black's *Franklin Delano Roosevelt: Champion of Freedom*, Kenneth Davis's five-volume biography of Roosevelt, and Jean Edward Smith's *FDR* formed the backdrop for my understanding of this seminal figure. FDR's campaign speeches from 1932, which Samuel Rosenman assiduously reprinted, were of enormous assistance. In addition, Raymond Moley's *After Seven Years* provided wonderful color from the 1932 and 1936 campaigns, as did Harold Ickes's *Secret Diaries*. Moley's volume laid out in crisp detail the speechwriting process for the 1932 race and the last-minute intervention of Louis Howe. The chaotic manner in which FDR's acceptance speech was written and the high drama of FDR's flight to Chicago is wonderfully reconstructed by not only Schlesinger but also Jonathan Alter's *The Defining Moment: FDR's Hundred Days and the Triumph of Hope*.

I am grateful to Stephen Neal's history of the 1932 convention, *Happy Days Are Here Again: The 1932 Democratic Convention, the Emergence of FDR—and How America Was Changed Forever*. Neal does a great job of placing the speech in the larger historical context of the 1932 election. For Hoover, few books I read were more instructive then the ones by the man himself, in particular *New Day*, a collection of his 1928 campaign speeches, and *American Individualism*. Several biographies of Hoover were helpful in producing this chapter, particularly Richard Norton Smith's *Uncommon Man: The Triumph of Herbert Hoover*.

Davis Houck's "FDR's Commonwealth Club Address: Redefining Individualism, Adjudicating Greatness" from *Rhetoric and Public Affairs* (Fall 2004), was revelatory for me when writing the section on FDR's Commonwealth Club speech. Even if I didn't always share Houck's conclusions, his skepticism about the strength of this address helped confirm my own feelings about a speech that has been universally praised more by acclamation than by the strength of Roosevelt's words.

The chapter on FDR's 1936 acceptance speech (probably my favorite in the book) would not have been possible without the detailed history featured in Schlesinger's *Years of Upheaval*. It was fascinating to see how many historians have cribbed generously from that seminal description of the speech. Both Schlesinger and Davis's biography of Roosevelt do a nice job of tracing the evolution of Roosevelt's rhetoric in 1936 as he began to cast his political appeal in far more populist terms. Moley's biography gives his side of the famous falling-out between the two men over the speech.

The literature around the 1940 and, in particular, the 1944 elections is paltry. A notable exception is Charles Peters's *Five Days in Philadelphia*, which provides a blow-by-blow account of the 1940 Republican convention and its impact not only on the campaign but also on American foreign policy. In a similar vein, the speeches of Wendell Willkie, while not nearly as eloquent as those of his opponent, were fascinating to read. His meteoric rise in American politics and the courage of his internationalist convictions are truly underappreciated in American history. In addition, the 1940 campaign featured some of Roosevelt's best rhetorical moments, not all of which, unfortunately, could be reprinted in this volume. For those so inclined, the *1940 Volume of Public Papers and Addresses of Franklin D. Roosevelt*, edited by Samuel Rosenman, is well worth a read.

So much has been written about Harry S Truman and the 1948 campaign it's now become a race more of folklore rather than of insightful historical analysis. Zachary Karabell's *The Last Campaign* stands in stark contrast to the mythic manner in which Truman is remembered today, puncturing, in part, the notion of Truman's homespun victory. Karabell's book was for me a confirmation of the conclusion that I drew from my own analysis—that Truman's campaign was mean-spirited, frequently vicious, and in the long run counterproductive for not only Democrats but also American foreign policy.

I am additionally grateful to Steve Neal's anthology of Truman's major campaign speeches, *Miracle of '48: Harry Truman's Major Campaign Speeches and Selected Whistle-Stops*. For anyone curious to get a true sense of the 1948 campaign, I recommend picking it up. In addition to these works, David McCullough's magisterial biography *Truman* was a wonderful resource, as was David Fromkin's *In the Time of the Americans*, which offered an important foreign policy context to the campaign and Truman's take-no-prisoners approach, and William Leuchtenburg's *In the Shadow of FDR: From Harry Truman to Ronald Reagan*, which demonstrated the extent to which Truman relied on FDR's legacy to win this election. It was pretty much my fundamental analysis for this chapter, but it's always nice when a preeminent historian such as Leuchtenburg confirms it.

## Chapter 7: HUMPHREY

Hubert Humphrey is hardly the most revered American politician today, but yet his speeches had an enormous impact in shaping the direction of the Democratic Party on both civil rights and foreign policy. There are a number of excellent biographies of this rather complicated and conflicted political figure. For the purposes of his 1948 address on civil rights at the Democratic National Convention, I am indebted to L. Patrick Devlin's scholarly article "Hubert Humphrey's 1948 Civil Rights Speech," from *Today's Speech* 16 (1968). It is one of the few scholarly analyses of the speech. In addition, I relied in great measure on Carl Solberg's *Hubert Humphrey: A Biography*, Dan Cohen's *Undefeated: The Life of Hubert Humphrey*, and Humphrey's autobiography, *The Education of a Public Man: My Life and Politics*. In addition, I am also grateful to Kari Frederickson's *The Dixiecrat Revolt and the End of the Solid South, 1932–1968*, which provided fascinating insight into the 1948 Dixiecrat ticket and in particular the Dixiecrat convention.

## Chapter 8: STEVENSON

There is a frustrating lack of good scholarly research about Adlai Stevenson. The obvious exceptions, and my research crutches for this chapter, are John Barlow Martin's *Adlai Stevenson of Illinois* and Porter McKeever's *Adlai Stevenson: His Life and Legacy*. Both of these volumes were instrumental in crafting this chapter. In particular, Martin's biography of Stevenson vividly recounts the tales of the Elks Club, and I relied heavily on his description of this unusual speechwriting process. In addition, Arthur Schlesinger's recently released *Journals 1952–2002* offers another insight into the fascinating Stevenson speechwriting process. McKeever's biography does a nice job of placing Stevenson's words in a larger historical context and in particular dramatizing the extent to which his words influenced an entire generation of young Democrats. I am also grateful to David Halberstam's *The Fifties*, which also offered a perspective on Stevenson's historical impact that I had not considered before drafting this chapter. Finally, Stevenson's own *Major Campaign Speeches of Adlai Stevenson* provided me with rich fodder and much indecision over precisely the best one of his speeches to use for my book. As was the case in so many of these chapters, it is the words of the candidates themselves that were the most important research I conducted.

## *Chapter 9:* NIXON AND CHECKERS

So much has been written about the Checkers speech that it's difficult to narrow down the single best sources of material. While I referenced innumerable histories of the speech, I was partial to several. Garry Wills's *Nixon Agonistes: The Crisis of the Self-Made Man* is a great book and really delves into the psychology of Nixon and his political motivation. The description here of the interplay between Nixon and Eisenhower over the fund issue is astonishing. *Agonistes* is one of the most unvarnished and honest political biographies I've ever read, and I can't recommend it highly enough, not only for its take on Nixon but also for its examination of American politics. Roger Morris's *Richard Milhous Nixon: The Rise of an American Politician* has exhaustive and vivid detail about the run-up to the speech and the back-and-forth machinations between the Nixon and Eisenhower camps. Also useful in this regard was Stephen Ambrose's biography *Eisenhower*.

David Greenberg's *Nixon's Shadow: The History of an Image* places the Checkers speech in appropriate historical context, as do, to a lesser extent, Kathleen Hall Jamieson's *Eloquence in an Electronic Age: The*

*Transformation of Political Speechmaking* and Eric Goldman's *A Crucial Decade*. Greenberg's book does a wonderful job of demonstrating how the image making that defined the Checkers speech became fundamental to the way Nixon approached politics. Nixon has become such a caricature today that we often forget how seismic his influence was on contemporary American politics. In this book, I write that we are living in FDR's America, but at the same time our political system and the means by which our national leaders communicate with the American people owe much to Nixon.

Nixon's own *Six Crises* provides the candidate's revealing, and at times self-serving, perspective on the Checkers speech. Martha Cook's "Ethos, a Cloth Coat and a Cocker Spaniel," which is featured in Rohler and Cook's *Great Speeches for Criticism and Analysis*, offers one of the best analyses of the Checkers speech, and one I relied upon greatly. Finally, the primary research I conducted on the coverage of the speech was instructive and provided a real sense of the unique nature and high drama of the Checkers speech. The Walter Lippmann quote in this chapter, from Richard Steel's biography *Walter Lippmann and the American Century*, is one of my favorites. The Steel book was actually not directly helpful for the writing of this book. I was surprised to find that I rarely consulted it. But I am forever indebted to my former professor Walter LaFeber, for assigning it to me during my sophomore year of college. It's a magisterial book and is as responsible as any major volume I've read for my understanding of twentieth-century American history.

## Chapter 10: EISENHOWER

Much has been written about Dwight D. Eisenhower the general and the president, but far less on Eisenhower the candidate. Amazingly, even less has been written about the "I shall go to Korea" speech even though it is one of the more influential campaign speeches in modern American history. The notable exception is Martin Medhurst and his book *Dwight D. Eisenhower: Strategic Communicator* and his scholarly article "Text and Context in the 1952 Presidential Campaign: Eisenhower's 'I Shall Go to Korea' Speech," from the *Presidential Studies Quarterly* (September 2000). These materials were essential for completing this chapter, and Medhurst provided the single best analysis of the speech. In addition, Dr. Medhurst was generous enough to take the time to speak with me, and I am appreciative of his wise counsel and advice.

William B. Pickett's *Eisenhower Decides to Run: Presidential Politics and Cold War Strategy* placed Eisenhower's candidacy in the historical context of the Cold War and offered compelling evidence about his motivation for seeking the presidency in the first place. This argument was fundamental to my analysis of the chapter, and I am deeply indebted to this book and Pickett's exhaustive research, which in many respects runs counter to the popular perception of Eisenhower as a disinterested candidate.

In addition to these notable texts, I also relied heavily upon David Fromkin's *In the Time of the Americans*, Michael Korda's biography *Ike: An American Hero*, Stephen Ambrose's *Eisenhower*, Eric Goldman's *A Crucial Decade*, and David Halberstam's *The Fifties*.

But most of all, I appreciate the fact that so many newspapers in 1952 reprinted Eisenhower's campaign speeches. Rereading the general's major campaign speeches provided me an important understanding of the evolution of Eisenhower's rhetorical approach on the campaign trail. In many respects, it is this evolution that is so fundamental to the effectiveness of the "I shall go to Korea" speech.

## Chapters 11–12: KENNEDY

My single greatest personal revelation about the political speakers in this book involved John F. Kennedy. Having not been alive during his presidency, I never fully appreciated his political salience, because his accomplishments as a senator and president seemed so meager to me. I always assumed that his mythic image was a result of his tragic death rather than his accomplishments as president. Rereading his campaign speeches quickly disabused me of that notion. Like few other candidates in this book, Kennedy understood the power of the bully pulpit, particularly on the campaign trail. Moreover, I was captivated by the courage of his campaign theme—national sacrifice in the face of enormous domestic and international challenges. It took a supremely self-confident and self-assured politician to so openly challenge the electorate in the manner he did. He deserves enormous praise for it, and I wish more politicians would demonstrate the conviction that Kennedy showed on the campaign trail.

The single most useful source for John F. Kennedy's 1960 presidential campaign was Theodore Sorensen's memoir *Kennedy*. From a speechwriter's perspective, Sorensen's book provides a fascinating perspective on the campaign and the nuts and bolts of the speechwriting process. Moreover, he provides great insight into the development of Kennedy's campaign message and the tactical thinking behind his Houston speech to the Protestant ministers. I am additionally indebted to Mr. Sorensen for taking the time to speak with me about the campaign and the drafting of the two speeches in this book. In addition, I relied significantly on Theodore White's *The Making of the President: 1960* and Robert Dallek's biography of Kennedy, *An Unfinished Life*, as well as my personal conversations with him. Barbara Leaming's *Jack Kennedy: The Education of a Statesman* and Thurston Clarke's *Ask Not: The Inauguration of John F. Kennedy and the Speech That Changed America* both helped me understand the evolution of Kennedy's political philosophy and the motivation for his courageous political message. Leaming's book is particularly noteworthy, as she lays out the extent to which Kennedy was influenced by Churchill and the interwar years in England. Also, Richard Slotkin's *Gunfighter Nation: The Myth of the Frontier in Twentieth Century America* was a useful reference tool for my discussion of the frontier in American politics and national mythology.

For the chapter on Kennedy's Houston speech, I am again grateful to Robert Dallek and Theodore Sorensen for their personal thoughts on the address. In addition, Thomas Carty's *A Catholic in the White House? Religion, Politics, and John F. Kennedy's Presidential Campaign* and Jon Meacham's *American Gospel: God, the Founding Fathers, and the Making of a Nation* gave perspective to the historic issue of Catholicism in American politics. Several academics have written excellent analyses of the Houston speech, including David Henry's "Senator John F. Kennedy Encounters the Religious Question: 'I Am Not the Catholic Candidate for President,'" Harold Barrett's "John F. Kennedy Before the Greater Houston Ministerial Association," and Lloyd Rohler's critical analysis

"I Am Not the Catholic Candidate for President." All were useful in confirming my initial analysis of this seminal address, which is one of the most courageous speeches featured in this book.

## Chapter 13: GOLDWATER

Barry Goldwater is a truly fascinating political figure and a man of rare political courage and conviction—even if I find those convictions largely abhorrent. Reading about him was one of the more enjoyable experiences of writing this book. The best history of Goldwater and the 1964 campaign, and the book I relied most heavily, on is Rick Perlstein's *Before the Storm: The Unmaking of the American Consensus*, which provided a stirring portrait not only of the man but also of the conservative movement. The subtitle to Perlstein's book sums up well his basic argument and the fundamental role that Goldwater played in American politics, offering a counternarrative to the basic postwar consensus of activist government at home and liberal interventionism abroad. In addition, I found fascinating Goldwater's autobiography, *Goldwater*, which really demonstrated his political tin ear. In his description of the 1964 campaign he comes across as a thin-skinned politician who viewed his race for the White House as more of a crusade rather than a crass political endeavor. It was revealing in ways that most politicians would likely not prefer. Also helpful was Robert Alan Goldberg's 1995 biography, *Barry Goldwater*, which offered great color about the writing of the acceptance speech itself.

As for histories of the 1964 election, Theodore White's *The Making of the President: 1964* is the virtual bible, but equally useful was *The Road to the White House: The Story of the 1964 Election*, a compilation of *New York Times* articles about the race. For the section on Lyndon Johnson's Great Society speech I relied largely on Robert Dallek's biography of Johnson, *Flawed Giant*, and Doris Kearns Goodwin's *Lyndon Johnson and the American Dream*. If I have one regret about this book it is that I did not have the opportunity to talk more about Lyndon Johnson, who I find to be the most fascinating president of the postwar years. I don't think we have truly come to appreciate Johnson's transformative impact on American politics. I suppose we'll all have to wait for Robert Caro's next volume. Jeremy Mayer's *Running on Race*, Thomas Edsall's *Chain Reaction*, and James Reston's reporting on the election for the *New York Times* helped me in drawing conclusions about the long-term impact of the Goldwater speech on American politics.

### Chapter 14: NIXON AND WALLACE

The 1968 race for the White House is without a doubt my favorite presidential election. While I have read virtually everything ever written about the campaign, one book above all must stand out: *An American Melodrama: The Presidential Campaign of 1968*, a chronicle of the race and its main protagonists as written by three BBC reporters. It's the single best campaign history ever written.

For the section on Wallace, I relied heavily on Dan Carter's excellent and unsympathetic biography of the Alabama governor, *The Politics of Rage: George Wallace, the Origins of the New Conservatism, and the Transformation of American Politics*, and his lecture "From George Wallace to Newt Gingrich: Race in the Conservative Counterrevolution." Carter does a great job of placing Wallace's ideas in a larger historical context and demonstrating the extent to which it influenced the political messaging of conservatism in 1968 and the four decades afterward. Carter's volume remains among the best political biographies that I've read. Also useful for the section on Wallace was Stephen Lesher's *George Wallace: An American Populist*, Lloyd Rohler's *George Wallace: Conservative Populist*, Jody Carlson's *George C. Wallace and the Politics of Powerlessness*, and Marshall Frady's wonderful piece of reportage, *Wallace: The Classic Portrait of Alabama Governor George Wallace*. Once again, Edsall's *Chain Reaction* and Mayer's *Running on Race* were incredibly useful for this chapter.

The aforementioned *American Melodrama* provided the backdrop for the 1968 campaign. I am also indebted to Lewis Gould's *1968: The Election That Changed America*, Garry Wills's *Nixon Agonistes*, Theodore White's *The Making of the President: 1968*, Charles Kaiser's *1968 in America: Music, Politics, Chaos, Counterculture, and the Shaping of a Generation*, David Greenberg's *Nixon's Shadow: The History of an Image*, and of course Joe McGinnis's seminal *The Selling of the President, 1968*.

## Chapter 15: HUMPHREY AND MCGOVERN

Though this chapter was fundamentally about the speeches of Hubert Humphrey and George McGovern, the political figure with the greatest influence on the evolution of Democratic thinking on foreign policy was Eugene McCarthy. For this reason, I am most grateful for Dominic Sandbrook's wonderful biography of the man, *Eugene McCarthy and the Rise and Fall of Postwar American Liberalism*. McCarthy was a principled if prickly man who maybe more than any other politician gave credibility to the liberal critique of U.S. foreign policy. As Sandbrook describes in vivid detail, without McCarthy the 1968 race would have been very different, and certainly it's hard to imagine the rise of George McGovern without him. In addition, Peter Beinart's *The Good Fight: Why Liberals—and Only Liberals—Can Win the War on Terror and Make America Great Again* does an excellent job of laying out the evolution of liberal thinking on American foreign policy and in particular the use of force. While I don't always agree with Beinart's conclusions, he makes a compelling argument that the shift toward a neo-liberal foreign policy approach had a disastrous impact on the Democratic Party as it ceded the issue of national security—from a political perspective—to conservative Republicans.

Carl Solberg's biography of Humphrey provided much of the fodder for the section in this chapter on the writing of the Salt Lake City speech. I relied on Theodore White's *The Making of the President: 1972*, and his supreme political insight for the anecdote about the mining of Haiphong harbor. This episode served as a confirmation of my basic thesis, and I am thankful that White understood thirty-five years earlier what this event said about the Democratic Party in 1972.

One of the best things about writing a book like this is the opportunity it gave me to peruse books about American politics that I normally never would have time to read. Hunter Thompson's *Fear and Loathing on the Campaign Trail 1972,* which had been sitting on my bookshelf unread for years, is just one of those books. Thompson was more than just an alcoholic speed freak; he was a great reporter and a rather insightful political observer. I loved this book and it helped me understand the almost surreal nature of the 1972 campaign and in particular the Democratic race for the nomination. Finally, Christopher Cooper and Greg Hitt's article in the *Wall Street Journal* in April 2004 titled "Democrats Are in an Odd Position on Iraq" provided me with the quote " 'It's never stopped being 1968' for Democrats" from a senior Bush administration official (my guess would be Karl Rove). It might seem like an exaggeration to suggest that a short sentence like this could pretty much sum up three and half decades of American politics, but it's not. This quote speaks volumes, and when I read it on a New York subway in the spring of 2004 it changed the entire way I think about modern American politics. But I'll save that discussion for my next book.

## *Chapter 16:* REAGAN

Even though I grew up during the Reagan years, I felt as though I knew less about his presidency and the 1980 election than nearly any other in this book. Maybe, as a Democrat, I was trying to blot it from my memory. However, in conducting research for this chapter I came away with enormous respect for Reagan and his speechmaking abilities. There are a few Democrats who could take lessons from Reagan's preaching of national greatness, a concept progressives too often look askance at.

For this chapter I am particularly indebted to my former student Reah Johnson, who did fantastic background research. She identified several of the key themes that I explored and took the time to page through the various reference tools that I used for this chapter. In particular, *The Pursuit of the Presidency*, a collection of articles from the *Washington Post* on the 1980 campaign, offered good background on all the key actors in the race. I relied heavily on Jeff Greenfield's examination of the campaign in *The Real Campaign: How the Media Missed the Story of the 1980 Campaign.* Jack Germond and Jules Witcover's *Blue Smoke and Mirrors*, Elizabeth Drew's *Portrait of an Election*, Stephen Hayward's *The Age of Reagan, 1964–1980: The Fall of the Old Liberal Order*, and of course Theodore White's *America in Search of Itself, 1956–1980*. Finally, thanks must go to my professional colleagues Jim Badenhausen and Don Nathan for taking the time to read this chapter and offer some very precise critiques of my analysis.

## Chapter 17: CUOMO AND JACKSON

In several of the chapters in this book I produced an analysis that runs particularly counter to the general historical interpretation. The chapter on the 1984 election is probably the clearest example. I have enormous respect for Mario Cuomo and Jesse Jackson, but I do believe that these speeches, while beautiful ruminations on the liberal vision of America, are flawed political documents. Even if I share most of the views expressed by both men, I tried to be honest to the vision of this book, and that is expressed, I hope, in my analysis.

For this chapter I relied heavily on Jack Germond and Jules Witcover's history of the 1984 campaign, *Wake Us When It's Over: Presidential Politics of 1984*, as well as Elizabeth Drew's *Campaign Journal: The Political Events of 1983–1984* and Peter Goldman and Tony Fuller's *The Quest for the Presidency, 1984*. All of these books provided me with the political backdrop for the convention speeches and explained the complicated nature of the 1984 Democratic primary for president.

In addition, I am indebted to Jeremy Rosner for taking the time to review this chapter and offer me some incredibly insightful comments. It helps that Jeremy shares my basic political outlook, but he also has one of the best political minds of anyone I know, and his comments really helped to make this a far better chapter.

From a critical standpoint, I also relied upon David Henry's "The Rhetorical Dynamic of Mario Cuomo's 1984 Keynote Address: Situation, Speaker, Metaphor," from the *Southern Speech Communication Journal* (Winter 1988), and the analysis of Jackson's speech by Martha Solomon and Paul Stewart in Lloyd E. Rohler and Roger Cook's *Great Speeches for Criticism and Analysis*.

## Chapter 18: QUAYLE AND BUCHANAN

The two speeches in this chapter were among the most obscure of the book, but in some respects we are feeling the consequences of these addresses more than nearly any others. Once again, Jack Germond and Jules Witcover's *Mad as Hell* provided much of the background material for this chapter. In addition, *Newsweek's* post-election issue about the

1992 election offered some of the best coverage of the writing of the Quayle speech and the political considerations of the vice president and his staff. In addition, Barbara Dafoe Whitehead's April 1993 article in the *Atlantic Monthly*, "Dan Quayle Was Right," helped guide some of my thinking on this chapter. In its own right, Whitehead's piece is a fascinating read. Finally, I am grateful to Lisa Schiffin taking the time to discuss the Murphy Brown speech with me.

## *Chapter 19:* CLINTON

I probably started out knowing more about Bill Clinton and his two campaigns for the White House than any other in this book. I worked on the 1992 campaign for President Clinton and I did a prodigious amount of research on the 1996 campaign working with Doug Schoen on his book *The Power of the Vote*. In addition, Mr. Schoen was kind enough to read this chapter and provide his thoughts. Jeremy Rosner also took the time to read this chapter and I am appreciative, once again, of his comments. This is one of the few times that Doug Schoen and Jeremy Rosner have worked on anything collaboratively, so I'm pleased to be the catalyst for this unlikely pairing.

Due to my background knowledge of these two elections, I spent less time on original research. However, Jack Germond and Jules Witcover's *Mad as Hell: Revolt at the Ballot Box, 1992* helped to refresh my memory of the 1992 election, as did the post-election roundups put out by *Time* and *Newsweek* magazines. For 1996 I relied on Doug Schoen's book as well as John Harris's presidential biography *The Survivor: Bill Clinton in the White House*. Bill Clinton's autobiography *My Life* helped to fill in some historical gaps on the 1992 race, and Jeremy Mayer's *Running on Race* did the same for the Sister Souljah speech. In addition, Gwen Ifill's coverage in the *New York Times* of the fallout from the Souljah speech was invaluable.

# PERMISSIONS

William Jennings Bryan, "The Cross of Gold" Speech. Source: *Boston Daily Globe*, July 13, 1896, 5.

Theodore Roosevelt, New Nationalism Speech, Osawatomie, Kansas, August 13, 1910. Source: Theodore Roosevelt, *The New Nationalism* (Englewood Cliffs, NJ: Prentice-Hall, 1961), 21–39.

Woodrow Wilson, Labor Day Speech, Buffalo, New York, September 2, 1912: Source: *A Crossroads of Freedom: The 1912 Campaign Speeches*, ed. John Wells Davidson (New Haven, CT: Yale University Press, 1956), 69–85.

Warren Harding, "Return to Normalcy" Speech, Boston, May 14, 1920. Source: Warren G. Harding, "Back to Normal: Address Before Home Market Club," in Frederick E. Schortemeier, ed., *Rededicating America: Life and Recent Speeches of Warren G. Harding.* (Indianapolis: Bobbs-Merrill, 1920), 223–29.

Herbert Hoover, "Rugged Individualism" Speech, October 22, 1928. Source: Herbert Hoover, *The New Day: Campaign Speeches of Herbert Hoover 1928* (Stanford, CA: Stanford University Press, 1929), 149–76.

Franklin D. Roosevelt, Acceptance of the Democratic Presidential Nomination, Chicago, July 2, 1932. Source: The Governor Accepts the Nomination for the Presidency, Chicago, July 2, 1932, *The Public Papers and Addresses of Franklin D. Roosevelt*, vol. 1: *The Genesis of the New Deal, 1928–32* (New York: Random House, 1938), 647–59.

Franklin D. Roosevelt, Speech at Commonwealth Club, San Francisco, September 23, 1932. Source: Campaign Address on Progressive Government at the Commonwealth Club, San Francisco, September 23, 1932, *The Public Papers and Addresses of Franklin D. Roosevelt*, vol. 1: *The Genesis of the New Deal, 1928–32* (New York: Random House, 1938), 742–56.

Franklin D. Roosevelt, "Rendezvous with Destiny" Speech, Philadelphia, June 27, 1936. Source: Franklin D. Roosevelt: Speech to the DNC, Philadelphia, June 27, 1936, *The Public Papers and Addresses of Franklin D. Roosevelt,* vol. 5: *The People Approve, 1936* (New York: Random House, 1938), 230–36.

Franklin D. Roosevelt, Campaign Address at Madison Square Garden, New York, October 28, 1940. Source: *The Public Papers and Addresses of Franklin D. Roosevelt,* vol. 9: *War—and Aid to Democracies, 1940* (New York: Harper & Brothers, 1941), 499–510.

Franklin D. Roosevelt, The "Fala" Speech, Washington, D.C., September 23, 1944. Source: *The Public Papers and Addresses of Franklin D. Roosevelt*, vol. 13: *Victory and the Threshold of Peace, 1944–45* (New York: Harper & Brothers, 1946), 284–92.

Harry S Truman, Speech Accepting Democratic Party's Nomination for the Presidency, Philadelphia, July 14, 1948. Source: *Miracle of '48: Harry Truman's Major Campaign Speeches and Selected Whistle-Stops*, ed. Steve Neal (Carbondale: Southern Illinois University Press, 2003), 53–60.

Hubert Humphrey, "The Bright Sunshine of Human Rights," July 14, 1948. Source: Hubert H. Humphrey Papers, Minnesota Historical Society. Reprinted with permission of the Minnesota Historical Society. Permission to reprint text transcripts granted from www.americanrhetoric.com.

Adlai Stevenson, Speech at the American Legion National Convention, New York City, August 27, 1952. Source: Box 136, Adlai Stevenson Papers. Reprinted with permission of Princeton University Library.

Richard Nixon, "Checkers" Speech, Los Angeles, September 23, 1952. Source: *New York Times*, September 24, 1952, 22.

Ronald Reagan, Speech Accepting the Republican Presidential Nomination, Detroit, July 17, 1980. Source: Ronald Reagan Presidential Library. Reprinted with permission of Ronald Reagan Presidential Library.

Mario Cuomo, Keynote Address to the Democratic National Convention, San Francisco, July 16, 1984. Source: Roger Cook and Lloyd E. Rohler, *Great Speeches for Criticism and Analysis,* 4th ed. (Greenwood, IN: Alistair Press, 1988), 56–62. Reprinted with permission of Governor Mario Cuomo.

Jesse Jackson, Speech to the Democratic National Convention on Unity in Party, San Francisco, July 17, 1984. Source: "The Rainbow Coalition: Young America, Dream," San Francisco, July 17, 1984, *Vital Speeches of the Day* 51, 3 (November 15, 1984): 77–81. Reprinted with permission of Jesse Jackson.

Dan Quayle, Address to the Commonwealth Club of California on Family Values, May 19, 1992. Reprinted with permission from the Dan Quayle Center & U.S. Vice Presidential Museum. Source: www.commonwealthclub.org.

Pat Buchanan, "The Election Is About Who We Are: Taking Back Our Country," Houston, Texas, August 17, 1992. Source: *Vital Speeches of the Day* 58, 23 (September 15, 1992): 712–15. Reprinted with permission of Pat Buchanan.

Bill Clinton, Acceptance Speech to the Democratic National Convention, 1992. Source: www.biblio.org/pub/academic/political science/speeches/clinton.dir/c2.txt.

# INDEX

Note: page numbers followed by "n" refer to footnotes

# A NOTE ON THE AUTHOR

MICHAEL A. COHEN is a professional speechwriter who has worked in both government and the corporate world. A senior research fellow at the New America Foundation, Cohen has taught speechwriting and political rhetoric at Columbia University's School of International and Public Affairs. He lives in Brooklyn.